COMMUNITY PLANNING
FOR AN AGING SOCIETY

COMMUNITY DEVELOPMENT SERIES

Series Editor: Richard P. Dober, AIP

Volumes Published

TERRAIN ANALYSIS: A Guide to Site Selection Using Aerial Photographic Interpretation/Douglas S. Way

URBAN ENVIRONMENTS AND HUMAN BEHAVIOR: An Annotated Bibliography/Edited by Gwen Bell, Edwina Randall, and Judith E. R. Roeder

APPLYING THE SYSTEMS APPROACH TO URBAN DEVELOPMENT/Jack LaPatra

DESIGNING FOR HUMAN BEHAVIOR: Architecture and the Behavioral Sciences/Edited by Jon Lang, Charles Burnette, Walter Moleski, and David Vachon

ALTERNATIVE LEARNING ENVIRONMENTS/ Edited by Gary J. Coates

BEHAVIORAL RESEARCH METHODS IN ENVIRONMENTAL DESIGN/Edited by William Michelson

STRATEGY FOR NEW COMMUNITY DEVELOPMENT IN THE UNITED STATES/Edited by Gideon Golany

PLANNING URBAN ENVIRONMENT/Melville C. Branch

LANDSCAPE ASSESSMENT: Values, Perceptions, and Resources/Edited by Ervin H. Zube, Robert O. Brush, and Julius Gy. Fabos

ARCHITECTURAL PSYCHOLOGY/Edited by Rikard Küller

THE URBAN ECOSYSTEM: A Holistic Approach/ Edited by Forest W. Stearns

URBAN PLANNING THEORY/Edited by Melville C. Branch

INSTRUCTIONAL MEDIA AND TECHNOLOGY: A Professional's Resource/Edited by Phillip J. Sleeman and D. M. Rockwell

NEIGHBORHOOD SPACE/Randolph T. Hester, Jr.

MIXED LAND USE: From Revival to Innovation/ Dimitri Procos

COMMUNITY PLANNING FOR AN AGING SOCIETY/Edited by M. Powell Lawton, Robert J. Newcomer, and Thomas O. Byerts

EDRA Conference Publications

EDRA 1/Edited by Henry Sanoff and Sidney Cohn

EDRA 2/Edited by John Archea and Charles M. Eastman

ENVIRONMENTAL DESIGN RESEARCH, Vol. I: Selected Papers/Edited by Wolfgang F. E. Preiser (EDRA IV)

ENVIRONMENTAL DESIGN RESEARCH, Vol. II: Symposia and Workshops/Edited by Wolfgang F. E. Preiser (EDRA IV)

MAN—ENVIRONMENT INTERACTIONS: Evaluations and Applications/Edited by Daniel H. Carson (EDRA V)

RESPONDING TO SOCIAL CHANGE/Edited by Basil Honikman (EDRA VI)

CDS/20

COMMUNITY PLANNING FOR AN AGING SOCIETY:
Designing Services and Facilities

Edited by

M. Powell Lawton
Philadelphia Geriatric Center

Robert J. Newcomer
San Diego Office of Senior Citizen Affairs

Thomas O. Byerts
Gerontological Society

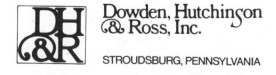

Dowden, Hutchinson & Ross, Inc.

STROUDSBURG, PENNSYLVANIA

Copyright © 1976 by **Dowden, Hutchinson & Ross, Inc.**
Community Development Series, Volume 20
Library of Congress Catalog Card Number: 75-45302
ISBN: 0-87933-195-X

78 77 76   5 4 3 2 1
Manufactured in the United States of America.

LIBRARY OF CONGRESS CATALOGING IN PUBLICATION DATA

Main entry under title:
Community planning for an aging society
     (Community development series/20)
        1. Aged—United States—Addresses, essays, lectures.
2. Old age assistance—United States—Addresses, essays,
lectures. 3. Aged—Dwellings—Addresses, essays,
lectures. I. Lawton, Mortimer Powell. II. Newcomer,
Robert J. III. Byerts, Thomas O.
HV1461.C65   362.6'0973   75-45302
ISBN: 0-87933-195-X

Series Editor's Preface

This is an important book in many respects. First, it comprehensively deals with preferential questions. How can we best set in motion processes and procedures that will improve the physical environment for older people? What substantive issues deserve special attention and, having been resolved, are likely to be most productive for those subjected to planning and design? Where are the frontiers in this special, but pervasive, area?

There are more than just answers in this valuable reference work. M. Powell Lawton and his colleagues are also advancing an important cause and effect relationship. Based on experience and experiment, they demonstrate that there are beneficial relationships—if not discernible links—between good planning, the delivery of social services, and the quality of the built environment.

Beyond these matters, one other comment should suffice to indicate why this book belongs in the professional library, close at hand for everyday use. The number of people 65 and over will grow from around 20 million to over 27 million in the next 15 years. Thus, population increase of the aged alone clearly points the way toward enlarged professional responsibilities in the near future.

Richard P. Dober, AIP

Preface

During the past decade and a half, a surge in concern for the problems of older people has occurred. Despite the immediate frustrations of a federal housing moratorium, cutbacks in research funding, and the capricious attention federal and local governments and voluntary funds have given to many services for older people, the national level of concern is markedly different from that of 1960. Increased Social Security benefits, Medicare and Medicaid, the Older Americans Act, federal housing programs, Office of Economic Opportunitity monies, and revenue sharing have transformed the national service picture. Programs for the elderly, such as the Retired Senior Volunteer Program (RSVP), Foster Grandparents, minibus and reduced-fare transportation services, adult protective services, home health aides, hot meals programs, and information and referral services, are now commonplace. Many began as demonstration projects and became widespread under Community Action programs or Model Cities categorical grants. Public response has been overwhelmingly favorable. As a consequence, revenue sharing and United Way Programs are increasingly called upon to perpetuate and expand existing service levels for the elderly.

Programs responding to the now visible needs of the older population have for the present greatly exceeded both the number of individuals trained to operate these programs and the number who can develop plans for efficient application. Most people involved in these efforts have been generalists or people trained in fields not previously emphasizing aging; they have had to pick up through practice whatever knowledge they could about older people.

Title III of the Older Americans Act, establishing Area Agencies on Aging (AAA), mandated that comprehensive service systems be planned and developed as a requisite to obtaining Title III program funds. The development of AAA's for each large metropolitan area and multicounty rural region has further magnified the manpower shortage while providing a stimulus for career development and professionalization within the field of aging.

In roughly this same period has occurred the interdisciplinary attempt to integrate knowledge about human behavior with knowledge about the environment. This field, variously called man–environment relations, social ecology, or environmental psychology, has had little direct effect on everyday practice, but it has stimulated appreciation for a wide range of environmental variables, even in nondesign disciplines. Thus the sociologist, psychologist, and social planner are increasingly apt to look beyond individual and demographic characteristics as the sole behavior predictors.

Such broadened perspectives have great potential for policy developers. Programs are now conceived that may be directed toward an alteration of "environment" as a demonstrated method for altering individual circumstances. This approach, when used with a clinical model (which when applied exclusively focuses all remedies on changing the individual), enhances programming flexibility. Closing the communication gap between physical and social planners and between environmentalists and clinical traditionalists is an issue of substantial importance to those concerned with the problems of the elderly. More than middle-aged adults, the elderly are often acutely vulnerable to environmental circumstances. Vulnerability increases as functional ability declines, as economic resources diminish, as a couple becomes a single-person household, as perceptual ability declines, as the automobile is no longer driven, or as friends and relatives die or move away.

Although much research on environmental influences on older people has been conducted, most has been addressed to institutional and group housing settings. Much remains to be learned about "normal," "typical" community residents who form the other 92 percent of the elderly population.

This book is designed to speak to both major issues raised here: the training needs of planners for the elderly, and the linking of environmental psychology to this process. An attempt has been made to define the skill and training needs within the context of the planning process and functions outlined in Title III of the Older Americans Act, and in light of the developing importance of the human-service program planning resulting from revenue sharing.

Within most communities there is a long tradition of social-service programming. However, these services have developed incrementally and often in response to crises. Consequently, there is an often-cited duplication and overlap in services. Even more important is a lack of coordination and gaps in services.

The 1973 amendments to the Older Americans Act established Area Agencies on Aging and charged them with examining the pattern of human services and developing a comprehensive system with respect to Title III funding priorities. Unlike the Community Action Agency and Model Cities program, which preceded this program, AAA's have county- or region-wide planning and coordination responsibilities. Their jurisdiction is limited only in terms of target populations, not geography.

Initially, each AAA operated under the mandate to coordinate and in some cases to finance several broadly stated services with high priority for older persons:

Information and referral
Transportation and escort
Outreach
Counseling
Health-related services
Homemaker and home health
Friendly visitors
Telephone reassurance
Protective services
Housing assistance
Recreational services
Continuing education
Legal services
Welfare services

Limited Title III direct-service funding has necessitated that service priorities be developed and that links be established with ongoing programs and other funding resources. Emphasis is placed on "tapping untapped resources."

The community organizational work, needs assessment processes, and priority systems that have been developed to meet the requirements of the Area Agency grants are now having a direct impact on local-level human-service planning. The stimulus for this has been both the success of area agencies and the politically draining process of allocating revenue-sharing funds, which have clearly demonstrated the need for an objective process for establishing priorities and area plans.

Because of the vast range of human services now claimed to be within the planning jurisdiction of area agencies and the necessity to work closely with other planning agencies and direct-service providers, many planning skills are required of AAA personnel. The following must be regarded as basic:

Information systems. The planning staff provides technical assistance to the program-development staff, including secondary data collection, literature searches, and maintenance of an inventory of human services. Many communities utilize computerized systems for the storage of data files and service inventories, so computer experience is also desirable.

Demographic analysis.   At the present time census data are the principal source of information for AAA's. Needs assessment methodologies, such as the one used in California (described by Glassman, Tell, Larrivee, and Helland in this volume), rely strongly on census data. Substantial familiarity with census documents and tapes and with population-forecasting techniques for updating these materials is essential.

Program evaluation.   The staff (1) reviews project proposals in terms of scope of service, desired pattern of services, and budgets; and (2) monitors programs and evaluates impact. Included in this latter process are skills in study design, data collection form and data procedure development, cost–benefit analysis, and other data analytic procedures. Implied too is a familiarity with computer and data-processing procedures.

Special study in each mandated service area is the most demanding and challenging of the responsibilities for the AAA planner. As part of a rational planning process, it is necessary to conduct in-depth analysis to determine the resources for, needs for, and barriers to service provision. The study design and analytic skills noted above also apply here. But two further elements are added: the necessity to gain quickly functional expertise in any one of 14 broad service areas, and the ability to work with community groups and other agencies in defining the problem, research strategy, and policy recommendations. These latter requirements are as much political as research skills.

Furthermore, each service area has many direct environmental implications. For example, housing needs are partially a function of individual competence, such as the ability to cook, but the presence of others, in the form of a spouse, relative, friend, or external service, can compensate for deficiencies in these areas. Mobility can be a problem. The circumstances underlying barriers to goods and services can be both individual—the inability to drive, walk, or use a bus, or environmental—excessive distance, heavy traffic, or the absence of transportation.

Sensitivity to the possible symbiosis between individual ability and environmental conditions as being essential in both problem definition and solution strategies is a continuing theme throughout the papers in this book. The skills discussed, particularly the synthesis of social planning and environmental psychology, are outside the experience of many now working in the field of aging. This book is structurally organized to introduce a number of very general planning problems that have special reference to old people. In this way, the generalist will be helped to understand both the unique problems of the aged and the way that universal problems can be dealt with in relation to older people. Second, the aspects of planning addressed are those that lie near the interface of the man–environment system: housing, institutions, zoning, resource location, transportation, and geographic mobility.

The assembly of such a book is a difficult task because little has been done in this area. Therefore, a great deal of the material presented is original. It was sought from individuals in fields related to planning, who were also known to have special expertise in aging. An integrative treatment of the field would be premature now, and the editors believe the most useful contribution to this new subarea is to provide a collection of material from the area's pioneers.

In planning such a book, it seemed wise to include a range of material wide enough to satisfy the diverse needs of planners, and to include enough material at the periphery of their interest to whet appetites and extend horizons. Thus the book contains some basic gerontology, many attempts to translate this gerontological knowledge into social and environmental prescriptions, a number of applications of population data use in planning, and some reports on moderately esoteric research methods. None are so technical as to cause difficulty in comprehension, however, and the reapplication of the methods and results in new situations should be perfectly feasible.

The basic division of content is between material that is standard for planners and material that represents an extrapolation of knowledge about older people, including suggestions regarding the design of the environmental resource package for them. The papers are grouped into four sections.

Part I begins by introducing the uninitiated to the basic facts about the aged and highlights the planning-related aspects of these facts. Included are an updated synthesis of demographic information about the older population, an examination of urban life style and life-cycle factors, and finally one of the most comprehensive treatments to date of the relation between subcultural variations, environmental planning, and service delivery for the aged.

Part II uses material that, although related principally to housing, presents a conceptualization of several issues in community planning and policy decisions that affect the life style of older people. Examined are federal and local decision-making processes as they impact local services, the effectiveness of previous federal housing programs in reaching their intended target groups, emergent legal trends showing promise of affirmative action directed toward increased assistance for older people, and finally the utilization patterns and the relative cost of alternative housing and services. The orientation of this part is to provide case material that illustrates the identification and definition of important variables which require monitoring as the future unfolds.

Part III relates directly to programmatic aspects of housing for the elderly. It provides a continuation of the preceding part by looking at a variety of the issues involved in planning housing for the elderly, such as demand estimation, housing preferences and satisfaction, the constant debate regarding age segregation versus integration, site-selection criteria, project size and service mix, and the potentialities of new towns as locales for serving older people. In sum, these chapters deal explicitly with several of the major determinants to housing design and location.

Part IV considers community service for the elderly, presented within the context of a social planning process. Each chapter illustrates a practical application of one element in this process; a recurrent theme stresses the importance of assessing and matching services to their community context. Specifically covered are the factors affecting service use and delivery, the influence and definition of neighborhoods, methods for service-need estimation and migration analysis, a background paper on intraurban transportation needs, and two case studies. One study identifies likely problems in program coordination; the other illustrates the utility and practicality of evaluation research.

Throughout the manuscript, the assumption is made that physical planners will do better work if they are aware of the problems of those who are concerned with the human aspects of service delivery,

and that those in the social area will be similarly enriched by a sense that proper use of the physical environment can actively enhance their efforts. It is hoped that this work will constitute the beginning of the end of the separation of the two disciplines.

The editors wish to acknowledge the early interest in the subject matter of this book that was expressed by Howard Ball and Jean Wasman of the Office of Community Planning and Development, U.S. Department of Housing and Urban Development. Their support through a contract to the Gerontological Society led to the publication of an abbreviated version of core material entitled *Community Planning for the Elderly,* edited by M. Powell Lawton and Thomas O. Byerts (National Technical Information Service publication number PB 232 000/AS).

Although most of the articles were written for this book and are published here for the first time, special thanks are due James Birren, formerly Editor-in-Chief of the *Journal of Gerontology;* Jerome Kaplan, Editor of *The Gerontologist;* and Charles B. Fowler, Editor-in-Chief, *Parks and Recreation,* for their permission to reprint certain articles. Many people generously provided photographs. We are particularly grateful to Olivia Coulter, Director of Public Information, Administration on Aging, U.S. Department of Health, Education, and Welfare; Dr. Sandra Howell, Department of Architecture, Massachusetts Institute of Technology; and Marilynn Wacker, Deputy Executive Director of the San Antonio Housing Authority, for providing a large number of photographs.

Much of the thread of our concern has developed under the support of the Administration on Aging, U.S. Department of Health, Education, and Welfare, through individual grants to the Gerontological Society, the Massachusetts Institute of Technology, and the Philadelphia Geriatric Center. We are particularly fortunate in having had the leadership of Jessie Gertman, Supervisory Specialist on Aging, in overseeing these projects.

The editors trust that this volume will be useful in improving the environmental condition of the elderly and unanimously encourage the dialogue—positive or negative—that will improve its utility.

M. Powell Lawton
Robert Newcomer
Thomas O. Byerts

Contents

PART I

**THE AGED POPULATION
IN A COMMUNITY SETTING**

THOMAS O. BYERTS

Thomas O. Byerts is Director of Architecture and Environment of the Gerontological Society.

Introduction

Part I presents an effective background for the general consideration of community planning for the elderly. In three papers we move from a comprehensive national demographic profile of the elderly, through a life-cycle-oriented physiological, psychological, and sociological overview of the older population, to specific findings from a study of cultural factors that affect the life styles of three ethnic subgroups of the aged in New York City.

Brotman's paper, "Every Tenth American: The 'Problem' of Aging," begins this book by tracing the generally negative consequences surrounding the national demographic shift toward extended longevity. Factors such as life expectancy at birth have increased since 1900 from 49.2 to 71.0 years; however, anticipated remaining years of life at age 60 has only modestly improved. Thus more people will be living into their sixties and seventies and more adults (some 60 percent) will have active parents and grandparents. Women fare better than men, married couples better than singles, and whites better than minorities. The declining birth rate will also contribute to the expected maturing of our population.

The shift toward extended years of life within our society is often accompanied by such negative aspects for the individual as a general decline in social status, growing obsolescence of work roles, diminished purchasing power, and dissolution of multigenerational households. Early retirement, loss of family and friends, inflation on top of fixed income, and declining health, sensory capacity, and mobility are additional concomitant factors facing people as they age. Clearly, the complex societal issues regarding the definition and active enhancement of appropriate standards for the quality of the life that is being extended must be resolved. A resolution favoring a stronger quality-of-life focus, not currently emphasized in our youth-oriented culture is the key factor that must be adopted before broad-ranging reform can be initiated.

On the positive side, some gerontologists argue that concepts such as the extended family are still very viable, that most urban elderly are not isolated in cities, and that many older citizens now have the best standard of living of their lifetime. Nevertheless, all would agree that far too many individuals are urgently in need of direct social, economic, and environmental services and facilities to assist them in overcoming the deprivations consequent to aging.

In "Urban Life Style and Life-Cycle Factors," Carp stresses that, whereas basic human needs are fairly constant across the life span, the appropriate means of meeting these needs vary generally by age group and specifically according to individual capability. Therefore, many environmental options require stress-inducing adaptation that is often more appropriate to younger cohorts who can more easily adjust than to older people.

Carp maintains that, although the urban scene exhibits many negative influences, the elderly (as well as other age groups) continue to congregate there because cities contain "compelling attractions." Beyond this, the need for continuity with past life style, the dictates of economics, the inability to plan for alternatives, or the fear of moving into an unknown and potentially worse situation are all factors that discourage change. Therefore, a developmental approach, based on an awareness of the individual's particular functional capacity, is necessary in analyzing population needs and structuring programs to meet those needs.

Age-related changes in sensory, physiological, social, and psychological characteristics that shape the way the individual relates to his or her environment are also discussed. The author concludes by focusing briefly on the elderly *in situ* within the complex urban scene. A better understanding of the complex resultant effects of various combinations of age-related changes is needed and would facilitate an effective planning approach to these problems.

The paper by Cantor, "Ethnicity and the Low-Income Urban Elderly," completely dispels any notion that the elderly population is homogeneous. The author demonstrates that subgroup membership (white, black, and Puerto Rican) is at least as important in determining the life style of the aging individual as chronological or physiological age. Meaningful social planning requires precise knowledge of both the basic processes of aging and the degree to which subgroups differ in their needs.

The New York City study was conducted in 1970 in 26 neighborhoods designated as poverty areas. Age, health, retirement patterns, income, use of financial aid, living arrangements, migration patterns, extended family structure, social contacts, and services for each of the three population subgroups were studied. The real lack of homogeneity demonstrated in individual behavior, cultural patterns, use of space, and service

needs should be kept in mind when reading the later papers of this book. Implications for responsive separate and integrated planning programs are discussed by Cantor.

NOTES TO PLANNERS

The three papers in Part I define the characteristics of older people, especially the urban elderly. All emphasize the diversity of subgroups and individuals. This diversity must be explicitly recognized. Generalized planning models usually mask the importance of individual differences, although amalgamation is enevitable in the real world. The Project Find study conducted by the National Council on the Aging (1970) interviewed 44,000 people in 12 communities. The project dramatically uncovered vast numbers of vulnerable persons who had previously "fallen through the cracks" of service-need estimates. Some, for example, were found to be paying 50 percent of their income for rent; 17 percent of the sample had had no visitors in the past week and had spent the last holiday alone. Conversely, the tendency for some social service agencies to overestimate and overrespond to service needs must also be guarded against.

Sound knowledge of the viable trends and details illustrated in Part I is especially important to planners and administrators since their decisions affect the lives of vulnerable segments of society. Reliable and detailed information can help refine thinking about the allocation of scarce resources within the complex, interrelated urban scene. Long-run economy and parity should result from conducting comprehensive baseline studies and monitoring changes over time. The resultant interactions and benefits to other population segments can also be identified and traced. There is, however, a tendency to deal with today's data when an anticipatory focus should be used. Researchers need to more clearly separate consistent trends from variable temporal patterns, and planners need to adopt new strategies to anticipate future trends.

A note of caution needs to be raised. Planners must consider that change of any kind can seriously affect the elderly, whether it be the massive dislocation of urban renewal, the addition of curb cuts on street corners for handicapped persons, or reduced fares on public transit. Involuntary change can have profound and even grave consequences, as seen in Pastalan's study (1973) conducted in Michigan, which documented the tragic results of relocating people from nursing homes that failed to meet fire codes. The research findings allowed him to estimate statistically that far more patients will die as a result of the relocation than die over the same period of time in nursing-home fires! This does not mean that change necessarily should be avoided but, if proved necessary, change must be dealt with in a sensitive, programmatic way. The negative consequences of necessary change can be reduced through efforts such as expanded public information, phasing the change over longer periods of time, direct counseling, family network involvement, and training of specialists to assist people in the readjustment process.

Finally, before moving into the balance of the book, the concise statement by Parr (1966, p. 45)

should be noted and reflected upon when ordering priorities:

It is high time to insist that the behavior of men, and the needs of the human mind, be also made the first objects of study in planning the environments in which our minds must function and our lives will be contained.

REFERENCES

National Council on the Aging. *The Golden Years: A Tarnished Myth*. Report on "Project Find," n OEO-sponsored contract. Washington, D.C.: National Council on the Aging, 1970.

Parr, A. E. Psychological aspects of urbanology, *Journal of Social Issues*, 1966, *22*, 39–45.

Pastalan, L. Relocation reports, nos. 1, 2, and 3. Institute of Gerontology, University of Michigan—Wayne State University, 1973.

HERMAN B. BROTMAN

Herman B. Brotman is a Consultant to the Senate Special Committee on Aging; formerly Assistant to the Commissioner on Aging, U.S. Department of Health, Education, and Welfare.

Every Tenth American: The "Problem" of Aging

With historical inevitability, economic development brings to each country in turn an increase in life expectancy and a growth in the proportion of older people in the population. Unfortunately, it also brings a drop in the physical, social, economic, and psychological attributes that make these older years desirable. It is both ironic and doubly frustrating that recent successes in the achievement of longer life should also produce the "problems of aging."

The very same "progress" that makes it possible for such a large proportion of our population to reach old age has produced the changes that make today's elderly essentially a dependent group, shorn of their traditional and most consequential functions, roles, and sources of status. The designation, "an elder," is no longer a title of respect and recognition of wisdom and experience. Instead, we search for euphemisms for old age, like "golden ager" or "senior citizen." No one is old, just aging.

The elder's loss of status, role, and function in society and family is an unplanned by-product of industrialization and urbanization, a necessary component of economic development. The rural (and small-town) multigeneration household has been supplanted by the urban nuclear family, with the elderly cut further adrift in separate households amid changing relationships with adult children.

The individually owned family farm or family craft or retail shop, to be inherited by the next generation in the family, has been replaced by an impersonal, absentee, corporate ownership in a cash wage system for the currently employed, in a crowded urban setting of small dwelling units. Even skills and know-how, until recently passed on from father to son or through a parallel system of apprenticeship, have been shifted to the responsibility of vocational education in the schools.

The wiping out of former satisfactions and status-giving roles and functions, without satisfactory replacements, has not only left the elderly without status but has also reduced their ties with the community and with their adult children. Worse, many elderly now accept society's negative image of old age—a self-fulfilling prophecy.

Meanwhile, the growing availability of retirement income arrangements and mandatory retirement regulations, the reduced relative manpower requirements due to technological change and the slower growth of the economy, and the obsolescence of old skills have combined to squeeze the vast majority of older per-

FIGURE 1
The physical proximity of multiple generations in sparsely setttled areas has been altered by increasing urbanization. (Photo by Thomas Byerts.)

sons out of the labor force whether or not they are physically, psychologically, or economically ready for retirement from their life's major activity.

As a corollary, almost all older people are dependent for most or a very high proportion of their incomes after retirement on retirement income payments of various kinds. If traced back far enough in the economic and political systems, all such payments can be shown to involve a social policy decision, conscious or accidental, and to depend on the willingness of the younger population in the so-called productive ages to share the current national product by transferring purchasing power to the elderly through a variety of fiscal and financial arrangements that help distribute the "burden."

LIFE EXPECTANCY

Life expectancy (more accurately, average remaining years of life) is a computed figure that summarizes the impact of medical, economic, nutritional, and environmental changes on death rates. Contrary to popular usage, life expectancy does not forecast survivorship in the future but merely provides a projection based on the current age–sex–color population mix, and only if there are *no changes* in the current age-specific death rates. For example, life expectancy at birth in 1900 was slightly over 49 years. If this had been a forecast of survivorship rather than a projection based on death rates in 1900 (which have since dropped drastically), very few people aged 75+ would be alive today. Actually, almost 8.3 million persons are aged 75+, close to 40 percent of the older population, and they form the fastest growing segment of our population, having increased 43 percent between 1960 and 1970.

Thus the changes that lowered death rates since the turn of the century have increased life expectancy at birth by almost 22 years, from 49.2 years in 1900 to 71.3 years in 1973. Although life expectancy for "Negro and other" races has increased faster than for whites, the nonwhite level in 1900 was so much lower than for whites that the gap has not yet been closed. It is interesting, however, that at ages 69 and over "Negro and other" life expectancy exceeds that of whites, perhaps as a result of the "survival of the fittest" among the sorely disadvantaged minority aged.

Study of life expectancy trends shows two additional developments of tremendous relevance to understanding the characteristics of the older population. First, the major improvements in life expectancy have occurred in infancy, childhood, and early adulthood. The medical conquest of many birth problems, early infancy disorders, and most of the contagious diseases, coupled with improved nutrition and sanitation, has meant that practically all children reach their adult years. Thereafter, the rate of improvement in life expectancy slackens and then falls off sharply at the ages when the major causes of death become chronic conditions, impairments, and diseases—all areas in which medical research has made little progress.

Thus, although many more people are now reaching the upper ages, once there they are not living much longer than did their ancestors when they reached these same ages. This could, of course, change substantially if breakthroughs in medical research into the major killers of older persons should materialize; three of these cause 75 percent of the deaths of persons aged 65+.

If all future deaths from cancer or stroke were eliminated for those persons now aged 65, it is estimated that average life expectancy for them would increase $1\frac{1}{2}$ years. Elimination of death from heart diseases for this group would add almost 5 years. Wiping out deaths from the prime killer of older persons, major cardiovascular–renal diseases, would add as much as 10 years to life expectancy at age 65. These estimates, however, do not take into account the possibility of an intervening death from other causes.

The second trend noted from the study of life expectancy is the considerably greater improvement in life expectancy for females than for males at all age levels, on top of an already somewhat greater life expectancy for females in 1900. The implications of the current almost 8 years greater life expectancy for females at birth (67.6 for males, 75.3 for females, in 1973) are examined later in this paper.

GROWTH IN THE SIZE OF THE OLDER POPULATION

The significant improvement in life expectancy (decrease in death rates) has resulted in a notable growth in the size of the older population. In 1870, we had 1.2 million persons aged 65+; in 1974, there were almost 22 million. Furthermore, the growth rate of the older population has been consistently faster than for persons under 65. Thus the *proportion* of the population aged 65+ has also increased.

In 1900, when 3 million of our 76 million population was age 65+, the elderly were 1 in 25; in 1974, with almost 22 million elderly in our 211 million total, the elderly are 1 in 10—thus, every tenth American. Compared with 1900, the under-65 population is now two and one half times as large, but the 65+ age group is six and one half times as large.

Projections of the size of the older population in the year 2000 can be prepared easily. All such persons are already born. The conservative assumption wolld be that there will be little change in death rates for the elderly and no change in net migration. Projections of the size of the *total* population are considerably more difficult because they require assumptions concerning future fertility rates.

The older population is expected to grow to 24.5 million by 1980, to 28.9 million by 1990, and to 30.6 million by 2000. If birth rates should continue at their currently low levels, the total population in 2000 might be 262 million (a total fertility rate of 2.11 children per female, zero growth or replacement rate); the 30.6 million persons aged 65+ would make up about 11.6 percent of the total. If, on the other hand, the birth rate should increase significantly, the total population in 2000 might be 287.0 million (a total fertility rate of 2.7 children per female) and the 30.6 million aged would make up 10.7 percent.

Thus all projections that do not assume a major medical breakthrough, like a cancer cure, agree that the older population will continue to constitute approximately one tenth of the total.

To describe 22 million people is a formidable undertaking. Even to grasp the concept of the sheer numbers involved is an awesome task. Twenty-two million is larger than the total number of people living in the eight largest cities in the United States or it is equal to the total population of the 21 smallest states in the United States.

Although we describe the older population as a "group," the term has only arbitrary validity; it is a statistical convenience, nothing more. The group includes the man born during the first decade of the twentieth century, who turned 65 just yesterday, as well as the man born before the Civil War who is on the Social Security rolls at age 126. What kinds of life histories, experiences, child rearing, and working lives can these two have in common?

Studies confirm the great diversity within the older population. In fact, a truism is that there is a greater range of differences within the older population than between the average of the older group and the average for any other age group. Finally, there is a whole range of differences within the older invididual himself—differences in both increments and decrements in tissue, organ function, and structure.

Moreover, the older population is not static in time. It is constantly changing and experiencing "turnover." Every day approximately 4,000 Americans celebrate their sixty-fifth birthday. Every day approximately 3,000 Americans aged 65+ die. Every day, therefore, there is a net increase of 1,000 in the older population, but the differences between the 4,000 newcomers and the rest of the older population are more meaningful than the mere 1,000 growth in numbers. When the 1971 White House Conference on Aging convened, it discussed a group of people more than 60 percent of whom had joined since the 1961 White House Conference; these newcomers had lived their whole lives in the twentieth century.

AGING OF THE OLDER POPULATION

As a result of changes in the rate of entry of persons into the age 65+ group and of small increases in life expectancy after age 65, the older population has been aging. In the 30 years since 1940, the median age of the elderly has risen almost $1\frac{1}{2}$ years (from 71.4 to 72.8). Projections based on present death rates indicate that the median age will increase by another year (to 73.9) by the end of the century.

Thus, while the older population has been increasing faster than the younger population, the older part of the older population has been increasing still faster. Between 1940 and 1970, the proportion of the older population aged 65 through 74 fell from almost 71 to just under 62 percent. The 75 through 84 segment rose from 25 to over 30 percent. The 85+ segment jumped from 4 to close to 8 percent, accounting for 1.5 million people.

Projections to the year 2000 indicate a general continuation of this trend during the next 30 years, with the median age of the older population rising to close to 74 years. The distribution for the year 2000 shows a further drop in the proportion aged 65 through 74 to under 56 percent, a further rise in the 75 through 84 group to almost 34 percent, and an increase in the 85+ segment to 10.5 percent, or 3.2 million persons.

The aging of the older population has serious implications for family structure, housing needs, medical-care services, transportation, home services, and the costs involved. Additionally, the presence of several

generations of retired persons in the same family will become increasingly common, each member struggling to live on a retirement income that is a fraction of preretirement income levels, and all looking to each other for financial and psychological support in emergencies.

SEX RATIOS

In the course of a year, about 105 boys are born for every 100 girls. Death rates for males, however, are greater than for females, beginning at birth. Thus, by the end of the "teens," the count of males and females at the same age is about even. Thereafter, females begin to outnumber males, and the size of the disparity increases with age.

At the turn of the century, there were still slightly more older men than older women (99 women per 100 men). By 1940, the situation had reversed itself, and thereafter the preponderance of older women grew rapidly. In 1970, there were 138 older women per 100 older men. Prospects are that this ratio will jump to 154 women per 100 men aged 65+ by 2000 unless the biologists can solve the puzzle of the greater vulnerability of the male.

These sex ratios, however, represent averages for the whole age 65+ group. Within the 1974 65+ population, there is a rapidly increasing disproportion, starting with 126 women per 100 men at ages 65 through 69, rising to 153 women per 100 men at 75 through 79, and jumping to 202 women per 100 men at 85+.

In addition to the effect on marital status, the increasing preponderance of older women requires special concern in the planning and design of housing, medical care, income arrangements, and family and social roles and opportunities.

MARITAL STATUS

Most older men are married; most older women are widows. Not only do women have longer life expectancies and thus outlive men, but they usually marry men older than themselves, compounding the chances for widowhood.

It has been calculated that for the middle-aged woman with a husband 5 years *younger* than herself the chances of widowhood at some time before death

FIGURE 2
Less than 1 in 5 older men are widowers. (Photo by Collas Smelser, courtesy of San Antonio Housing Authority.)

are about even. For the middle-aged woman married to a man of the same age, the chances of widowhood increase to 2 out of 3. For the more usual case, the middle-aged woman with a husband five years *older* than herself, the chances of widowhood jump to 3 out of 4. Widowhood brings an array of social, physical, economic, and psychological problems resulting from the loss of two central roles—wife and mother.

In 1974 about 79 percent of the older men but only 39 percent of the older women are married, whereas 52 percent of the older women and only 14 percent of the older men are widowed. The remaining 10 percent of both sexes are single or divorced.

Of every 100 noninstitutionalized older persons, 64 are between 65 and 74 years old and 36 are 75+. Of the 64 aged 65 to 74, 23 are married men, 17 are married women, 15 are widows, 2 are widowers, and 7 are single or divorced. Of the 36 aged 75+, 15 are widows, 9 are married men, 6 are married women, 3 are widowers, and 3 are single or divorced.

Comparing the age of husbands with that of their wives shows a further potential for growth in the number and proportion of widows. Less than 1 percent of the age 65+ wives have under-65 husbands, but 38 percent of the 65+ husbands have under-65 wives. About 63 percent of the age 65 to 69 husbands have under-65 wives; about 66 percent of the 70 to 74 husbands have under-70 wives and 30 percent have under-65 wives; and 55 percent of all age 75+ husbands have under-75 wives and 12 percent have under-65 wives.

LIVING ARRANGEMENTS

Living arrangements of the older population reflect such obvious factors as marital status, income position, and availability of housing choices, but also such strong psychological considerations as intensity of family ties, and a desire for independence or to avoid burdening adult children or other family members.

In broad terms, about 8 out of 10 men and 6 out of 10 women aged 65+ live in a family setting of some kind, 16 percent of the men and 36 percent of the women live alone or with nonrelatives, and less than 4 percent of the men and about 4.5 percent of the women live in institutions. These averages ignore the changes with advancing age within the 65+ group.

Of all older men, 86 percent live in households that they head—72 percent as heads of families (68 percent with wives present) and 14 percent alone or with a nonrelative present (less than 1 percent). Another 14 percent are not household heads; most (8.5 percent) live in a relative's household, a few (1.9 percent) live in the household of a nonrelative, and almost 4 percent live in an institution. It should be remembered that almost 40 percent of 65+ husbands have under-65 wives.

The situation for living arrangements for older women is quite different. About 44 percent live in households where they are the family head (no husband present) or are married to the family head. More than one third live alone or with nonrelatives and another 16 percent live in a relative's household. Almost 5 percent are in institutions.

Most widows live in their own households (68 percent); over half live alone or with nonrelatives. Of all older women who are heads of households better than 80 percent are widows. Similarly, two thirds of the older women in institutions are widows.

EDUCATIONAL ATTAINMENT

As a consequence of more limited availability and less emphasis on schooling when the current aged population was of school age (especially among the 15 percent who are foreign born), the amount of schooling completed by the older population averages about 3.5 years less than that of the younger population (aged 25 to 64) who have completed their schooling. Older women have more schooling than older men.

The median for the younger group is just above completion of high school; the median for the older population is less than 1 year of high school. More than one in every eight older persons is functionally illiterate (less than 5 years of schooling). At the other end of the educational scale, twice the proportion of younger persons (28 percent) have some college as do older persons (14 percent). It is reasonable to assume that the quality and relevance of educational content have improved over this long period.

The impact of high turnover in the older population, resulting from the large numbers of people reaching age 65 (with more schooling) and the death of people already 65+ (with less schooling), produces the projection of a rapid rise in the level of educational attainment of the older population in the future. The median number of completed years of schooling of older persons rose $\frac{1}{2}$ year during the 1960s, will gain 1 year during the 1970s, and will jump more than 2 years in the 1980s as the better-educated cohorts reach age 65 and the less educated aged die off.

"BURDEN" OF THE OLDER POPULATION

As previously indicated, the older population exists economically by sharing in the current national product, produced primarily by the part of the population in the so-called productive-age group, aged 18 through 64, largely through the willingness of the latter to provide purchasing power to the aged.

Before examining the economic status of the elderly, it might be well to examine the burden thus placed on the productive-age population. One measure is a simple dependency ratio showing the number of 65+ persons per 100 persons aged 18 to 64. Also, since children are "dependent" on this productive-age population as well, the same ratio must be considered for this younger end of the age scale.

The rapid and recent growth in the size and proportion of the older population is reflected in the increase in the ratio over the last 40 years from 9 to about 18 per 100. However, in view of the tremendous increase in productivity during this period, both the growth rate and the higher level of the ratio of older persons may be considered a very minor burden on the 18 to 64 group. Thus it is not the size of the economic burden that has prevented the provision of a more adequate standard of living for the elderly.

Considering the shape of the population pyramid, the dependency ratio for the under-18 population is considerably larger than for the older population and rose in the last 40 years from 59 to 61 per 100. However, the trend has varied and the recent drop in birth rates is reflected in the final level of the ratio.

Projections to the year 2000 indicate that, regardless of the assumptions concerning future birth rates, the total dependency ratios will remain relatively stable. And since productivity is sure to increase, the "burden" on the productive-age group will probably decline.

INCOME POSITION OF THE OLDER POPULATION

Work represents not only a major source of status and role satisfaction but also the best single source of income for most people. It is estimated that retirement brings a reduction of between one half and two thirds in money income as retirement benefits replace earnings as the principal source of income. Over the years, the median money income of older families has been consistently just under half the median for families headed by younger persons ($6,426 versus $12,935 in 1973). Older persons living alone or with nonrelatives fare even worse; their median averages less than half that of their younger counterparts ($2,725 versus $5,547 in 1973).

In 1973, of the 7.9 million families headed by persons aged 65+, 3.9 percent had incomes under $38.50 a week, 23.2 percent had incomes under $77 a week, and 71.4 percent had under $192 a week. At the other end of the income scale, almost 29 percent of the older families had $10,000 or more for the year and 4.4 percent had more than $25,000. Of the 6.3 million older persons living alone or with nonrelatives, 5.3 percent had incomes of less than $20 a week, 28.0 percent had less than $38.50, and 72.8 percent had less than $77. Only 4.8 percent had $10,000 or more for the year.

A survey in 1967 showed that about one quarter of older units (economic units such as couples, single persons, etc.) had some earnings from employment during the year, and, although most of this employment was part time and low pay, these earnings made up almost 30 percent of the total aggregated income of all older persons. On the other hand, the total of payments to the 9 out of 10 older people receiving retirement benefits added up to considerably less than half the aggregate income.

Half the older units had some income from assets (interest, dividends, rents, etc.), but it totaled only one seventh of the aggregate income and went mainly to the affluent aged, since the major asset for most elderly is the owned home. All other sources of income combined, including veterans benefits, public assistance, and contributions from relatives, provided only 10 percent of the aggregate income.

This quick summary points to the low relative income position of the aged. On the average, they are provided a level of purchasing power that permits only half the standard of living enjoyed by the rest of the population.

One of several attempts to measure the actual, rather than relative, adequacy of the income of older people is the federal poverty concept. This approach establishes a poverty or minimum subsistence level by using as a base the Department of Agriculture's economy food budget (originally developed to provide for subsistence over a limited period of time). The food budget was priced out with numerous variations by type, age of household head, size of family, number of children, and farm—nonfarm location of the household. Then, using data on the relationship between expenditures for food and all other consumption costs for low-income families, a matrix of "poverty thresholds" is computed to define poverty levels in dollar amounts. These dollar amounts are adjusted each year for the annual change in the consumer price index.

The application of poverty thresholds to data on annual income permits the designation of poor households for the noninstitutional population and thus the identification and study of the poor persons residing in such households.

The 3.4 million older people living in poor households in 1973 made up one sixth of all older people not in institutions. The aged poor constitute more than one seventh of the total poor of all ages as compared to making up one tenth of the total population. Within the aged, the largest proportion of poor are among those living alone, women, and minority members.

Another approach to measuring the adequacy of income arbitrarily establishes a detailed budget for an elderly, retired couple—a budget judged by a group of experts using all available information on consumption patterns to provide a "modest but adequate" standard of living. Pricing out all items in a large number of locations across the country produces a dollar figure that represents the amount required for this specific level of living for an elderly couple. This Bureau of Labor Statistics Retired Couple Budget has been priced out or computed from changes in the Consumer Price Index almost every year since 1967. Comparison with income data for elderly couples has consistently shown that at least half the couples could not afford the "modest but adequate" standard of living (estimated to cost $5,414 in the autumn of 1973).

Price inflation hits persons on fixed incomes especially hard. Even harder hit are older persons with little potential for improving their personal income by themselves. Generally, adjustments in retirement benefit levels, even if they are large enough to restore purchasing power, lag some distance in time behind price increases and cause great difficulties to older persons, who rarely have enough savings to carry them over. Formulas for automatic adjustment of retirement benefits for price increases tend to be illusions unless they start with a base level of benefit payments that provide an adequate standard of living, and unless they recognize the older population's right to share in the general improvement of the nation's standard of living.

Current inadequacies are reflected in the differences in consumption patterns of the older and younger portions of the population. Shelter and health costs of older persons must be paid first and use up a higher proportion of the lower income available to them. The remainder, necessarily, is small and dictates minimal expenditures for "necessities" like food and clothing, and minute expenditures, if any, for "luxuries" like transportation and recreation.

THE OLDER PERSON IN THE LABOR FORCE

Work and earnings play very important social and psychological roles as well as remaining the single best source of income. Compulsory retirement or pressures that have the same effect are serious problems for older persons on both counts, although changing social attitudes and new patterns for use of leisure time may change future values if the income problem can be alleviated.

At the turn of the century, two thirds of men aged 65+ were in the labor force; now less than one quarter are. Older women, sharing in the general movement of women into the labor force, increased their labor force participation rate slightly, from 8 to 10 percent.

The 2 million older men and 1 million older women working or actively seeking jobs are, however, disadvantaged by overrepresentation in the lower-paid pursuits. While only 4 percent of under-65 workers are in agricultural employment, almost 15 percent of the 65+ are thus employed. Part-time jobs are held by 16 percent of the under-65 workers but by 44 percent of the older. And only 8 percent of the under-65 are self-employed but 29 percent of the 65+ are.

The impact of this overrepresentation in low-income sectors is demonstrated by the fact that in 1973 families with a fully employed aged 65+ head of household had a median income only 83 percent of that of families with a fully employed head aged under 65 as was also true for persons living alone or with nonrelatives.

The advantage of income from employment, however, is still considerable. Those older families with a fully employed 65+ head (about 11.7 percent of all older families) had a median income 89 percent larger than the median for all older families. Similarly, the median income of fully employed 65+ workers living alone or with nonrelatives (5 percent of all these 65+ individuals) was two and one half times that of all the older individuals.

PHYSICAL HEALTH AND HEALTH-CARE COSTS OF THE OLDER POPULATION

Contrary to a troublesome but widely held stereotype, only 5 percent of the older population lives in institutions. The other 95 percent lives in the community, frequently with great difficulty owing to the shortage of all kinds of facilities and community and home services. The problem is compounded by the fact that the health-care needs of the elderly arise from the greater prevalence of chronic conditions and

FIGURE 3
Only 1 in 20 older people lives in an institution. (Photo by Sam Nocella.)

impairments (incurable, by definition) rather than accidents or contagious diseases, and require long-term medication, treatment, care, and special facilities. In addition, the individual's income is cut at the same time as his medical-care needs increase.

About 86 percent of the noninstitutionalized aged have one or more chronic conditions but the vast majority suffer no interference with their mobility and independence. Adding the 14 percent of older persons with no chronic conditions to the 67 percent who have chronic conditions that have no effect on their mobility gives a total of about 81 percent of older persons with no hindrance to mobility. Of the remaining one fifth, 8 percent need mechanical aids, 6 percent need personal help to get around, and 5 percent are homebound.

In 1973, the death rate for persons aged 65+ was 59 per 1,000 (4 per 1,000 for the under-65 population); the 65+ male rate was 72 and the female rate 49 per 1,000. It is important, however, that 80 percent of the total of 1.3 million deaths of older persons were caused by three chronic conditions: dis-

FIGURE 4
The great majority of old people live independently and have
no limitations on their mobility. (Photo by Mort Savar.)

eases of the heart and blood vessels (50 percent), malignant neoplasms (16 percent), and cerebrovascular diseases (14 percent).

Older persons have more restricted-activity and bed-disability days than do younger persons. They have twice as many general hospital stays and stay in the hospital twice as long. They visit their physicians 50 percent more often.

As a result, the personal health-care bill for the older population in the fiscal year ending June 30, 1974, was $26.7 billion or 29.5 percent of the $90.3 billion total for the population as a whole. The aged are 10 percent of the population but use close to one third of the health care.

On a per capita basis, personal health-care expenditures were $183 per person under 19 years of age, $420 for those aged 19 through 64, and $1,218 for the 65+ group. Of this $1,218, $734 or 60 percent was paid by public programs and $484 or 40 percent came from private sources, including $415 paid by the older person himself.

Of the $1,218 per capita expenditure for health care for older persons, $573, or almost half, went for hospital care ($458 or 80 percent paid by public

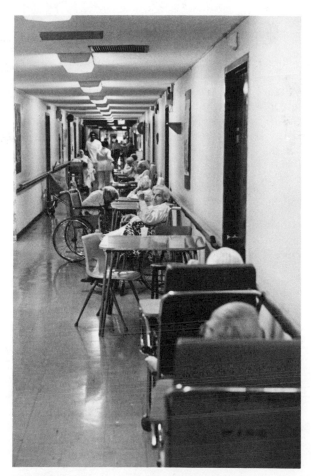

FIGURE 5
About one fourth of the nation's health-care expenditures are for the elderly. (Photo by Jonathan Harris.)

programs); $182, or 15 percent, went for physician services ($103 or 56 percent paid by public programs); $289, or about one fourth, went for nursing-home care ($142 or 49 percent from public programs); $103, or less than one tenth, went for drugs and drug sundries ($14 or 13 percent from public programs); and about $20 each was spent for dentists, for other professional services, and for eyeglasses and other appliances, almost entirely paid from private sources.

In fiscal year 1966, just prior to the beginning of the Medicare program, personal health-care expenditures per older person were $441 and 30 percent came from public programs. In fiscal year 1974, expenditures per older person were $1,218 and 60 percent came from public programs. Even allowing for the rapid increase in medical-care prices, it is clear that older people are getting considerably more health care, although their out-of-pocket expenditures may have remained about the same in nominal dollars. Whether the care is completely adequate in quality and quantity is a separate question.

MIGRATION

For the major part of the total population, residential mobility is closely related to the employment of the family head, a reflection of the vaunted mobility of the American worker. Older persons, in general, show considerably less mobility both out of choice (roots, family and friends, neighborhood ties) and because of economic considerations (lack of assets of potential for income, ownership of very old or unsalable home, etc.).

In March 1971, 91 percent of older persons lived in the same house as they had the year before. Of the less than 9 percent (1.7 million) who had moved during the year, 6 percent (1.2 million) moved within the same county, 1.3 percent (259,000) moved to a different county within the same state, and 1.4 percent (280,000) moved to a different state. Of the last group, less than 1 percent (176,000) moved to a noncontiguous state.

Comparable data for a 4-year interval (residence in 1974 compared with residence in 1970) showed that about 83 percent of older persons still lived in the same house, 10 percent had moved within the county, 3.5 percent had moved to a different county in the same state, and only 3.3 percent had moved to a different state.

The illusion of a larger interstate movement of older persons results from the fact that the flow of the comparatively small number of interstate migrants is concentrated into a very small number of states, primarily Florida, Arizona, and Nevada. Although the prime attractions are climate and health factors, many older persons are not very satisfied with the change after it has been made but find a return to a previous residence or another change too complicated.

Some older interstate migrants find that very few of the expected opportunities for supplementing retirement income actually exist. Many find that lack of accustomed seasonal changes, distance from friends and relatives, and scattered health-care facilities and services are handicaps. Many find the new state's residence and elgibility requirements more burdensome. Some find that expected or advertised lower living costs do not materialize because quoted costs for housing, transportation, shopping, and services were based on the experience of long-time residents with older housing and much greater familiarity with the facilities and customs in the community.

As is true of every other aspect of aging, data for the total 65+ population represent averages and mask significant cohort and age-related differences within the group. Space does not permit full discussion of detailed age differences here, but it should be noted that increasing widowhood and institutionalization after age 80 brings more movement of residence within the same state but no increase in the movement across state lines. By the same token, the proportion with an unknown address as of 5 years ago also increases. After age 80, only two thirds of the persons questioned in the 1970 census had the same address as in 1965.

DISTRIBUTION OF THE OLDER POPULATION AMONG THE STATES

In a pattern generally similar to that of the total population of all ages, older people are clustered in the larger and more populous states. One quarter of the older population in mid-1974 (5.3 million out of 21.8 million) lived in just three states (New York, California, and Pennsylvania). Adding five more states (Florida, Illinois, Texas, Ohio, and Michigan), with another 5.4 million older people, brings the total for these eight states to 10.7 million, or almost half of all older people in the United States. It takes 11 more states (a total of 19) to account for three quarters of the older population. Eleven more states (total of 30) are needed to account for 90 percent, and the remain-

ing 21 states have the remaining 10 percent of the older population.

New York and California each had just under 2 million older people in 1974. Pennsylvania, Florida, Illinois, Texas, and Ohio had numbers ranging from 1.3 to 1.0 million. Michigan, New Jersey, Massachusetts, Missouri, Indiana, and Wisconsin ranged between $\frac{3}{4}$ and $\frac{1}{2}$ million. At the other end of the scale, Delaware, Nevada, Wyoming, and Alaska each had less than 50,000, with Alaska estimated to have only 8,000 older persons.

PROPORTION OF OLDER PERSONS IN STATE

In spite of the rough correlation between the rankings of the states in total and in older population, there is sufficient variation to produce a wide spread in the proportion of each state's total population that was 65 years of age or older.

Florida, with substantial in-migration of older persons, led all states with 15.8 percent of its population aged 65+ in 1974. Seven states, Arkansas, Iowa, Kansas, Nebraska, Missouri, South Dakota, and Oklahoma (all highly agricultural states losing their younger populations), came next with between 12 and 13 percent. Another 15 states were at the U.S. average of 10.4 percent or between 10.4 and 11.9 percent. The remaining 28 states had less than 10 percent, ranging down to 7.3 percent in Nevada, 6.7 percent in Hawaii, and 2.6 percent in Alaska.

RATE OF GROWTH IN STATES' OLDER POPULATIONS

In the 4-year period from 1970 to 1974, the U.S. older population increased 8.5 percent. About half the states grew at a faster rate and half slower. The fastest growth in the older population occurred in four states, with increases of about 20 percent or more (Nevada, 33.9; Arizona, 30.2; Florida, 27.7; and New Mexico, 21.5) as a result of the *current* in-migration of older persons or the large in-migrations of young persons in the early 1900s now reaching age 65. On the other hand, seven states had older population growth of less than half the national average (South Dakota, 4.4; Nebraska, 4.1; Massachusetts,

FIGURE 6
Not all elderly households are as well equipped as this one.

3.8; Illinois, 3.5; Iowa, 2.8; New York, 1.6; and the District of Columbia with a loss of 0.1).

DISTRIBUTION OF THE OLDER POPULATION BY RESIDENCE

Analysis of 1970 census counts by the traditional definitions of urban and rural residence indicates that a very slightly higher proportion of older persons live in rural areas than do under-65 persons (27.1 versus 26.5 percent), and that a higher proportion of older persons live in towns (places of 1,000 to 2,500 inhabitants) than do younger persons (4.5 versus 3.1 per-

cent). Thus a somewhat smaller proportion of older persons live in urban areas than do younger persons (72.9 versus 73.5 percent), but higher proportions of older than of younger persons live in central cities and in towns and cities with over 2,500 inhabitants. Higher proportions of younger than of older persons (27.4 versus 21.2 percent) are found only in the "urban fringe."

The metropolitan–nonmetropolitan classification system, closer to present-day residential patterns, shows a higher proportion of older than of younger persons living in nonmetropolitan areas (35.8 versus 30.9 percent). Within the nonmetropolitan areas, the pattern of higher proportions of older than of younger persons showed these variations: urban, 15.4 versus 12.7 percent; rural nonfarm, 16.2 versus 14.2 percent; and farm, 4.3 versus 4.0 percent. Some 64 percent of older persons lived in metropolitan areas as compared with 69 percent of the younger. Within these metropolitan areas, however, 55 percent of the younger people lived *outside* the central cities, whereas 53 percent of the older persons lived *inside*.

Black aged are much more heavily concentrated in the nonmetropolitan areas and in the central cities of metropolitan areas.

OWNERSHIP OF ASSETS AND MAJOR APPLIANCES

Scattered studies show that the only widely held asset among older persons is a home. About 7 out of 10 households headed by an older person are owner occupied and about 80 percent of these homes are debt free. The median value of the family homes in this category in 1970 was about $14,500; that of single-person households was about $11,000. Not all of these, however, could be considered equivalent to liquid assets. Many homes are located in "changing neighborhoods," need extensive maintenance and repair work, are partially unoccupied, and are expensive to heat, light, and keep clean. Furthermore, in most cases, sale would not produce enough to purchase substitute housing or pay rental costs over a period of time.

A 1967 study of sources of income indicated that about half of older consuming units (families and unrelated individuals living alone or with nonrelatives) had some income from assets but that the *average* amount was quite small. Total income from assets accounted for only 15 percent of the aggregate income of all older units.

As is true for most major household appliances,

ownership of automobiles by older households is considerably below that of households with younger heads, but most of the explanation rests with current income level. A 1972 survey showed the lowest proportion of households owning an automobile to be those with aged 65+ heads (58 percent) and the highest to be those households with aged 35 to 44 heads (88 percent). However, only among households with under $5,000 incomes was there an actual decrease in automobile ownership with advancing age. In the over $5,000 per year income households, there were practically no differences by age. In fact, 92 percent of elderly households with $15,000+ annual incomes owned at least one automobile.

A WARNING

Any attempt to describe a large group of individuals necessitates the use of measuring instruments—arbitrary yardsticks and definitions—and statistical summarizations like measures of central tendency. Such generalizations, no matter how convenient and useful, tend to stress averages and "typical" cases but gloss over the tremendous range within the older age group—a range usually much larger than the differences between the averages of the two age groups. Similarly overlooked are the differences in change and in the rates of change within the single older individual and his organs and tissues and skills and capacities, as if the whole individual suddenly became old like the one-horse shay.

Finally, and perhaps most important to the community planner, this discussion is based on national data, on national averages. Planning must be based on thorough knowledge of the community situation. It is unlikely that your community will be exactly like the national picture; it may, in fact, show none or few of the characteristics presented here.

FRANCES M. CARP

Frances M. Carp is Project Director, The Wright Institute, Berkeley, California.

Urban Life Style and Life-Cycle Factors

At present, most old people live in cities. In 1970, nearly three quarters of those aged 65 and over lived in urban areas (U.S. Bureau of the Census, 1973). The tendency for the elderly to congregate in the cities will probably continue (Gibbs and Davis, 1958). Planning, which must be concerned with the future in order to be timely, must accept the urban environment as the usual setting for older adults in this country.

Undeniably, American cities at present are in many ways deleterious life settings for the old as well as for other population groups (Whalen, 1965; Morris, 1969; Milgram, 1970; Michelson, 1970). Nevertheless, the urban milieu may have unique potential for meeting the needs of old people and for supporting life styles appropriate to the later years of life. It is important to explore these potentials. The very fact that old people as well as those of other ages congregate in cities suggests that the urban situation contains compelling attractions, despite its obvious faults, and therefore provides encouragement for the exploration.

In this paper we present life-cycle considerations that are relevant to life styles in the later years and, to the extent possible, view them in terms of the urban scene context. The final section is a summary of some of the major disadvantages and potential advantages of that context; it is hoped that the reader will be stimulated to conceive of specific ways in which the urban environment can be made a more salutory milieu for the elderly resident.

LIFE STYLES OF THE ELDERLY

Psychologists agree about very few things. One of that small number is that individual differences increase with age: the older a person, the more unique is he likely to be (Kelly, 1955). Infants are fairly similar; 2-year-olds are becoming "real persons"; how much more clearly differentiated are octogenarians, each with his extensive life history of unique experience. The point is crucial here because the first principle must be that *there is no one best life style* for the elderly but instead a rich variety; consequently, the goal is not to discover *the* ideal housing and living situation for old people, but rather to design and create the *wide range of environments* necessary to support the rich variety of life styles that are appropriate among older people.

Although individual differences become accen-

19

tuated with age, development is, nevertheless, to be expected throughout the life span. To understand the life styles of later years, we must look at (1) the changes later years usually bring, which constitute common modifiers with aging, regardless of differences among those who are growing older, and (2) the constancies across age—the relatively invariant human factors that old people hold in common with people of all ages.

AGE-RELATED CHANGES

Taking a life-cycle viewpoint, we are interested in how a person, as he moves through time, adapts to the situation in which he finds himself, with the capacities he has available. Progress through the life cycle entails both normal aging and cumulative damage. Even if biochemists should stop biological aging, every individual will continue to age in the sense of living longer and being changed by that living. Also, the longer a person lives, the more opportunity he has to be damaged—physically, psychologically, socially, and emotionally. We must distinguish damage from normal aging.

Thus we need to separate context effects from essentially age related changes. Many external influences so regularly accompany aging that we mistake their effects for those of age. Poverty, substandard and socially isolating housing, and inadequate transportation are common among the old. How differently would these people age in conditions of adequate incomes, good housing and living situations, and easy access to community resources and to other people?

To understand the life styles of the elderly, many intrapersonal factors must be considered. Among them are sensation and perception—the avenues of awareness of self and situation; the mechanisms of response—the ways in which a person reacts to a situation; and the capacities for learning, remembering and thinking—the ability to acquire new information and new skills and to make use of old ones. It is also necessary to consider motivation and emotion—the power sources for action and reaction, for learning, and for performing or not performing learned behaviors. Finally, we must consider attitudes—the residuals of past experience that orient a

FIGURE 1
Failing senses may be bolstered by either human or mechanical aids. (Photo courtesy of Administration on Aging. U.S.D. H.E.W.)

person to new situations; adjustment techniques—the habits of performing life's tasks, solving problems, meeting challenges, and withstanding stress; and personality—the self.

Sensation and Perception

Generally, with age there is loss in sensory acuity. It takes a stronger signal to get through. However, there is not a one-to-one relationship between the amount of sensory loss and consequences in behavior.

People have the capacity to compensate for losses, and environments can assist this compensation. People extend their arms and wear glasses to compensate for visual changes; much less willingly, they put on hearing aids. Sometimes the compensation makes use of other senses, other modes of perception to help them perform better. To adapt to auditory loss, some people learn to read lips without being aware that they are doing it. As people age, they may begin checking on what they are doing with their body parts by looking at them. The visual signal is necessary to let them know for sure the position of a foot or hand. Older people do many things, consciously or unconsciously, that help to compensate for losses of acuity in the various senses.

However, all the habits of everyday living have been built up on the basis of earlier levels of sensory acuity. For example, a lifetime of habit has been based on 20–20 vision and now the person no longer has it. He receives visual information incorrectly or partially, which leads him to make mistakes, because his response repertory was built up on the basis of accurate reception of visual signals. This, in turn, makes him hesitant and unsure. He loses confidence and tends to give up trying to do some of the everyday things he has always done.

In addition to the loss of sensory acuity, the aging person has increasing difficulty in dealing with complex stimuli. If confronted with a number of "signals" at one time, he tends to become more confused

FIGURE 2
Environmental aids such as corrective lenses and proper illumination provide continuing opportunity for enrichment. (Photo by Richard Mowrey, U.S.D.H.U.D.)

than he would have been at an earlier age. Also, and very importantly, if rushed, he is even more likely not to "get his signals straight." These statements hold true generally for all sense modalities.

Vision. The eyes are usually considered the most important sense organs. Paradoxically, although vision becomes less accurate, aging people become increasingly dependent on vision. They begin to use visual cues to augment or correct kinesthetic, proprioceptive, and auditory cues—which are also becoming less clear and accurate. Lipreading is an example. Or when stepping down from a curb, many old people look at the foot, because they are not really sure where it is. At earlier ages, looking was not necessary.

Vision deteriorates in several ways. The pupil becomes smaller and less light is let into the retina. Good illumination is some help as an environmental compensation. However, lens opacity increases with age and cataracts are more common, so glare is increasingly a problem. With age, the muscles of the eye lose elasticity and tone, so focusing becomes less accurate. Glasses help, as do clearly demarcated "edges" in the environment. Inaccurate focusing is less of a problem when forms are sharply delineated and objects are clearly distinguished one from another.

Color vision holds up better than shape perception, although some hues tend to fade owing to lens opacity. Color coding the environment is especially helpful to the old.

Dark adaptation becomes slower and less effective with age. As a person ages, it takes more time before he can see well enough to find a seat in a dark theater. Sudden plunging from a brightly lighted to a darkened area, in a residential or transportation situation, can be dangerous and frightening to an old person.

The size of the visual field tends to constrict with age; that is peripheral vision is reduced. Visual "signals" outside the central range of vision are not received. This age change has particular relevance to the design of signaling and signing systems, and may account in part for the fear, which is common among old people, that they may not be able to find their way about the city (Carp, 1971a).

Hearing. With age, audition becomes less sensitive, especially for high frequencies; but it also occurs for low frequencies. Men tend to have more loss than women. The level at which auditory loss is handicapping to a person depends on many things. For example, a very bright person may interpret speech sounds even though he is quite deaf, in the sense of hearing pure tone, while a dull or disinterested person is unable to understand what is said. The behavioral effect of hearing loss depends upon interest, listening habits, and intellectual ability.

Hearing also depends upon the "noise climate." People with hearing problems receive auditory messages more clearly in quiet surroundings. Background noise seriously impedes their ability to hear. Thus, receiving a reply to a request for information may be very difficult at a busy intersection. In a multipurpose recreation room, other activities may interfere with listening to television or carrying on a conversation to a far greater extent for old people than for young (Carp, 1966).

The consequences of the inability to hear are serious, particularly if the person does not acknowledge the auditory decrement. He may then think that others are not making any effort to include him or even that they are trying to exclude him. Some old persons become withdrawn and suspicious as a result.

Kinesthesis. Perceptions of change in body position and of orientation in space become less accurate with age. Body sway also increases: when people stand up, put their feet together, and shut their eyes, the older tend to lose their balance more quickly. These proprioceptive and kinesthetic changes probably cause the increased use of visual checks on feet and hands. Together with reduced visual acuity, these changes no doubt contribute to the increasing tendency to fall as people age.

Temperature. Sensitivity to temperature declines, especially to cold. Temperature-regulation mechanisms become less effective, so that older people's bodies are less capable of adapting. Older people may be unaware that the ambient temperature has fallen to levels which are dangerous for them. Obviously, then, dependable and adequate heat and control of temperature within a fairly narrow range are essential components in environments for old people.

Other senses. There usually is not much change in taste sensitivity until about age 50 and no very large change until 70; the same is probably true of smell.

FIGURE 3
This pathway from a building housing the elderly to the local shopping center is a hazard for those with visual, kinesthetic, or ambulation problems. (Photo by Gerald Falls.)

Awareness of thirst also diminishes. There is little alteration in sensitivity to pain until past 70. Generally, there is slight sensory-perceptual decrement with age, and marked change at about 70 years of age. As we age, the world impinges on us less clearly and less accurately, unless signals are strengthened and provided in several sense modalities.

Mechanisms of Response

With age, strength and agility decline. Perhaps the most impressive change is in the slowing of response.

The reaction time between a stimulation and a simple response to it starts slowing shortly after age 20. On the other hand, movement time, for example, tapping as rapidly as you can between signals to start and stop, does not decline until after age 70. Spontaneous speech holds up also; people aged 70 can talk as fast as those who are 17. However, performance of other complex tasks, such as writing, slows.

Anything unfamiliar in a task further reduces speech, as does any extraneous stimulation that does not have to do with the task (such as other nearby activities). Trying to hurry a person only makes him slower and less accurate. If the task cannot be completed in a certain amount of time, the older person seems to "lose" the instructions, and he may not complete the task at all unless the instructions are repeated to him or are left where he can refer to them.

Old people are less adaptable in changing speed. For example, if you tell people to write very slowly, then very rapidly, then at their usual speed, young adults and children write, as requested, at quite different rates, but old people tend to write at the same speed for all instructions.

There are some general principles to use to get old people to respond well. First, they need plenty of time to get ready and a preparatory signal to let them know that the task is about to begin. This need is clearly expressed, for example, in their difficulties in getting off public transit vehicles at the correct stop (Carp, 1971b). Old people need a reminder of what the task is, particularly if it extends over quite a period of time. "People-movers," such as that in the Tampa airport, may be especially helpful to the old because information is repeated throughout the ride.

Old people also need plenty of time to respond. Ideally, they should be allowed to perform at their own rate. Therefore, signals paced for the convenience of automotive traffic give older pedestrians particular difficulty (Carp, 1971c; Carp, 1972a). Similarly, the most serious problem for older drivers is the speed of traffic (Carp, in press a).

Old people do less well with unfamiliar material and tasks. It is desirable, then, to introduce new situations gradually or to relate new situations to familiar ones. Finally, because of the sensory-perceptual changes discussed, old people always need a strong, clear signal and an environment without distractions, in order to perceive the environment accurately so that they can respond to it appropriately.

Locomotion. There is a very high accident rate, especially with falls, among persons past the age of 65. Most accidents occur at home, so they are not because of unfamiliarity. There are also many pedestrian accidents. Because perceptions become less acute and responses slower, and because habit patterns have been built up on the perception and reaction capacities of younger years, an older person can experience considerable difficulty in getting around. Many become discouraged and stay at home.

Some find ingenious solutions. For example, there is what Lawton and Azar (1966) call "convoy behavior." An older pedestrian at a busy corner starts and then pulls back, until finally he spots a younger

FIGURE 4
The hazards of being a pedestrian are lowered by curb cuts such as this. (Photo courtesy of Administration on Aging, U.S.D.H.E.W.)

person who looks competent and follows him across the street. Old people resort to this because they cannot get all the signals, the visual checks on the position of the feet, and the necessary motions timed and coordinated together to proceed across the street before the signal changes—or at least they fear they cannot.

In 1966, people aged 65 and older comprised less than 10 percent of the population but accounted for 25 percent of the nation's pedestrian fatalities (National Safety Council, 1967). Either we must design better pedestrian accomodations or we will kill even more oldsters as signals increase in complexity, and traffic, in speed.

In driving automobiles, accident rates decline until about age 50; then they begin to increase. Accident rates are not closely related to age until about 65, but by the time a person is 70 he is more likely to have a wreck than is a teen-ager. There are characteristically different types of accidents at different ages. For drivers under 30, most accidents are caused by driving too fast. Over 65, speed is not a factor, but older drivers tend to get in trouble over the right-of-way and to have problems with complex stimuli such as several traffic lights and signals. For example, if there are three lights, two of them for cars going straight ahead and one for a left turn, an older driver may go ahead when a left turn is signaled, or turn left when the lights signal "go" for straight ahead. He has three lights to watch in a complex visual and temporal pattern; there is time pressure and a complex background of traffic sights and noises. Older drivers also have accidents involving turns. Apparently, again, there is difficulty in pacing and coordinating the stimulus—response patterns. It is no wonder that driving in an urban area is difficult for older drivers and that many limit their driving to local streets (Carp, 1971a), which seriously impedes their access to the community.

For this reason and for reasons of income, health, and licensing, older people tend to be transit-dependent (Vollmer et al., 1972). Unfortunately, the use of public transportation is unusually difficult for them in a number of ways—negotiating the stairs and dodging the doors, keeping their footing, managing packages, knowing when to prepare to get off, and the attitude of other travelers who press them to hurry,

FIGURE 5
In the absence of clear signals, heavy traffic poses a problem for the elderly pedestrian. There are simply too many quickly changing stimuli. (Photo by George Gardner.)

will not give them information, and may rob or attack them (Carp, 1971a).

Occupational skills. In view of the difficulty old people have in getting work, mention might be made of occupational skills. Studies in agriculture report that the kinds of accident which can be avoided by using good judgment tend to occur among young farmers; the old farmer has those which could be avoided by rapid, evasive action. These findings may have relevance to some urban jobs.

Industrial accidents are generally lowest among older workers, with those 65 and older having the lowest rate of industrial accidents, as well as low absenteeism and high accuracy. However, the industrial worker past 65 is a highly selective phenomenon. He probably was among the best all his life. Perhaps he must be above average to retain a job past normal retirement age. Therefore, the findings on older workers cannot be generalized to indicate that *most* people 65 and older would have a low industrial accident

FIGURE 6
Pedestrian signals are mandatory near senior-citizen housing. Not only is the rough sidewalk on the left a hazard, but in general, a bar so close to such housing is undesirable. (Photo by George Gardner.)

rate. Among "old" airline pilots—those 40 to 60—the accident rate goes down with age.

Learning

There is little evidence of a change in learning ability with increasing age. Other age changes may simulate loss in learning ability. For example, what is learned is affected by sensory input. If the signal is too weak, the person cannot learn from it. In laboratory or test situations to assess ability to learn, scores are affected by the slowing of response that comes with age. Often, in these situations, there is pressure for speed, and anxiety blocks learning for older peo-

ple. They have been convinced that they cannot learn and are motivated by "fear of failure" rather than "hope of success." Old people's performance at learning tasks is reduced further by lack of interest in what is given them to learn and by lack of motivation to learn it. Such problems for a time made it appear that learning ability declined with age. Now it seems that this is not true (Jarvik, Kallman, and Falek, 1962; Birren, 1967; Green, 1969).

As an example, over 200 old people moved into a new apartment house that had very modern kitchen stoves (Carp, 1966). The staff was afraid that the old people would be unable to prepare hot meals. However, one demonstration sufficed. Motivation was strong, the task was relevant, and the demonstration was clear; there was no problem in learning.

In another study, Belbin (1968) compared 12-year-olds with older workers on two kinds of learning tasks. One was rote learning and the other was problem solving. Belbin gave two different types of instruction: in one, he described exactly how they had to do the task; in the other, he put them on their own. When the learning procedure was predetermined, the 12-year-olds did better; but when the person approached the learning task in his own way, the old were superior.

Belbin also found that any kind of continuing education—making baskets, baking pots, studying engineering—was associated with a good capacity to learn in old age. Maybe we should get back to that concept psychologists tell people to forget, the idea of "strengthening the mental muscles." Of course there are no "mental muscles," but there is something that needs exercise for people to continue to learn as well as they ever did or in some instances perhaps better.

Societal Context

As a person moves through live, his adjustment tasks change according to the developmental period; his capacities and the situation alter; the rewards and disappointments differ. All are related to society's "norm" for the age at which he finds himself. How does society define old age? Often, to be old is also to be poor. One third of those 65 and older exist below the poverty line, and that "line" is lower for them than for younger persons (Orshansky, 1965). Almost universally, to be old is to be poorer than in previous years. Even good retirement incomes are sharply less than working incomes. As Rosow (1967) so graphically put it, at retirement income typically is "chopped in half." This relative and absolute poverty affects all aspects of life—housing, transportation, hobbies, community service, church attendance, and contact with friends and family. It limits all aspects of independent action, self-esteem, and usefulness. It makes dependence an ever-present threat.

To be old is to sense the world less clearly and respond to it less quickly and with reduced strength. It is to have more ailments and less adequate medical care, because the old are poor, have chronic ills, and do not know that they can feel better. The physician's "What do you expect at your age?" is spoken too readily and taken too literally (Ostfeld, 1968).

To be old is to be useless to others and to be devalued by them. Studies show consistently that people of all ages—old people, too—hold negative views of old age. No one wants to be old. Few want to serve the old. A small fraction of the national resource dollar is spent on improving the lot of the nation's elders. Generally, their status in the society is low.

CONSTANCIES ACROSS AGE: BASIC NEEDS

Despite the many changes that old age typically entails—in sensory acuity, motor skills, sensory-motor coordination, financial capability, social context, and societal status—old people are, first of all, people. Recognition of the characteristics that they continue to share with other human beings of all ages is essential to the design of optimal environments for the old.

Basic needs seem to remain remarkably similar throughout the life span. However, the appropriate means for meeting these needs varies from stage to stage in the life cycle, and from one person to another within one life-cycle phase. The design of environments for the elderly must be based on an understanding of these common human needs as they operate in later life.

Physical Life-Support Needs

The most basic needs, obviously, are those whose fulfillment at some minimal level is necessary to the continued physical existence of the individual. Life is most quickly threatened by the absence of *air* to breathe, and next most quickly by lack of *water*. All people need an environment that provides good-quality air and water. This need may be more acute among the old because of increased vulnerabilities. For example, larger proportions of older residents of the San Francisco Bay Area report being "bothered by" air pollutants.[1] Rates of emphysema and other respiratory diseases increase with age. For various reasons, physicians are more likely to recommend distilled drinking water for older patients. Thus pure air and water may be especially important environmental factors for the old. In some instances, regardless of age, air conditioning (for its cleansing as well as cooling function) can be justified as a medical expense for income-tax purposes. Equipment to cleanse water and air may be a necessity rather than a luxury in housing for old people.

Food is another obvious physiological need, and eating, in addition, may entail important social and psychological satisfactions. An adequate environment provides good nourishment in ways that are at least physically manageable and hopefully also psychologically acceptable. Old men may never have learned to plan meals, shop, and cook. Old women may live on tea and toast, not out of ignorance or preference but because they must fetch their groceries on foot (Carp, 1971c, 1971d). Old people of either sex may eat poorly because they are alone and eating has been a life-long social occasion. Older people want to maintain the autonomy represented by their own kitchens, but many would welcome the service of one hot meal a day at a price that they could afford. Needless to say, poor nutrition is also a function of the fixed incomes of old people in a situation of continuing inflation.

Just as at any age, old people need good nourishment; for many reasons, they are unlikely to receive it unless the environment is especially designed to provide it. In addition to the considerations mentioned, old people are more likely to have special dietary requirements. For example, diabetes and high blood pressure rates increase with age; for persons with these disorders, life expectancy is heavily dependent upon carefully controlled food intake. In addition, the dental status of many old people makes it difficult to consume a well-rounded diet.

Although there are medical reasons for many older people to have bland diets, reduced sensitivities to taste and smell—both important to the enjoyment of food—argue for stronger cues to make food attractive enough to ensure consumption of appropriate nourishment. This extra stimulation may need to make use of other senses. When strong seasoning is not advisable, particular attention should be paid to provide variety and interest through the texture and color of foods.

Shelter is another basic need. Once more, the old

FIGURE 7
An inexpensive meal out is good for both nutrition and social needs. Another of the city center's frequent resources is benches for rest or for watching other pedestrians. (Photo courtesy of Administration on Aging, U.S.D.H.E.W.)

tend to be more vulnerable than young persons. They tend to be less adaptable to extremes in heat and cold, particularly the latter. Relative insensitivity to cold may constitute a special danger for the old in

FIGURE 8
Shelter from sun and rain, plus opportunity for conversation, are given by this otherwise dismal ground-floor area of a public housing project. (Photo by Lois Jean Tiskur.)

view of a reduced capacity to adapt to low temperatures (Anderson, 1973). Therefore, the thermostats in their residential areas may need to be more accurate and dependable than those in other homes, if "shelter" is to provide equitable protection.

Shelter also carried the connotation of *safety*. The home area should be one in which the individual, at any age, can carry out normal activities without fear

of accident. But a "safety" feature for one age group may be an unusual hazard for persons at another point in the life cycle. For example, one residence for the elderly went to great pains to specify "safety ranges" for apartment kitchens. Unfortunately, "safety" had been determined for toddlers. Therefore, the controls were at the back of the cook-top, quite possibly the most unsafe of all possible locations for old people. Reduced visual acuity coupled with increased unsteadiness, particularly of older women (Lawton and Azar, 1966), makes these "safety stoves" unusually inconvenient and dangerous for the old (Carp, 1966).

Living areas—not just homes—must be designed to provide physical safety for the residents; the environment must support the individual's ability to perform normal tasks and minimize the likelihood of injury in the course of ordinary activities. Planning environments for safety must take into account the life-cycle status of residents. For example, pedestrianism holds a certain amount of risk for everyone, but the very large majority of injuries from automobiles are to preschool children and old people (National Safety Council, 1969).

Security of person and property is another basic need. Today, fear of attack and of property loss or damage are prevalent in urban areas. For example, data collected recently in the San Francisco Bay Area indicate that, of a random sample of 2,541 persons 18 years of age and older, 13 percent are afraid in the area immediately around their homes "often" or "most of the time." The figure is slightly higher for those 65 and older (17 percent).[2] Over one third (36 percent) of the total sample was "very" or "extremely" concerned with being attacked on the street in their residential areas. The old tend to be especially vulnerable to robbery and mugging because they are relatively powerless to fight back, are less fleet of foot, and tend to go about alone or in pairs rather than, as at some younger ages, in groups that afford the protection of numbers. Furthermore, the consequences of robbery or assault are likely to be more serious for the old person. His (and even more, her) fragile bones are more likely to break, recovery from injury is slower, and the loss of money or property is greater, in relative terms.

Old people are more likely to be dependent upon walking and on public transit to get them where they need to go (Carp, 1971a); these forms of transportation offer far less security than a private automobile. One result of the fear of crime is further reduction in mobility. In addition to lack of automobiles and problems with driving, poor pedestrian facilities and inadequate public transit, and little money for transportation, the old are further inhibited from going

FIGURE 9
Purse snatchers find this pathway leading from a housing site an excellent location. (Photo by Ralph Huff.)

about, especially after dark, by fear of attack. Even within their own homes, many elderly people feel insecure.

Psychological Needs

Prolongation of physical existence is only part of any reasonable societal goal for older citizens; there must also be concern for good *quality* of life. Old people share with those of other ages a variety of social and emotional needs whose satisfaction determines the level of function of the individual. Frustration of these needs leads to the wasting of the individual's unique potential, to his dependence upon society rather than contribution to it, and to his suffering a consequent sense of failure or guilt.

These basic psychological needs are closely tied to the environment. The specific forms of their expression and satisfaction were determined in person—environment interactions early in life, as is clearly documented by cross-cultural studies. It is perhaps inadequately emphasized that, even late in life, the physical and social environments determine the extent to which these common human needs can be met.

One need which is unquestionably dependent for satisfaction upon the environment is that for appropriate *sensory experience*. Developmental theory and practice stress the requisite for adequate sensory stimulation for the infant and child to develop normally in motor behavior, intellect, and relationships with others. For an infant with a sensory deficit, care must be taken to provide stronger stimulation in the defective sense modality and/or compensatory stimulation in others.

Even in adult life, the loss of sensory input is a danger to normal behavior. The adult who loses his vision, for example, may be in some ways even more greatly disadvantaged than the congenitally blind. Even laboratory studies of sensory deprivation have serious behavioral and experiential consequences. Normal persons become disorientated, withdrawn, and may experience hallucinations if they are temporarily deprived of normal sensory input. Apathy and lack of motivation have been identified as part of the sensory-deprivation syndrome (Hebb, 1958).

The reduced sensory acuity that comes with age may produce a sort of sensory deprivation which should receive compensation in terms of stronger signals from the environment. This necessity is recognized to some extent. For example, in deference to reduced visual acuity, environments for the old usually include stronger visual cues to indicate a change in grade, such as that involved in going up or down stairs. It is possible that other information and enjoyment provided in the visual environment is not received because of the reduced sensitivity of old eyes or ears. Research suggests that signaling and decorating should provide not only strong cues but also cues in several sense modalities. Then old persons will have the opportunity to compensate for losses by using the best combination of remaining sensitivities rather than being dependent upon only one. Signaling, signing, and decorating should be assessed by persons similar to those who will live in a residence or use a park or a transportation facility, rather than only by designers, who tend to be younger.

One great advantage of the urban milieu may be the richness and intensity of sensory stimulation that it provides. The city may be an environment that supports direct (within-sensory modalities) and indirect (across-sensory modalities) compensations for the reduction in acuity which comes with age.

Audition is a special problem, and the urban scene may accentuate it. Old people accept eyeglasses more readily than hearing aids, yet auditory losses often accompany aging. One unfortunate consequence is feeling left out of things and even that others are talking about one. The physical environment can magnify or minimize problems with hearing. The old person who has a hearing deficit has the least trouble hearing what someone is saying when there is the least background noise. A noisy dining room or recreation center is not a setting for social interaction among people with hearing problems. The high background noise in the city makes it more difficult for old people to hear signals clearly and to communicate with others. Sound conditioning of indoor and outdoor areas used by the old will allow them to receive auditory signals more accurately, to function more compentently, and to enjoy life more fully.

Tactile and *kinesthetic* stimulation is an area of relative ignorance in regard to the old. Indeed, recognition of the importance of touch and movement to normal development and adequate functioning at earlier ages is comparatively recent. The work of Harry Harlow and his associates at the University of Wisconsin suggests that cuddling and moving an infant are as important to normal social and psychological development as feeding is to continued life. A cloth "surrogate" mother serves the development of the infant rhesus monkey nearly as well as does the presence of its own mother, particularly if the surrogate moves about. There is recent evidence that premature human infants gain weight faster if they are gently swung about within their incubators (Sutton, 1972), and experiments are under way to determine the possibly beneficial effects upon intellectual, emotional, and social development.

The rhesus monkey deprived of tactile–kinesthetic stimulation resorts to body rocking, as do sensorially deprived human children, such as those raised in institutions, who are touched and carried infrequently (Spitz, 1946). Use of the rocking chair is

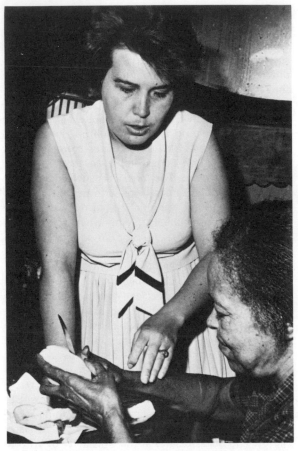

FIGURE 10
The elderly, especially those with sensory losses, may respond positively to the sense of touch. (Photo courtesy of Administration on Aging, U.S.D.H.E.W.)

FIGURE 11
Shopping gives an opportunity for pleasant social contact. (Photo courtesy of Administration on Aging, U.S.D.H.E.W.)

beneficial to the circulation of old people, and it may also serve to meet the basic human need for kinesthetic experience.

Old people have less opportunity to touch and to be touched because of the loss of or distance from those persons with whom such behavior is acceptable, such as parents, siblings, spouses, and children. Pets sometimes are used to meet this need. However, pets are a serious problem in many urban areas, and special living arrangements for the elderly ordinarily exclude dogs and cats. The physical environment, to some extent, may provide substitutes. For example,

the hot whirlpool may provide satisfaction for basic tactile needs in addition to relief for the discomforts of arthritis or muscle spasms that sometimes plague the old. Variation in the textures of such items as furniture coverings, bedclothes, cutlery, napery, and dishware may also help to compensate for reduced tactile experience. Attention to variation in texture should focus on furnishings that people normally touch, not upon such items as wall covering and drapes.

Interaction with other people is a lifelong, basic need; unfortunately, it is often frustrated by the

LEGEND

1 ENTRY
2 FOYER
3 LOBBY
4 RECEPTION
5 WORK ROOM
6 SEWING
7 CRAFTS
8 LIBRARY
9 OFFICE
10 RECREATION
11 OFFICE
12 LOBBY
13 LOUNGE
14 KITCHEN
15 PRIVATE DINING
16 DINING AREA
17 COLD STORAGE
18 OFFICE
19 SERVICE DOCK
20 TERRACE

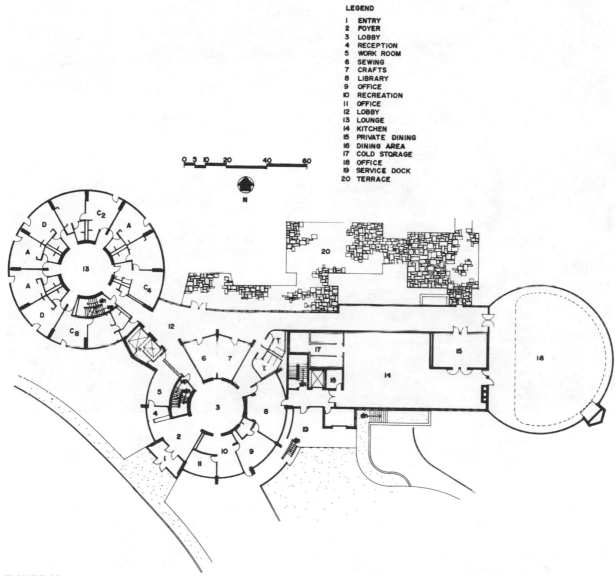

FIGURE 12
Social interaction can be encouraged by architectural design. The central area of each of the Wesley Woods (Atlanta) towers gives occupants of the apartments added opportunity to encounter one another. (Charles Edward Stade, architect. Photo by Hedrich-Blessing.)

environments of the old. Death takes more and more of the "meaningful others" as age advances, and limitations on mobility and finances increasingly restrict contact with those who remain. However, even very old people are capable of forming new relationships and enjoy doing so (Carp, 1966). Furthermore, the formation of new relationships has a beneficial effect on old bonds that remain. Older people often are

FIGURE 13 *(above and right)*
Beauty in the living environment is frequently ignored in the planning of new housing for the elderly. Victoria Plaza, planned under the direction of Marie McGuire Thompson and designed by Thomas Thompson, is a notable exception. (Photos by Collas Smelser, courtesy of the San Antonio Housing Authority.)

aware of their need to be with others. For example, although walking and public transit are in many ways highly unsatisfactory as modes of transportation, some old people prefer them "because you are with other people" (Carp, 1971a). These findings suggest that widespread loneliness, alienation, and anomie among the old (Bracey, 1966; Turnstall, 1966) could be greatly alleviated by creating environments for them that include convenient access to other, suitable people.

This raises the issue of age segregation versus age integration. Rosow (1967) has made an eloquent case for the availability of age peers in his demonstra-tion that older people who lived in apartment build-ings with larger numbers of other old people had more friends among the residents than did old people who lived in apartment buildings with fewer elderly residents. However, Rosow's "age-homogeneous" liv-ing situations were apartment houses in which per-haps 40 percent of the residential units included an older person. Such neighborhoods are less segregated by age, from the viewpoint of the older person, than is the typical area in which only about 10 percent of the population are age peers; but the situation Rosow studied is scarcely that of an age-homogeneous popu-lation such as occurs in housing for the elderly. Truly

age homogeneous living situations do not seem to be especially advantageous to the old (Carp, in press b).

Perhaps the most important point for planning and policy purposes is that, exactly like people of all ages, the old person needs friends and acquaintances and he forms these associations most readily with people with whom he has something in common (Merton, 1957). Similarity in age is *one* commonality, but there are others. Too limited a supply of age peers may too greatly restrict the supply of potential friends and confidants. Conversely, the availability of none other than age peers may too greatly restrict other important commonalities that could provide bases for the development of valuable interpersonal bonds.

It is useful to refer back to the important point about individual differences and the tendency for age to accentuate these differences. Some people form associations with others based largely on time since birth, but others find new friends among those who share some other trait, such as a current hobby or community service. Therefore, age-segregated living situations may be the best milieu for some older persons, but not necessarily for all. The provision of options is necessary to meet individual needs. Again, the urban milieu may be advantageous because it contains a larger number and variety of potential friends, acquaintances, and coparticipants in various activities.

People need people, but they also need *privacy* (Warren and Brandeis, 1890; Maslow, 1954). Lack of privacy has been demonstrated to be an important factor in nervous breakdown and physical collapse (Westin, 1967). Privacy is essential to good functioning and to a sense of well-being. For older people, at least, the feeling of privacy is highly dependent upon the physical environment (Pastalan, 1970). Obviously, privacy invasions must occur when a grandparent shares a bedroom with a grandchild or when (s)he shares a bathroom and/or kitchen with other tenants of an "apartment house" (Carp, 1966). However, having one's own apartment in a building designed for the elderly is no guarantee of privacy. The placement of windows with respect to passageways; the type of window draping; the location of mailboxes, balconies, and elevators; and the presence or absence of doors between living and sleeping areas within apartments are all relevant design features (Carp, 1966).

New experience is essential to alertness and good functioning at all stages of life. One reason for the lassitude, fatigue, and poor intellectual functioning so often observed among the old may well be simply the dullness and apathy that come from uninterrupted routine. The human organism is attracted by the novel, and variety is essential to the maintenance of good function. "Perhaps the greatest gift the city has to offer is not what you seek and find, but what you constantly come upon unexpectedly, and would have

FIGURE 14
A trip may be for a necessary errand or simply for a change of scene. Wheelchair-accessible vehicles are available. (Photo courtesy of Administration on Aging, U.S.D.H.E.W.)

gone without if you did not live in metropolis" (Parr, 1971, p. 24).

The life styles of old age tend to be routine and monotonous, which may result partly from situational factors and not be completely a matter of choice. For example, the old would like to travel more than they are able (Carp, 1972b); "a trip" is the prototype of variety and new experience. The most common deterrent is lack of funds. In Western Europe, and more recently in this country, programs have been developed that provide inexpensive "vacations" to the retired by arranging for the swap of homes. This can be done between countries for relatively little cost and with great benefit in terms of revitalizing the travelers. The benefits of "change of scene" might accrue from even less costly exchanges of residence between persons in different parts of one metropolitan area.

Several types of built-in variety in the day-to-day pattern are eliminated by retirement. At younger ages, the alternation between work and leisure is salutary and enjoyable. Fishing (or whatever) is much less fun when it is no longer a "break" from the job. Retirement eliminates this source of a change in pace from work to play. The trip to and from work, itself, stimulates the senses. The place of work is a different environment from the home, and the people in the two are different. At retirement, automatic exposure to all these sources of variety is eliminated.

Budgets often restrict or preclude the continuation or undertaking of nonwork activities that would make one day in retirement different from the next. To maintain interest, alertness, and enjoyment of life, it may be necessary, in creating environments for the old, to build in variety and change. The city obviously has an advantage in any attempt to do this. However, how to ensure variety and change without creating confusion and disruption is a challenge.

The problem is especially acute because all people need the security of *predictability* regarding the environment, of "knowing where things are" (Lynch, 1960). Indeed, the old may be especially vulnerable to environmental unpredictability because of their reduced sensory–motor capabilities and deeply ingrained habits. Nevertheless, if old people's needs are to be met in such a way as to allow them to enjoy a good-quality later life as well as a long one, environments must provide both the security of predictability and the stimulation of variety and change.

Solutions to this seeming paradox should be sought among old people. I have found them remarkably insightful into the design inadequacies of housing (Carp, 1966) and transportation (Carp, 1971e), and conclude that they have a great deal to contribute—if only they are included in the planning process and brought in early. Unfortunately, society generally

thinks it knows what is best for the old. Thereby we lose the benefits of their wisdom and experience, and they suffer further loss of *self-esteem*—another essential human need.

Gans (1971) stresses that "policy-oriented research must be particularly concerned with the values of all those participating in or affected by a specific policy, not only to discourage the policy designer from imposing his own or his sponsor's values on the beneficiaries of the policy, but also to make sure that the designed policy bears some relevance to the aspirations of those affected by it" (p. 31). It should become routine for local and regional commissions, town councils, health and welfare groups, and others to contact organizations of older people to seek counsel as they begin to plan housing and other neighborhood and community changes that will affect the elderly.

This brings us to the final "need" that will be discussed: *autonomy*. The most dreadful possibility to an old person is that of becoming a burden on others; the most desired personal attribute is independence. As long as a person can take care of his own physical-maintenance needs, he has a sense of independence. Therefore, every environmental support to the capacity for independent living is directly fulfilling of the basic need for autonomy. For example, bathroom handholds guard not only against physical injury but also against dependence.

Special environmental design features that extend and prolong *independent living* are not usually considered by old people to be demeaning. To some extent the assistance of a paid staff member is not perceived as "dependence," although the same service from a friend or a family member would be. For example, older people recommend "transit aides" to help them to negotiate bus stairs and doors, manage packages, and know when to get off; they perceive this service as an extender of their independence and freedom of action, not as a sign of increasing dependency (Carp, 1971b).

Autonomy connotes not only the absence of dependence but also the capacity to make choices and decisions. This is possible only when *options* exist (Sussman, 1972). Perhaps the most negative aspect of the usual living situation for older people is the narrow range or nonexistence of alternatives. This constricted situation may be difficult, but old people tend to make the best of it because they are powerless to effect a change. There is evidence that, far from complaining, old people with problems tend to underreport them (Blenkner, 1961; Ostfeld, 1968; Carp, 1969).

Here again, old people react in a normal human fashion for ego defense. Just as submariners refuse to complete negative items in sociometric questionnaires regarding crew mates while they are on long voyages (although they will complete them when land based) (Sells, 1963), older people turn away from the negative aspects of the lives into which they feel locked.

The introduction of options has an immediate effect. For example, applicants for public housing for the elderly who lived in substandard and socially isolating or emotionally damaging situations (Carp, 1964) generally rated their present living arrangements as "all right," although they were doing everything in their power to get out of them. However, when those selected were notified that they would have apartments in the new building, they rated their present situation at the negative extreme of the scale; unsuccessful applicants continued to say that their present living arrangements were "all right."

Many studies have shown the deleterious effects of moving old people from one nursing home to another; yet many other studies show favorable results from the move of community-resident old people to better quarters, and some show beneficial effects even for those in poor health. It seems likely that autonomy is involved. The voluntary move, after consideration of alternatives and exercise of choice, must have far different mental and physical health consequences than does passive transfer. People decide and act; objects are decided about and acted upon. The most pervasive human need is *to be a person*. This status is defined for each of us by the way other people deal with us. The "decided about and done to" status of the old is perhaps the most flagrant violation of their first right as human beings.

THE URBAN SETTING

In many ways the urban environment is especially difficult for the old. It is noisy, crowded, dangerous,

rushed, and confusing. People in the city tend to be not only uncaring and inconsiderate of the old, but even actively hostile. However, the city has great potential for meeting the needs of persons in the later parts of the life cycle. First, it stimulates the senses, is varied and changing, and provides some options even to the person with limited physical and financial resources. People are available in vast supply, although how to make meaningful contact presents a problem (Riesman, 1950).

Obviously, delivery of services, although not easy, is not so difficult as in rural areas. In cities more services exist, but their existence has no reality to the old person until he has access to them. Service delivery is crucial.

Walking is perhaps not the ideal mode of transportation, but it provides far wider access to services, community facilities, and other people for city dwellers than for suburbanites or country residents. Also, the problem of vehicular transportation is at least more amenable to solution where people and facilities are relatively close, as they are in urban compared to rural areas.

The difficulties of the urban environment are staggering. However, it may be profitable to speculate upon ways the city's problems can be solved that will greatly benefit the old—with their reduced sensory acuity; diminished strength, speed, and agility; accumulated health problems; curtailed incomes; and demeaned status—yet who share with others of all ages the need not only for life-support services but also for variety and change, social interaction, independence, self-esteem, and demonstrable value to others. The urban environment can be designed and managed not only to prolong lives but also to allow and support satisfying and useful life styles for the elderly.

NOTES

1. Data from Bay Area Rapid Transit Residential Impact Study, collected by the Institute of Urban and Regional Development, the University of California. Berkeley, under a contract with the U.S. Department of Transportation.

2. Data from Bay Area Rapid Transit Residential Impact Study, collected by the Institute of Urban

and Regional Development, the University of California, Berkeley, under a contract with the U.S. Department of Transportation.

REFERENCES

Anderson, W. F. The spectrum of housing and environments required by older adults. Paper presented at the *International Symposium on Housing and Environmental Design*, Washington, D.C., December 1973.

Belbin, R. M. Implications for retirement of recent studies on age and working capacity. In F.M. Carp (ed.), *The Retirement Process.* Washington, D.C.: Government Printing Office, 1968.

Birren, J. E. Increments and decrements in the intellectual status of the aged. Paper presented at a regional research conference on *Aging in Modern Society: Psychological and Medical Aspects*, at the University of California, San Francisco Medical Center, March 1967.

Blenkner, M. Comments. In R. W. Kleemeier (ed.), *Aging and Leisure.* New York: Oxford University Press, 1961.

Bracey, H. E. *In Retirement.* Baton Rouge, La.: Louisiana State University, 1966.

Carp, F.M. *A Future for the Aged: The Residents of Victoria Plaza.* Austin, Tex.: University of Texas Press, 1966.

_____. Housing and minority-group elderly. *Gerontologist*, 1969, *9*, 20–24.

_____. The mobility of retired people. In E. Cantilli and J. Shmelzer (eds.), *Transportation and Aging.* Washington, D.C.: Government Printing Office, 1971(a).

_____. Public transit and retired people. In E. Cantilli and J. Shmelzer (eds.), *Transportation and Aging.* Washington, D.C.: Government Printing Office, 1971(b).

_____. Walking as a means of transportation for retired people. *Gerontologist*, 1971, *11*, 104–111 (c).

_____. Pedestrian transportation for retired people. *Highway Research Record*, 1971, *356*, 105–118 (d).

_____. Automobile and public transportation for re-tired people. *Highway Research Record*, 1971, *348* (e).

_____ The older pedestrian in San Francisco. *Highway Research Record*, 1972, *403*, Part 1, 66–72 (a).

_____. Retirement travel. *Gerontologist*, 1972, *12*, 73–78 (b).

_____. Driving an automobile in retirement. In press (a).

_____. Neighborhood age composition. In press (b).

Gans, H. J. Social science for social policy. In I. L. Horowitz (ed.), *The Use and Abuse of Social Science.* New Brunswick, N.J.: Transaction, Inc., 1971.

Gibbs, J. P., and Davis, K. Conventional versus metropolitan data in the international study of urbanization. *American Sociological Review*, 1958, *23*, 504–514.

Green, R. F. Age-intelligence relationship between ages sixteen and sixty-four: a rising trend. *Developmental Psychology*, 1969, *1*, 618–627.

Hebb, D. O. Motivating effects of exteroceptive stimulation. *American Psychologist*, 1958, *13*, 109–113.

Jarvik, L. F., Kallman, F. J., and Falek, A. Intellectual changes in aged twins. *Journal of Gerontology*, 1962, *17*, 289–294.

Kelly, L. Consistency of the adult personality. *American Psychologist*, 1955, *10*, 659.

Lawton, A. H., and Azar, G. J. Consequences of physical and physiological change with age in the patterns of living and housing for the middle-aged and aged. In F. M. Carp (ed.), *Patterns of Living and Housing of Middle-Aged and Older People.* Washington, D.C.: Government Printing Office, 1966.

Lynch, K. *The Image of the City.* Cambridge, Mass.: MIT Press, 1960.

Maslow, A. H. *Motivation and Personality.* New York: Harper & Row, 1954.

Merton, R. Patterns of influence: local and cosmopolitan influentials. In R. Merton, *Social Theory and Social Structure.* New York: Free Press, 1957.

Michelson, W. H. *Man and His Environment: A Sociological Approach.* Reading, Mass.: Addison-Wesley, 1970.

Milgram, S. The experience of living in cities: a psychological analysis. In F. F. Korten, S. W. Cook and J. I. Lacey (eds.), *Psychology and the Problems of Society*. Washington, D.C.: American Psychological Association, 1970.

Morris, D. *The Human Zoo*. New York: McGraw-Hill, 1969.

National Safety Council. *Accident Facts*. Washington, D.C., 1967.

____. *Accident Facts*. Washington, D.C., 1969.

Orshansky, M. Counting the poor: another look at the poverty profile. *Social Security Bulletin*, January 1965.

Ostfeld, A. M. Frequency and nature of health problems of retired persons. In F. M. Carp (ed.), *The Retirement Process*. Washington, D.C.: Government Printing Office, 1968.

Paar, A. E. The child in the city. *Yale Review*, New Haven, Conn., 1971.

Pastalan, L. Privacy as an expression of human territoriality. In L. A. Pastalan and D. H. Carson (eds.), *Spatial Behavior of Older People*. Ann Arbor, Mich.: Institute of Gerontology, University of Michigan, 1970.

Riesman, D. *The Lonely Crowd*. New Haven, Conn.: Yale University Press, 1950.

Rosow, I. *Social Integration of the Aged*. New York: Free Press, 1967.

Sells, S. B. *Stimulus Determinants of Behavior*. New York: Ronald Press, 1963.

Spitz, R. A. The smiling response: a contribution to the ontogenesis of social relations. *Genetic Psychology Monographs*, 1946, *34*, 57–125.

Sussman, M. B. An analytic model for the sociological study of retirement. In F. M. Carp (ed.), *Retirement*. New York: Behavioral Publications, 1972.

Sutton, L. *Touching*. 17 minute color-sound film. National Sex Forum, Multi-Media Resource Center, San Francisco, 1972.

Turnstall, J. *Old and Alone*. London: Routledge & Kegan Paul Ltd., 1966.

Tyler, L. E. *The Psychology of Human Differences*. New York: Appleton-Century-Crofts, 1950.

U.S. Bureau of the Census. *We the American Elderly*. Washington, D.C.: Public Information Office, June 1973.

Vollmer, H. M., Jaffe, F., Steffens, H., Seabrook, M. E. (eds.). *Conference on Transportation and Human Needs in the 70's, June 19–21*. The American University, Washington, D.C., August 1972.

Warren, C., and Brandeis, L. The right to privacy. *Harvard Law Review*, 1890, *4*, 193.

Westin, A. *Privacy and Freedom*. New York: Atheneum, 1967.

Whalen, R. J. *A City Destroying Itself: An Angry View of New York*. New York: Morrow, 1965.

MARJORIE H. CANTOR

Marjorie H. Cantor is Director of Research for the New York City Office for the Aging.

Effect of Ethnicity on Life Styles of the Inner-City Elderly

Just as individuals are clearly distinguished from one another by physical, social, and psychological characteristics, so aggregates of people in our society can be differentiated by virtue of their shared culture, ethnicity, and socioeconomic status. As we move toward greater acceptance of the value of a pluralistic society, the importance of understanding differences becomes even more critical for environmental or social planning. Increasingly, decision makers are faced with the need for subgroup analysis as they attempt to fairly balance the competing interests of various ethnic and nationality groups. Nowhere is this need more evident than in large urban areas characterized not only by high density of population but by wide diversity of the backgrounds of its citizens.

Yet in planning services for the elderly there has been a tendency to view older people as a homogeneous group, set off from the rest of society by virtue of a single determinant, age.

But older people on reaching 65 (or whatever arbitrary figure a society chooses to signify as old age) do not shed their identity as members of racial, ethnic, or socioeconomic subgroups. Rather, it may well be that this subgroup membership is the crucial factor in conditioning how older people grow old and

in determining the social, physical, and psychological needs to which the planning process should be addressed.

In all stages of life, morale and well-being are related to an individual's ability to successfully perform the tasks set forth for his age group by society. In childhood, control and mastery of environment is a gradual process, with considerable dependency upon adults as mediating agents. Adulthood presumes the ability, skills, and competence to effectively control environment and determine the course of one's own daily existence. The degree to which this is possible determines to a considerable extent the individual's mental health and integrity of personality. A sense of powerlessness is anathema to successful adulthood in industrialized societies.

Similarly, in old age, although social roles change, the basic drives for independence, competence, and mastery of environment remain. At the same time, with deteriorating health and reduced income, frequent concomitants of old age in our society, a countertrend of gradual diminution of mastery occurs. To the extent that an older person can continue to exercise considerable freedom of choice and control, morale will be high and aging successful.

But the form in which the basic needs of all older people are expressed and the relative role of the family and community in providing the necessary assistance for independent living are heavily conditioned by cultural, economic, and kinship patterns. When family structure continues to be strong and cohesive, more help from that source can be expected. When family is dispersed or nonexistent, the community role is of increasing importance. Meaningful social planning requires precise knowledge of both the extent to which the aging process is similar for all older people and the degree to which racial, ethnic, and socioeconomic differences require varying types of community facilities and services to sustain older people independently in the community for as long as possible.

The Urban Elderly Poor

A review of the gerontological literature confirms the paucity of data about the urban poor and particularly the minority-group elderly. In general, much stress has been placed (not inappropriately) on discovering the broad patterns of the aging process. Where subgroups of elderly have been singled out for study, the sample too often consists of white middle-class respondents in medium-sized or suburban communities. Yet, increasingly, the concentration of elderly in all industrialized societies is in the largest cities—most frequently in the older central or inner city where poverty and social and environmental blight are common conditions of life.

New York City is the home of three major racial ethnic subgroups—white, black, and Spanish-speaking (mainly Puerto Rican). Although at present the vast majority of older New Yorkers are white, there are growing numbers of black and Puerto Rican elderly; this trend is expected to continue. In an attempt to document the basic similarities, but more importantly the differences, in the life styles and needs of the three major groups of elderly and thereby provide the specificity of data needed for immediate and long-range physical and social planning, the New York City Office for the Aging undertook in 1970 one of the first and most comprehensive cross-cultural studies of the urban elderly poor living in the inner city

FIGURE 1
Urban decay is part of the proximate environment of many older city dwellers. (Photo by George Gardner.)

(Cantor et al., 1975). Findings in several major areas of particular interest to planners will be discussed and the social policy implications highlighted.

Although New York City is in many ways *sui generis*, particularly with respect to size and complexity, the findings have considerable implications for other major urban areas. Perhaps more important than any specific findings, the New York City study provides a case history in the use of subgroup analysis as a tool for meaningful planning.

Study Goals, Population, and Methodology

The study goals were as follows:

1. To describe the life of urban elderly residing in neighborhoods characterized by poverty, decay, and high risk. Highlighted were problems of income maintenance, social isolation, the unique nature of housing and environmental conditions, and patterns of mobility.

2. To determine the effects of subgroup membership on the aging process among white, Spanish, and black elderly and to document areas of similarity and difference.

Particular emphasis was placed on identifying the factors that enable the elderly to cope with and effectively control their environment. The relative roles of the individual, family, and community were considered for the population as a whole and for each subgroup.

3. To document the needs of the three major subgroups of elderly for supportive community services with a view toward enhancing mastery over environment. Where possible, differential needs were identified and related to the desirability for new services or the improved delivery of existing services.

4. To explore the degree to which positive feelings of mastery over environment are related to the concepts of high morale and successful aging as presently employed in the gerontological literature.

The focal point of the study was the elderly of the inner city rather than a citywide sample for three major reasons:

1. First, much is known about middle-class older people but little about the life styles and support systems of the urban elderly poor. Yet it is among the urban poor that one would expect to find the greatest need for community assistance.

2. A principal goal of the study was to document the effects of subgroup membership on aging and identify the commonalities and differences among the life styles and coping mechanisms of the three major ethnic subgroups found in New York. Most of the black and Spanish elderly reside in the inner city, yet the majority of older people in these core neighborhoods are white, as is the case for the rest of the city.

3. In the belief that environment was a key vari-

FIGURE 2
Parks and public seating places in safe locations are important aspects of the urban community. (Photo courtesy of Administration on Aging, U.S.D.H.E.W.)

able in life styles, it was desirable to limit the universe to older people living in similar conditions of neighborhood blight and deterioration.

Defining the inner city in New York was somewhat more difficult than in other urban areas of the country. Typically, a central city is an easily identifiable geographic entity with all the classic atrributes of environmental and social decline, surrounded by concentric rings of middle-class communities to which the more affluent have fled. In New York, on the contrary, each borough has its blighted areas interspersed amid middle- or upper-class neighborhoods. Sometimes, even on a single block, tenements stand next to luxury apartments.

FIGURE 3
Crime and vandalism in the city disturb the relationship of older people to their most critical resources. (Photo by George Gardner.)

The central city of New York was, therefore, defined operationally to be the 26 neighborhoods designated as poverty areas by the Human Resources Administration. These areas have the highest incidence of crime, infant mortality, welfare case load, and deteriorated housing, and clearly duplicate the objective conditions found in the inner city of other urban centers in the United States.

The criterion of aging was purposely set at 60, rather than at the more usual 65 years, to enable the gathering of information about the life styles and needs of those entering the aged cohort as compared with the "older" elderly. The sample was limited to noninstitutional elderly living in the community.

A replicated probability sample was employed, that embodied five randomly selected, stratified, interpenetrating matched samples. Through a two-step enumeration process, 2,180 households were identified as having one or more older persons. Six callbacks ultimately yielded 1,552 interviews, a completion rate of 71 percent—quite good considering the areas in which the study was conducted and the possible fears of older people about opening doors to strangers.

The final sample of 1,552 respondents proved to be highly representative of the approximately 400,000 older persons living in the 26 neighborhoods in 1970 when interviewing took place. The ethnic distribution of the sample is remarkably accurate with, if anything, a slight overrepresentation of black and Spanish elderly—the very groups usually underrepresented in most studies. Where possible, any discrepancies arising from sample selection or interviewing were compensated for through weighting. Interviews were held in the home, ran from 1 to 2 hours, and elicited information on virtually all aspects of the lives of older New Yorkers.

FINDINGS

An aging population can be subdivided in many ways: well versus sick, the young elderly versus the older elderly, or institutionalized versus community based. From the beginning the cross-cultural approach was chosen. It was hypothesized that the influence of ethnicity and culture on the life styles of older people is crucial, particularly in the areas of greatest interest to us—the support system and the relative roles of family and community in enhancing the lives of older people. Furthermore, little or nothing is known about the similarities and differences in life styles of the aged among the major ethnic groups in urban society. Finally, inasmuch as New York City contains the largest number of white, black, and Spanish elderly in the country, it seemed most appropriate to place our initial stress on ethnicity and culture.

However, not unmindful of the importance of socioeconomic class, the final study report will attempt to identify the relative importances of ethnicity, culture, and class. The fact that the study population is limited to poverty-area elderly acts to narrow the range of socioeconomic class. But particularly in the case of the white elderly, social-class status prior to old age may be unrelated to current income and may well be a determining factor in attitudes and life style. In addition, the white population is not as homogeneous with respect to culture as the black and Spanish. Finally, ethnicity and culture are used interchangeably in this discussion of the findings.

A Brief Profile of the Inner-City Elderly

Who then are the inner-city elderly, what are their general characteristics, and to what extent does ethnicity affect these characteristics? (see Table 1).

First the inner-city elderly are clearly not a homogeneous middle-class white population. Rather, the study population is a low-income, urban elderly sample encompassing three distinct ethnic groups. Although inner-city neighborhoods are increasingly nonwhite, at the present time whites still predominate among both young and old alike. Thus, in the sample, 49 percent of the respondents were white, 37 percent black, and 13 percent Spanish-speaking, principally of Puerto Rican origin.

Ethnicity has a considerable effect on age distribution. If old age is conceptualized as a continuum having a beginning, middle, and ending period, the Spanish elderly are the youngest, tending to cluster in the initial period. Two thirds of the Spanish elderly were under 70. Black elderly tended to be more in the middle, older than the Spanish but younger than whites. Nearly 60 percent of the blacks were under 70; among white respondents, the oldest of the three groups, 40 percent were under 70 and 60 percent were 70 or older. Several cultural factors contribute to these age differences. The most important is differential longevity. Black life expectancy is 7 years less than that of whites; although exact data with respect to mainland Puerto Ricans are lacking, it is believed that a similar differential exists. In the past, another factor contributed to ethnic differences in age distri-

bution in the city—the tendency for blacks and Puerto Ricans to return "home" upon reaching old age. This out-migration factor is expected to fade in succeeding generations of black and Spanish elderly.

With respect to the presence of a spouse, more Spanish married originally and as the youngest group more were still married and living with spouse (43 percent). Whites were next most likely to still be married (36 percent). Although blacks had the second highest rate of marriage originally and were younger than the white respondents, at this point in their lives they were least likely of the three subgroups to report still being married and living with spouse. Persons who reported never having been married were most likely to be found among the whites.

The health of the inner-city elderly is poorer than older people generally, as measured both by self assessed health and the Townsend Index of Functional Ability (Shanas et al., 1968). Although younger, Spanish and black elderly appeared to have significantly more health problems than whites, and a higher proportion was found to be severely impaired or incapacitated (see Table 1). However, although most respondents reported at least one chronic illness, they were not homebound and were able to get around. (Only approximately 7 percent were in wheelchairs or bedridden.)

The inner-city elderly, like all older New Yorkers, had lived in the city and in their immediate neighborhoods for a long time. They had deep roots and considerable feelings of belonging, although they recognized the urban blight around them and were often very fearful of the "strangers in the neighborhood." As expected, whites had the longest tenure in the city (mean residency of 52 years), followed by blacks (mean residency of 39 years). Relatively recent arrival was characteristic only of the Spanish elderly, most of whom came to the mainland when they were 40 years old or more. But even the Spanish in the sample had lived in New York an average of 25 years.

The late arrival of the Spanish has had serious implications affecting their ability to learn English, their employment opportunities, and their Social Security coverage, to say nothing of the psychological problems attendant upon uprooting and moving to an alien culture in the middle and later years of life. It is noteworthy that 86 percent of the Spanish elderly

TABLE 1

Major Demographic Characteristics of Inner-City Elderly Respondents
(percentages)

	Total	White	Black	Spanish
Age				
60–64	22.0	15.2	26.2	35.8
65–69	28.2	25.1	31.8	30.0
70–74	22.1	22.3	23.5	17.2
75+	27.2	36.9	17.9	17.0
Sex				
Male	41.0	45.2	35.2	41.9
Female	59.0	54.8	64.8	58.1
Ethnicity				
White	49.4	49.4		
Black	37.4		37.4	
Spanish	13.2			13.2
Religious affiliation				
Protestant	43.5	18.3	86.0	17.4
Catholic	35.3	43.2	9.6	78.7
Jewish	14.9	29.5	0.8	0.4
Socioeconomic status				
Hollingshead's ISP (IV and V: working and lower class)	74.7	63.8	85.3	85.3
Income: under $2,500/yr (est. per capita)	63.8	55.6	71.3	73.6
Occupation: manual	67.6	57.3	79.4	72.4
Education: 8th grade or less	59.9	50.1	65.3	80.4
Marital status				
Married	34.3	35.9	29.3	42.6
Widowed	42.0	39.9	45.2	41.1
Never married	13.4	17.3	10.8	6.1
Separated or divorced	10.3	6.8	14.8	10.3
Living arrangements				
Live alone	39.2	47.4	33.1	26.2
Live with spouse	33.4	34.7	29.0	41.0
Live with others (not spouse)	27.4	17.9	37.9	32.8
Health				
Have health problem(s)	67.3	62.8	72.1	70.6
Self-perceived health as poor	23.8	20.6	25.2	31.4
Incapacity index: severely impaired or incapacitated	15.4	13.6	15.5	22.2
Nativity: born on U.S. mainland	53.3	46.5	80.2	3.4
Total respondents	1.552	766	580	205

Source: Cantor et al., *The Elderly in the Inner City*, New York City Office for the Aging, in press.

spoke Spanish at home. In the case of most other foreign-born elderly, whether white or black, English was the language in the home.

Although it is common to think of the present generation of white elderly in big cities like New York as largely foreign born, this was far from the case. Almost half the white respondents were native-born, and of this group 40 percent were at least second-generation Americans. The inner city is apparently the home of a substantial number of white

Americans of old stock, mainly Protestant, who are living in hidden "genteel" poverty.

Because they grew up during the period when higher education, including high school, was mainly for the well-to-do, it is not surprising to find little formal education among the inner-city urban poor. Most of the sample had a grade school education or less, with the least amount of formal education being reported by the Spanish. (This lack of education coupled with minority-group status has severely limited the job opportunities available to most black and Spanish elderly during their adult years.)

Although there is considerable occupational and social-class spread among the inner-city elderly, par-

FIGURE 4
Despite its obvious negative characteristics, the urban neighborhood affords many pleasures to its residents. (Photos by Jeanne Bader.)

ticularly in the case of the whites, 64 percent of the sample was classified according to the Hollingshead Index of Social Position (Hollingshead and Redlich, 1958) as being in the two lowest categories (i.e., working or lower class), and most respondents were involved in skilled or unskilled occupations during their working years. Spanish and black elderly almost exclusively held unskilled or semiskilled jobs, with only a handful reporting employment in skilled or clerical/sales occupations. White elderly showed a somewhat greater occupational spread. Although the bulk were skilled workers during their adult years, 15 percent held managerial or professional positions and 20 percent were owners of small businesses or held sales or clerical jobs. As is to be expected, there were relatively few upper-middle- or upper-class elderly living in the inner city, no matter what their ethnic backgrounds.

Retirement and Income

If older people, regardless of their ethnicity, are to live independently in the community, two essential requirements are the ability to buy what they need and the physical strength necessary to permit an adequate level of functioning. Since poverty areas contain more families with lower earnings, lower Social Security coverage, and less savings, one might expect that economic pressures would operate to keep more poverty area elderly at work than is usual among older people in general. This was not so. Inner-city elderly were far less likely to be working after 65 than their peers nationally.

Even though all males and 70 percent of the female respondents reported gainful employment sometime during their adult years, 78 percent of the inner-city elderly sample were retired. Ethnicity clearly influences the point at which an older person leaves the labor market. The Spanish were forced out of the labor market earliest. Among Spanish males 60 to 64, 61 percent were no longer working. With respect to black males the picture was slightly better than among the Spanish but still very bad; 50 percent of black male respondents in the 60 to 64 age cohort were no longer working.

Among whites in our sample the picture was very different and corresponded to the national labor force participation statistics for the age group. Only a relatively small proportion (25 percent) of those 60 to 64 were retired. Whites continued to work much longer. Of those in the 65 to 69 age cohort, over 25 percent were still working, as compared with only a very small proportion of black and Spanish males. Even among whites 70 and over, 13 percent of the sample were still working.

These patterns clearly reflect the close link between ethnicity and work status; persons in professional, managerial, and higher-skilled jobs tended to continue working longer than the less skilled. Thus a greater proportion of white male respondents was still working in their late sixties and the early seventies than was true for the other two groups. Sadly enough, the very groups in the elderly population with the lowest incomes during adult working years, and therefore the lowest Social Security benefits in old age, were, because of lack of skill and minority-group status, the first groups forced out of the labor market.

It has been pointed out that poor health may also be a cause of early retirement. In our sample, Spanish reported the greatest health deficiencies, followed by blacks; whites reported the best health. Health of course was related to low income.

It is interesting that among nonworking men in the 60 to 64 age group, black and Spanish elderly were two and one-half times more likely to consider themselves retired rather than unemployed as compared with similar-aged white men. This undoubtedly represents a reality orientation. Black and Spanish males are more likely to experience chronic unemployment in their adult working years and, therefore, correctly consider themselves out of the labor market by age 60.

Whereas black men tended to be out of the labor market earlier, black women continued to work longer, certainly through their sixties. Of the black women 60 to 64, 39 percent were still working; in the 65 to 69 age cohort, 20 percent of the black women still worked as compared with only 9 percent of the black men.

From this picture of work status, it is no surprise to learn that the income levels of the inner-city elderly were far below those required for adequate living in a city of high costs. Respondents' incomes were abysmally low, significantly below the citywide levels for older people, and sharp ethnic differences existed. In 1970, the median income for white respondents was $2,746, for blacks, $2,166, and for the Spanish, $1,946. Increases in Social Security since 1970 do not appear to have altered the relative income positions of the inner-city elderly or of the three subgroups.

If these figures do not fully convey how poor the inner-city elderly are, New York City's rent increase exemption program set $5,000 as the upper income eligibility limit for elderly households, and the Bureau of Labor Statistics (U.S. Department of Labor, 1969–1970) considered that a retired couple in 1970 needed $3,080 to maintain a minimum living standard and close to $4,700 for a moderate living standard in New York City.

Although Social Security was the principal source of income for all inner-city elderly (73 percent were receiving Social Security), what was less expected was the extent to which Social Security was the *only* source of income. Relatively few elderly received income from pensions, investments, or savings (30 percent), and fewer still, as we have already mentioned, from employment. Despite the low income levels, only 20 percent received Old Age Assistance and only 11 percent reported financial aid from families.

There were major differences among ethnic groups in regard to income sources, which reflect differential occupational history and minority-group status. White elderly were more likely to receive income from Social Security than either of the other two groups—82 percent as compared with 70 percent of the blacks and 50 percent of the Spanish elderly. And the benefit received by whites was larger in the fall of 1970—$139 monthly for white elderly, $118 for blacks, and $107 for Spanish. Inasmuch as some of the elderly (or their spouses) were still working, the proportion receiving income from Social Security is not necessarily identical with coverage. But similar differentials were found with respect to coverage; 93 percent of the whites reported being covered by Social Security compared to only 87 percent of the blacks and 73 percent of the Spanish. The study data raise the question as to whether Social Security should not begin at age 55 for Spanish and black

elderly, especially since so many are out of the labor market earlier and their life expectancy is so much shorter than whites.

Far fewer black and Spanish elderly received retirement pensions than did whites. One third of the whites reported pensions compared to only 25 percent of the blacks and 11 percent of the Spanish elderly. Whites were far more likely to have income-producing savings and investments (43 percent) as compared to black (8 percent) or Spanish elderly (9 percent). However, this income was rarely a large amount or a substantial part of the total income of the poverty-area respondent.

In view of the lower coverage of black and Spanish elderly by Social Security and pensions, the fact that more of these two groups received Old Age Assistance (OAA) than did whites is not surprising. Forty-five percent of the Spanish respondents received OAA as compared with 25 percent among Blacks and only 9 percent among whites. Considering the low level of income, it is indeed surprising that more of the respondents were not recipients of OAA.

The question of Old Age Assistance and by the same token the newer Supplemental Security Income (SSI) program appears fraught with cultural implications. Spanish elderly, whose incomes were lowest, seemed to have the least hesitation accepting OAA—most of those eligible in our sample were covered. Among the black elderly, although a large proportion (60 percent) of those estimated to be eligible were covered, there was a sizable group of apparent eligibles, 40 percent, still uncovered. Some of these undoubtedly were still working, and in answer to a question on whether or not they would turn to OAA in case of need, most blacks indicated a willingness to use the program.

It is among the white elderly that one finds the greatest resistance to entitlement such as OAA or SSI. Thus only 30 percent of the white respondents estimated to be eligible actually used the OAA program, and almost 25 percent flatly said they would never turn to such a program even if in need. In the case of white respondents, some small few may be precluded from OAA because of unwillingness to surrender meager savings, but far more important seems to be the culturally conditioned feeling of lack of dignity and surrender of independence involved in turning to welfare. Early reports on SSI enrollment indicate that this new program also is having difficulty in attracting many of the white elderly who so desperately need the assistance. As long as such programs are seen as based on means tests and as welfare handouts, the potential for reaching the needy eligible of the inner city appears severely limited.

Living Arrangements

A crucial factor affecting an older person's sense of independence and personal integrity is his or her living arrangements. Does the older person live in his own household or is the older person living in the home of a child or other family member? Certainly, in our culture to give up one's home is viewed as a move away from independence toward dependency. Whether or not one lives alone affects the need for support in time of crisis and the potential for social isolation. What is the picture in the inner city today and what trends are discernible?

First, whose household is it? The vast majority of older persons in the poverty areas, as in the rest of the city, live independently in their own homes; 91 percent of the sample reported that they or their spouse were head of household; only 8 percent lived in the household of another, usually a child. However, a higher proportion of the inner-city sample maintained their own homes than is true in the city as a whole, and fewer have moved in with families. Thus, although 84 percent of noninstitutionalized elderly 65 and older in the city live in their own homes, 91 percent live independently in our sample. Some part of the differential is due to the presence of 60- 64-years-olds in the study sample, but not much. More important is the changing nature of the populations of these areas, with considerable out-migration of younger white families and replacement by blacks and Puerto Ricans. As noted previously, the older population is, however, still predominantly white. This white population appears to consist of fiercely independent elderly who prefer to remain in their own homes rather than move in with their children, as well as older persons who have no choice in the matter, either because they cannot afford homes elsewhere or have no families with whom to live.

The strong desire of older people to maintain their own homes is compatible with the cultural norms of

FIGURE 5

The great majority of older people live in their own households. As long-time owners or renters of a familiar dwelling, they are loathe to or unable to leave when the neighborhood deteriorates. (Photo by George Gardner.)

the nuclear family so cherished by the dominant white population. Among ethnic groups more accustomed to extended family patterns, one would expect to find a higher proportion of older people giving up

FIGURE 6
The urban fabric is dotted with "project housing," where viable ethnic mixtures are the rule. The security of this site is low because of the rows of hedges on either side of this much-used pathway. (Photo by Karen Ouzts.)

their independent residences and moving in with their families. Such was the case among the respondents of Spanish background and to some, although lesser, extent among blacks; 95 percent of the whites and 89 percent of the blacks continued to maintain their own homes. But the proportion of Spanish living independently dropped significantly to 82 percent, in spite of the fact that the Spanish were the youngest of the three groups and more still had a living spouse.

Although Spanish and blacks were less likely to maintain their own homes than their white peers, the proportion who cling to independence was higher than might be expected, given the extended family tradition and the pressures of poverty. With the continuing acculturation of the younger Spanish population and the difficulties of finding suitable apartments for large families, it is likely that in the future few if any older people will live with children, no matter what their ethnic background. As will be noted later, there is evidence of considerable interaction between older people and children despite the existence of separate households. Perhaps urbanized society is developing a new kind of extended family based on mutual help rather than joint domicile.

But living in one's own household is not the whole question. Whether or not an older person lives entirely alone without anyone else in the household has implications for assistance in time of crisis as well as for morale and degree of social isolation. Although a live-alone is not necessarily an isolate, the likelihood of isolation is greater and the potential need for community intervention is increased.

New York City has more older people living alone than is the case throughout the country (30 percent as compared with 22 percent nationally), and the problems of live-alones are particularly acute in the inner-city neighborhoods.

Among persons 65 and over in New York City as a whole, 30 percent live alone; in the inner city the proportion was 41 percent. The proportion of live-alones in the sample as a whole was 39 percent, but this included younger elderly 60 to 64, who are far more likely to be still married. Thus 4 out of 10 of New York's inner-city elderly 65 and over had no one else in the dwelling unit with them. This is a much greater proportion of live-alones than found in two other urban poverty samples; only 26 percent lived alone in the low-income areas of Philadelphia (Kent and Hirsch, 1971), and in the model-city neighborhoods of Los Angeles the proportion was 28 percent (Gelwicks et al., 1971). Although age and sex affected the likelihood of living alone (women were more apt to live alone than men and the oldest elderly were more often found alone), ethnicity was perhaps the most decisive factor. As noted previously, white elderly were far less inclined to move in with their children and, instead, cling to independent living

FIGURE 7
New York City has a relatively high proportion of people who live alone. The live-alone is more vulnerable, but not necessarily isolated. This man maintains contact by watching sidewalk traffic. (Photo courtesy of Administration on Aging, U.S.D.H.E.W.)

composition of their neighborhoods only compounds the objective conditions of aloneness and isolation. But even among black and Spanish, where the pattern of living alone was not yet as prevalent, a surprisingly high proportion were alone—27 percent among the Spanish and 34 percent among the blacks. It is, therefore, likely that large numbers of older persons living alone will characterize inner-city neighborhoods, even if there should be a continued decline in white residents. Providing support for these live-alones, many of whom are the oldest, frailest, and most isolated elderly, will continue to be a challenging community responsibility.

Family Relationships in the Inner City: Extent of Contact Between Elderly and Children

In urban industrial society, the support system of the elderly increasingly involves an amalgam of services provided by the family and significant others and services offered by large-scale governmental or voluntary organizations. As kinship structure evolves from the extended family to the modified extended family (i.e., a coalition of separately housed semi-autonomous nuclear families in a state of partial dependency; Litwak, 1965), the importance of the familial versus societal role shifts. Thus today it is government that provides the floor of basic services for older people in such crucial areas as income maintenance, health, and transportation. But the family and significant others still retain considerable importance, particularly in meeting the more idiosyncratic human needs of the individual. An elder person without a circle of significant others can be severely disadvantaged.

In most societies, children and immediate kin are looked to as the first line of support in time of crisis. Particularly as freedom of movement is curtailed owing to increased frailty, poorer health, and the resultant lessened capacity to manage one's own life wholly independently, the circle of significant others—children, siblings, friends, and neighbors—becomes increasingly significant. It is, therefore, important to know to what extent older inner-city residents have living children, how close they are to these children, and the degree to which relationships are

in their own households, even when loss of spouse occurs. Thus many more white than black or Spanish elderly in the inner city were found living alone. Among white respondents, 47 percent lived alone as compared with 37 percent among blacks and 27 percent among Spanish. The highest incidence of single-person households was found among the frailest segment of the white population, older people in their seventies and eighties, particularly among widowed or single women. For such elderly the changing ethnic maintained. And, perhaps most crucial, if there are relationships, what is the quality and form that they take?

Contrary to myths that circulate widely about today's parent–child relationships, most inner-city elderly had children and had not been abandoned by their children. Two out of three had at least one living child. Spanish elderly were significantly more likely than either black or white to have had children in the first place, to still have a child in the household, and to have larger families. (Spanish mean number of children was 4.7 as compared with 3.2 for blacks and 2.7 for whites.)

The majority of the children of all three ethnic subgroups lived relatively near their parents, and the two generations had frequent face-to-face and telephone contact with each other. In view of the frequently described flight of children to suburbia, it is significant that 28 percent of all children were within walking distance, living either in the building or immediate neighborhood, while 26 percent lived elsewhere in the five boroughs of New York. Only 13 percent resided in the suburbs, and 32 percent were beyond the metropolitan area. (It should be noted that the sample was heavily weighted toward the working and lower-middle classes. It is likely that among older people in the city as a whole the proportion of children living in suburbia would be greater. Even in our more limited sample there was a significant difference between the proportion of children in suburbia among the highest-income elderly and the lower-income groups.)

According to the respondents, they see half of their children at least once and a week and two thirds at least monthly. Even though more white children live in the suburbs (19 percent white, 11 percent Spanish, and 8 percent black), while the children of Spanish and black elderly tend to reside more frequently in the neighborhood or within city limits (47 percent white, 62 percent black, 55 percent Spanish), there was little difference with respect to the proportions of the three groups of children who saw their parents regularly (50 percent white, 48 percent black, 53 percent Spanish). Apparently, the greater affluence and mobility of white children enabled them to keep in contact with parents even though they lived farther away.

But although children as a group may have lived in relatively close proximity and had a high level of interaction with parents, this does not go to the heart of the question of availability of familial support in time of need. The crucial question is how many older people in the inner city are in contact with at least one or more children on a frequent and regular basis.

The study data indicate that the majority of respondents with children (68 percent) saw at least one child once or more per week. In the case of the Spanish elderly, whose children live the closest, the proportion seeing at least one child weekly was over 80 percent; among blacks the figure was 70 percent, and among whites, 62 percent. At this point we do not know whether the frequent visitor was the same child, perhaps a daughter, or whether the responsibility for the weekly or biweekly visitation was shared among all the children. Whatever the case, the majority of all older persons in the sample had a regular weekly visit from at least one child. In addition, face-to-face contact was supplemented by frequent telephoning, especially between white parents and children, who used telephone contact more frequently than Spanish and black families. The greater frequency of telephoning among white respondents and their children was probably a matter of both greater affluence and greater distance rather than availability of telephones, since 87 percent of the whites and blacks in the sample had a phone in their own household, as did 76 percent of the Spanish.

Although most of the sample had considerable contact with living children, one cannot overlook the fact that there was a sizable minority of older people without living children for whom primary support may have had to be from neighbors or the community. One third of both the white and black poverty-area respondents indicated that they were without children. Among the Spanish elderly, more of whom initially married and had larger families, there was only 18 percent who were childless.

Type of Relationship

An older person can see children frequently and not have close, meaningful relationships. When the respondents were asked to evaluate the closeness of their relationships with their children and to delineate what closeness means behaviorally, a fascinating system of mutual assistance emerged. Although many older people may find it difficult to state to an interviewer that they are not close to a child, and favorable responses may, therefore, be somewhat inflated, white and Spanish respondents felt very close to somewhat more than 75 percent of their children and fairly close to most of the remainder. Black respondents reported somewhat less closeness, indicating that they felt very close to 66 percent of their children, fairly close to 17 percent, and not too close to 16 percent. Here it is likely that the strains of long-term poverty and institutionalized racism have had their effects on the family.

Contact between parents and children is not limited to mere visiting or "checking up," valuable as this type of support may be psychologically. In attitudinal questions the respondents expressed strong feelings about the appropriateness of assistance within the kinship structure and the desirability of mutual

interdependency between parents and children. The behavior of the generations appears consonant with these attitudes and involves concrete patterns of mutual help between generations, but clear cultural differences in kinds of assistance emerge.

Respondents were given a series of common types of assistance and asked which they performed for their children, which their children did for them, and the frequency of assistance. Four broad categories of help were involved: (1) ongoing assistance in chores of daily living; (2) advice giving, (3) crisis intervention, and (4) gift giving (see Table 2).

Over 75 percent of the elderly reported helping children in some manner, and this type of involvement of children with parents was even greater; 87 percent of the respondents reported that their children helped in some way.

Looking first at the flow of assistance from parents to children, among all three ethnic groups, the giving of gifts, baby-sitting, and helping in times of

TABLE 2
Patterns of Mutual Assistance Between Inner-City Elderly of New York and Their Children (percentages)

	Parents to Children				Children to Parents			
	Total	White	Black	Spanish	Total	White	Black	Spanish
Crisis intervention	50.7[a]	50.5	49.2	54.8	67.8	67.4	67.7	69.1
Assistance in chores								
of daily living	38.3	35.2	40.9	41.7	65.1	63.1	66.6	67.7
Baby-sit	22.7	21.0	21.9	29.2	—	—	—	—
Shop, errands	17.6	14.0	21.4	19.4	50.5	42.3	57.9	57.5
Fix things in house	11.3	9.5	10.9	17.5	39.4	38.3	42.1	42.1
Keep house	13.0	8.1	17.8	16.0	21.7	13.9	25.9	34.4
Meal preparation	—	—	—	—	16.1	11.5	21.6	17.1
Take away in summer	—	—	—	—	19.2	23.3	10.2	27.2
Drive to store, doctor	—	—	—	—	28.5	33.3	22.1	29.3
Giving advice	35.5	26.7	36.3	52.8	26.0	24.6	27.0	27.9
On child rearing/home								
management	27.3	20.2	29.2	43.5	—	—	—	—
On major purchases	9.4	9.0	8.5	12.8	12.2	15.1	8.7	11.9
On jobs, business, money								
matters	17.1	13.8	18.2	24.3	21.7	17.5	26.0	23.8
Gift and giving	66.6	72.3	64.0	55.2	81.6	83.7	77.9	82.7
Gifts (nonmonetary)	65.0	70.2	63.1	54.1	79.1	82.2	76.5	76.1
Money	19.9	20.6	21.2	14.9	29.0	20.1	33.4	44.8
No assistance	21.6	19.1	23.2	24.9	13.3	10.5	16.1	15.1
Total respondents	1,020	480	374	166	1,020	480	374	166

[a]Respondents could give more than one response in a category. Totals of subcategories are therefore greater than that for the category itself.
Source: Cantor et al., *The Elderly in the Inner City*, New York City Office for the Aging, in press.

illness were the most often reported forms of parent–child assistance. Spanish parents less frequently gave gifts involving money than did white and black parents, reflecting unquestionably to some degree their lower income. But, more importantly, the Spanish elderly still appeared to have a more direct role in the family than their black or white peers, and were far more often involved in giving advice with respect to running the home, child rearing, and making major decisions on such things as jobs or substantial purchases. They were also involved in helping to raise grandchildren than were white or black grandparents. Whites and blacks, on the other hand, although available for help to children in times of illness and for occasional baby-sitting, appeared to play a more passive role with respect to family operations. Their main form of assistance on a regular basis appeared to be gift giving.

A similar pattern with respect to degree of actual involvement in day-to-day chores of life is seen when we look at what children did for parents (as reported by the parents). Help from children was, if anything, even more extensive than parents helping children. Almost 9 out of 10 older people having children reported such help (see Table 2).

As one might expect, gift giving and crisis assistance were the principal forms of assistance reported by respondents of all three ethnic groups. Among all three ethnic subgroups similarly high proportions of respondents received gifts from children (78 percent black elderly, 84 percent white and Spanish). There were, however, some significant differences in the form of gift. Spanish elderly, with the lowest incomes, more frequently received monetary gifts, followed by blacks. Among the white respondents, gifts were generally in the form of objects (a coat or refrigerator) rather than money.

The difference in type of gift may well reflect the greater need for money on the part of Spanish and black elderly, and a reluctance on the part of white elderly to accept monetary gifts that connote greater dependency.

Children of all three ethnic subgroups assisted equally in time of illness; the proportions of respondents receiving crisis intervention were virtually identical (67 percent white, 68 percent black, 69 percent Spanish) (see Table 2).

Although a similarly high proportion (approximately two thirds) of each subgroup reported receiving some assistance from children in the chores of daily living, there were noticeable differences in the form of the assistance. Spanish and black children appeared to be significantly more involved than white children in such things as shopping and running errands, keeping house, and preparing meals. This greater involvement undoubtedly is partially a reflection of the closer geographic proximity of black and Spanish parents to children, but it is probably also a manifestation of the continuing influence of the extended family structure.

Even more significant with respect to the nuclear family and independence, far fewer white respondents reported that children gave advice in matters of daily living than was the case among the black and Spanish elderly. Among blacks and Spanish, at least one quarter received advice regularly from their children.

Our data clearly indicate that the Spanish elderly, and to some extent the black elderly, are still part of an extended family network encompassing frequent contact and much direct mutual assistance. White elderly, although involved with their children, are less directly involved in day-to-day household activities and have a less time-consuming, a less specified, and a less direct role with respect to the lives of their children. It is, of course, impossible to predict how long this extended protective family system will continue for the Spanish and black elderly. From the attitudinal material in our study, it would appear that the impact of the dominant culture is already having its effect and that the Spanish elderly more than any other group are feeling the strains of attempting to bridge two cultures.

DISCUSSION AND IMPLICATIONS

The foregoing findings point to the important strengths held and difficulties faced by the inner-city elderly of New York.

First, with respect to the newest arrivals, the Spanish elderly as a group are at the younger end of the elderly continuum and have fewer years of residency in the city, although still a substantial amount. Spanish elderly tend to be still married and living with a spouse and may even have a younger child still in the household. Economically, they are the worst off, both with respect to when they leave the labor force and to their level of job skills. Because of relative lack of skill and education they held the lowest paying jobs during their adult years and, if covered by Social Security, receive only minimum benefits. Many, however, are not even covered by Social Security, and they are less likely to be covered by Medicare. However, the Spanish elderly, although suffering from communication difficulties (many still speak only Spanish), have turned to Old Age Assistance and, therefore, Medicaid to a much greater degree than either their black or white peers. The municipal hospitals tend to function as their doctors, and without Medicare coverage they use private physicians to a lesser degree than do the black and white elderly. Low incomes and poor nutrition have undoubtedly contributed to their self-assessed poorer health, but here cultural factors are important, for illness is not considered something to hide but rather to talk about widely (especially among the women). But balanced against severe handicaps of language, economic privation, and lack of Social Security coverage is the fact that the Spanish elderly, more than their peers, are still functioning within the protective environment of the extended family. Many indicate that they still have rights as elders, and they tend to interact strongly with their children in giving both advice and assistance in a variety of tasks from baby-sitting to shopping to fixing things in their childrens' homes. With less money, they are not as apt to give children material gifts but appear to have outlets for giving of themselves and a role to play within the family circle. However, this picture is being eroded as the younger generation of Spanish-background adults becomes more acculturated. Already 27 percent of the Spanish elderly live alone rather than within the extended family, and Spanish elderly show signs of mental stress and worry to a far greater degree than do black or white elderly. The very thing they worry most about—children and family matters—is indicative of the strains that are evident in the changing family situation among New Yorkers of Spanish background. It would appear that the future holds considerable uncertainty for the Spanish elderly, who in coming generations will probably be caught up in the same dilemma of role crisis presently faced by their peers.

The black elderly are facing many of the same economic and minority-group problems as the Span-ish elderly without some of the redeeming features of close-knit, extended family life. Although slightly better off economically than their Spanish peers, they too suffer from extremely low incomes, job discrimination, and forced early retirement for the men. Social Security coverage is far from complete, particularly among women, many of whom continue to work into their late sixties and early seventies. Like the Spanish, black elderly tend to receive minimum or near-minimum Social Security benefits. They are more likely to be covered by Medicare and when ill tend to use private physicians or the clinics of the voluntary hospitals.

Because of poverty and discrimination in childhood and adulthood, blacks have 7 years less life expectancy than whites and report poorer health and a greater incidence of chronic illness than white elderly. A somewhat different family pattern is evident among the black elderly. Although most married at one time, fewer blacks in old age are still married and living with a spouse than among the other two subgroups. The incidence of divorce and/or separation is more frequent among blacks, and widowhood is as prevalent as among whites. As a result, there are more female-headed homes with younger family members living in the households of the grandmother. Blacks report slightly less emotional closeness to children, although the majority of their children live within the city limits or in the immediate neighborhoods of the elderly and there is contact between the generations. Black parents help children out somewhat less often than Spanish elderly but seem to play a more direct role in the functioning of their childrens' households than do white elderly. They give gifts as freely as their white peers, although they have less income, and in turn children are available for assistance in time of crisis. However, intervention on the part of children on a day-to-day basis is not as frequent as among Spanish families. Black elderly in need seem more willing than whites to accept Old Age Assistance, but not all black respondents estimated as eligible for income maintenance assistance are getting such help. Among the blacks, increasing numbers appear to be living alone in old age, and it is likely that in the future the problem of live-alones will reach proportions similar to that found among the white population.

Of the three subgroups, black elderly express the

greatest satisfaction with their lives in old age and worry the least. It is impossible to determine the exact meaning of this higher level of life satisfaction. Are such attitudes genuinely indicative of present happiness or are they perhaps a reaction formed in response to the discrimination suffered by blacks in this country, a psychologically protective stance adapated early in childhood and carried over into old age? Certainly, black elderly face severe problems of low income, poor health, inadequate housing, and difficulty in obtaining supportive assistance from both the community and often from their families; their high scores on measures of life satisfaction must be accepted with some hesitation. However, just reaching 65 may indeed be a cause for considerable satisfaction.

The white elderly in the poverty areas of the inner city present a conflicting picture. Most have been lower-middle or middle class during their adult years; old age for them brings not only role loss but severe economic and often social discontinuity. Living longer, many more are found living alone; the incidence of live-alones is particularly high in the case of women, who far outnumber men and are not as likely to remarry upon loss of spouse. Residing in changing neighborhoods, often among hostile neighbors whom they cannot understand, there is considerable fear of crime and of persons different from one's self.

On the other hand, the white elderly have lived in New York a long time; they have strong feelings of belonging and are particularly appreciative of the easily accessible neighborhood facilities and the richness and variety of city life. They are staunch New Yorkers and speak about the city with considerable affection, although recognizing the problems inherent in deteriorating neighborhoods.

The white elderly, although slightly better off than their Spanish and black peers, are truly New York's hidden poor. They have strong feelings of pride and are unwilling to accept easily the help available, such as Old Age Assistance, if it means any loss of independence or dignity. Although most have living children in the area with whom they feel close and are in contact, the separation between the generations is complete in most cases. Children and parents help each other in times of crisis, but involvement in the details of daily living is neither expected nor desired on the part of white elderly nor does it appear to be

forthcoming from children, many of whom live outside the immediate neighborhood. Love and affection is shown through gifts, money, visiting, phoning, and emergency help or occasional baby sitting; other types of more direct intervention, including advice giving, are rare. Parents and adult children function as two separate nuclear families, and this separation is both accepted and real.

For the black and Spanish elderly the community must be prepared to accept considerable financial responsibility to compensate for low retirement incomes and poor work histories. The entire cost of adequate housing, health, nutrition, and the variety of services needed by older people certainly cannot be assumed by most black or Spanish elderly, given their low incomes. White elderly, given rising Social Security benefits and pensions, may in the future be better able to assume a greater part of the cost of their needs. But problems of greater isolation from family and higher incidence of living alone will continue to require supportive community services for them as well; particularly in the case of the older and more frail elderly and the unattached women, the two groups of white elderly most often found living alone and with the lowest incomes. In addition, many white elderly need economic assistance, but it must be given in a way that does not strip pride and destroy independence. Hopefully, the assumption of Old Age Assistance by the Social Security system will mean greater economic security for the elderly of all three ethnic groups, coupled with a consideration for personal feelings and for a sense of personal dignity. The elderly of the inner city and their peers throughout the city have contributed long hard years of work and they deserve an old age of respect, dignity, and freedom from want. If today's older New Yorkers fail to realize such a life, neither will coming generations.

Acknowledgment

The research reported here was supported by Administration on Aging Grant AA-4-70-089-02.

REFERENCES

Blau, Z. S. *Old Age in a Changing Society, New Viewpoints*. New York: Franklin Watts Press, 1973.

Cantor, M. H., and Mayer, M. *Health Crisis of Older*

New Yorkers. New York: New York City Office for the Aging, 1972.

____. et al. *The Elderly in the Inner City*. New York: New York City Office for the Aging, 1975 (in press).

Clark, M., and Anderson, B. G. *Culture and Aging*. Springfield, Ill.: Charles C Thomas, 1967.

Gelwicks, L., Feldman, A., and Newcomer, R. J. *Report on Older Population: Needs, Resources and Services*. Los Angeles: Los Angeles Gerontology Center, University of Southern California, 1971.

Hollingshead, A. B., and Redlich, F. C. *Social Class and Mental Illness*. New York: Wiley, 1958.

Kent, D., and Hirsch, C. *Needs and Use of Services Among Negro and White Aged*, Vols. I and II. University Park, Pa.: Pannsylvania State University, July 1971 and October 1972.

Litwak, E. Extended kin relations in an industrial democratic society. in E. Shanas and G. Streib (eds.), *Social Structure and the Family*. Englewood Cliffs, N.J.: Prentice-Hall, 1965.

Rose, A., and Peterson, W. A. (eds.). *Older People and Their Social World*. Philadelphia: F. A. Davis, 1965.

Rosow, I. *Social Integration of the Aged*. New York: Free Press, 1967.

Shanas, E., Townsend, P., Wedderburn, D., Friis, H., Milhøj, P., and Stehouwer, J. *Old People in Three Industrial Societies*. New York: Atherton Press, 1968.

Townsend, P. *The Family Life of Old People*. London: Routledge & Kegan Paul Ltd., 1957.

U.S. Bureau of the Census, 1970 Census of Population. Washington, D.C.: Government Printing Office.

U.S. Department of Labor, Bureau of Labor Statistics. *Three Budgets for A Retired Couple in Urban Areas of the United States, 1969–70*. Washington, D.C.: Government Printing Office.

PART II

COMMUNITY PLANNING
AND POLICY DECISIONS
AS THEY AFFECT OLDER PEOPLE

ROBERT J. NEWCOMER

Robert J. Newcomer is Senior Research Analyst for the County of San Diego Human Resources Agency, Senior Citizens Affairs, San Diego, California.

Introduction

Among the responsibilities facing planners today is the traditional function of attempting to develop an overall scheme of arrangement for housing and services. Critical to this task is a sensitivity to those decisions and trends that can have a lasting impact on a proposed project or program. If decisions for the future are made in relation only to today's needs, priorities, and resources without consideration of likely future events or population preferences, the buildings and environments produced will probably constitute serious handicaps as the future unfolds. It is essential that flexibility be programmed into plans and service systems, while incorporating as much as can be known of future contingencies.

The planning and provision of housing for the elderly illustrates a major current shortcoming of both social and physical planning—a failure to think beyond rhetoric and the problems of the present generations of aged persons. The very low economic status of today's older population cannot, of course, be ignored, but neither should it obscure an assessment of how the present generation may differ from the next and the generation after that.

Today's problems arise from a combination of factors that may not be relevant in the future. Among these are a rapid relative and absolute increase in the number of older persons during the past 40 years. Society simply did not set aside ample income to meet this demand. Moreover, today's older individuals come primarily from blue-collar, farm, and self-employed small business occupations. They have had small past earnings from which to set aside for themselves.

The proportion of older people in the total population will increase more slowly among the next generation. Increased numbers will come from higher socioeconomic backgrounds, and most will have better pensions and retirement incomes. For the first time, too, these people will come in large numbers from suburban rather than rural or central-city areas.

To the extent that future generations are healthier, wealthier, and more leisure-oriented, changes can be expected in the demand for services and housing and in life styles generally.

The effects of these demographic changes on our cities and service-delivery programs have been given scant consideration in most community planning. Take, for example, the housing element of a city's comprehensive plan. Virtually all efforts to date have concentrated on structural quality and the access of

FIGURE 1
Will tomorrow's elderly be more accustomed to the good life? (Photo by Linz, courtesy of Leisure Technology Corporation.)

low-income and minority populations to the housing market. Typically, remedies have been sought in subsidized housing and rehabilitation of current stock. But when one considers that roughly one quarter of all housing units in our cities are headed by someone over the age of 65, and that the proportion may reach over 40 percent in some sections of a city, there is a major problem that has to be considered. Furthermore, because the private sector cannot easily provide housing for older persons whose income is below $5,000, it becomes clear that the housing problem is not limited to those defined as low income, but to the majority of older people.

The federal government has made superficial efforts to solve some of the needs for low-rent housing. The Housing and Community Development Act of 1974 is one example, but the actual number of units to be provided during any given year is far below the estimated need. An equally serious problem is that the projects built for the low-income population have mortgages of up to 40 years. People will obviously be expected to occupy these units from 10 to 40 years. Will units designed today, addressed to today's income groups and located in terms of today's political expediencies, remain suitable to future residents? Will these people be similar to the present residents? Will this housing become obsolete? If so, to whose use will it fall?

Existent tools and knowledge can help us to plan and provide much needed housing that can remain vital and appropriate over time. But we must be prepared to use these tools, to be creative in programming, and to conduct contingency planning.

The same reality of changing circumstances applies

to all service programming. It is essential that programs be continually monitored, updated, and modified as required by changing circumstances.

The papers contained in Part II, although directed to the functional area of housing, are intended to conceptualize four issues affecting all service programming and to provide an introduction to some of the specific subsequent programmatic recommendations in this book.

Robert Newcomer reviews the literature regarding the federal and local decision-making processes as they affect housing and other service programs. Many shortcomings and possible bottlenecks to be anticipated in project or program implementation are painfully apparent from this analysis: local communities are extremely incremental and consensus-oriented in their approach to planning; senior-citizen involvement and influence have until now been much needed though absent catalysts to innovative programming; professional organizations and agencies too are described as being meagerly prepared and passive in their approaches to problems of the aged. These circumstances are shown to have combined to cast many responsibilities by default back to the federal government. However, in spite of the good intentions of federal programming, it becomes clear that administrative guidelines and legislative intent do not always symbiotically produce the best end products.

In short, from this paper emerges an appreciation for the dynamics of this decision-making process and some of the critical variables to be addressed in the program-development process. For the research-oriented reader, a discussion of data shortcomings will be of added interest.

In spite of problems in project development and implementation, many housing units have been provided. Yet, as is often true of many programs, opinions can be divided over whether enough is being done. William Baer, through a creative manipulation of secondary data, poses the question of who benefits from federal housing for the elderly. The performance of virtually all federal housing programs is traced. Included are conventional FHA and VA home-purchasing mortgage insurance and federal income-tax benefits from ownership, as well as the basic home-purchase and rent-subsidy programs. In light of his appraisal, Baer attempts to assess likely consequences for the elderly and those interested in providing such housing that might arise from the Housing and Community Development Act of 1974. This paper, while providing information useful to advocates of additional projects and legislation, also provides an illustration of how one might begin to evaluate the benefits derived from many other programs.

In an era when the public and the courts are schizophrenically asserting affirmative action one day and equalitarianism the next—depending of course on the issue and those affected by the action—it is not surprising to find confusion over determining the best procedure for the advocacy and evaluation of programs. As pointed out in Newcomer's paper, one of the greatest shortcomings of existent housing policy is the lack of authority to prescribe locations. Instead, authorities can only react to what has been proposed. Until social planning becomes combined with an ability to mandate services and programs, this problem will be a plague. Area plans as produced under Title III of the Older Americans Act do have the authority to mandate, at least for Title III funded programs. As these plans gain local credibility, they may become influential in the allocation of additional funds, hopefully in a prescriptive rather than reactive way.

During the evolution of such planning efforts, legal challenges must be anticipated. Robert Gillan, although again focusing on a housing-related concern, zoning, considers several constitutional and statutory limitations as applied to preferential treatment of the elderly. He concludes that the time is fast arriving when communities *must* rather than *can* accord the elderly special treatment. For the most part, this trend has stemmed from situations where attempts were made to exclude particular housing locations from a community. But precedents have been established that may prove useful in opening program eligibilities, reducing restrictions, and enlarging service districts in an effort to broaden quality controls. Gillan's article should provide cause for both optimism and advocacy in program development.

The final two papers in Part II, both by William Pollak, shift the housing focus from independent to supportive settings, and to the realm of concerns commonly known as "alternatives to institutionalization." These papers provide an insightful conceptualization of the issues that must be considered in the utilization of alternative care settings for the elderly. The point is repeatedly raised that existing patterns of utilization and cost vary geographically, with income, race, and other variables, and that standardization of criteria is essential. These papers form an excellent basis for the initiation of a monitoring system for dependent housing. From that basis they provide a needed complement to the preceding materials and to David Sears' paper appearing later in this book. Perhaps the primary significance of these papers comes from their illustration of the importance of standardization and definition of measurable units in any program-monitoring process.

In short, the papers presented in Part II each address specific issues broadly relating to housing for the elderly, and also direct attention to a multitude of issues for community planning and policy decisions affecting the lives of older people. More research into all program areas is apparently needed, but enough information has been provided here to stimulate consciousness of our present shortcomings and of the parameters that must be considered in future-oriented program decision making.

ROBERT J. NEWCOMER

Robert J. Newcomer is Senior Research Analyst for the County of San Diego Human Resources Agency, Senior Citizens Affairs, San Diego, California.

Meeting the Housing Needs of Older People

The quality of our current housing for aging citizens is one indication of how society has dealt with the past and present problems of older people. Of the more than 20 million persons over age 65, 95 percent live in households (boarding homes, apartments, houses, housing for the elderly projects, mobile homes, and with relatives). Two thirds of these people live in their own homes. The remaining 5 percent live in institutions (nursing homes, homes for the aged, and mental hospitals). This occupancy pattern is not wholly reflective of either housing preferences or needs. Federal housing programs, for example, have produced over 500,000 multifamily units for the elderly, which house about 650,000 older people (U.S. Senate, 1974). This total represents just over 3 percent of all older people, but the waiting lists for these projects could easily double or triple the number of persons housed by federal programs. The principal attraction of this housing is its low rent. Specialized housing related to health needs is also unable to provide a wide enough range of suitable alternatives for the semi-independent needs of the middle- and low-income aged population. At any given period of time, as many as 12 percent of the older population is in need of supportive services for major daily activities (Shanas et al., 1968). (For low-income groups, the proportion is perhaps 20 percent.) In other words, today's pattern of occupancy is a reflection of the alternatives, not necessarily of need.

Since the mid-1960s the acute housing problems among older people have received increasing attention. In some years, up to half of all federally subsidized new construction has been for this group. However, in many ways the acceleration in building has proceeded with too little forethought about what was being provided for whom and about its long-range viability. Too little was known by those responsible for design and implementation about the housing preferences and needs of older people, the changing tenant characteristics and operational demands, over time, within projects, the importance of neighborhoods to a project's viability, and the special needs of today's older people and those of the next generation.

As a consequence of this collective ignorance, many programs and administrative policies worked counter to national housing objectives with respect to low-income groups. Housing and Urban Development administrative restrictions on Section 236 housing are illustrative. Overall project costs, including land and site improvement, was limited to $2,400 per room in family units and $2,500 per room in elderly units. (Special increases of up to $750 per room were allowed for elderly units in exceptionally expensive locations.) Site selection and building type were the realistic trade-offs if anything was to be built. Frequently, these constraints necessitated that family units be located in areas which did not have enough open space for children or were in slums, urban-renewal areas, or transitional areas (Keith, 1968).

Another incentive for the provision of housing for the elderly was an attempt by civil rights groups and others to use housing projects as a device for integrating neighborhoods. For a time in the early 1960s, cities were threatened with cutbacks in federal funds if housing projects were not sited to achieve integration.

Access to predominantly white suburban areas was hampered for projects that were to house people who were poor, culturally different, or who exhibited a nonconforming life style. Elderly projects typically did not generate as much local opposition (Schermer, 1968; Taggert, 1970; Peel et al., 1970). As of 1970, for example, only 12 percent of the Sections 221 (d) (3) and 236 units were in suburbs, while significantly more Section 202 housing for the aged was so located (Peel et al., 1970; Druker and Shouldberg, 1970; U.S. Senate, 1971).

These problems are now recognized, but as this country evolves another housing policy, it must become sensitive to the special dimensions and complexities of the elderly submarket. Older persons, although totaling but 10 percent of the national population, head 27 percent of all households (U.S. Bureau of Census, 1970). Within a decade this proportion could easily surpass 33 percent with a lowering of retirement age to 60 or 55. This magnitude of people, with generally higher incomes than the retirees of today, will be placing many demands on the housing market for more alternatives.

The present generation of aged has lived most of its life in either rural settings, small towns, or center-city areas. The next generation of elderly will begin coming in substantial numbers from the suburbs. Their willingness to move to inner-city (or central-city) housing projects is an unresolved issue.

Within existing facilities for older people (e.g.,

housing and homes for the aged) the increasing need for supportive services that can aid the individual and reduce transfers to nursing homes is now being recognized. Under these circumstances, women residents who enter at age 65 will have an estimated length of residence exceeding 15 years. Men who enter at the same age would have at least 10 years in residence. This fact, coupled with the advent of home-delivered services, will significantly affect the demand for existing projects. It has been observed that the average age of project residents increases with the age of the project, and that the average age of new residents correspondingly tends to increase. Projects that had residents with a median age of 65 when opened had a median age over 70 ten years later (Koff, 1973). Service demands have also been shown to increase with age; therefore, operational costs have tended to rise.

Another phenomenon that appears to be developing is that projects located in transitional areas (in the sense of deterioration or increasing blight) will have attractiveness for only those persons whose income leaves them no other alternative. Over time, relative increases in income (especially as provided by housing-allowance programs) should reduce the attractiveness of this housing for even those with low incomes. In other words, housing in marginal locations will filter out of the elderly housing market altogether.

The notion of filtering may be pervasive in all existing housing for the elderly. Facilities housing middle-income persons may cease to be alternatives to the middle class within 10 years. Stable mortgage rates and moderate increases in operational costs may permit this housing to come within the means of "low-income" groups. (This assumes that the minimum low income in 10 years will be relatively higher than that known today.)

At the time of writing, housing assistance to the individual renter (the housing allowance), as contrasted to the programmatic project-type, multiunit housing of the past 30 years, is the major type of assistance on the horizon. Although one cannot predict its viability as the nation's political leadership changes, the immediate future seems certain to maximize the role of private-market housing. Emerging too are provisions that allow local housing authorities, using the 1937 Housing Act, Section 23 (now

FIGURE 1
Deterioration may begin with the selection of an unfavorable
site location. (Photo by Jeff Cooper.)

Section 8 of the 1974 Housing and Community Development Act), to contract with private owners for
the leasing of units to individuals and families meeting the financial criteria for public housing. As in
earlier applications of Section 23, HUD pays the
difference between the market rental for the unit and
the amount the occupant is judged able to pay. This
plan covers both existing and new housing. Whether
better housing will result for low-income families is
problematic. In the case of the elderly, it is by no
means self-evident that their housing situation will
improve. For these programs to be successful, it is

essential that mechanisms be made available for
matching people with needed housing, for quality
control over site selection and building design, for
monitoring rent levels and their fair market value, and
for ensuring that needed supportive services such as
homemakers, meals, and home health aids are available.

Judged on the basis of their performances, most
communities have much to do in anticipation of these
new responsibilities. This paper will review issues related to subsidized housing, giving particular attention to local regulatory and goal-setting systems.

Hopefully, uncovering past weaknesses will help to identify needed areas for further study and direct attention to remedial policies.

THE HOUSING SUBSIDY SYSTEM

The housing subsidy system, defined within the context of public housing and mortgage subsidy programs, has four basic actors: local housing authorities, profit and nonprofit sponsors, the Department of Housing and Urban Development (HUD), and money lenders. The following discussion is limited to the first three.

Local Housing Authorities

Established by the Housing Act of 1937, it is the responsibility of local housing authorities (LHA's) to manage all public housing units within their jurisdiction. Ostensibly, these organizations are free from the political control of elected officials, although some if not all members might be their appointees.

A few studies of LHA's have examined their composition and policy attitudes. These studies raise a serious question about both the objectivity and independence of LHA's. Housing authorities, except in larger cities, are described as being small and rarely capable of affording a highly trained professional staff. Most LHA's rely almost entirely on the abilities of inexperienced and part-time citizens serving on their boards. Even if a staff exists, policy matters are generally decided by the board.

Board members are usually appointed by the mayor or board of supervisors. Some evidence suggests that these boards are neither responsible to the will of the public nor to their tenant clientele (Schwartz, 1969). Furthermore, current controls are inadequate and ineffective in obtaining the most efficient production of low-rent housing.

Most board members are white males—business executives, lawyers, real estate men, and bankers. Demographically these individuals are not representative of the clientele served by public housing. Investigation of board attitudes toward such particular housing policy issues as the desirability of tenant unions and the need for more housing has found that board members most often indicated no desire for tenant unions and believed that there was an ample supply of housing.[1]

Schermer (1968) describes the composition of LHA boards and their behavior as indicating a high sensitivity to the consensus interests of the local political structure, the opinions and values of the business and middle-class community, and the interests of the building trade unions. Rarely did he find an indication that the authority was sensitive or committed to the needs and interests of the poor. As an example, only a few LHA's were found that developed their own data pertaining to overall low-income-housing needs. None had developed a comprehensive plan or general strategy for interpreting problems to the community, involving citizen groups in their programs, or testing out a variety of approaches.

It was Schermer's conclusion that LHA interests were directed toward the management of existing properties rather than improving the city's overall housing situation. And in recent years they had apparently found it much easier and less controversial to develop housing for the elderly than housing for families. Respondents in these studies tended to view their chief responsibilities for the elderly in terms of special design and equipment features in the housing. The majority also believed that there should be a program dealing with the social problems of elderly tenants, but that these programs should be determined primarily by the availability of services outside the project. The current financial pressures on LHA projects would require that any ancillary services be financed by outside agencies.

Subsidized Housing Sponsors

The relative shortcomings of the LHA and the statutes in many communities that require public referenda on public housing support the rationale for alternative housing programs that bypass the LHA. Nonprofit and limited-dividend sponsors have to date been the personification of this alternative for the development of low-income housing.[2] From 1954 to 1968, nonprofit sponsors were the only vehicle for subsidized housing sponsorship for low- to moderate-income older people. These sponsors consisted primarily of churches and other religious organizations who developed and operated the completed projects. In essence, this pattern was but a continuation of earlier church responsibilities toward the aged (Gold, 1970).

The 1968 Housing Act, Section 236 program, allowing limited-dividend sponsors, was an attempt to promote more involvement from the private sector. Typically, limited-dividend sponsors consisted of two groups—packagers, that is, people who acquired the site, prepared plans, and arranged financing, and those who were prepared to manage the facility (often a nonprofit group).

In the 1968 Housing Act, Congress left the definition and evaluation of "sponsors" to the FHA. But there were no criteria in FHA regulations that expressly defined limited-dividend sponsors, no guidelines to test motivation or experience in dealing with members of the community to be served, no required prespecified plan for providing social services to housing residents, and no requirement for a commitment to long-range management by the developer or owner.

Such criteria do exist for nonprofit sponsors, who have to prove their community involvement or community roots and to have an established history of social-service activity (Tone, 1970).

The vagueness of criteria and guidelines for evaluating sponsors did not prove to be a serious operational obstacle because, as will be detailed shortly, FHA evaluation of project applications rested mainly on technical and financial considerations. For this reason, limited-dividend sponsors were preferred because they were usually better able to get a project underway and to build much faster. Quality control over a sponsoring group eventually was exercised by favoring those projects proposed by sponsors and architects with whom FHA had good previous experience.

HUD Project-Selection Criteria and Their Administration

Despite the maze of federal and local organizations, research, and other inputs to the design process, the major mechanism for a project's quality control rested with the Department of Housing and Urban Development (HUD). HUD had the tools (in the form of project-evaluation criteria and minimum property standards) for quality control based on the best technical knowledge, but this was apparently not fully utilized with respect to site selection. A proposed project would be rejected when the project was inappropriate, but there was little that could be done to encourage builders to construct projects where they were most needed. The major limitation on these controls was that they were negative rather than affirmative.

Other limitations are attributable to the application of the six criteria employed by HUD in evaluating subsidized housing project suitability (including LHA projects) (U.S. Department of Housing and Urban Development, 1971). In theory, each criterion had equal weight. A rejection on the basis of one criterion supposedly would void the whole project. In practice, economic constraints dominated decisions. The six criteria and their major limitations are summarized here:

1. *Suitability of the site in relation to the surrounding neighborhood and the city plan.* The site must be conducive to residential living, not affected by environmental hazards, and accessible to needed services and facilities. There was no explicit method for balancing these elements against each other, no real specificity for the selection of sites for the elderly versus families, and no uniformly applied definition of suitability or accessibility.

2. *Physical character of the site.* Basically, the concern was whether or not the topography and surface conditions would support the building. This was a technical problem for which reliable quantitative data could be obtained. This criterion was unambiguously applied.

3. *Site dispersion, that is, the use of scattered sites as opposed to the use of single sites.* Operationally, for any one project this was usually unfeasible because of the loss of scale economies in production, coupled with limitations on per unit cost. A more realistic criterion regarding the same general issue concerned "impaction," that is, the allocation of too many projects or units within any given area, especially one that was highly segregated by race or income. Each locality apparently could establish its own benchmarks on this criterion, thus reducing its salience.

4. *Cost of site and required improvement costs.*

Statutory per unit costs of $2,400 per room for family and $2,500 per room for elderly units were generally applied. Normally, the LHA and potential sponsors had some latitude in balancing site acquisition and building costs. (Extra allowances of up to $750 per room would be granted in areas of excessive need or high cost.) Urban-renewal areas and Model Cities areas, where land costs could be reduced through other subsidies, were also often encouraged as potential sites. Special zoning provisions for elderly housing that permitted high building-to-land coverage ratios was another strategy used to reduce per unit costs. In short, the economic constraint was effectively applied. Flexibility was mainly obtained by juggling site locations. This fact was one of the paramount weaknesses in the site-selection criteria.

5. *Feasibility of relocation of all site occupants to standard housing.* Most potential housing sites were on vacant land so this criterion typically did not apply.

6. *Suitability of the site for facilitating racial integration.* The site integration criteria required that sites be located so as not to deny a racial minority the opportunity to locate outside areas of minority-group concentration. But according to Peel et al. (1970), the nondiscrimination criterion was the last to be applied when evaluating a site and was infrequently used to void a project. For example, if an LHA could show that no site was available outside racially mixed areas, the nondiscriminatory requirement could be waived for a site acceptable by the other criteria. High land cost and zoning were the principal constraints used to argue for a site's availability. Turnkey, leased housing, and nonprofit and limited-dividend projects were likely to be more leniently evaluated than public housing, because in these cases a site was often already owned by the proposed developer. If the site was rejected, the whole project would likely die.

Not all subsidized projects were subject to these controls. Outlined here are the basic project-evaluation procedures used by HUD officials regarding these other facilities.

1. Conventional public housing: local housing authorities drew up a set of preliminary plans and standards and selected a site. After approval of site and plans by the city and HUD, the authority submitted the project to competitive bidding and financed the project through the sale of short-term notes.

2. Direct acquisition since the 1950s and turnkey since the 1960s have been the primary methods of developing public housing. Through this procedure, a private developer built a project on his own land and sold the completed project to the LHA. Final price and broad specifications of the project were stated in an initial contract; there was, however, no detailed project approval by the LHA and no competitive bidding.

3. Leased housing, like turnkey, required no detailed site-selection or project-evaluation process by HUD as long as the number of units in a single building was less than 25.

4. Sections 235, 221(d)(3), and 202 housing for both families and elderly were subsidy programs, negotiated independently from the LHA between either limited-dividend or nonprofit sponsors and HUD. It was up to the sponsors to acquire land, start-up funding, and zoning, and to prepare preliminary plans for the project. This proposed package was then reviewed and evaluated by HUD.

Regardless of the program, of all the criteria cost carried the greatest weight. The most significant result of the heavy emphasis on cost has been the proportionate increase in production of housing for the elderly. These projects were not bound to the density and building coverage limitations of family units. The net coverage and density limits would be waived for elderly housing, subject to local approval. Moreover, greater per room building allowances and reduced parking requirements allowed elderly projects to compete more successfully outside ghetto areas for available sites than did family housing.

A final factor favoring housing for the elderly was its greater acceptability by neighborhoods and public officials. HUD for some time tried to apply pressure on suburbs to introduce low-income housing. In fact, at one time HUD threatened to withhold all HUD funds to cities that did not comply (Franklin, 1971; Frederick, 1970; Potvin, 1969; Dutsch, 1970; *U.S. News and World Report,* 1970a and b, 1971a and b). Housing for the elderly appears to have been a convenient compromise for many committees.

Local governments and goal setting. That the

HUD project-evaluation process essentially bypassed direct local controls is in some measure an artifact of the national approach to housing programs, which have, since their inception in the Housing Act of 1937, bypassed local government. This was evident first in the designation of local housing authorities as administrators of public housing (Farkas, 1971). More recently, Sections 202, 221(d)(3), and 236 programs have bypassed the LHA's, involving negotiations between the sponsoring organization and HUD. The actual decision making and operational independence of these groups has varied widely across the country.

Local governmental controls stem from a variety of sources. Zoning and building codes illustrate explicit regulatory devices. Additional community processes also merit attention. This section reviews existing literature evaluating the capabilities of local government in the exercise of these controls, especially as applied to policies for the aged.

Local controls. Manvel (1968) through a survey of local planning, zoning, and building regulation activity in county government, municipalities, and townships found most regulatory agencies to be small, often without a full-time staff. Even in large departments there were few individuals who had had training in the special needs or problems of older people. Staff have few available guidebooks to call upon. (Kaufman, 1961; Belos, 1972; Lawton and Byerts, 1973; Lawton, 1975; and Gelwicks and Newcomer, 1974, are virtually the only sources of professional guidelines.) As a consequence, few communities had an operant procedure for such planning. In spite of these shortcomings, communities typically have developed guidelines, often expressed by the zoning ordinance, for project evaluations. These ordinances usually were directed to the issues of parking ratios, room sizes, lot-coverage ratios, and special design features for the handicapped (Spicer, 1971). Their apparent effect is to reduce land costs and therefore rent levels. In other words, the intention of these special ordinances or variance provisions was generally to facilitate the provision of low- to moderate-income housing.

Secondary effects of such controls do not appear to have been considered in the application of the procedures. It is likely, for example, that locations and buildings which are highly supportive in terms of the type of services available (particularly medical and meal services) attract persons of high physical dependence (Lawton, 1970). The interaction between a building and neighborhood resource utilization also is seemingly ignored. Convenient access to diverse outdoor areas reduces the utilization of on-site common areas (Lawton, 1968; McDonald and Newcomer, 1973). High crime in the neighborhood, on the other hand, reduces tenant mobility both within and outside the building (Lawton and Simon, 1968). Failure to recognize these secondary effects may have contributed to the provision of a building unsuited to its location.

Goal setting and policy planning. In addition to land-use planning, many social-service agencies and volunteer groups are involved in the establishment of community policy. The relationships among these groups is illustrative of how older people have been ignored in the planning process. The active involvement of the elderly in decision making relating to housing and services appears to be an ideal sought by many, but is perhaps even less realized than in the case of minority groups and the poor. Research on this specific matter, however, is not extensive.

A study of voluntary organizations in seven communities (Morris and Randall, 1965) provided the first example of research into this system, particularly with respect to programs for the elderly. Voluntary association memberships were found to be typically drawn from three local sources—socially influential individuals, economic influentials, and scattered representatives from civic organizations. Generally excluded were minority and ethnic groups that did not control traditional social agencies and those individuals and organizations exclusively committed to one cause. Narrow commitment, such as to problems of the aged, made an organization difficult to absorb into an association clearly committed to a balanced theory of resource allocation (e.g., welfare planning council). Labor and senior-citizen associations were found to function almost completely outside health and welfare planning councils. Even if they were nominally affiliated with comprehensive agencies, they continued to carry on their major efforts in the political arena and not within the association.

The established welfare planning councils, because

FIGURE 2
This ground-floor area of public housing for the elderly is an effective deterrent to social behavior and mobility. (Photo by Wilbur Jackson.)

of their value for balanced versus cause-oriented resource allocation, had a limited capacity to develop or conduct programs that required major readjustment of resources in light of altered circumstances.

Community Action and Model Cities programs were partially designed to help bypass the existing service infrastructure and to bring about greater input from community representatives. But these efforts too, until recently, ignored older people.

Fraser (1969) presented a typical report on citizen participation in the administration of a variety of programs, including Model Cities and Community Action programs. He found that participatory boards

were generally unrepresentative of those groups and interests affected by these programs and, further, that commitment to participatory boards or units involved conflict with local "old-line" agencies.

Such studies, and another by de St. Lenkass (1969) that examined the issue of citizen participation, have generally done so on a global level and were concerned principally with income and race, not age. Thus the full extent of the exclusion of the elderly has not been well documented.

A particularly glaring illustration of narrowly focused research can be found in Kaplan et al. (1970). Seattle, which was one of the cities evaluated for the

FIGURE 3
Proximity to an attractive shopping area with weather protection and helpful "extras," such as the exaggerated stopsign, might be used as a positive criterion for site selection. (Photo by Thomas Byerts.)

manner and effectiveness of citizen participation in the planning process, was exemplary in its concern for elderly Model Cities residents. Yet the report failed to comment on the extent of elderly involvement, if any, in program planning.

As a subpopulation, the elderly continued its low profile well into the "war on poverty." Cities found older people disproportionately residing in target areas but allocated relatively few funds for their needs. This pattern changed somewhat after President Johnson mandated that older people be given special consideration.

The congressional hearings on the "Usefulness of the Model Cities Program to the Elderly" (U.S. Senate, 1969) gave testimony to the poor Model Cities response, while highlighting a few specific instances of elderly involvement. In general, neither concern for nor involvement of older people was strikingly high in spite of the fact that the proportion of older people in Model Cities areas tended to be high. Of 72 original demonstration cities, 42 had areas where elderly population constituted more than 20 percent of the population. Yet only 4 percent of these cities specifically mentioned the aged as a priority problem in their original applications. Almost one half of the funded cities, however, did indicate their desire to research the problems of older persons.

Elderly involvement in Model Cities Planning generally included membership on the task forces established by the City Demonstration Agencies (CDA).[3] There have been no data reported to quantify this involvement.

The City of Boston with its Council of Elders is perhaps the premier example of citizen participation of older people. This group grew out of an elderly housing project in which the tenants organized to obtain grants needed for the improvement of the services that they were receiving. Subsequently, they also developed pilot projects and hired staff. As the organization expanded, they were invited to become involved with the larger CDA program planning.

Part of the problem of gaining wider participation for the elderly, aside from the initial apathy of CDA and CAP organization groups, was the process by which planning groups were chosen. The predominant manner was through neighborhood elections. This required extensive electioneering, aggressiveness, and the necessity of building a cohesive power group, tasks for which the elderly were usually at a disadvantage except in areas where there were age-congregate housing projects.

There is promise for more participation in the future because of volunteer and employed elderly working on projects such as Foster Grandparents, RSVP, Day Care Centers, Senior AIDES, and in multipurpose centers. Agencies are increasingly delegating one or more staff members as specialists on aging. These people, if they assume an advocate role, help to generate momentum for participation. Title III of the Older Americans Act (as amended in 1973) establishing Area Agencies on Aging throughout each state should further accelerate these trends.

Research as a substitute for participation. By far the most visible mechanism for feedback and input to the policy planning and design process of housing for the elderly has been research. However, serious questions can be raised regarding the filtering of this information to the local level.

McGuire (1969), then Special Assistant for Problems of the Elderly and Handicapped in HUD, identified several reasons for the poor rate of research utilization in design: (1) feedback between research and practice was ineffective because practitioners were not trained in methodology and could not directly apply research findings, (2) policy makers did not coordinate and focus research in the most effec-

tive manner, and (3) research was overlapping, redundant, and isolated from other efforts. Anderson and Stone (1969), reviewing research on nursing homes, identified similar shortcomings.

On a more specific level, Morris and Binstock (1966) showed that social planning programs for the elderly had evolved sporadically, expediently, and haphazardly. Rarely was technical knowledge employed to allocate resources. Less than 50 percent of the program goals studied gave consideration to whether goal accomplishment would enhance the welfare of the aged. Less than 5 percent of the goals was selected from among a set of possible alternative measures for improving the welfare of older people. Perhaps most startling, less than 10 percent of the goals made substantial distinctions among the varying characteristics of older persons: sex, marital status, health, income, or residential environment. Only about 25 percent of the goals were chosen on the basis of data with regard to the needs of older people. Only a handful of goals were developed with attention to the power variables that could determine the success or failure of an attempt to establish a program of service.

Goal formulators were local welfare agencies and planning councils. A primary consideration of these groups, as suggested previously, was maintenance of community consensus in goal formulation, not advocacy planning.

More recently, a study of three federal planning organizations all claiming to deal specifically with problems of the elderly in one community found that the activities of planning coordination and research were clearly secondary functions (see the chapter by Estes, page 309). Instead these organizations assumed the roles of labeling the aged as a social problem of consequence, advancing work in the field of aging as a legitimate profession, developing and presenting for public acceptance the participants in the planning organizations as a core of "experts" in aging, and attempting to secure the recognition that would enable these professionals to influence any future planning activities. In actual outcomes, planning activities were described as more symbolic than instrumental, and more oriented toward validation and legitimation of the members' work than toward actual accomplishment.

These two studies do not of course describe comprehensively all local communities in their approach to planning for older people, but they do illustrate consistency with the organizational problems that the Community Action and Model Cities programs tried to circumvent. The advent of Area Agencies on Aging hopefully will rectify these shortcomings. However, several years must be allowed before these agencies will have developed competent staffs and the community and organizational links that can make them effective.

In the meantime, emergent research will find its most interested audience to be national agencies and consulting firms. Substantial information related to housing facilities for older people has been developed, including publications specifying design standards: National Council on Aging (1961), Nierstrasz (1961), Rutherford (1963), Beyer and Kira (1966), Urban Land Institute (1968), Weiss (1969), U.S. Department of Housing and Urban Development (1970), and Gelwicks and Newcomer (1974).

Research is under way that may considerably broaden the evaluation of critical man—environment relationships. Illustrative are those which examine elements of project design (Lawton, 1970, 1972; Lawton and Simon, 1968), site suitability (Newcomer, 1975; Lawton, 1972; Rosenberg, 1970; Schooler, 1970), management practice (Lawton, 1972; Perrow, 1971; Lempert and Sheda, 1970), and problems of crime (Newman, 1972). Numerous studies have also been done on the issue of age segregation (Rosow, 1967; Messer, 1967; Mangum, 1970; Sherman et al., 1968; Hamovitch et al., 1969; Levin, 1970; Butterick, 1969) and the effects of relocation (Carp, 1966; Blenkner, 1967; Aldrich and Mendkoff, 1963; Bennett and Nahemow, 1965). Attention has also recently been given to neighborhood cognition and utilization (Regnier, 1973; Eribes, 1973; Newcomer, 1975).

CONCLUSIONS

Local housing authorities and planning agencies were found to be generally meager in technical skill and passive in their approach to problems of the aged. Local communities were found to be extremely incremental and consensus-oriented in their approach to planning. This propensity, coupled with the dearth of

FIGURE 4
Even under the cost constraints of public housing, design can be beautiful and functional. (Louis Sauer Associates, architects; photo by David Hirsh.)

influence and involvement of senior citizens or their advocates, has resulted in little innovation in programs for the aged.

Of the six project evaluation criteria employed by HUD to determine the suitability of a project's building and site acquisition, costs were shown to be the most important. This factor, coupled with the racial problems associated with the dispersal of low-income projects for families, caused projects for the elderly to be both more feasible and politically expedient for construction in white areas. Family projects correspondingly were disproportionately built in segregated areas. In addition to the political pressures against a more integrated dispersal plan was the pressure of the infrastructure of the housing system. Relatively few affirmative controls were applied to sponsors to encourage them to build housing where it was most needed. Reliance on limited-dividend and turnkey projects heightens this problem because in most instances these developers intended only to provide buildings; other groups had to assume the responsibility of management. The only real quality check on sponsors has apparently been through ex post facto experience with sponsors and architects, rather than through a priori evaluation criteria.

A few final comments are needed to summarize general themes evidenced in the literature, to raise questions about its quality, and to highlight areas for further investigation.

Federal and state level. The studies and writings done in this area are primarily descriptions of housing programs, prominent lobby groups, and important political figures. An insider's view of the relative weight of these actors in any given decision or policy and the trade-offs made in reaching policy consensus are lacking.

HUD and its subsidiary FHA have been shown to form an important link between legislation and local realities. Application of the HUD project selection criteria clearly suggested the presence of a political system not covered in this paper, that of budget appropriations. Budgeting has played an important role in HUD's concern with building many housing units rather than building consistently high quality units. This was seen first in the preference for limited-dividend sponsors and in the disproportionate allocation of housing for the elderly.

A concomitant pressure alluded to in the materials reviewed is that of racial integration. Powerful civil rights groups and congressmen have received and applied pressure to broaden the dispersion of low-income housing throughout the nation's cities. The

adminstration, through HUD, sought for a time to accomplish this task, but local reality (and the statutory limitation on per unit costs) has forced a compromise in which elderly housing was again found to be used to meet the letter, but not the spirit, of the integrationist pressure. When and how this pressure may emerge relative to new housing finance programs remains an open question.

Local level. There is no extensive systematic appraisal of how local communities operated to bar low-income housing in white areas or how housing for the elderly was compromised in this dispersal pattern. Most conclusions apparently have been reached from limited descriptive studies of housing allocation and a few accounts from HUD or other local officials.

Needed research would include studies of city councils, zoning boards, and realtors regarding their receptivity to zoning changes, the quality of available land, cost of these sites, and the economic feasibility for low-income housing for families versus housing for the elderly.

In contrast to housing, other services for older people apparently have had low priority among existing agencies and even among Community Action and Model Cities programs unless there was outside pressure for them. The elderly or their spokesmen seemingly have had little independent impact on the incremental consensus politics of local government and agencies. More information on citizen participation among the elderly and about the politics of all services for older people is needed. The current literature on this subject has only the experience of a few communities as its referent. The involvement of the aged in service organizations and boards of directors and the influence and pervasiveness of "militant" senior groups and other advocates for the aged have been only sketchily traced.

Sponsorship and grantsmanship. Limited-dividend sponsorship of housing, as well as turnkey and leased housing, has expanded federal housing programs to the private sector. But the composition of most LHA's, planning commissions, and zoning boards suggests that the established system for monitoring housing policy is one of peers rather than of organizations representing divergent views. Divergence broad enough to encompass the needs of the intended service recipients is almost totally absent. Existing litera-

FIGURE 5
A concentrated shopping area accessible to tenants is an asset that can compensate for location of a housing project in a poor neighborhood if the pedestrian pathway to it are safe.

quality of housing and site selection by profit versus nonprofit sponsors in order to contrast properly these two development strategies.

It is somewhat disturbing that the fundamental questions cited here persist even as a new housing policy is being debated. We do not know all the parameters and constraints affecting the adequate provision of suitable housing for the elderly. Yet we seem to be reluctant to evaluate previous policy in an attempt to point out its strengths and weaknesses and to highlight those factors which contributed to these conditions. New programs such as the housing allowance method of rent subsidy may resolve or bypass several significant problems such as segregation and unsuitable site selection. But our basic ignorance of housing needs and our piecemeal reactive approach to housing provision remain. These problems cannot be solved with a housing allowance. Further research appears to be justified, but enough is now known to attack comprehensively many of the diverse issues affecting the quality and quantity of housing and services.

NOTES

1. These attitudes may change as tenant groups and community representatives gain board membership. The pervasiveness and rate of such changes, however, have not yet been documented.
2. Section 8 leased housing and turnkey projects are other programs operated through LHA's. The quality controls applicable to these programs are discussed in the following section in relation to HUD project evaluation criteria.
3. Problem-area task forces were the principal vehicle for citizen input in most Model Cities programs. Membership was determined through a variety of modes: elections, appointment, simple participation. In most cases, technical assistance was also provided to the task forces either from the CDA staff or by outside persons.

REFERENCES

Aiken, M., and Alford, R. Community structure and innovation: the case of public housing. *American Political Science Review*, 1970, *13*, 843–864.

ture on this subject is again basically descriptive. There have been few, if any, inquiries into possible systematic bias or impropriety, but much research is needed in the whole area of the politics and possible corruption of sponsor selection. Needed too, as a part of this research, is a comparative evalauation of the

Aldrich, C. K., and Mendkoff, E. Relocation of the aged and disabled: a mortality study. *Journal of the American Geriatrics Society,* 1963, *11,* 185–194.

American Institute of Architects Journal. Proposals on housing for the elderly, 1972, *49,* 46.

Anderson, N. N., and Stone, L. B. Nursing homes: research and public policy. *Gerontologist,* 1969, *9,* 214–218.

Belos, N., *Model Cities and the Aging.* Washington, D.C.: U.S. Department of Health, Education, and Welfare, Administration on Aging, 1972.

Bennett, R., and Nahemow, L. Institutional totality and criteria of social adjustment in residence for the aged. *Journal of Social Issues,* 1965, *21,* 44–70.

Beyer, G. *Housing and Society.* New York: Macmillan, 1965.

_____, and Kira, A. Housing for the aged. In J. Callender (ed.), *Time-Saver Standards: A Handbook of Architectural Design.* New York: McGraw-Hill, 1966.

Binstock, R. What sets the goals of community planning for the aging? *Gerontologist,* 1967, *7,* 44–46.

Blecher, E. M. *Advocacy Planning for Urban Development.* New York: Praeger, 1970.

Blenkner, M. Environmental change and the aging individual. *Gerontologist,* 1967, *7,* 101–105.

Booz-Allen and Hamilton, *Citizen Participation in the Model Cities Program.* Washington, D.C.: Department of Housing and Urban Development, 1972.

Brincefield, J. The low-rent housing program: some observations, suggestions and predictions. *Urban Lawyer,* 1971, *3,* 31–60.

Butterick, S. M. *Interaction Patterns, Housing and Morale of the Aged.* Washington, D.C.: Catholic University, 1969.

Cahn, E. (ed.). *Citizen Participation: Effecting Community Change.* New York: Praeger, 1971.

Carp, F. M. *A Future for the Aged.* Austin, Tex.: University of Texas Press, 1966.

Cassidy, R. Government in the suburbs: housing black workers. *New Republic,* 1971, *57,* 16–17.

Davis, J. W. Decentralization, citizen participation and ghetto health care. *American Behavioral Scientist,* 1971, *65,* 94–107.

Druker, G., and Shouldberg, T. A locational analysis of low income housing in Seattle and King County. *Urban Law Annual,* 1970, **3,** 85–101.

Dutsch, R. W. Backing the suburbs. *New Republic,* 1970, **56,** 8–9.

Eribes, R. *The spatio-temporal aspects of service delivery: a case study,* unpublished Master of Architecture Thesis, University of Southern California, Los Angeles, 1973.

Farkas, S. The federal role in urban decentralization. *American Behavioral Scientist,* 1971, *65,* 15–35.

Franklin, H. M. Federal power and subsidized housing. *Urban Lawyer,* 1971, *3,* 61–77.

Fraser, S. A. *Citizen Participation in Decision-Making by Federal Agencies. Selected Service Systems: Bureau of Land Management, Office of Equal Opportunity, Department of Housing and Urban Development.* Baltimore: Johns Hopkins University, 1969.

Frederick, B. The legality of affirmation measures to achieve and maintain integration in a new town. *Georgetown Law Journal,* 1970, *59,* 335–353.

Freeman, L. *Public Housing: The Politics of Poverty.* New York: Holt, Rinehart and Winston, 1967.

Friedly, P. H. Welfare indicators for public facility investment in urban renewal areas. *Socio-Economic Planning Sciences,* 1969, *3,* 291–314.

Friedman, L. M. *Government and Slum Housing.* Chicago: Rand McNally, 1968.

Gelwicks, L., and Newcomer, R. *Planning Housing Environments for the Edlerly.* Washington, D.C.: National Council on the Aging, 1974.

Gold, J. G. Development of care for the elderly: tracing the history of institutional facilities. *Gerontologist,* 1970, Part 1, *10,* 262–274.

Green, N. J. *Low and Moderate Income Housing in the Suburbs: An Analysis for Dayton Ohio Region.* New York: Praeger, 1972.

Hamovitch, M. Social and psychological factors in adjustment in a retirement village. In F. Carp (ed.), *The Retirement Process.* Washington, D.C.: Public Health Service, Department of Health, Education, and Welfare, 1966.

_____, Peterson, J. A., and Larson, A. E. Perceptions and fulfillment of housing needs of an aging population. Paper presented at the *Eighth Inter-*

national Congress of Gerontology, Washington, D.C., 1969.

Hartman, C., and Carr, G. Housing authorities reconsidered. *Journal of American Institute of Planners,* 1969, *35,* 10–21.

Hersch, B., Statement in hearings before the subcommittee on housing for the elderly, in U.S. Congressional Hearings on the *Adequacy of Federal Responses to Housing Needs of Older Americans,* Washington, D.C., 1971, 265–272.

Journal of Housing. Public housing for the elderly, 1963, *23,* 77–92.

____. Five public housing projects for elderly win HUD award, 1968, *28,* 504–507.

Kaplan, B., and Hammond, W. Public housing of elderly in Chicago. *Geriatrics,* 1961, *16,* 655–663.

Kaplan, M., Gans, H., and Kahn, H. *The Model Cities Program: A Comparative Analysis of the Planning Process in Eleven Cities.* Washington, D.C.: Department of Housing and Urban Development, 1970.

Kassabaum, G. E. Housing for the elderly. *Journal of the American Institute of Architects,* 1962, *39,* 65–68; 1962, *39,* 61–65; 1962, *39,* 51–52.

Kaufman, J. *Planning and an Aging Population.* Chicago: American Society of Planning Officials, 1961.

Keith, N. *Housing Americans, Low Income and Moderate Income Families; Progress, Problems and Prospects in the Federal Act of 1968.* Research Report of National Commission on Urban Problems, Washington, D.C., 1968.

Koff, T. Service needs and delivery. In R. Davis (ed.), *Housing for the Elderly.* Los Angeles: Andrus Gerontology Center, University of Southern California, 1973.

Lawton, M. P. Social and medical services in housing for the elderly, progress report (mimeo), Philadelphia Geriatric Center, Philadelphia, 1968.

____. Planning environments for older people. *Journal of the American Institute of Planners,* 1970, *36,* 124–129.

____. Assessing the competence of older people. In D. Kent, R. Kastenbaum, and S. Sherwood (eds.), *Research, Planning and Action for the Elderly.* New York: Behavioral Publications, 1972.

____. National survey of housing for the elderly (study in progress), Philadelphia Geriatric Center, Philadelphia, 1972.

____. *Planning and Managing Housing for the Elderly.* New York: Wiley–Interscience, 1975.

____, and Byerts, T. *Community Planning for the Elderly,* Washington, D.C.: U.S. Department of Housing and Urban Development, 1973.

____, and Simon, B. B. The ecology of social relationships in housing for the elderly. *Gerontologist,* 1968, *8,* 108–115.

Lempert, R., and Sheda, K. Evictions from public housing: effects of independent review. *American Sociological Review,* 1970, **35,** 852–860.

Levin, J. Bureaucracy and the socially handicapped: a study of lower status tenants. *Sociology and Social Research,* 1970, **54,** 209–219. 1973.

Mangum, W. P. *Adjustment in Special Residential Settings for the Aged, an Inquiry Based on the Kleemeier Conceptualization.* Unpublished doctoral dissertation, University of Southern California, Los Angeles, 1970.

Manvel, A. *Local Land and Building Regulations.* Research report of the National Commission on Urban Problems, Washington, D.C., 1968.

Marshall, D. R. *The Politics of Participation in Poverty: A Case Study of the Board of the Economic and Youth Opportunity Agency of Greater Los Angeles.* Berkeley, Calif.: University of California Press, 1971.

McDonald, A., and Newcomer, R. Differences in perception of a city park as a supportive or threatening environment. In D. Gray and D. Peligrino (eds.), *Reflections on the Recreation and Park Movement.* Dubuque, Iowa: William C. Brown, 1973.

McGuire, M. The utilization of research data. *Gerontologist,* 1969, part 1, **9,** 37–39.

Messer, M. The possibility of an age-concentrated environment becoming a normative system. *Gerontologist,* 1967, *7,* 247–251.

Metro Regional Council, *Low-Income Public Housing in the Region: An Assessment of Low-Income*

Public Housing Units and Local Housing Authorities in 22 Counties, New York, 1970.

Morris, R., and Binstock, R. *Feasible Planning for Social Change.* New York: Columbia University Press, 1966.

_____, and Randall, O. A. Planning and organization of community services for the elderly. *Social Work,* 1965, *10,* 1–10.

National Council on the Aging, *Building for Older People—Financing, Location, Construction, Administration.* New York, 1961.

Nelson, E. L. *Evaluation of Federal and State Legislation Aiding Housing for the Elderly in New York.* Syracuse, N.Y.: Syracuse University, 1962.

Newcomer, R. *Group Housing for the Elderly: Defining Neighborhood Service Convenience for Public Housing and Section 202 Residences.* Unpublished doctoral dissertation, University of Southern California, Los Angeles, 1975.

Newman, O. *Defensible Space: Crime Prevention Through Urban Design.* New York: Macmillan, 1972.

New York State Division of Housing. *New York State's Housing Program for Senior Citizens.* New York: Executive Department, Division of Housing and Community Renewal, 1965.

Nierstrasz, F. (ed.). *Buildings for the Aged.* New York: American Elsevier, 1961.

Peel, N. D., Pickett, G. E., and Buehl, S. T. Racial discrimination in public housing site selection. *Stanford Law Review,* 1970, *22,* 63–147.

Perrow, B. *Life Goals of Retirement Home Residents and Applicants in Selected Organizational Climates.* Unpublished doctoral dissertation, University of Southern California, Los Angeles, 1971.

Potvin, D. J. Suburban zoning ordinances and building codes: their effect on low and moderate income housing. *Notre Dame Lawyer,* 1969, *44,* 123–134.

Progressive Architecture. Houses and housing for the elderly, 1967, *47,* 124–136.

_____. Dignity in housing for the elderly, 1969, *49,* 124–129.

Regnier, V. *Neighborhood Cognition and Older People: A Comparison of Public Housing Environ-* *ments in San Francisco.* Unpublished Master of Architecture Thesis, University of Southern California, Los Angeles, 1973.

Rosenberg, G. S. *The Worker Grows Old.* San Francisco: Jossey-Bass, 1970.

Rosow, I. *Social Integration of the Aged.* New York: Free Press, 1967.

Rutherford, R. B. (ed.). *Architectural Designs: Homes for the Aged, the European Approach.* Peoria, Ill.: Howard, 1963.

St. Lenkass, H. de. *Citizen Participation in a Technically Oriented Government Decision-Making Process: A Study of the Development of a Neighborhood Plan for the Adams-Morgan Project Area.* Unpublished doctoral dissertation, American University, Washington, D.C., 1969.

Schermer, G., and Associates, *More than Shelter: Social Needs in Low and Moderate Income Housing.* Research report 8 for National Commission on Urban Problems, Washington, D.C., 1968.

Schooler, K. S. *Residential Physical Environment and Health of the Aged.* Final Report, U.S. Public Health Service, Grant EC 00191, Florence Heller School for Advanced Studies in Social Welfare, Brandeis University, Waltham, Mass., 1970.

Schwartz, S. *Control of Local Housing Authorities.* New York: New York University Press, 1969.

Shanas, E., Townsend, P., Wedderburn, D., Friis, H., Milhøj, P., and Stehouwer, J. *Old People in Three Industrial Societies.* New York: Atherton Press, 1968.

Sherman, S. R., Mangum, W. P., Dodds, S., Walkley, R. P., and Wilner, D. M. Psychological effects of retirement housing. *Gerontologist,* 1968, *9,* 170–175.

Spicer, R. B. *Zoning for the Elderly.* ASPO Planning Advisory Service. Chicago: American Society of Planning Officials, 1971.

Taggert, R. *Low Income Housing: A Critique of Federal Aid.* Baltimore: Johns Hopkins Press, 1970.

Tone, R. W. Sponsorship of subsidized housing for low and moderate income families under the National Housing Act. *George Washington Law Review,* 1970, *38,* 1073–1090.

U.S. Bureau of the Census. *Census of Housing: 1970*

Subject Reports, Final Report Housing of Senior Citizens (HC[7]-2). Washington, D.C.: Government Printing Office, 1973.

U.S. Senate, Special Committee on Aging. *Usefulness of the Model Cities Program to the Elderly,* Parts 1–7. Washington, D.C., 1969.

____. *Adequacy of Federal Response to Housing Needs of Older Americans,* Hearings, Parts 1–5. Washington, D.C., 1971.

____. *Developments in Aging, 1970* and *January– March 1974,* Washington, D.C., 1974.

U.S. Department of Housing and Urban Development, *Housing for the Physically Impaired, a Guide for Planning and Design.* Washington, D.C., 1968.

____. *1970 Annual Report of the Department of Housing and Urban Development.* Washington, D.C., 1970.

____. *Project Evaluation Criteria.* Washington, D.C., 1971.

U.S. News and World Report. Battle to open the sub- urbs, new attack on zoning laws. 1970, *68,* 39– 40 (a).

____. Furor over a drive to integrate the suburbs. 1970, *68,* 23–24 (b).

____. Shift in policy on housing? 1971, *70,* 63 (a).

____. Government renews pressures for integrated suburbs. 1971, *5,* 47–48 (b).

Urban Land Institute. *The Community Builders Handbook.* Washington, D.C., 1968.

Weiss, J. D. *Better Buildings for the Aged.* New York: Hopkinson and Blake, 1969.

Wolman, H. *Politics of Federal Housing.* New York: Dodd, Mead, 1971.

Zimbalist, S. The function of the private builder, manager, and owners in evolution of the low- rent housing project. *Urban Lawyer,* 1970, *2,* 175–185.

WILLIAM C. BAER

William C. Baer is Assistant Professor of Planning and Urban Studies, School of Urban and Regional Planning, University of Southern California, Los Angeles.

Federal Housing Programs for the Elderly

National concern for the elderly's housing problems has been exhibited in a variety of ways over the last 25 years. To cite the Housing Act of 1949, with its declaration of a "decent home and suitable living environment for every American family," is by now a commonplace, but other examples exist as well.

In 1950 the first National Conference on Aging urged the commencement of housing programs specifically designed for the needs of the elderly. Not until 1956 was such legislation enacted by Congress. Other special provisions for the elderly were added in 1959. Nevertheless, in 1961, the White House Conference on Aging felt compelled to reemphasize the older population's need for adequate housing, and reiterated the call for elderly-oriented housing programs that would "enrich their way of life and offer a future to the many who now have have none." The Housing Act of 1964 saw additional special programs enacted to assist the elderly's housing needs, yet the Older Americans Act of 1965 still stressed the entitlement of older people to "suitable housing, independently selected, designed and located with reference to special needs and available at a cost which older people can afford." Also, the Housing and Urban Development Act of 1965 enacted the now well-known rent supplment and rehabilitation grant program, both of which served the elderly. In 1968 still more programs were enacted assisting the elderly, among which were the Sections 235 and 236 interest-subsidy programs. Despite these numerous programs, the President's Task Force on Aging in 1970 recommended special attention to the particular housing needs of the older population.

Examining the exhortations of the legislative preambles and the national conferences and task forces on aging over the years, one gains the impression that little has been done for the elderly in the way of housing. On the other hand, examining the numerous housing programs passed during the 1950s and 1960s, either designed especially for the elderly or to serve income groups of which the elderly comprise a significant portion, one concludes that the housing problems of the elderly are being, or will soon be, largely met. The truth appears to lie somewhere in between: legislated programs *have provided* housing for the elderly; the elderly's housing problems *are still* a long way from being solved.

In this paper we shall examine the effectiveness of the federal housing programs available to the elderly. The examination will include loan assistance (e.g.,

81

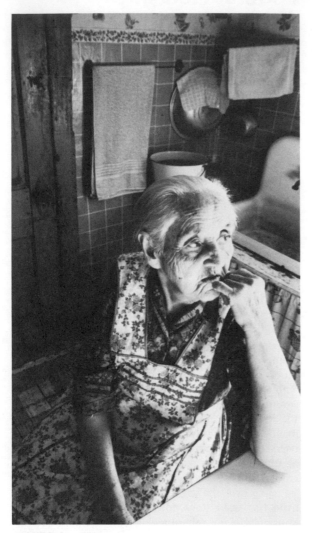

FIGURE 1
"A decent home and suitable living environment for every American family"? (Photo courtesy of Administration on Aging, U.S.D.H.E.W.)

FHA), direct subsidy (e.g., public housing), and the indirect assistance provided through federal income tax provisions available to homeowners. Unfortunately, data on these programs and the elderly are somewhat limited. Analysis will be confined largely to the number (and proportion vis-à-vis other age groups) of elderly housholds assisted and, where possible, the age and income distribution of these elderly households. In some instances, estimates of the annual amount of assistance will also be provided. Because of the variety of sources, the data will pertain to the early 1970s.

A number of the direct-subsidy programs described here were terminated by the Nixon administration in the housing moratorium of January 1973. Housing allowances were proposed by the administration as a substitute approach. No new housing programs were enacted, however, until the fall of 1974 when Congress approved a multiyear program permitting local governments to devise many of their own programs. Thus the state of federally assisted housing programs is currently in ferment. A final purpose here will be to reflect upon the probable effectiveness of some of the proposed programs in light of the experience with past programs.

OWNER-OCCUPANT COMPARED WITH RENTER HOUSEHOLDS

A basic distinction to be made at the outset is between owner occupants and renters. Our society accords considerable status to the homeowner. This status consists of the psychological effect of self-esteem; the inherent freedom from landlord–tenant disputes, and the added responsibilities of the property-tax payer. As an offset, homeowners must also bear the burden of property maintenance, which becomes increasingly onerous for the elderly. In addition, there are very real economic differences between owners and renters, that is, the value of the equity. There are substantially different kinds of federal housing programs for each group as well. Not only do the federal programs differ in legal form and implication, but they also differ markedly in the amount of subsidy per household that they provide. Thus, before the housing programs themselves can be discussed, brief mention must be made of the relative proportions of the elderly living in owner-occupied and rental housing.

There are two pertinent measures of the relationship of the elderly to the owner- versus renter-occupied housing: (1) the percentage of the age group that occupies each kind of housing, or (2) elderly owner-occupied housing as a percentage of all elderly housing units. By either measure, a higher percentage of the elderly lives in owner-occupied housing than is true for the remainder of the population. Slightly more than 70 percent of those 65 or older lived in owner-occupied housing in 1970, whereas less than 67 percent of the remainder of the population did so. To be sure, some older persons lived in owner-occupied units owned by someone else, but even when the head of the household was 65 or older, 67 percent of the housing units occupied by such households were owner-occupied (U.S. Department of Housing and Urban Development, 1973c). In other words, despite the low incomes of the elderly, a substantial number own their housing. As will be suggested shortly, however, this housing in most cases is of decidedly lower value than the rest of the nation's owner-occupied housing and is frequently of poorer quality (Robins, 1971; U.S. Department of Housing and Urban Development, 1971).

Why is it important to distinguish between owner- and renter-occupied housing? A number of issues have been alluded to, but for our purpose the chief distinction is that ownership, particularly for the elderly, is an important index of economic well-being. Furthermore, ownership makes one eligible for particularly advantageous federal assistance programs that are not available to renters.

Since earned income diminishes after retirement, the amount of income-yielding assets possessed by the elderly takes on increased significance. In most cases, the single most valuable asset owned by the elderly is the equity in their homes. This equity is important in two ways: (1) it can be converted into cash by sale of the unit, by renting all or a portion of it, or by borrowing against it, and (2) homeownership, particularly ownership with a large equity (i.e., no mortgage or one largely paid), generates income with unique income tax advantages: it is tax-free since the income is in the form of housing services rendered. The amount of this income is roughly equivalent to the rental value of the house less such expenses as mortgage interest (if any), property taxes, maintenance costs, and depreciation (Rolph, 1973). A rule of thumb holds that the monthly gross rent of a house should be approximately 1 percent of its value; hence in many instances the value of these housing services can amount to several thousand dollars a year, yet no tax need be paid on this amount.

Another advantage is that the homeowner is allowed to deduct mortgage interest payments (if any) and property taxes from his income even though he has not declared the income accruing from owning his house. As will be shown, substantial subsidies accrue to the elderly homeowner, as well as all other homeowners, even though these income tax provisions are not normally thought of as subsidy programs.

An important factor, of course, is whether or not the home is owned "free and clear." The older the owner occupant, the higher the probability that the house is mortgage-free (Table 1). For all principal owners 65 and over, 85 percent owned their properties free of mortgage.[1] Furthermore, those principal owners 65 years and older who owned mortgaged residences had a higher equity percentage than the other age groups.

But some questions remain. How valuable is the

TABLE 1

Percentage of Homeowners with Nonmortgaged Properties and Median Equity Percentages for Mortgaged Properties by Age of Principal Owner, 1970

Age of Principal Owner	Nonmortgaged Properties: Percentage of Total Properties	Mortgaged Properties: Median Equity as a Percentage of Value
Less than 25	10	23
25 to 34	7	33
35 to 44	13	46
45 to 54	29	56
55 to 64	55	66
65 or over	85	71

Source: U.S. Bureau of the Census, *Residential Finance*, Tables 1a and 13.

TABLE 2
Median Value of Mortgaged and Nonmortgaged Properties by Age of Principal Owner, 1970

| | Median Value | |
| | Mortgaged | Nonmortgaged |
Age of Principal Owner	*Property*	*Property*
Less than 25	$17,300	$16,400
25 to 34	20,600	12,500
35 to 44	23,000	15,700
45 to 54	22,600	16,600
55 to 64	19,700	16,500
65 or over	17,700	13,800

Source: U.S. Bureau of the Census, *Residential Finance*, 1973, Tables 11 and 12.

TABLE 3
Median Income of Principal Owners for Mortgaged and Nonmortgaged Properties by Age of Principal Owner

| | Median Income of Principal Owner | | |
| | Mortgaged Properties | | |
Age of Principal Owner	*Acquired Prior to 1967*	*Acquired 1967–1971*	*Nonmortgaged Properties*
Less than 25	$ 9,400	$ 9,400	$ 7,900
25 to 34	11,400	11,500	9,400
35 to 44	13,200	13,400	10,300
45 to 54	13,500	13,000	10,800
55 to 64	11,300	11,000	9,100
65 or over	6,200	5,900	3,900

Source: U.S. Bureau of the Census, *Residential Finance*, 1973, Tables 14, 15, and 16.

housing owned by the elderly? What is the burden of the property tax, which, unlike a mortgage, can never be paid off? How likely is it that an elderly homeowner can obtain a mortgage should he or she desire to do so?

As Table 2 shows, the elderly owner occupied decidedly lower valued properties than did most other age groups, whether or not the mortgage had been completely paid. On the other hand, the elderly who were still paying their mortgage had properties worth substantially more than did those elderly owners with paid-up properties (this was true for the other age groups as well).

In addition to the age of the owner, an equally important consideration is the comparison of property characteristics with the socioeconomic characteristics of owners. How able is the elderly homeowner to meet his housing expenses in light of a reduced income? Is ownership for the elderly only a burden in disguise? Can the elderly with their reduced incomes obtain a mortgage? The data are not sufficiently detailed to wholly satisfy these concerns, but they do provide some indication of the elderly homeowners' economic well-being.

Table 3 presents data with respect to income for the different age groups on the basis of whether the property was mortgaged, mortgaged between the years 1967 and 1971 (which indicates the recent ability of the elderly to obtain mortgages), or nonmortgaged. The elderly had the lowest median in-

come regardless of the mortgage status of their property. Furthermore, the median income of the elderly with mortgages was almost 50 percent higher than for the elderly without mortgages. Thus those elderly who still had to meet mortgage payments were better able to afford it than those who did not. Even with decidedly low incomes, elderly and near-elderly persons were able to obtain mortgages. From 1967 to 1971, 236,000 elderly persons obtained first mortgages, even though their median income was only $5,900. These constituted only 3 percent of all mortgages made during that period, however.

A related issue is the amount of the mortgage. As Table 4 shows, of all age groups that obtained a first mortgage between 1967 and 1971, the elderly obtained mortgages in an amount considerably less than most others. One would expect lower incomes to be associated with lower mortgages. It is not clear from the data, however, whether other factors, such as the ability to make a larger down payment with proceeds from an earlier house sale or from other assets, might also account for these differences.

Another major concern for the homeowner is the property tax, which is always a major source of homeowner expense. The reduced income of the elderly makes this aspect of home ownership particularly burdensome. Indeed, as Table 5 shows, property taxes for the elderly exceed 8 percent of their in-

TABLE 4
Median Amount of First Mortgage for Properties Acquired
Between 1967 and 1971 by Age of Principal Owner

Age of Principal Owner	Median Amount of First Mortgage
Less than 25	$12,800
25 to 34	15,400
35 to 44	16,500
45 to 54	13,600
55 to 64	9,400
65 or over	7,100

Source: U.S. Bureau of the Census, *Residential Finance,*
1973, Table 9.

TABLE 5
Percentage of Income Paid for Real Estate Taxes by
Age Group, 1971

Age of Principal Owner	Proportion of Income Paid in Real Estate Taxes (%)
Less than 25	4.01
25 to 34	3.95
35 to 44	3.86
45 to 54	3.94
55 to 64	4.80
65 or over	8.11

Source: U.S. Bureau of the Census, *Real Estate Tax
Data by Homeowner Properties in the United States
and Regions,* Supplementary Report, HC(51)-17,
1973.

come; for most other age groups it is about 4 percent. Thus, even though the elderly have lower-valued properties than do other age groups, they still pay a substantially greater percentage of their incomes as property taxes because their incomes have dropped so drastically. Recent state efforts to ameliorate these effects through property-tax exemptions or "circuit breakers" should help considerably (Shannon, 1973).

Although elderly homeowners are potentially in a better economic position than most elderly renters, they face problems. For one, the value of their homes is considerably lower than for other age groups and threatens to drop still further. For another, they continually face the prospect of property taxes that will consume a substantially greater proportion of their income than for other age groups. Finally, they are frequently unable to perform comparatively minor maintenance tasks because of the physical difficulties involved.

FEDERAL HOUSING PROGRAMS FOR THE ELDERLY OWNER OCCUPANT

FHA and VA Programs

Given the preceding basic considerations regarding homeownership and the elderly, it is important to examine the federal housing programs that assist elderly owner occupants to acquire housing. The best known of these programs (although they are not normally thought of as providing federal housing assistance for the elderly) are the Federal Housing Administration (FHA) mortgage insurance and the Vet-

erans Administration's (VA) mortgage guarantee programs. These programs have been in existence long enough so that many of the elderly are assisted by them, even though the assistance was first rendered when the homeowner was not an older person. But are the elderly assisted as much by these federal programs as other mortgagors? Table 6 suggests that the FHA and VA programs aid the youngest households in the greatest proportion, in terms of both the number of households served and the amount borrowed. Since use of the FHA program is largely at the option of the lender, there might be a systematic bias in the program against older borrowers. The purpose of the VA program, to assist returning veterans, means that the program is aimed at the younger age groups. Taken together, the two programs do not assist elderly home buyers in the proportion to their numbers. Conventional mortgages are the rule for older groups (Table 6).

Within the overall FHA program, there are several different kinds of homeowner assistance. The best known is the Section 203(c) program. This section insures loans made by lending institutions on FHA-approved single-family units and tends to serve moderate-income families by virtue of the upper limit placed on the amount of loan insured. Older persons may take advantage of this assistance by qualifying as mortgagors on the basis of income, that is, as long as their current and expected future incomes appear sufficient to cover all necessary housing expenses and

TABLE 6
Percentages of Federally Assisted and Conventional First Mortgage Loans by Age Group, 1970

Age of Principal Owner	FHA		VA		Conventional		
	Total Mortgages	Total Debt	Total Mortgages	Total Debt	Total Mortgages	Total Debt	Total
25	37	41	13	15	49	44	100
25 to 34	29	29	14	16	57	55	100
35 to 44	21	20	16	17	63	63	100
45 to 54	17	18	17	14	66	68	100
55 to 64	15	16	11	10	74	74	100
65 and over	17	17	6	6	78	77	100

Source: U.S. Bureau of the Census, *Residential Finance*, 1973, Table 4a.

other obligations. In addition, a special provision for the elderly relieves them of some of the cost of the down payment. Nevertheless, Table 7, which compares the 203 program with others, suggests that the proportion of elderly served by this program (in terms of recently placed mortgages) is disproportionately small for both new and existing housing units. The number of elderly households served by

TABLE 7
Percentages of FHA Mortgages in 1972 by Program and Age Group

| Age of Principal Owner | FHA Program | | | | | |
| | 203(b) | | 221(d)(2) | | 235(i) | |
	New	Used[a]	New	Used[a]	New	Used[a]
Less than 25	18.5	20.8	29.3	28.2	32.5	27.8
25 to 34	51.0	47.1	44.5	42.5	40.3	39.7
35 to 44	17.1	19.1	15.1	17.2	16.9	20.2
45 to 59	12.0	11.7	10.0	10.6	8.1	9.6
60 and over	1.4	1.3	1.1	1.4	2.2	2.7
	100	100	100	100	100	100

Source: U.S. Department of Housing and Urban Development, *1972 HUD Statistical Yearbook*, Tables 208, 209, 227, 228, and 233.
[a]Existing unit refinanced.

this program in the first 9 months of 1972 was only 3,055.

A lesser program designed to assist low- and moderate-income persons displaced from their existing residence by government action or natural disasters, the Section 221(d)(2) program, also failed to assist the elderly in proportion to their numbers as homeowners. Indeed, although this program was specifically designed to assist families in lower-income classes, as Table 7 shows, the elderly's proportion of the total was, if anything, smaller than for the 203 program. The number of elderly households served by this program in the first 9 months of 1972 was 92, or about 3 percent of the 203 program. This program was being phased out in 1972.

A third program designed for low- and moderate-income families was the Section 235(i) program, which subsidized a major portion of the homeowner's interest rate. Enacted in 1968, it became scandal-ridden by 1972 and died in the housing moratorium of 1973. Here, however, the elderly made up a slightly larger proportion of occupants than in the 203 or 221(d)(2) programs, as shown in Table 7. In all, 2,700 elderly households were served by this program in the first 9 months of 1972.

In addition to the age proportions served, it is also important to know what economic groups within the elderly population are served: the relatively well-to-do elderly or the moderate-income elderly? Data are available only for the 203 program (Table 8). As is clear, the 203 program served largely those elderly mortgagors with incomes in excess of $10,000 annually. In comparison, the 235 program seemed to reach elderly households of more moderate incomes. Although data on the utilization of the 235 program by income and age were not available, the income distribution for all ages of households served by this program ranged from 1.8 percent earning less than $3,000 to 1.8 percent who earned in excess of $10,000; the modal range was $5,000 to $5,999. Whatever the income distribution of the elderly within this program, it clearly served elderly of decidedly lower incomes than did the 203 program.

The Sections 203 and 221(d)(2) programs provide assistance indirectly through, among other things, mortgage insurance, which serves to lower mortgage costs and make mortgage funds available that would otherwise go to other borrowers. The monetary value of the assistance is exceedingly difficult (if not impossible) to calculate (Aaron, 1972). The 235 program, on the other hand, lends itself more readily to calculation since the subsidy is direct. In 1972 the annual subsidy ranged between $720 and $864 for all ages, depending upon income and family size. Given the generally lower income of the elderly household (and its smaller size), the average annual subsidy for the elderly may be estimated as about $750.

TABLE 8
Income Distribution of Section 203 Mortgagors Age 60 or More

Annual Income of Mortgagor ($)	New Homes (%)	Existing Homes (%)
Less than 6,000	5	12
6,000–6,999	5	10
7,000–7,999	5	10
8,000–8,999	8	10
9,000–9,999	8	10
10,000–14,999	38	29
15,000 or more	32	10
	100	100

Source: U.S. Department of Housing and Urban Development, *Housing, 1971*, White House Conference on Aging, 1971, Tables 25 and 26.

Two additional federal programs for homeowners available to the elderly are the Section 115 rehabilitation grant and the Section 211 rehabilitation loan programs. Originally restricted to urban-renewal and concentrated code enforcement areas, their application has been broadened to other areas as well. As of 1968 (later information not available), a high proportion of the elderly participated in these programs: 64 percent of the grants and 20 percent of the loans were to owner occupants over 62 years old (McGuire, 1970). Assuming that the proportions held for 1972 as well, over 4,400 grants averaging $3,200 were made to older homeowners for rehabilitation in that year. Similarly, 1,100 rehabilitation loans averaging in excess of $7,600 were made to elderly homeowners in 1972 (U.S. Department of Housing and Urban Development, 1974). Clearly, these two rehabilitation programs have devoted a considerably larger percentage of their total resources to the housing needs of the elderly than have other homeowner programs.

Fewer data are available for VA loans. In 1971 the average VA mortgagor over 60 years had an income of $9,360, assets of $5,801, and purchased a house valued at $21,263 using a $20,459 loan. It would appear that this federal program also mostly assisted moderate-income elderly; but only 583 of these loans were made to older people in 1971. Given the eligibility requirements and the age of the recipients (i.e., the veteran is only eligible for such a loan), it is likely that most veterans in this age group have already exercised their option.

Housing Subsidies Through the Federal Income Tax

Finally, a very important subsidy program to the older owner occupant is that established through special provisions in the federal income tax. The value of the income derived from net housing services is not declared as income by the owner occupant; that is, there is no declaration of "imputed" rent. The homeowner of any age can also deduct that portion of his mortgage that goes toward interest and the amount of his yearly property taxes. The total amount of subsidies accruing from these income tax provisions may well have exceeded $12 billion in 1972 (U.S. Department of Housing and Urban Development, 1973a). Here we shall be concerned only with the amount of subsidy derived from homeowner income tax deductions, which constituted $6.2 billion for all homeowners (regardless of age) in 1972.

In brief, the value of these deductions to the homeowner is equivalent to his income tax bracket percentage times the amount of his total homeowner deductions. Thus, if the homeowner's adjusted gross income placed him in the 20 percent bracket, for every dollar he paid in mortgage interest and property tax (assuming he itemized deductions) 20 cents would be saved on his income tax payment. If he was in the 50 percent bracket, he would "save" 50 cents in tax payments on every dollar deducted.

Table 9 shows the number of elderly (65 or older) homeowners by income class who availed themselves of these deductions and an estimate of the average amount "saved" by each income class, both for property taxes and mortgage interest. As one would expect, the number of elderly who claimed property-tax deductions greatly exceeded those declaring mortgage interest. Only 25 percent of those deducting property

taxes also deducted mortgage interest. Of more importance, however, is the fact that 2.7 million elderly (60 percent of all elderly homeowners) benefited in 1970 in some degree from these indirect subsidies. In other words, this form of assistance dwarfs any of the other housing programs in terms of number of elderly households served.

Of even more interest is the average amount of benefit received by each income group. Unlike the other federal programs mentioned, this subsidy serves all income classes. Indeed, the higher the income class, the higher the amount of subsidy received per household. It is a remarkably regressive housing assistance program. *The least needy receive the largest per household subsidy*. This finding is not unique to the elderly homeowner; the same is true for the nation's other homeowners (Aaron, 1972).

Furthermore, the total amount of subsidy is considerable; $1.7 billion accrued to elderly homeowners through this income tax "expenditure" for 1970 alone. This is a considerably larger sum than for all the other housing programs (homeowner as well as renter) put together.

TABLE 9
Estimated Average Federal Income-Tax Subsidy for Homeowners 65 Years or Older by Income Class and by Type of Deduction, 1970

	Elderly Homeowner Deductions			
	Property Tax		Mortgage Interest	
Adjusted Gross Income Classes	No. of Elderly	Average Amount of Subsidy	No. of Elderly	Average Amount of Subsidy
$ 1,000–4,999	928,646	$ 69	191,345	$ 64
5,000–9,999	949,956	87	252,214	83
10,000–14,999	353,768	138	112,118	135
15,000–24,999	250,646	197	65,619	169
25,000–49,999	141,135	455	29,420	364
50,000–99,999	47,339	874	9,262	570
100,000–199,999	12,987	1,431	2,500	700
200,000–499,999	3,853	2,560	775	938
500,000–999,999	629	5,000	135	1,500
1,000,000 or more	236	12,500	59	1,000
	2,696,444		665,740	

Source: U.S. Internal Revenue Service, *Statistics of Income—1970: Individual Income Tax Returns*, Table 68.

FIGURE 2
The public housing program has provided almost half a million older people with modern dwelling units. Many such tenants come from rented dwellings such as the one pictured here, and worse. (Photo by Powell Lawton.)

Finally, there is one special provision in the income tax for elderly homeowners with respect to the sale of their house. Any capital gain on a house sold for under $20,000 is not taxed; and only a portion of the gain for a house sold for more than $20,000 is taxed. It is not known what the magnitude of this tax savings is, but it is probably not great, given stagnant or declining house values for many elderly homeowners.

FEDERAL HOUSING PROGRAMS FOR THE ELDERLY RENTER

HUD Direct-Assistance Programs

Federal programs for renter households take a somewhat different form. In most programs, the assistance is funneled to the builder or landlord and not directly to the household. Obviously, this kind of assistance does not enable the occupant to accumulate equity in the way that mortgage assistance or rehabilitation loans and grants do. The assistance is for housing services, not for the housing stock per se. The renter, possessing fewer property rights, participates less fully in the system. Should the assistance program be terminated or should the renter wish to move to a nonsubsidized unit, future benefits have been lost while past benefits have been fully consumed.

Public housing is the largest and best known of all the federal housing assistance programs for renters. Although public housing was initiated in 1937, the elderly as a class were not singled out for special attention until 1956. By 1972, 954,000 units were occupied and over 392,000, or 41 percent, were occupied by elderly families. Seven years earlier, only 28 percent of the total units had been so occupied; hence the proportion of units occupied by elderly families increased markedly by early 1972. Elderly units, on average, cost less to construct than did units for other persons—$16,166 for the elderly in 1972 compared with $17,903 for other units. This difference was accounted for, in part, because elderly units were approximately two rooms smaller (3.34 rooms on average for the elderly in 1972 compared to 5.39 for others). On the other hand, special equipment for the elderly partially offset these potential savings (U.S. Department of Housing and Urban Development, 1974).

Of more immediate importance are the characteristics of the elderly assisted by public housing. How do they fare compared with other occupants? As already noted, the elderly constitute over 40 percent of all public housing occupants. The age breakdown of the heads of families (as distinguished from the ages of all occupants) is shown in Table 10. Not only do the elderly constitute a high proportion of all public housing tenants, but the very elderly (those over 75) are also well-represented. Fully 24 percent of all elderly families moving into public housing during 1972 had heads of families over 75 years of age (U.S. Department of Housing and Urban Development, 1974).

FIGURE 3
This individualized three-unit public housing structure blends in perfectly with its new nonsubsidized neighboring houses.

These superior units in West Helena, Arkansas, replaced dwellings of the type shown in Figure 5-2. (Photo by Powell Lawton.)

By definition, public housing occupants are poor. This is especially true for the elderly. While 68 percent of the nonelderly households were receiving assistance or benefits over and above public housing, if one includes Social Security, fully 97 percent of the elderly were. The income distribution of the two groups is shown in Table 11. Clearly, the elderly in public housing have far lower incomes than do other households. The median income for elderly families was $1,990 compared with $2,816 for the nonelderly in 1972. Mean monthly rent for the public housing units was $40 for the elderly and $55 for the nonelderly. The mean subsidy for all households ranged from $504 per year to $1,044 in 1972, depending upon income and household size. The elderly subsidy is unknown, but $750 would be a reasonable estimate.

Despite the fact that the poorer circumstances of the elderly in the nation as a whole would suggest that a higher percentage would live in substandard housing, of those recent occupants admitted to public housing, 43 percent of the nonelderly families previously occupied substandard housing, whereas only 35 percent of the elderly families occupied such housing (U.S. Department of Housing and Urban Development, 1974).

The other major federal rental program designed for low- and moderate-income families is Section 236 housing, which, like Section 235, provides an interest subsidy to the owner so as to enable eligible families to live in housing that would otherwise consume more than 25 percent of their income. Some elderly are assisted by this program, but they are not as heavily represented as in public housing.

Table 12 shows the age distribution of all Section 236 tenants; Table 13 shows the income distribution of elderly tenants compared with the income distribution of all occupants.

Whereas the 236 program overall failed to serve as high a proportion of elderly as public housing, those that were served had a median income of only $2,826, compared with a median income of $5,209 for all nonelderly households occupying 236 housing. In 1971 the approximately 20,000 elderly households in this program paid a mean gross rent of only $90 per month. For those households also receiving rent supplements, the actual rent paid would be considerably less. By way of comparison, the median income for elderly households residing in 236 housing was 44 percent higher than that for the elderly occupying public housing; their gross rent was 100 percent higher than that for public housing. The annual subsidy for all households ranged from $950 to $1,455 in 1972. Again, the subsidy specifically provided to the elderly is unknown, but $1,100 would not be an unreasonable estimate.

The rent supplement program, a payment by the federal government to make up the difference between 25 percent of the occupants' income and the fair market rent of the unit, also assisted the elderly. Table 14 shows the age distribution of households served. Clearly, the rent supplement was one of the better programs for assisting elderly renters. A quarter (almost 10,000) of all the units assisted went to the elderly—a substantially higher proportion than any other direct federal housing program save public housing. Those elderly served by this program had median incomes of $1,969 in 1971 and paid a gross rent of slightly over $50 per month. The subsidy for all rent supplement tenants in 1972 ranged from $1,342 to $1,845; for the elderly, $1,500 would be a reasonable estimate.

Data on other federally assisted rental projects are confined to the number of units produced under the respective programs. Only where the program is specifically designed for the elderly is the number of elderly households known. In cases where the only

TABLE 10
Age Distribution of Public Housing of Heads of Families who Moved in During 1972

Age of Head of Family	Distribution (%)
Under 25	26
25 to 44	35
45 to 61	12
62 to 74	20
75 and over	8

Source: U.S. Department of Housing and Urban Development, *1972 HUD Statistical Yearbook*, Table 100.

FIGURE 4 *(above and right)*
Exterior style and dwelling-unit warmth were achieved in
Victoria Plaza at relatively low cost. (Photos by Collas Smel-
zer, courtesy of San Antonio Housing Authority.)

eligibility criterion is income, households of all ages
occupy the units. Tenant turnover is much higher
than for owner-occupied units, and HUD apparently
does not keep (or at least publish) information on
household characteristics for many rental programs.
Accordingly, only the number of units produced under each program can be reported in many instances.

Section 207, multifamily rental housing is the
rental equivalent to Section 203 housing, and consists
of the bulk of the multifamily housing insured by
FHA. Section 231, senior-citizen housing, is a special
mortgage-insurance program for the elderly and the
handicapped. Together, these two programs accounted for 43,593 units of elderly housing (cumula-
tively) by 1970. The relatively high failure rate of
231 projects led to its virtual abandonment.

The Section 202 program provided loans for
senior-citizen housing made directly by the federal
government (rather than insuring privately made
loans as was done for Section 231); they were pro-

vided to nonprofit groups to build housing. By 1971 this program had provided 45,000 units for the elderly and handicapped, although the program ceased to be funded from 1969 to 1974.

For those elderly in need of nursing care, Section 232 provides mortgage insurance for construction or rehabilitation of facilities for 20 or more patients requiring skilled nursing care and related medical facilities. Over 56,000 beds had been provided by 1972, with about a 13 percent "vacancy" rate due perhaps to the high cost of the beds. The median charge per bed was $527 per month in 1971. Almost 39 percent of the total payments for this cost was

TABLE 11

Income Distribution of Elderly and Nonelderly Families Moving into Public Housing in 1972

Annual Income ($)	Elderly (%)	Nonelderly (%)
Less than 1,000	4	2
1,000–1,999	47	15
2,000–2,999	30	24
3,000–3,999	13	26
4,000–4,999	5	17
5,000 and over	2	15
	100	100

Source: U.S. Department of Housing and Urban Development, *1972 HUD Statistical Yearbook*, Table 114.

FIGURE 5
In subsidized housing the public lobby is often the center of social life. (Photo by Collas Smelzer, courtesy of San Antonio Housing Authority.)

from private funds; the remainder was paid by some form of governmental assistance (Medicaid, Medicare, welfare, etc.). The average age of the occupants was over 75 years, as Table 15 shows. Clearly, this program was assisting the very elderly.

ELDERLY RENTERS AND THE FEDERAL INCOME TAX

There are no explicit federal income tax provisions for renters, whether elderly or not. Indirectly, however, the income tax does provide some housing bene-

fits to renter households. By allowing a standard deduction in lieu of itemizing deductions, the government implicitly allows a portion of that deduction to go toward housing expenses. But the standard deduction is also available to homeowners should they choose not to itemize; thus this provision does not single out renters. Another means is the provision for accelerated depreciation of apartments by owners. Insofar as the depreciation claimed exceeds the depreciation actually realized, it provides additional tax savings to the landlord; in a competitive market, these savings would be passed on to the tenants. There is no

TABLE 12
Age Distribution of Section 236
Tenants, 1971

Age of Head of Household	Distribution (%)
Under 25	39
25 to 34	37
35 to 44	9
45 to 54	5
55 to 64	4
65 and over	16
	100

Source: U.S. Department of Housing and Urban Development, *1972 HUD Statistical Yearbook*, Table 134.

TABLE 14
Age Distribution of
Rent-Supplement-Assisted Tenants

Age of Head of Household	Distribution (%)
Under 25	29
25 to 34	23
35 to 44	10
45 to 54	6
55 to 64	8
65 and over	25
	100

Source: U.S. Department of Housing and Urban Development, *1971 HUD Statistical Yearbook*, Table 138.

way of estimating the amount of this benefit, however.

SUMMARY

Contrasting themes emerge from this analysis. The elderly who own their own residences are potentially in better economic condition that those elderly who rent. This is especially true in times of inflation, with rising land prices, construction costs, and interest rates. The relatively fixed costs of owning, save for property taxes (but even here tax abatements for the elderly are becoming common), compared with rising

rents makes homeowning attractive for elderly with fixed retirement incomes.

However, federal housing assistance programs that aid homeowners have not provided as much assistance for the elderly as for other age groups. The only exception is the equal amount of indirect assistance provided all homeowners through homeowner deductions in the federal income tax. The amount of subsidy provided and the number of households served through this assistance, however, makes this exception extremely significant.

TABLE 13
Income Distribution of Elderly and All Tenants of Section 236 Housing, 1971

Annual Income ($)	Elderly (%)	All Occupants (%)
Under 1,000	1	—
1,000–1,999	17	8
2,000–2,999	23	11
3,000–3,999	21	15
4,000–4,999	19	20
5,000–5,999	10	19
6,000 and over	8	27
	100	100

Source: U.S. Department of Housing and Urban Development, *Housing, 1971*, White House Conference on Aging, Table 30, and *1971 HUD Statistical Yearbook*, Table 137.

TABLE 15
Age Distribution of Nursing
Home (Section 232)
Occupants, 1972

Age	Percentage
Less than 60	6.5
60 to 69	11.9
70 to 74	14.6
75 to 79	18.9
80 to 84	22.1
85 to 89	17.1
90 or older	8.9
	100

Source: U.S. Department of Housing and Urban Development, *1972 HUD Statistical Yearbook*, Table 129.

RENTERS

Rent Supplement (10,000)   ▣

Sec. 236 (20,000)   ▣

Sec. 232 (34,000)   ▣

Sec. 207 & 231 (44,000)   ▣

Sec. 202 (45,000)   ▣

Public Housing (392,000)   ▣

OWNERS

Sec. 221 (d) (2) (7,500)   ▪

Sec. 235 (9,000)   ▣

FHA Sec. 203 (55,000)   ▣

Income Tax Deductions
(2,696,000)

FIGURE 6
Relative magnitude of the number of elderly households served annually by each housing program, 1971.

Elderly renters had available to them a number of federal housing programs that provided substantial annual housing subsidies. The amount was usually in excess of that provided to elderly homeowners. In addition, many housing programs, particularly public housing, devoted a disproportionate share of units to the elderly. The total number of assisted units available to the elderly, however, was still not sufficient to meet the need, nor did it compare with the number of assisted units for elderly homeowners, if one counts income tax assistance. The situation was not helped by the housing moratorium, which suspended so many of these programs.

The variety of programs and the different forms the assistance takes makes overall comparison between the benefits provided for owners and renters difficult; only an approximation is possible. The two basic measures for comparison are the number of households assisted and the amount of assistance provided. The second measure is available for only some of the programs. In general, it appears that the low- and moderate-income elderly households who rent receive a larger annual subsidy than those who own. On the other hand, many more owner households are assisted than are renters, and this proportion is greatly in excess of the proportion of owner and renter elderly households in the nation. This is shown in Figure 6, which provides an estimate of the relative number of elderly households assisted by each of the programs discussed. Clearly, the homeowner deductions available from the federal income tax comprise the most significant housing assistance program for the elderly. This is particularly noteworthy since those provisions are not usually thought of as a housing program. Their sheer magnitude makes them the standard for comparison, both for existing and for proposed programs in the future.

THE ELDERLY AND THE NEW FEDERAL HOUSING PROGRAMS

Since the housing moratorium of early 1973, there have been two major developments in the federally funded housing programs. The first was the Nixon administration's announcement that public housing and other subsidy programs were to be converted to the Section 23 Leased Housing Program.

The second, the passage of the Housing and Community Development Act of 1974, altered the first by permitting the gradual phasing out of low-rent public housing and Section 23 leased housing, both to be replaced by a general housing assistance plan to be administered by public housing authorities and other local agencies Section 8.

In both cases, the moves had little to do with the elderly per se, although they will be affected. Rather, the concern was over the most efficient and effective way of providing housing for low- and moderate-income households under the direct supervision of federal and local authorities. These changes were largely based on past inefficiencies experienced in running the programs.

An even more innovative effort, still in the experimental stage, is the housing allowance program. Here either cash or a rent certificate is provided to needy households, and they in turn seek their own accommodations in the private market. A proposal has been made to expand this program to include all the elderly assisted by federal programs in subsequent years.

In addition, special emphasis was also placed on the elderly in the 1974 Housing Act. Assessment of the housing needs of the elderly by local communities is one requirement of the act. Section 202 housing assistance for the elderly and handicapped was revived and a special $800 million was authorized to accomplish this purpose. With respect to FHA, the new legislation increased the maximum amount of FHA-insured mortgage allowable on single-family homes.

How will these revised programs affect the elderly, particularly in light of the assistance provided by the other programs? First, commitment to the elderly is very much in evidence. Second, the housing assistance programs would seem to provide a flexibility that local governments will find useful in matching the unique needs of their inhabitants.

Third, on the negative side, the changes in the FHA mortgage insurance minimums would seem to benefit the elderly very little, since they usually do not purchase housing requiring a large mortgage. Fourth, the changes for the elderly appear to be largely brought about through dissatisfaction with the programs in general, not through any particular analysis of the impact of the federal programs on the elderly as a special class. This is an area that will require considerable attention before appropriate program modification will be forthcoming. Finally, the new housing programs suggest a political dimension that has not yet been discussed. It may well be that the political commitment to providing a "fair share" of assisted units to the elderly is as important as the ingenuity of the programs themselves. The decision to devolve program design to state and local levels is very important in this regard. The groups interested in housing for the elderly will also have to decentralize their efforts. The necessary political lobbying for these interests will have to be increased in legislative chambers, mayors' and governors' offices, and bureaucrats' cubbyholes. The opportunities are great, but they will have to be seized at the state and local level if improvement is to be made.

NOTE

1. Data from the Census publication *Residential Finance* is collected on a *property* basis rather than the *housing unit* basis as used in the *Census of Housing.* Since the number of housing units on a one-unit homeowner property may exceed one, the number of one-unit homeowner properties is less than the one-unit, owner-occupied housing units reported in other census reports. Furthermore, the derived percentages by age group may differ if there is a different ownership between age groups; for example, the elderly may own a disproportionate share of small, income properties. Finally, data on residential finance were collected in 1971 rather than 1969.

REFERENCES

Aaron, H. J. *Shelter and Subsidies.* Washington, D.C.: Brookings Institute, 1972.

McGuire, M. *Hearings Before the Subcommittee on Housing for the Elderly.* U.S. Senate, Special Committee on Aging, 91st Congress, 1st Session, Part 4, Homeownership Aspects, 1970, p. 759.

Robins, I. S. *Housing the Elderly: Background and Issues.* 1971 White House Conference on Aging, Washington, D.C., 1971.

Rolph, E. R. Discriminating effects of the income tax treatment of owner-occupants. *National Tax Journal,* 1973, *26,* 471–484.

Shannon, J. Residential property tax relief—a federal responsibility? *National Tax Journal,* 1973, *26,* 499–513.

U.S. Bureau of the Census. Census of Housing: 1970, Vol. V. *Residential Finance,* Washington, D.C., 1973.

U.S. Department of Housing and Urban Development. *Housing, 1971.* White House Conference on Aging, Washington, D.C., 1971a.

_____. *Housing in the Seventies.* Washington, D.C., 1973a.

_____. *1971 HUD Statistical Yearbook.* Washington, D.C., 1973b.

_____. *Older Americans.* Washington, D.C., 1973c.

_____. *1972 HUD Statistical Yearbook.* Washington, D.C., 1974.

U.S. Department of the Treasury, Internal Revenue Service. *Statistics of Income—1970: Individual Income Tax Returns.* Washington, D.C., 1972.

ROBERT B. GILLAN

Robert B. Gillan is Director of Litigation for the National Senior Citizens Law Center, Los Angeles, California.

Zoning for the Elderly

This paper is a discussion of the legal framework within which zoning considerations, as an aspect of community planning for the elderly, must be viewed. The legislative authority of states, counties, and municipalities in the zoning field is broad and a community can do pretty much what it wants, subject to certain constitutional and statutory limitations. We shall consider those limitations and thus provide the legal canvas upon which the planner must paint in formulating zoning policies and practices. The authorities discussed deal, in general, with zoning questions that are of particular relevance to the elderly. To a large extent, however, the principles cut across all age brackets.

As a class possessing unique characteristics, the elderly are entitled to individualized treatment in the creation of zoning patterns. For example, a zoning ordinance that requires a given number of parking spaces per residential unit should contain special exceptions for elderly housing since the ratio of cars to household unit is different than for that of the population in general. Typically, such exceptions do exist in zoning ordinances around the country.[1] Nevertheless, the need for such individualized treatment has seldom been judicially articulated.

In this connection, it is interesting to contrast the views of two lower New York courts. In *Central Management Co. v. Town Board*,[2] the court reviewed the refusal of a town zoning authority to grant a special exception permit for the construction of garden apartments for the elderly in a business zone. The local board had refused the permit because, in its judgment, the location was inappropriate for elderly residents due to traffic and other problems. In reversing the town board and ordering that the special exception be granted, the court observed:

The question here is whether a town board . . . may properly consider the *age* of people who may some day occupy a garden apartment in determining whether or not to grant a special exception permit for the apartment itself. I believe, and it is here held, that age, in and of itself, is just as irrelevant a consideration insofar as zoning is concerned as is race, color, creed, or physical condition. The determination must be made according to traditional zoning concepts, as to whether a garden apartment is suitable "for the purpose of promoting the health, safety, morals, or the general welfare of the *community* . . ." and the board's findings here would appear to have no bearing whatsoever upon these traditional objectives of zoning.[3]

Subsequently, another New York court was presented with the argument that a zoning ordinance amend-

99

ment designed to permit the construction of low-income and elderly housing was invalid because the classification violated the equal protection clause of the U.S. Constitution. The court dismissed the argument in the following language:

Classifications predicated upon natural factors such as age and income have long been recognized as permissible in many legislative forms such as Social Security, income tax, housing, welfare, labor, motor vehicle laws, Selective Service requirements, voting franchise requisites, etc. . . . Consequently, differentiation based upon age and income factors is permissible as long as it is rational and does not result in invidious discrimination. . . .[4]

The *Central Management* case is largely of historical interest. In point of fact, numerous communities accord elderly housing special treatment in zoning ordinances with respect to building characteristics, parking, and density measured in terms of room area, lot area, and height requirements.[5] In addition, the concept of special treatment for elderly housing in terms of site selection, design, and the provision of ancillary supportive services is deeply ingrained in federal housing legislation.[6] It can no longer be seriously questioned that zoning formulations tailored to elderly housing are valid. Indeed, as will be shown, the development of the law is in the direction of whether a community *must* rather than *can* accord the elderly (as well as other categories of people possessing special needs) special treatment for zoning purposes.

WHAT IS ZONING?

An understanding of the constitutional limitations and obligations surrounding the subject of zoning requires an understanding of the concept itself and its historical legal background. Briefly, zoning is the classification by a governmental entity of private property in terms of permissive use. Early zoning laws were relatively uncomplicated, defining uses in broad terms, for example, residential, commercial, and industrial, and providing for cumulative zoning (residential and commercial uses permitted in an industrial zone and residential uses permitted in a commercial zone). Modern zoning laws tend to be more sophisticated, creating numerous use zones and often providing that within each zone the permissive use

shall be exclusive. In addition, devices such as variances are utilized to ensure that the literal application of a zoning law to a specific case does not frustrate the purpose of the law, and administrative machinery is established to accord due process and relief from hardship.

THE "POLICE POWER"

The power to restrict the use of private property in the public interest is an attribute of sovereignty reserved to the states under the Tenth Amendment to the U.S. Constitution. In the cornerstone decision, *Euclid v. Amber Realty Company*,[7] the U.S. Supreme Court, in 1926, held that comprehensive zoning was a legitimate exercise of a state's police power and that the corresponding restriction upon individual property rights did not, as such, violate the Fourteenth Amendment to the U.S. Constitution. In the language of the court:

Building zone laws are of modern origin. They began in this country about 25 years ago. Until recent years, urban life was comparatively simple; but with the great increase and concentration of population, problems have developed, and constantly are developing, which require, and will continue to require, additional restrictions in respect of the use and occupation of private lands in urban communities. Regulations, the wisdom, necessity and validity of which, as applied to existing conditions, are so apparent that they are now uniformly sustained, a century ago, or even half a century ago, probably would have been rejected as arbitrary and oppressive.

The ordinance now under review and all similar laws and regulations must find their justification in some aspect of the police power, asserted for the public welfare. The line which in this field separates the legitimate from the illegitimate assumption of power is not capable of precise delimitation. It varies with circumstances and conditions. A regulatory zoning ordinance, which would be clearly valid as applied to the great cities, might be clearly invalid as applied to rural communities.[8]

The traditional judicial approach to zoning views it as a balancing act between the property rights of the landowner and the police power of the state to impose restrictions upon those rights in the interest of public health, safety, morals, and general welfare. For example, in an early decision, the U.S. Supreme Court had no difficulty upholding a municipal ordinance prohibiting the erection of billboards in a residential district without the consent of a majority of the interested landowners; the direct relationship between the existence of billboards and the safety of the streets was found a sufficient basis to bring into play a valid exercise of the police power:

Upon the question of the reasonableness of the ordinance, much evidence was introduced upon the trial of the case, from which the supreme court finds that fires had been started in the accumulation of combustible material which gathered about such billboards; that offensive and unsanitary accumulations are habitually found about them, and that they afford a convenient concealment and shield for immoral practices, and for loiterers and criminals.[9]

Conversely, when a land-use restriction cannot be related to any valid public interest, the restriction is invalid. Thus the Supreme Court declared unconstitutional an ordinance that authorized the construction of a philanthropic home for the aged in a residential district, but conditioned that authorization upon written consent by the owners of two thirds of the property within 400 feet of the proposed home. The vice inherent in the ordinance, according to the court, was that

The section purports to give the owners of less than one-half the land within 400 feet of the proposed building authority—uncontrolled by any standard or rule prescribed by legislative action—to prevent the trustee from using its land for the proposed home. The superintendent is bound by the decision or inaction of such owners. There is no provision for review under the ordinance; their failure to give consent is final. They are not bound by any official duty, but are free to withhold consent for selfish reasons or arbitrarily, and may subject the trustee to their will or caprice.[10]

THE PRESUMPTION OF VALIDITY

The judicial philosophy reflected in the early zoning decisions was characterized by a jealous regard for the sanctity of private property rights; laws that infringed upon those rights, either by diminishing values or by restricting use, were viewed with a jaundiced eye and upheld only if the court found "a substantial relation" to the public welfare. The absence of such a relation was deemed a denial of "substantive due process." With the advent of the New Deal and the growing complexity of social and economic relationships, a new judicial philosophy evolved. Zoning statutes and municipal ordinances were presumed valid, and if any conceivable state of facts or circumstances could be postulated that would justify the land-use restriction in terms of public welfare, it was upheld. The actual existence or nonexistence of those facts was deemed a legislative question not subject to judicial second-guessing:

A zoning ordinance passed in the exercise of the police power is clothed with a presumption in favor of its validity. It will not be disturbed where there is ground for a legitimate difference of opinion concerning its reasonableness, and the burden of showing it unreasonable and oppressive rests upon the party attacking it. But courts do not inquire into the facts or reasons which motivate the passage of a zoning ordinance, and all questions relative to the wisdom or desirability of particular restrictions in the ordinance rest with the legislative body creating it. When the reasonableness of an ordinance is challenged, the question for the court is not whether it thinks the ordinance wise, but whether the ordinance has a rational relation to public health, safety or general welfare.[11]

CONTEMPORARY DEVELOPMENTS

Until quite recently, the common thread running through zoning decisions was the standard police power analysis; that is, zoning ordinances are presumed constitutional and will be upheld unless their opponent can prove the complete absence of a relationship to the public welfare. The focus was upon the welfare of the existing inhabitants of the zoned area viewed in relation to the restrictive effect of the zoning ordinance upon private property rights.[12] Several recent cases now herald a judicial concern for the rights or potential future inhabitants and hold that, as a matter of law, a zoning authority is under an affirmative obligation to make provision for all segments of society.

Appeal of Girsh[13] involved a municipal zoning ordinance in Pennsylvania that restricted residential zones to single-family dwellings with fairly large minimum lot sizes (called "snob zoning"). The case arose when an individual purchased land within the residential zone and applied for a building permit to erect an apartment house, which permit was denied by the municipal authorities. Litigation was instituted and ultimately an appeal was taken to the state supreme court, which ordered that the permit issue, using the following language:

The question posed is whether the township can stand in the way of the natural forces which send our growing population into hitherto undeveloped areas in search of a comfortable place to live. . . . A zoning ordinance whose primary purpose is to prevent the entrance of newcomers in order to avoid future burdens, economic and otherwise, upon the administration of public services and facilities cannot be held valid.[14]

The Court also observed:

Perhaps in an ideal world, planning and zoning would be done on a *regional* basis so that a given community would have apartments, while an adjoining community would not. But as long as we allow zoning to be done community by community, it is intolerable to allow one municipality (or many municipalities) to close its doors at the expense of surrounding communities and the central city.[15]

Likewise, a New Jersey court recently declared unconstitutional a township's zoning ordinances that prohibited multifamily dwellings except on farmland, excluded mobile homes and trailers, and required minimum lot sizes for single-family dwellings; the court held that the municipality was guilty of economic discrimination and ordered that it undertake a study to reformulate its zoning patterns.[16] In another current decision, a federal court enunciated a zoning authority's obligation as follows:

Surely, if the environmental benefits of land use planning are to be enjoyed by a city and the quality of life of its residents is accordingly to be improved, the poor cannot be excluded from enjoyment of the benefits. Given the recognized importance of equal opportunities in housing, it may well be, as a matter of law, that it is the responsibility of a city and its planning officials to see that the city's plan as initiated or as it develops accommodates the needs of its low income families . . . .[17]

The preceding decisions, which were based upon the equal protection clause, reflect a judicial awareness of the critical importance of zoning as a social planning device. All members of society are entitled to reasonable housing opportunities, and the failure of a municipality or other zoning authority to provide them is subject to challenge in the courts. From the standpoint of the elderly, the cases are significant because to a large extent the elderly have unique housing needs. To repeat a familiar example, zoning ordinances that require a minimum number of parking spaces in relation to residential units may be inappropriate for elderly housing projects; the failure to rezone or to grant a variance to accommodate such

a project would, in light of recent judicial developments, be of questionable legality.

SPECIFIC PROBLEMS

Prejudice Against Mobile Homes

Having discussed the historical development of judicially formulated zoning law, we shall now address several zoning problems of relevance to the subject of elderly housing and their legal solutions. Consider first the question of mobile home parks. Customarily, a developer will wish to locate such a project on the fringes of the community where the land is zoned for nonresidential use. If the zoning authority, whether city or county, refuses to grant a variance or to effect a zoning change, precedent exists for judicial recourse. As pointed out previously, although a zoning ordinance will be sustained even if it results in an appreciable diminution in the value of affected property, the presumption of validity will be overcome where the value is almost totally destroyed *with no corresponding public good*. In a recent case, the owner of a 160-acre tract that was zoned agricultural applied for a zoning change to permit construction of mobile homes. When the change was refused by the zoning authorities, suit was commenced; the evidence demonstrated a substantial need for low-cost housing in the area and that the land was unsuitable for agricultural use. The court held that the refusal to rezone the property, in light of the need for low-cost housing and the absence of any corresponding public benefit in the existing zone, was arbitrary and in excess of the zoning prerogatives of the county:

The presumption of validity which arises from enactment of a zoning ordinance can be overcome by clear and convincing evidence that the ordinance, as applied to the subject land, was arbitrary and unreasonable and without real or substantial relation to the public health, safety, morals and welfare.

Thus zoning authorities may not frustrate the development of needed housing unless they can justify the law with a valid land-use reason:

[I]t is not the mere loss in value alone that is significant, but the fact that the public welfare does not require the restriction and resulting loss. . . . The law does not require that the subject property be totally unsuitable for the purpose classified but it is sufficient that a substantial decrease in value results from a classification bearing no substantial relation to the public welfare.[18]

"Spot-Zoning" Argument

A plethora of litigation surrounds the subject of "spot zoning," which results when an isolated parcel of land is subject to more or less restrictive zoning than surrounding properties.[19] The vice inherent in spot zoning is denial of equal protection; one man should not be treated differently than his neighbors when all other circumstances are equal. However, attempts by property owners to frustrate the construction of elderly housing by challenging zoning changes that permit higher density spots in residential districts have proved unsuccessful,[20] and it is likely that in the future the hallowed shibboleth "spot zoning," as a device to block construction of needed elderly housing, will receive little judicial sympathy.

"Preemption" Solution

The "spot-zoning" problem arises when community zoning authorities, through either variances, conditional use permits, or zoning changes, expressly sanction the construction of high-density housing. What happens if the zoning authorities refuse to make such a change in the face of demonstrated need? The problem has arisen where municipalities have resisted public housing commissions and declined to accommodate their zoning patterns to desired public housing. Under the legal doctrine of "preemption," a subordinate political entity, such as a municipality, may not enact legislation inconsistent with existing statutes promulgated by a higher political entity, such as a state. This axiom has been utilized by courts to permit the construction of elderly housing in areas zoned for low-density residential housing. It has been held that state statutes providing for the creation of housing commissions, either state or municipal, which are empowered to construct elderly and low-income housing preempt municipal zoning ordinances and that such a public body can disregard the ordinances in selecting sites for construction.[21]

"Blood-Relative" Problem

Typically, ordinances that create residential zones define single-family dwelling units in terms of blood or marital relationship among the occupants. A common situation is that of an elderly homeowner living on a low, fixed income that is insufficient to pay property taxes and other expenses of home maintenance and at the same time provide for the common necessities of life. Many of these people supplement their income by taking in roomers or boarders, a practice that might conflict with the applicable zoning ordinance, since the roomers or boarders are not blood relatives. The theoretical justification for ordinances defining single-family dwellings in such a manner is that family units are inherently stable, less transitory, own fewer cars, and do not possess the disruptive potential of a group of unrelated undesirables, for example, "hippies." The difficulty with such justification is that the regulation of antisocial behavior is not the province of zoning authorities and, in addition, a definitional attempt to do so would necessarily embrace many innocuous land uses; it has been so held:

> Zoning ordinances are not intended and cannot be expected to cure or prevent most antisocial conduct in dwelling situations. When intensity of use, i.e., overcrowding of dwelling units and facilities, is a factor in that conduct . . . consideration might quite properly be given to zoning or housing code provisions which would have to be of general application, limiting the number of occupants in reasonable relation to available sleeping and bathroom facilities or requiring a minimum amount of habitable floor area per occupant.[22]

The hypothetical elderly homeowner who takes in roomers in contravention of a zoning ordinance utilizing a blood relationship definition may, however, have some troubles because of a very recent decision by the U.S. Supreme Court. In *Village of Belle Terre v. Boraas*,[23] decided April 1, 1974, the Court upheld the validity of such an ordinance promulgated by "a village on Long Island's north shore of about 220 homes by 700 people." In addition to being contrary in philosophy to the above-quoted expression, the decision also strikes a blow for "snob zoning." It will be recalled that several courts (of lesser authority) had condemned that practice where its effect was to exclude entire classes of people. It is the author's opinion that the *Belle Terre* case will be narrowly construed by future courts as limited to its particular facts. There is an obvious distinction between a tiny village situated within a larger geographical region that accommodates all housing needs and a large municipality that is self-contained in terms of varieties of land use.

POLITICAL REALITIES

The central theme of this paper has been judicial response to various zoning practices, policies, and problems. An analysis of the legislative aspect of zoning, that is, substantive zoning provisions and procedures for obtaining variances, conditional use permits, and zoning changes, is the province of the legislator and the planner, rather than the lawyer. Nevertheless, it seems appropriate to comment briefly upon the political realities underlying the question of housing for the elderly, particularly subsidized or public housing. In the author's experience, the subject of housing for the elderly generally meets with sympathetic reaction in Congress, state legislatures, city councils, voters, and surrounding homeowners. In the language of one commentator,

There are several factors which encourage the local authorities to build these specially designed projects and units for the elderly. First, there is much less objection to racial integration in the elderly housing projects, and thus the local authority and the federal government can meet their "obligations" in the race relations field without arousing too much resentment. A second factor is that with the increasingly vociferous objections to the large projects, the local authority can meet the demands for scattered housing by building for the elderly. Neighborhoods which will not tolerate a huge low-rent project packed with Negroes on Aid for Dependent Children may go along with a high-rise for sweet but impoverished old folks. These elderly families are most often "white, orderly, and middle-class in behavior," and more than likely will be "grateful, docile and unseen." They are never vandals, and "they do not whore and carouse."[24]

A good case in point is a recent experience in the city of Los Angeles. California has a constitutional provision that prohibits the construction of low-income housing without voter approval through a referendum. Quite recently, in a general election, the voters approved construction of a substantial number of elderly housing units scattered throughout the city.

Accordingly, when a proposed housing project for the elderly, or when some other housing arrangement involving the elderly, conflicts with existing zoning ordinances, the chances of obtaining a variance or a zoning change are generally good. Of course, that generalization does not fit the truth in all cases and thus the courts must occasionally play a role. The purpose of this paper has been to provide an explica-

tion of that role and to point the way toward judicial solutions to zoning problems that the planner might face.

REFERENCES

1. Spicer, R.B., *Zoning for the Elderly*, Planning Advisory Service Report 259, July 1970, A.S.P.O.
2. 262 N.Y.S. 2d 728 (Sup. Ct. 1965).
3. 262 N.Y.S. at 731.
4. *Marino v. Town of Ramapo,* 326 N.Y.S. 2d 162 (Sup. Ct. 1971).
5. Spicer, R.B., *supra* n. 1.
6. 42 U.S.C. §1415 (12); *H.U.D. Low-Rent Housing Preconstruction Handbook*, HPMC-FHA 7410.8, pp. 3–30, 3.31; H.U.D. PG 46, *Minimum Property Standards, Housing for the Elderly*.
7. 272 U.S. 365 (1926).
8. 272 U.S. at 386, 387.
9. *Thomas Cusack Co. v. Chicago*, 242 U.S. 526 at 529 (1917).
10. *Washington ex rel. Seattle Trust Co. v. Roberge*, 278 U.S. 116 at 121, 122 (1928).
11. *Sinclair Refining Co. v. Chicago*, 178 F.2d 214 at 217 (7th Cir. 1949).
12. Comment, "A Survey of the Judicial Responses to Exclusionary Zoning," 22 *Syracuse L. Rev.* 537 (1971).
13. 263 A.2d 395 (Pa. 1970).
14. 263 A.2d at 397.
15. 263 A.2d at 399.
16. *Southern Burlington County N.A.A.C.P. v. Township of Mount Laurel*, N. J. Superior Ct., Burlington County, L-25 741-70-PW (S-2597), digested in 2 *Pov. L. Rep.* ¶15,567.
17. *Southern Alameda Spanish Speaking Organization v. Union City*, 424 F.2d 291 at 295, 296 (9th Cir. 1970).
18. *Lakeland Bluff, Inc. v. County of Will*, 252 N.E.2d 765 (Ill. App. 1969).
19. Anno., 51 A.L.R.2d 263 (1957).
20. *Marion v. Town of Ramapo*, 326 N.Y.S.2d 162 (Sup. Ct. 1971).
21. *Peters v. New York Urban Development Corp.*, App. Div., 20503, May 31, 1973, digested 2

Pov. L. Rep. ¶17,078; *Renshaw v. Coldwater Housing Comm.*, 165 N.W.2d 5 (Mich. 1969).

22. *Kirsch Holding Co. v. Borough of Manasquan*, 59 N.J. 241, 281 A.2d 513 (1971); *cf. City of Des Plaines v. Trottner*, 34 Ill.2d 432, 216 N.E. 116 (1966).

23. U.S., 94 S.Ct. 1536 (1974).

24. Ledbetter, W. H., Jr., "Public Housing—A Social Experiment Seeks Acceptance," *Law and Contemporary Problems*, Duke University School of Law (1968).

WILLIAM POLLAK

with the assistance of
JOANNE HILFERTY

William Pollak is on the Senior Research Staff of the Urban Institute, Washington, D.C. Joanne Hilferty was formerly with the Urban Institute, and is currently a graduate student in the Woodrow Wilson School of Public and International Affairs, Princeton University.

Utilization of Alternative Care Settings by the Elderly

Basic policy perspectives on alternatives to institutions are shaped, if not determined, by conceptions of the magnitudes of different target populations. For example, one's impression of the need for chronic care programs will be quite different if the share of persons thought to be unnecessarily placed in nursing homes is 60 percent rather than 20 percent. Similarly, the function and expected impact of a program of home care will be different if the majority of its anticipated users are persons who otherwise would be in nursing homes or mental hospitals rather than in the community. The program may be justified in either case but the estimate of expected users greatly affects the total net costs foreseen for the program. Yet, in spite of its central importance, accurate information about the size of different population groupings is rare, and planners and policy makers have no choice but to use figures whose meaning is unclear.

One can, in fact, cite estimates alleging that the percentage of nursing-home residents who are inappropriately placed is a vast 63 percent (Morris, 1971) or only 19 percent (Berg et al., 1970). Both figures may be accurate for the geographical areas to which they refer, but they are only confusing when no analysis exists to reconcile and explain their differ-

ences. Similar confusion relating to population magnitudes can be created verbally. Morris (1971) titles an interesting and innovative program of home care *Alternatives to Nursing Home Care*. Yet that title is misleading, since the program, according to his own figures, has a potential eligible elderly population of 2.54 million, of which 89 percent would be persons now in the community and only 11 percent would be persons who now are in institutions. If the program's actual users matched its potentially eligible users, the program would be a disappointment to those who see a reduction in the utilization of nursing-home care and a possible reduction in total care costs as a major objective. The program might well reduce the costs of caring for persons who otherwise would be in institutions. However, if the majority of its users were persons who otherwise would receive no formal care, the program would make a significant net addition to total care expenditures.

The following discussion will identify problems contributing to the confusion and lacunae identified, and will suggest appropriate research to be conducted by the Social and Rehabilitation Service and other federal agencies. Target populations are discussed under two issues: (1) *normative estimates* of the number of elderly persons who should be cared for in particular services, and (2) *current utilization*, which, instead of identifying placements that ought to occur, explains the placements and care utilization which do occur under existing programs—specifically the influence that income, location, family status, and program characteristics have on appropriate and inappropriate utilization of nursing homes, mental hospitals, home care, and other elements of the chronic care system. Projections of utilization of different forms of chronic care under specified changes in the programs that finance or provide chronic care for elderly persons would have important implications for future program costs.

NORMATIVE SYSTEMS OF UTILIZATION

Existing Studies

Estimates of the number of elderly persons most appropriately cared for in particular settings are important, especially when they are compared with the actual number of persons now served in those settings. They can identify gaps in the care spectrum, identify problems in the placement process, and enrich understanding of utilization patterns. Several published and unpublished studies have, in fact, examined the optimal and actual placement of functionally impaired elderly persons, in both particular settings (e.g., nursing homes) and groups of settings. Prominent are two studies concerned with care needs of the elderly in different parts of upstate New York: *An Areawide Examination of Nursing Home Use, Misuse and Nonuse* (Davis and Gibbon, 1971) and *Health Care of the Aged Study* (Hill, 1968). The Hill and Davis studies are not strictly comparable because they employ differently structured samples and because setting and service definitions and the arrays of settings used in specifying optimal placements are different. For example, the Hill study includes a random sample of old people in the community whereas the Davis study does not. The Hill study also identifies at the low-service-need end of the care spectrum "congregate living" and "public health nursing at home"; the latter is approximately equivalent to the service group described elsewhere in this report

as community or home care. The Davis study includes neither of these categories but does include "intermediate care facility" and "other" categories not included in the Hill work.

However, the broad outlines of their conclusions are similar. Both identify vast overutilization of mental hospitals by persons requiring less intense supervision and services. Of those in mental hospitals, Hill identifies only 10 percent and Davis only 25 percent who require such care. In addition, both identify some misuse of nursing homes, but this problem is thought to be much less severe. Thus Davis estimates that 73 percent of persons in nursing homes are appropriately placed and Hill places this figure at 79 percent. If appropriate placements were achieved overnight, neither study would dictate a major change in total nursing-home utilization, since the removal from nursing homes of residents not requiring nursing care would be roughly offset by the placement in nursing homes of inappropriately placed mental-hospital residents.

As indicated, the Hill study provides some detail about elderly persons in the community and other less intense forms of care. Contrary to the common view that there are many persons residing in the community who need but do not obtain acute medical and nursing-home care, the Hill study found that this was not a significant problem. In their age-adjusted sample of persons living at home, the Hill researchers found 3 percent who, according to their criteria, required a congregate living setting and 7 percent who needed public health nursing services. Of those living in residential clubs, Y's, boarding homes, and proprietary homes for adults, 6 percent required public health nursing and 31 percent needed to be placed in a congregate living setting.

In fact, except for the conclusions regarding nursing-home and mental-hospital utilization, the most striking results of the Hill study related to the underutilization of congregate living facilities and public health nursing services in the home. Thus, in the view of the authors, most persons who are inappropriately placed in nursing homes and mental hospitals and 3 percent of elderly persons living at home should be placed in congregate living settings. These groups, together with those already living in congregate settings, constitute 5.9 percent of the Monroe County

FIGURE 1
The presence of a caretaker—spouse frequently provides an alternative to institutionalization. (Photo courtesy of Administration on Aging, U.S.D.H.E.W.)

elderly, a figure that contrasts greatly with the 1.9 percent of the elderly now living in such settings. Public health nursing, similarly, now serves only 2.4 percent of the area's elderly but should, according to the Hill study, serve 6.7 percent. Significantly, virtually all persons who optimally would be located in their homes and served with public health nursing are persons now residing in the community, either in their own homes, residential hotels and clubs, or Y's. In other words, very few people residing in nursing homes were thought to be more appropriately placed in the community and served with public health nursing.

Research Needs

Both studies are significant, and their general conclusions are all the more interesting because of their similarities. The report of the Hill study, in particular, is a carefully prepared document that should be read by everyone interested in a rational policy of providing alternative forms of care for the elderly. Clearly, the studies must be replicated because of the crucial policy importance of normative estimates and the limitation of present studies to specific geographic areas, which are likely to differ from other parts of the country in terms of the economic, mental, and physical characteristics of their elderly populations and the programs that now determine the disposition of the care needs of their elderly. Replication, however, must be planned with recognition of the structure of normative estimates, since differences in the procedures and criteria employed could result in the ascription of quite different care needs even to areas with identical needs.

Statistics on the distribution of persons in each setting by their optimal placements (and services) are derived through the application of (1) service-need criteria to the distribution of persons by levels of mental and physical functioning to create a distribution of persons by service-need categories; and (2) placement criteria to the derived distribution of persons by service need to create a distribution of persons by optimal placements.

These steps are illustrated in Figure 2. Matrix A in Figure 2 presents a hypothetical classification of a sample of elderly persons by functional impairments.[1] Such a classification (in a more highly developed form) could be applied to a sample of persons in nursing homes, mental hospitals, the community, or any other setting; the number in any cell would indicate the number of persons in that setting with a particular level of functional competence. It is apparent that persons enumerated in lower cells have successively greater impairments.

Since a person's service and supervision needs are basically determined by his functional impairment, a particular package of services should be provided (formally or informally) to persons enumerated in a particular cell. For example, persons in the middle cell of the functional-impairment classification would appear to need part-time housekeeping, occasional meal preparation, personal care, and transportation.[2]

Once the level of service appropriate to each level of functioning is established, it is possible to transform the distribution of matrix A into a distribution of persons by required level of supervision and service need, such as the one illustrated by the headings of the left column of matrix B. Each person in a particular row of matrix B has a service—supervision package to suit his needs. Each person, however, also has a level of available family support, ranging from none to a healthy spouse or child who is willing and able to provide several services. The row distribution of persons by service needs in matrix B can, therefore, be modified to account for levels of available family support through the addition of a second dimension, illustrated by the headings at the top of matrix B. The number entered in a particular cell of matrix B, then, indicates the number of persons with a particular set of service needs and a particular level of available family support.

The setting deemed appropriate for any particular individual is determined by the impacts that the non-service aspects of different settings are expected to have on the individual and the costs of providing care in different settings. These, in turn, will be different depending on the needs of the individual and the availability of family members who might provide service were the person placed in the community. Since each cell of matrix B identifies service needs and family supports, the application of some placement criteria, based on assumptions or knowledge about setting costs and impacts, enables the transformation of the service-need/family-support distribution of matrix B into a distribution of the same persons by the placement that is most appropriate for them. Such placement criteria, for example, might specify that persons in cell IIc of matrix B be placed in their own residence and that persons in cell IIb be placed in an intermediate care facility.[3]

Although this progression from functional impairments to service needs to appropriate placements may not always be explicit, it is implicit in the development of all normative estimates of optimal placements and services for functionally impaired elderly persons. Thus a study may indicate only that a given percentage of all mental-hospital patients should be placed in nursing homes, but such a statement is inevitably based on (1) assessment of the mental and physical functional impairments of the patients, (2) identification of both the service and supervision needs associated with those impairments and the available family support, and (3) opinions on appropriate placements for persons with specified needs and family supports.

Two studies of exactly the same sample might, therefore, arrive at quite different optimal-placement distributions because they attribute different service needs to the same impairments and/or because they identify different placements as appropriate for persons with the same service needs.[4] The results of different studies can therefore be meaningfully compared and aggregated only if each handles the several steps in similar fashions. With respect to the first step, the creation of a distribution of persons by levels of mental and physical impairment, comparability among studies requires (1) the development and adoption of a uniform classification of mental and physical functional competencies and (2) a consistent method of assessing these competencies. The promulgation of a standard classification is, therefore, of considerable importance and should be given attention.

Comparability among studies also requires agreement concerning the service needs associated with different functional impairments. This is problematic for two reasons. First, opinion must play a role, and opinions will inevitably differ on the level of supervision, personal care, physical therapy, and other services an individual needs, even when there is agreement on the individual's mental and physical competencies. Second, these problems are compounded when considering the level and mix of home care, transportation, and other services needed by those functionally impaired elderly persons who, it is thought, are most appropriately placed in the community. If an individual is in a mental hospital, nursing home, or intermediate care facility, the client's total needs are relevant since virtually all these are provided for in the formal program of the setting.

B.   Classification by Service Need and Available Family Support

SERVICE NEED	FAMILY SUPPORT		
	I Family can house and provide continuous support	II Family can provide intermittent support	III No family, or family can provide no support
a. Occasional housekeeping and transportation			
b. Part-time housekeeping and occasional transportation			
c. Part-time housekeeping and meal preparation; occasional personal care and transportation			
d. Full-time supervision: housekeeping and meal preparation; part-time personal care, occasional transportation			
e. Full-time supervision: personal care, house-keeping and meal preparation; occasional transportation			

A.   Classification by Functional Impairment

FUNCTIONAL IMPAIRMENT	NO.
Ambulatory and unconfused; cannot clean house or manage own transportation	
Ambulatory and generally unconfused; cannot manage finances, clean house, or travel independently	
Ambulatory with difficulty and generally confused; can manage physical self-maintenance, except bathing, independently; cannot shop, clean house, prepare meals, manage finances, or travel independently	
Ambulatory with difficulty and confused much of the time; can toilet and feed self but cannot bathe or manage other physical self-maintenance tasks independently	
Ambulatory with difficulty and confused all of the time; cannot toilet or feed self, or manage other physical self-maintenance tasks	

Original Sample
(persons in community, nursing homes, boarding homes, mental hospitals, or other settings of groups of settings)

FIGURE 2 (*above and right*)
Decision-making chart for older people in need of service.

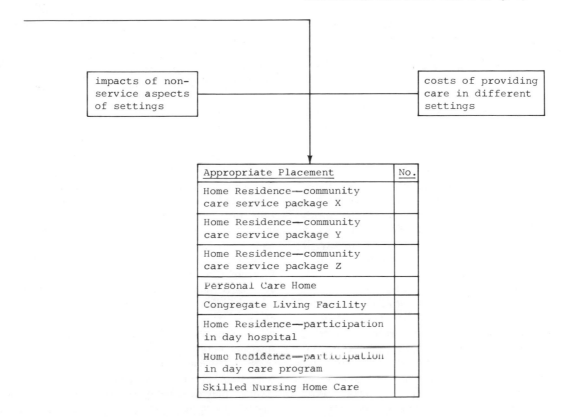

Appropriate Placement	No.
Home Residence—community care service package X	
Home Residence—community care service package Y	
Home Residence—community care service package Z	
Personal Care Home	
Congregate Living Facility	
Home Residence—participation in day hospital	
Home Residence—participation in day care program	
Skilled Nursing Home Care	

Community care programs for impaired elderly persons residing in independent housing, however, may be designed to meet only those impairment-created needs that are not met informally by relatives or friends or by purchasing services. If this is the case, the extent of unmet needs, even with total needs constant, will not be fixed but will vary, since the proportion of given needs that will be met through purchases, own efforts, and the assistance of relatives is likely to be influenced by the existence and terms of a particular home care program.

In the absence of a home care program, a child or sibling may provide shopping, transportation, and other services, and/or the old person may purchase maid or other services in the market. If a home care program is initiated, the level of the relatives' support and the quantity of services purchased may decline and produce an increase in the level of needs left to be met by the formal program; the degree of decline

can be influenced by the terms (prices) on which the home care services are provided.

For persons with family or financial resources, needs for home care services are not absolute and fixed such services are, to some degree, substitutes for services that can be purchased or provided informally. This ambiguity in service needs must obviously be recognized in designing and projecting utilization of home care services.[5] It also must be considered in the preparation and comparison of normative estimates of the number of elderly persons who ought to be placed in the community and provided with home care services.

Comparability of the results of different normative populations studies requires, finally, uniformity of the criteria employed in determining hypothetical optimal placements of persons with specified service needs. The existence of options for the placement of an impaired individual indicates that there are several settings in which the individual's service needs can be satisfied. Consequently, variations in nonservice characteristics of settings—their scale, familiarity to clients, responsiveness to individual needs, and flexibility in general activities—cause different settings (1) to have different expected impacts on the physical and mental well-being of clients, and (2) to incur different costs in providing the package of services needed by a client.

The criteria used in a normative study to make hypothetical placements of elderly persons with given service needs and family support could be based solely on a concern for the clients' welfare. This would dictate selection, in each instance, of the setting with the best expected impact on the clients' physical and mental well-being, regardless of cost. Conversely, if based solely on cost, criteria would dictate selection in each instance of that setting which could provide the needed package of services at least cost.

The criteria used in actual studies are likely to lie somewhere between these two extremes. Thus even the most client-oriented study, when considering placements of the severely impaired, is almost certain to restrict attention to settings that are not prohibitively expensive; for example, home care will not be considered for bedridden and incontinent individuals without family even if it is physically possible and known to be best for and preferred by the client. Nonetheless, there is considerable room for variation between criteria based solely on client welfare and criteria based solely on costs, and that leeway is a potential major source for noncomparability among studies of "optimal" placement. When client welfare and cost economy dictate selection of the same care setting, this problem does not arise. However, when they dictate selection of different settings, the priority to be attached to client welfare as opposed to cost economy can be settled only with an explicit value judgment; it cannot be avoided through appeal to or use of benefit—cost ratios.

Even if there were agreement on the priority to attach to client welfare and cost economy, placement criteria could still differ among studies because of disagreement (at least partially born of ignorance) about the impacts that nonservice aspects of different settings have on their residents and about the costs incurred in providing specified services in different settings.

To date, empirical evidence on the different physical and mental consequences of care provided in alternative settings is fragmentary—it is almost entirely focused on the nursing-home/community-living (with no service) comparison—and inconclusive. For example, mortality rates are higher and psychological adjustment worse among nursing-home clients than among elderly living in the community; but the accumulated research and data do not identify whether the differences are due to initial differences in the two populations, to the impacts of the different settings, or to the environmental changes associated with institutionalization. Furthermore, some negative effects of as well as bias against institutional care may result from inadequate service provided in a particular facility rather than from characteristics that are inevitable correlates of care in the generic setting.

It is evident that placement criteria based solely on client welfare cannot now be developed from empirical information. The evidence does not cover all settings (congregate living, services provided in the homes, day care, and hospitals have not been carefully studied) and is inconclusive with respect to the settings that have been covered. This does not argue against placement criteria based on client welfare but does indicate that such criteria will be derived from assumptions and beliefs rather than empirical evidence.

Although it is far easier to develop evidence about costs than about physical and mental impacts, current ignorance will cause placement criteria based on costs also to be based on assumption rather than empirical evidence. Allegations that one or another settings is "least" expensive abound. However, because the relative costs of providing care in different settings will be different depending on the services that must be provided, it is evident that the least expensive setting will not be fixed, but will differ depending on the particular impairments of the individual. Since evidence on the relationship between care costs and services (or impairments) in different settings is meager, cost-based placement criteria will, at least for a while, be based on conjecture.

The criteria that are used to make hypothetical

placements in normative studies must be based on some judgment about the relative significance of client welfare and cost economy, where those objectives compete, and, in the absence of empirical evidence, on assumptions about the merits and costs of care provided in different settings. This leaves considerable room (and justification) for choice in the selection of placement criteria. Comparability among studies could still be attained by imposing a common set of placement criteria. However, it would seem wiser instead to forego standardization of criteria and substitute in its place a requirement that all studies include, in addition to data on the distribution of persons in different settings by their optimal placements, explicit distributions of those persons by their mental and physical impairments by use of a standard classification. Users of different studies could then, if desired, bypass the placement criteria of individual studies in order both to aggregate the results of studies that use different criteria and to independently examine the implications of alternative placement criteria for the utilization and total costs of different settings.

Although this entire discussion of research needs has concentrated on the analysis of persons currently in particular settings, the analysis applies equally well to studies of the optimal placements of persons entering different settings. For example, a problem of overutilization revealed by a finding that persons in nursing homes are inappropriately placed could be dealt with by removing people from the setting (shifting the stock) *or* by reducing the flow of persons into the setting. The psychic strains of environmental change favor the latter solution; furthermore, the high mortality rates of nursing-home clients suggest that such a policy of reducing utilization by reducing inflow could be effective in correcting misutilization in a relatively short period of time.

CURRENT PATTERNS OF UTILIZATION

Several program failings are regularly cited in discussions of the utilization of chronic care facilities by the elderly: (1) placement procedures in which decisions are generally made with inadequate knowledge both of the clients' functional competence and of the number and type of alternative care options; (2) the absence of any program to finance long-term chronic care (in any setting) for middle- and lower-middle-class elderly, unless the cost of care depletes assets or raises medical costs to the point where the individual is eligible for Medicaid; (3) the absence of a program to finance community-based chronic care for low-income elderly on equal terms with the funding of care for such persons in nursing homes and intermediate care facilities (home care is almost impossible to fund under the restrictive conditions of Medicaid and is provided, with great variations among places, only to the very poor under the social-services element of the welfare programs); (4) Medicaid nursing-home reimbursement rates (and rate structures) in many states that will not remunerate care of satisfactory quality and may result in fewer nursing home and intermediate care facility beds than are needed; and (5) an unavailability of homecare services, day care, congregate living quarters, and other community settings and services, even when adequate means to finance them are present.

Some of these problems submit to direct investigation. Others are best studied inferentially through analysis of the utilization of care by the elderly. The following pages present and examine data of a type that can and should be used in such studies.

Data on the Utilization of Institutional Care

Changes over time. Table 1 presents data on the number of old persons in all types of institutions in 1960 and 1970 and reveals that nursing-home populations increased by 105 percent, that the absolute use of mental hospitals by the elderly actually declined by 36 percent, and that the use of all institutions by the elderly increased by 58 percent over the decade. Figure 7-3 demonstrates that, within the group of all institutionalized elderly persons, the percentage in mental hospitals fell precipitously from 29 to 12 percent and the percentage in nursing homes rose from 63 to 82 percent.

Between 1960 and 1970 the number of elderly persons in nursing homes (including personal care homes and homes for the aged) increased by 408,000,

TABLE 1
Old People in Institutions, by Type of Institution, 1960 and 1970

| | 1960[a] | | 1970 | | |
	Number	%	Number	%	Percentage Change, 1960–1970
Total number of people 65+	16,560,000[b]		20,066,000[c]		+21
Total 65+ in institutions	615,100	100	971,600[d]	100	+58
In nursing homes, personal care homes, and homes for the aged	388,000	63	795,800[e]	82	+105
In mental hospitals	177,800	29	113,000[f]	12	−36
In correctional institutions	800	—[g]	4,300[h]	—[g]	+432
In TB hospitals	14,200	—[g]	5,100[i]	—[g.]	−64
In chronic-disease hospitals (other than TB)	23,200	8	35,200[i]	4	+52
In other institutions	11,000	—[g]	18,300[i]		+66

[a]Figures for inmates of different institutions for 1960 are from U.S. Bureau of the Census, *Census of Population: 1960, Final Report, Inmates of Institutions*, PC(2)-8A, Tables 3–7.
[b]*Census of Population: 1960, op. cit., Vol. I, Characteristics of the Population*, p. 1–148.
[c]*1970 Census of Population, General Population Characteristics, U.S. Summary*, PC(1)-B1, Table 52.
[d]*1970 Census of Population, Persons in Institutions and Other Group Quarters*, PC(2)-4E, Table 19.
[e]*Ibid.*, Table 6.
[f]*Ibid.*, Table 4.
[g]Less than 1 percent.
[h]*1970 Census of Population, Persons in Institutions and Other Group Quarters*, Table 3.
[i]*Ibid.*, Table 26.

from 388,000 to 796,000. This 105 percent increase is attributable to several factors whose separate effects can, to some degree, be isolated quantitatively, as shown in Figure 4. These factors include the following:

1. *Increase in the number of people aged 65 and over.* Between 1960 and 1970 the number of old people increased by 21 percent. If there had been no change in this group's rate of utilization of nursing homes, this increase would have raised nursing-home populations by 21 percent or 81,000. This accounts for 20 percent of the total increase in nursing-home populations over the decade.

2. *Changes in the age structure of the elderly population.* The 21 percent increase in the population of people over 65 was not evenly distributed over the age brackets making up that total. The rate of increase was smallest (12 percent) for the age 65 to 69 group and was successively greater for each older group, rising to a 63 percent increase for the 85 and over age group (see Table 2). Since the percentage of persons in nursing homes rises greatly with age (from less than 1 percent for the 65 to 69 group to 17 percent for the 85-and-over group in 1970; see Table 3), the changed age composition of the elderly also increased the use of nursing homes.

If population within each age bracket had increased at the rate that did occur, while nursing-home utilization rates within each age bracket remained at

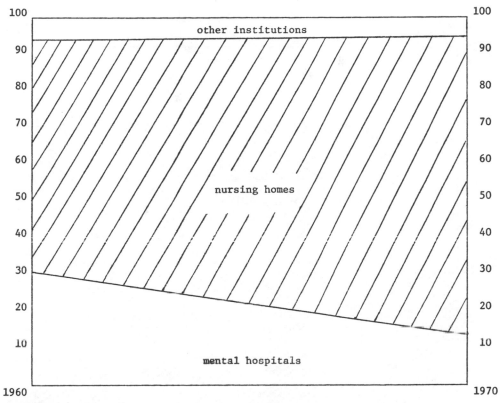

FIGURE 3
Distribution of institutionalized elderly by type of institution, by percent (1960–1970).

their 1960 levels, nursing-home use by the elderly would have increased by 137,000. This figure represents the total increase resulting from the combined effects of population increase and age-structure change. Since population increases alone have been shown to account for an 81,000 increase in nursing-home populations, the remainder of the 137,000, or 56,000, is the increase that is attributable to changes in the age structure of the over-65 population. This 56,000 figure represents 14 percent of the total increase in nursing-home populations over the decade. It is important to note that, because the age composition of the elderly will change little between 1970 and 1980 (see Table 2), this factor will have a smaller effect on nursing-home use over the coming decade.

3. *Increase in utilization rate of nursing homes within each age bracket.* Table 3 shows, for example, that between 1960 and 1970, nursing-home utilization within the 65 to 69 age bracket rose from 0.6 to 1.0 percent and that for people 85 and over it rose from less than 11 to over 16 percent. These increases must account for all the increases in nursing-home populations unaccounted for above, that is, for 271,000 persons or 66 percent of the total increases. Changes that help to explain this increased utilization within age brackets include the following:

(a) *Substitution of nursing-home for mental-hospital care.* Previously, many persons were placed in mental hospitals who now would be placed in nursing homes. This substitution has occurred for a variety of reasons that are both controversial and difficult to disentangle. Chemotherapy has enabled the care of

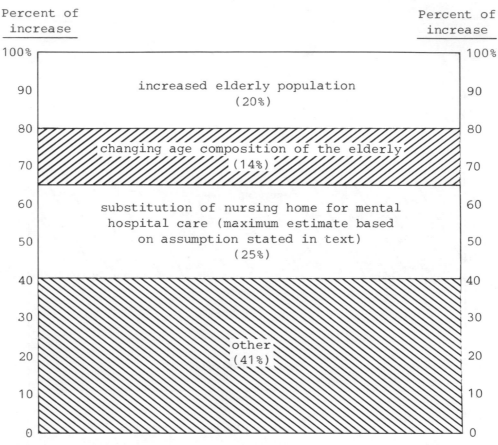

FIGURE 4
Increase in nursing home population, by cause (1960–1970).

some persons in less service intense settings than formerly was required. Other persons, who are not or are minimally mentally ill, are now cared for in nursing homes although they might once have been placed (inappropriately) in mental hospitals. Finally, although they require and once would have received mental-hospital care, some persons may now be cared for in nursing homes because it is less expensive.

If all the reduction in the rate of mental-hospital utilization by the elderly were reflected in increased utilization of nursing homes, it would account for 102,000 or 25 percent of the increased use of nursing

homes.[6] This would leave 169,000 or 41 percent of the total increase in the use of nursing homes to be explained by the factors listed next and by other forces.

(b) *Implementation of federal–state and federal programs that finance long-term and convalescent care of the elderly in nursing homes.* Under the Medicaid program, participating states are required to cover nursing-home care for those persons who need care but have insufficient resources to pay for it. Previously, such persons either would not have received formal care or would have depended on less well

TABLE 2
Population Aged 65 and over by Age Groups: Totals and Percentages

	1960		1970			1980	
Population Group	*Number (1,000's)*	*Population 65+ (%)*	*Number (1,000's)*	*Population 65+ (%)*	*Increase 1960–1970 (%)*	*Number (1,000's)*	*Population 65+ (%)*
Total 65+	16,560	100	20,066	100	21	23,932	100
65 to 69	6,258	38	6,992	35	12	8,161	34
70 to 74	4,739	29	5,444	27	16	6,778	28
75 to 79	3,054	18	3,835	19	26	4,459	19
80 to 84	1,580	9	2,284	11	45	2,761	12
85+	929	6	1,511	8	63	1,773	7
65+ as a % of total U.S. population	9.2		9.3			10.1	

Source: U.S. Bureau of the Census, *1970 Census of Population, General Population Characteristics U.S. Summary*, PC(1)-B1, Table 52, and *Projections of the Population of the United States, by Age and Sex, 1970 to 2020*, p-25, No. 470, Nov. 1971, p. 55. On the advice of people at the Census Bureau, we have built up projections from 1970 data using survival-rate figures presented in the projections volume rather than employing the projections figures given in that volume.

funded and more variable state programs. No accurate data are available on the percentage of nursing-home patients partly or fully financed by Medicaid, but estimates place this figure at around 65 percent.

Medicare will finance nursing-home care for the elderly regardless of economic status. The Medicare nursing-home benefit, however, is directed at convalescent care and is limited to post-hospital care of no more than 100 days. These limitations mean that Medicare is far less important in the financing of nursing-home care than Medicaid.

(c) *Changing social and cultural patterns.* Such

TABLE 3
Breakdown of Population 65 and over in Nursing Homes, 1960 and 1970

	1960			1970		
Age Group	*Population in Nursing Homes (1960)[a]*	*Population, (1960)[b]*	*Ratio: Nursing Home to Total Population*	*Population in Nursing Homes (1970)[c]*	*Population Total (1970)[d]*	*Ratio: Nursing Homes to Total Population*
65+	388,000	16,560,000	0.023	796,000	20,066,000	0.040
65 to 69	40,000	6,258,000	0.006	70,000	6,992,000	0.010
70 to 74	66,000	4,739,000	0.014	107,000	5,444,000	0.020
75 to 79	89,000	3,054,000	0.029	164,000	3,835,000	0.043
80 to 84	95,000	1,580,000	0.060	207,000	2,284,000	0.091
85+	98,000	929,000	0.105	249,000	1,511,000	0.165

[a]U.S. Bureau of the Census, *Census of Population: 1960, Final Report, Inmates of Institutions*, PC(2)-8A, Table 7.
[b]*Ibid., Census of Population: 1960, Vol. I, Characteristics of the Population*, p. 1–148.
[c]*Ibid., Census of Population: 1970, Persons in Institutions and Other Group Quarters*, PC(2)-E4, Table 6.
[d]*Ibid., Census of Population: 1970, General Population Characteristics, U.S. Summary*, PC(1)-B1, Table 52.

TABLE 4
Raw and Adjusted Percentages of Population 65 and over in Nursing Homes, by State, 1970

State	Population 65+ in Nursing Homes[a] (%)	Adjusted Percentage of Population 65+ in Nursing Homes[b]	Index of Nursing Home Utilization[b]
United States	4.00	4.00	1.0
Alabama	2.93	3.02	0.8
Alaska	4.30	4.43	1.1
Arizona	1.81	2.04	0.5
Arkansas	4.11	4.08	1.0
California	4.69	4.61	1.2
Colorado	7.35	6.90	1.7
Connecticut	4.78	4.67	1.2
Delaware	3.08	3.07	0.8
District of Columbia	4.95	5.01	1.3
Florida	1.95	2.16	0.5
Georgia	3.33	3.44	0.9
Hawaii	2.28	2.46	0.6
Idaho	4.66	4.41	1.1
Illinois	4.20	4.19	1.0
Indiana	4.04	3.91	1.0
Iowa	6.40	5.80	1.5
Kansas	5.86	5.37	1.3
Kentucky	3.31	3.26	0.8
Louisiana	3.44	3.63	0.9
Maine	3.73	3.53	0.9
Maryland	3.48	3.63	0.9
Massachusetts	5.67	5.44	1.4
Michigan	4.07	4.12	1.0
Minnesota	7.18	6.78	1.7
Mississippi	1.75	1.79	0.4
Missouri	3.72	3.58	0.9
Montana	4.84	4.33	1.1
Nebraska	6.30	5.75	1.4
Nevada	2.27	2.59	0.6
New Hampshire	4.89	4.74	1.2
New Jersey	2.88	2.98	0.7
New Mexico	2.14	2.22	0.6
New York	3.07	3.20	0.8
North Carolina	2.71	2.88	0.7
North Dakota	7.49	7.01	1.8
Ohio	4.22	4.12	1.0
Oklahoma	5.63	5.46	1.4
Oregon	4.95	4.73	1.2
Pennsylvania	3.32	3.36	0.8
Rhode Island	4.08	4.07	1.0
South Carolina	2.71	2.92	0.7
South Dakota	6.63	6.18	1.5
Tennessee	2.08	2.11	0.5
Texas	4.72	4.83	1.2
Utah	3.43	3.41	0.9
Vermont	4.51	4.24	1.1

TABLE 4 *(continued)*
Raw and Adjusted Percentages of Population 65 and over in Nursing Homes, by State, 1970

State	Population 65+ in Nursing Homes[a] (%)	Adjusted Percentage of Population 65+ in Nursing Homes[b]	Index of Nursing Home Utilization[b]
Virginia	2.86	2.95	0.7
Washington	5.62	5.28	1.3
West Virginia	1.62	1.62	0.4
Wisconsin	5.56	5.38	1.3
Wyoming	6.33	6.27	1.6

[a]*Sources for total population:* U.S. Bureau of the Census, *1970 Census of Population, General Population Characteristics, U.S. Summary*, PC(1)-B1, Table 62; for nursing-home population: U.S. Bureau of the Census, *1970 Census of Population, Persons in Institutions and Other Group Quarters*, PC(2)-E4, Table 36.
[b]These figures were calculated by multiplying the national utilization percentage by an age-adjusted state index of nursing-home utilization. This index is the ratio of actual to "expected" nursing-home utilization, where "expected" utilization is the number who would be in nursing homes in a state if, within each age bracket, the state had the same percentage in nursing homes as did the country as a whole.

changes have likely resulted in substantial substitution of formal nursing-home care for care formerly provided by relatives. This cause is frequently cited in discussions of the increased utilization of nursing-home care. It is traced to increased mobility, which separates the old from their children, and to the general decline of the multigeneration family. These social changes and the economic factors mentioned under (b) undoubtedly account for most of the otherwise unaccounted for 41 percent in the increased use of nursing homes.

(d) *Advances in medical care.* Such advances may have enabled persons to survive with greater impairments than was formerly possible. If this is so, the share of persons at each age who have severe impairments will have increased and raised the need for nursing care.

(e) *Changes in age structure within 5-year age brackets.* This repeats for 5-year intervals the argument presented above (p. 114). It undoubtedly accounts for some effects of age-structure change that are not picked up when using 5-year brackets.

Interstate differences in utilization. The 796,000 older persons who were in nursing and personal care homes in 1970 represent approximately 4.0 percent of the elderly population of the United States. This figure, however, conceals considerable variation among states in the share of older persons who are in nursing homes. The first column of Table 4 shows the variation in this percentage among 50 states and the District of Columbia. It goes from a low of 1.62 percent in West Virginia to a high of 7.49 percent in North Dakota.

These raw figures are ambiguous. The variations they identify may reveal significant underlying differences in the propensity of states to utilize nursing-home care, or they may merely reflect differences among states in the age structure of their elderly populations—rising in states where an unusually old elderly population necessitates a high level of nursing-home utilization and falling where an unusually young population of people over 65 reduces the need.

The data of column 2 of Table 4 adjust for the age composition of the states' elderly population in order to separate from the total variation in utilization that part of the variation which is due to real differences in the propensity of states to use nursing homes. Thus the age-adjusted percentage of the elderly in nursing homes would be lower than the unadjusted figure for states with an unusually old population of people 65 and over and, conversely, higher for states with un-usually young populations of elderly persons. The third column of Table 4 is an index that measures the propensity of a state to use nursing homes after adjusting for the age structure of its elderly population.

Although several states at both extremes of nursing-home utilization are brought slightly closer to the national average when account is taken of age composition, most of the variation of column 1 is preserved in column 2. Thus most of the interstate variations in nursing-home utilization represent real differences among states in the way that the care problems of elderly people are handled. It is impossible to know without further analysis, however, to what these differences are attributable—to know, for example, whether low utilization rates are due to unusual propensities of families to care for their old, to high availability of home care, to negligence in the provision of any form of care, to the substitution of boarding-home for nursing-home care, or to some other factor.

Variations in utilization by sex and marital status. The 4.0 percent figure that indicates the share of elderly persons who are in nursing homes also conceals significant differences between the nursing-home utilization rates of men and women, married and unmarried persons, rich and poor, and black and white.

Those familiar with nursing homes often note how women outnumber men in such institutions. This is normally attributed to the numerical dominance of women in the population 65 and over and their rising dominance as age increases into the older elderly brackets for which nursing-home use is very common. In Table 5 the figures of rows 4 and 5 are more analytically useful than these assertions, for they show that not only do women outnumber men in nursing homes, but that the rate at which women use nursing homes is significantly greater in all age groups except the youngest shown. Numerous forces beyond those visible in the simple cross-classification of Table 5 are obviously required to explain this difference in utilization between men and women. Nonetheless, the importance of a spouse in preventing institutionalization is evident in the table and goes a long way toward explaining why women use nursing homes at higher rates than men. First, rows 2, 3, and 6 to 9 make it clear that for both sexes in all age brackets the presence of a spouse makes placement in a nursing home less likely. Rows 7 and 9 also show

TABLE 5
Utilization of Nursing-Home Care Within Age, Sex, and Marital-Status Groupings (in percentages)

Population Characteristics	Age							
	65–74			*75–84*				
	Total	*65–69*	*70–74*	*Total*	*75–79*	*80–84*	*85+*	*Total 65+*
1. Total population	1.4	1.0	2.0	6.0	4.2	9.1	16.6	4.0
2. Married	0.3			1.8			5.4	0.8
3. Not married	3.0			8.8			19.7	7.1
4. Male	1.2	1.0	1.6	4.2	3.1	6.3	11.7	2.8
5. Female	1.6	1.0	2.2	7.2	5.0	10.8	19.4	4.8
6. Male—married	0.3			1.4			4.6	0.8
7. Male—not married	4.3			9.2			16.8	7.7
8. Female—married	0.4			2.4			7.1	1.0
9. Female—not married	2.5			8.7			20.8	6.9

Source for total population: U.S. Bureau of the Census, *1970 Census of Population, General Population Characteristics, U.S. Summary*, PC(1)-B1, Table 62; for nursing-home population: U.S. Bureau of the Census, *1970 Census of Population, Persons in Institutions and Other Group Quarters*, PC(2)-E4, Table 36.

TABLE 6
Differentials in Health Characteristics of the Aged by Color

	Limitations of Activity (%)	Number of Bed-Disability Days per Person per Year	Number of Restricted-Activity Days per Person per Year
White	45.3	11.8	33.9
Nonwhite	54.3	18.6	41.9

Source: National Center for Health Statistics, Series 10, Number 56, *Differentials in Health Characteristics by Color, U.S., July 1965–June 1967*, U.S. Department of Health, Education, and Welfare, Washington, D.C., 1969.

that within the class of nonmarried persons (who represent 89 percent of all nursing-home residents) the rate of nursing-home use is remarkably similar for men and women—within age brackets and among all persons over 65. It is, therefore, evident that the higher rate of nursing-home placements among women than men in all elderly age brackets arises primarily because women are more likely to be unmarried (widowed, divorced, or never married) than men in each age bracket. As noted above, a number of other forces are required to explain fully the different nursing-home use of men and women, but this analysis of Table 5 suggests that the greater likelihood that men will have a living spouse is the dominant one.

Variations in utilization by income. It is apparent that the elderly in institutions are poorer than the elderly living in the community. In 1970, approximately 9 percent of all Old Age Assistance recipients and less than 5 percent of the elderly population were in institutions.[7] It is also apparent in figures showing the distribution of income among persons in and outside of institutions. For example, 50 percent of nonmarried persons living in institutions in 1967 had income below $1,000. This contrasts with the ap-

TABLE 7
Nursing Home Utilization by Region

	Total Population 65+	Nursing-Home Population 65+[a]	Nursing-Home Population as a Percentage of Total 65+ Population[b]
Northeast			
New England	1,269,517	64,367	5.07
Middle Atlantic	3,929,867	122,505	3.11
North Central			
East North Central	3,810,977	164,908	4.32
West North Central	1.916,447	93,149	4.86
South			
South Atlantic	2,936,717	76,812	2.61
East South Central	1,269,634	32,593	2.56
West South Central	1,836,282	84,055	4.57
West			
Mountain	695,221	26,020	3.74
Pacific	2,400,840	97,066	4.04

[a]U.S. Bureau of the Census, *1970 Census of Population, General Population Characteristics, U.S. Summary*, PC(1)-B1, Tables 61, 62.
[b]U.S. Bureau of the Census, *1970 Census of Population, Persons in Institutions and Other Group Quarters*, PC(2)-E4, Table 36.

TABLE 8
Nursing-Home Utilization Rates by Race and State

State	White Nursing-Home Population as a Percentage of Total Population over 65	Black Nursing-Home Population as a Percentage of Total Population over 65
Alabama	3.72	0.73
Alaska	5.42	0
Arizona	1.82	2.49
Arkansas	4.47	2.49
California	4.85	3.13
Colorado	5.30	2.19
Connecticut	4.83	3.29
Delaware	3.41	0.51
District of Columbia	7.09	2.07
Florida	1.99	1.36
Georgia	3.99	1.25
Hawaii	0.25	0
Idaho	4.68	5.74
Illinois	4.35	2.29
Indiana	4.09	3.19
Iowa	6.39	6.92
Kansas	5.99	2.80
Kentucky	3.35	2.80
Louisiana	4.22	1.54
Maine	3.72	2.25
Maryland	3.66	2.36
Massachusetts	5.67	6.48
Michigan	4.16	2.97
Minnesota	7.19	7.43
Mississippi	2.60	0.22
Missouri	3.88	1.67
Montana	4.85	6.52
Nebraska	6.35	3.43
Nevada	2.35	0.57
New Hampshire	4.90	5.63
New Jersey	2.92	2.30
New Mexico	2.14	3.21
New York	3.16	1.74
North Carolina	3.02	1.47
North Dakota	7.50	22.72
Ohio	4.31	3.01
Oklahoma	5.82	3.82
Oregon	4.99	3.51
Pennsylvania	3.42	1.71
Rhode Island	4.08	5.04
South Carolina	3.25	1.32
South Dakota	6.69	0
Tenneessee	2.23	1.18
Texas	5.04	2.37
Utah	3.48	0
Vermont	4.52	0
Virginia	3.08	1.84
Washington	5.67	3.26
West Virginia	1.64	1.31
Wisconsin	5.56	5.70
Wyoming	3.94	10.34

proximately 30 percent of nonmarried people in the community with incomes below that threshold and the 24 percent of all married elderly couples with incomes below $1,000 per capita.[8] It is not clear, however, to what degree this statistically observed disproportionate institutionalization of the poor is due to (1) greater impairments among the poor, which cause or result from poverty or the preconditions of poverty, (2) the scarcity of noninstitutional care for the poor, and (3) the absorption of wealth and the elimination of employment opportunity, which are associated with institutionalization and the impairments that necessitate institutionalization.

Variation in utilization by race. Among persons over 65, census data show that 2.3 percent of black women and 1.9 percent of black men are in nursing homes, whereas 5.1 percent of white women and 2.9 percent of white men are in nursing homes. These differentials are most striking when note is taken of two considerations. First, the black aged have considerably lower incomes than the white aged. As we have shown, low income predisposes persons to nursing-home placement. Second, nonwhite elderly tend to be in poorer health than white elderly. This is revealed in Table 6, which shows that elderly nonwhites are more likely to have limitations in their activities and on average have more disability days and days of restricted activity than do whites. Obviously, this poorer health would tend to increase the use of nursing homes by nonwhites relative to whites.[9]

What then accounts for the strikingly lower rate of utilization of nursing-home care by nonwhites? One possibility is suggested by Table 7. It shows that nursing-home use is generally low in the southeast, where a disproportionately high percentage of all blacks live. Perhaps, then, the low rate of nursing-home utilization by blacks is to be explained by their tendency to reside where nursing-home use is generally low. The inadequacy of this explanation is demonstrable in many ways, perhaps most interestingly with the data of Table 8. From this table it is evident that *within* every state with sizable numbers of black elderly (more than 5,000 black elderly) except Massachusetts, the rate of nursing-home utilization of blacks is lower than that of whites. It is thus apparent that the low aggregate rate of nursing-home utilization among blacks is not due to the pattern of their location but rather to forces that operate in most states and in the states which account for 98.5 percent of all black elderly.

Two plausible explanations together probably explain this phenomenon. First, it is possible that the stronger survival of the extended multigenerational family among blacks causes their families to more frequently take care of their impaired elderly. Second, there may be considerable institutionalized and individual racism in the operation of nursing homes and the public programs that finance care. This may make the probability of nursing-home use by blacks lower than that of whites even where they are identically disposed to use such care.

Research Needs

Several problems of current utilization of institutional care by the elderly can be observed directly. For instance, examination of existing statutes reveals an absence of public programs to finance long-term chronic care of any kind for lower-middle-income elderly and reveals restrictive clauses that inhibit or prevent the utilization of home care.[10] The severity and consequences of other program problems, however, are most efficiently studied through the analysis both of utilization data and of data produced by normative population studies.

For example, as we have seen from the previous section, the poor are disproportionately represented in nursing-home populations. Analysis of the socioeconomic characteristics of populations inappropriately placed in nursing homes should reveal whether such overrepresentation is due to a greater incidence of impairments among the poor, to a care system that is particularly biased toward nursing homes in its treatment of the poor, or to the impoverishment of persons that can result from costly placement in nursing homes. Similarly, analyses of the incidence, by income class, of the unmet care needs of the elderly in the community can aid in identifying the

---

Sources for Table 8: U.S. Bureau of the Census, *1970 Census of Population, General Population Characteristics, U.S. Summary,* PC(1)-B1, Table 62, and *1970 Census of Population, Persons in Institutions and Other Group Quarters,* PC(2)-E4, Table 36.

extent to which community needs can be met with expanded resources under the existing organization of supply and the extent to which supply organization must also be manipulated. Finally, analyses of inter-state variations in the misplacement of persons and care deficiencies among elderly in the community can shed light on numerous issues. Two examples are considered here: if some states have disproportion-ately fewer inappropriate placements and low unmet community care needs, an examination of socioeco-nomic and program characteristics of those states designed to identify causes would be in order. Ana-lyses of utilization data should also reveal whether states that now make relatively limited use of nursing homes and mental hospitals do so by providing com-munity alternatives or by simply neglecting care.

Although the studies mentioned would be based on data developed in normative studies, similar ques-tions could also be addressed through cross-sectional multivariate analysis of the influence of social and economic population characteristics, state social-ser-vice funding, nursing-home reimbursement rates, and other variables on the utilization of mental hospitals, nursing homes, and other forms of chronic care by the elderly.

Projections of utilization. Many problems in the financing and provision of long-term chronic care for the elderly are widely recognized, even though the magnitude and distribution of such impacts is poorly understood. Recognition of the problems, however, has stimulated the generation of numerous proposals for major changes in the chronic care system.[11] Not surprisingly, at this stage, major program proposals are unaccompanied by estimates of their expected costs or the distribution of their expected benefits, even though it is impossible to select rationally among competing proposals without such estimates.

Projections of utilization of different care settings and services under alternative, long-term care pro-grams obviously are the foundation for cost estimates and thus are a priority research need. It is difficult here, however, to go beyond this simple assertion of importance because the research required for utiliza-tion projections depends on the particular program at issue. Consider, for illustrative purposes, changes in the chronic care system designed to eliminate two problems identified earlier.

1. The long-term chronic care of low-income el-derly persons in nursing homes and intermediate care facilities is now financed by Medicaid, whereas the care of such persons residing in their own, relatives', and boarding homes is financed out of Supplemental Security Income and social-services funds. It is often argued that these arrangements result in excessive reliance on nursing homes, mental hospitals, and in-termediate care facilities to the neglect of the home care option. Restoration of an appropriate utilization pattern might be sought through adjustments of Med-icaid to facilitate the funding of home care, or through the consolidation of all chronic care pro-grams serving low-income impaired persons into a single chronic care program, which might be more likely than existing disparate programs to consider the appropriateness, benefits, and costs of different care settings when determining the placement of indi-viduals.

The use which would be made of different settings and services under either of these changes cannot be forecast on the basis of estimates of the unmet needs that the programs are designed to meet. For utiliza-tion will depend on the "supply" characteristics of the program, which include the eligibility standards established, the matching requirements set, and, if expenditure ceilings are established, the level of the ceilings. On the demand side, utilization is likely to be affected, particularly at the home care end of the spectrum, by the propensity of clientele to substitute program services for informally provided services. This may be desirable, since providing care for an impaired elderly person may impose a great burden on a spouse or child, which society may well wish to partially or completely relieve. But the possible sub-stitution of program care for informal care is an important consideration that must obviously be rec-ognized in any projection of utilization.

2. The potentially enormous financial burdens of chronic care for elderly persons whose incomes ex-ceed Supplementary Security Income eligibility levels now fall on the impaired individuals unless the level of their care payments makes them eligible for Medic-aid. The financial and other problems that this creates could be alleviated in numerous ways. Medicare might be modified to cover long-term chronic care, or a consolidated chronic care program might set income

eligibility levels higher than those now in effect under Medicaid.

Attempts to project utilization and costs under these and other possible changes in the financing and provision of chronic care are difficult at best. To some degree, forecasts may be based on data and relationships observed in utilization under current programs; for example, utilization of nursing-home care benefits under an altered Medicare program might be forecast using relations observed in the past among Medicaid eligibles. But when the proposed changes involve the extension of coverage to community care, these difficulties are twice-compounded, once because of the substitution issue raised above and once because virtually no broad home care experience exists on which to base forecasts. These comments, then, suggest that the costs and care-utilization impacts of many proposed changes will be predictable only if carefully structured demonstrations (experiments) are established, monitored, and analyzed prior to the implementation of such changes.

NOTES

1. The simplified classifications (of functional competence, service need, and settings and services) used in this diagram are included to illustrate the logical structure of normative estimates and are not intended for actual use. Richer classifications with more categories and more clearly defined categories are explicitly employed, for example, in the work of Hill (1968).

2. The Hill study does not show the transition from levels of functional competence to levels of service and need because the study works throughout with a classification based on physical and mental care needs. We prefer to make that transition explicit in this example since, at least at lower impairments levels, there may be disagreement about an individual's service needs even when there is agreement concerning his or her functional competence.

3. It is apparent that, unless the functional-impairment and service-need classifications are sufficiently detailed to capture all characteristics relevant for placement decisions, different persons listed in the same cell may have different appro-

priate placements. It will then be necessary to supplement the information given by location in a specific matrix cell with individualized information when determining optimal placement.

4. The potential for noncomparability among studies is evident in a recent study (Tobin et al., 1972, p. 129) in which protocols of 10 randomly selected clients on the waiting list to a sectarian home were submitted to 38 judges (board members and professionals) who were asked to consider alternative plans in arriving at recommendations to "admit now," "defer admission," or "not admit." In only 4 of 10 cases did more than 60 percent of the judges agree on which placement was appropriate.

Recommendation for Disposition of Case
(Percentage of Judges)

Client	Admit Now	Defer Admission	Not Admit
1	2	63	34
2	5	53	42
3	21	58	21
4	3	44	53
5	84	3	13
6	0	74	26
7	11	71	18
8	8	50	42
9	16	58	26
10	53	42	5

Within both the Hill and Davis studies care was taken to assure that hypothetical placements made by different participants in the study would be comparable.

5. In an interesting study, Bell (1971) prepared estimates of the utilization and costs of a proposed community care demonstration project, based on questions whose ambiguity illustrates some of the issues discussed in the text.

Survey responses were obtained to questions such as "Could you use help with things like housecleaning? and "About how often do you think you could use this kind of help? With respect to responses to these questions, two issues must be raised. First, which kind of service need concept is represented in the responses of surveyed individuals? It seems reasonable to expect that people responded in terms of their presently unmet needs. However, this is not certain since some individuals may feel that they "could use" programmatic services to replace services they now get from friends or relatives, and others may respond by suggesting the need for services to satsify nonimpairment related needs. Thus the actual meaning of the survey responses are known to refer to unmet needs, but it is not clear that these needs will be expressed in service use when a program is implemented. Once the program is operating, it is quite possible that much informal support would be cut back and that clients would seek satisfaction of a new and larger set of unmet needs.

6. The 102,000 figure in the text is the difference between the number of old people in mental hospitals and the number of old persons who would have been in mental hospitals in 1970 had mental-hospital utilization rates of the elderly remained at their 1960 level. It obviously represents a maximum estimate of the impact that the reduced use of mental hospitals could have had on nursing-home utilization, since some persons who formerly would have entered mental hospitals now remain in the community or enter some form of institution other than a nursing home. Indeed, where strong service programs supported reductions in mental-hospital utilization by the elderly, a majority of those diverted from mental-hospital care did not enter nursing homes (see the discussion of the San Francisco Geriatric Screening Project in Cutler, 1971).

7. This figure is from Table 14, "Findings of the 1970 OAA Study, Part I, Demographic and Program Characteristics," Social and Rehabilitation Service, 1972. For nonmarried persons in 1967, the differential was greater: 16 percent of nonmarried public assistance recipients and 9 percent of nonmarried nonrecipients were in institutions (Murray, 1971).

8. These figures are all derived from figures in Table 7 of Muarry (1971), p. 10.

9. Because reporting practices vary, comparisons between nonwhites and whites are related here to comparisons of blacks and whites. Blacks, however, constitute 91 percent of the nonwhite el-

derly so that their experience should dominate in the nonwhite figures, and should keep broad comparisons from being invalid.

10. See, for example, the direct analysis of the home care aspects of the Medicare and Medicaid legislation in Trager (1972).

11. For example, the Chronicare proposal of the American Nursing Home Association and the personal care organization proposals advanced by the Levinson Gerontological Policy Institute at the Florence Heller School of Social Welfare at Brandeis University.

REFERENCES

Bell, W. G. *Community Care for the Elderly: An Alternative to Institutional Care for Functionally Impaired Low Income Older Persons in Florida*. Tallahassee, Fla: Florida State University, 1971.

Blenkner, M. Environmental change and the aging individual. *Gerontologist*, 1967, *7*, 101–105.

Cutler, D. The San Francisco Project: Complexities and Rewards of Prevention. In *Mental Health Care and the Elderly: Shortcomings in Public Policy*, a Report by the Special Committee on Aging, U.S. Senate, November, 1971.

Davis, J. W., and Gibbon, M. J. An areawide examination of nursing home use, misuses, and nonuse. *American Journal of Public Health*, 1971, *61*, 1146–1155.

Hill, J. G. *Health Care of the Aged Study*. Co-sponsored by the University of Rochester School of Medicine and Dentistry, the Patient Care Planning Council, and the Council of Social Agencies of Rochester and Monroe Counties, Inc., 1968.

Klonoff, H., and Kennedy, M. A comparative study of cognitive functioning in old age. *Journal of Gerontology*, 1966, *21*, 239–243, reported in Kasl, 1972.

Morris, R. *Alternatives to Nursing Home Care*. Prepared for use by the Special Committee on Aging, U.S. Senate, by Staff Specialists at the Levinson Gerontological Policy Institute, Brandeis University, Waltham, Mass., October 1971.

Murray, J. Living arrangements of people aged 65 and older: findings from 1968 survey of the aged. *Social Security Bulletin*, 1971, *34*, 3–14.

National Center for Health Statistics. Xerox of the printer's copy of *Findings of the 1969 Survey of Nursing and Personal Care Homes*.

National Institute of Mental Health, Biometry Branch. Unpublished reference tables on patients in mental health facilities.

_____. *Reference Tables on Patients in Private Mental Hospitals*, Washington, D.C.: Government Printing Office, 1969.

_____. *Veterans with Mental Disorders: 1968–1970*, Washington, D.C.: Government Printing Office.

Riley, M. W., and Foner, A. *Aging and Society*, Vol. I. New York: Russell Sage Foundation, 1968.

Social and Rehabilitation Service. *Findings of the 1970 OAA Study, Part I, Demographic and Program Characteristics*. DHEW Publication No. (SRS) 73-03805, NCSS Report OAA-(70), Washington, D.C.: Government Printing Office, 1972.

Scott, T., and Devereaux, C. P. Relatives' role in the habilitation of elderly psychiatric patients. *Journal of Gerontology*, 1963, *18*, 185–190, reported in Riley and Foner, 1968.

Tobin, S., Hammerman, J., and Rector, V. Preferred disposition of institutionalized aged. *Gerontologist*, 1972, part I, 129–133.

Trager, B. *Home Health Services in the United States*, a report to the Special Committee on Aging, U.S. Senate, April 1972.

U.S. Bureau of the Census (a). *Census of Population: 1960, Final Report, Inmates of Institutions*, PC(2)-8A.

_____ (b). *Census of Population: 1960, Vol. I, Characteristics of the Population*.

_____ (c). *1970 Census of Population, General Population Characteristics, U.S. Summary*, PC(1)-B1.

_____ (d). *1970 Census of Population, Number of Inhabitants, U.S. Summary*, PC(1)-A1.

_____ (e). *1970 Census of Population, Persons in Institutions and Other Group Quarters*, PC(2)-E4.

_____ (f). *Current Population Reports, Population Characteristics, Marital Status and Living Arrangements*, March 1971.

_____ (g). *Projections of the Population of the United States, by Age and Sex, 1970 to 2020*, p-25, No. 470, November 1971.

WILLIAM POLLAK

with the assistance of
JOANNE HILFERTY

William Pollak is on the Senior Research Staff of the Urban Institute, Washington, D.C. Joanne Hilferty was formerly with the Urban Institute, and is currently a graduate student in the Woodrow Wilson School of Public and International Affairs, Princeton University.

Costs of Alternative Care Settings for the Elderly

Information about the costs of providing chronic care to the elderly in different settings is important both as an input to major policy decisions at all levels of government about the direction in which chronic care should move and as one of several considerations in determining the setting most appropriate for the care of individual elderly persons. Nonetheless, accurate information about chronic care costs is rare. A few studies have analyzed the cost of providing care for the elderly in one setting, most notably nursing homes (Ruchlin and Levy, 1972; Skinner and Yett, 1970), but few studies have analyzed the costs of providing care in different settings in a way that permits even qualified cost comparisons across settings. Assertions about costs abound, but these tend to appear in newspapers and other reports prepared by advocates with interest in demonstrating the economy of a particular setting. Such estimates do not provide a suitable basis for making policy decisions.

This general ignorance about the cost of providing chronic care for the elderly results from a scarcity of research on chronic care costs and from the neglect of conceptual issues that inevitably arise when measuring the cost; the impairment levels that clients are assumed to have, the valuations assigned to inputs,

the care quality provided, and the cost concepts employed all significantly affect the measured relative cost of care in various settings. Past cost comparisons have not analyzed these matters nor, in many cases, have they even explicitly indicated the relevant assumptions underlying the cost figures presented.

In this paper, therefore, we analyze significant issues in the development of cost comparisons, present selected data on the cost of providing care in different settings, and discuss research possibilities and priorities. Throughout the paper it is assumed that total social costs should be the initial basis for cost comparisons.[1] These register the full value of what society must sacrifice when care is provided in alternative ways, and are independent of the distribution of the cost burden among different elements of society: clients, family of clients, philanthropic agencies, and federal, state, and local governments. Various components of total social cost (e.g., governmental expenditures) ignore some costs and reflect the distribution as well as the level of cost. Thus home care may be very costly to society if it prevents employment of an employable spouse, although it will appear inexpensive if only government costs are counted because the major portion of the costs of

128

care are absorbed by family. Similarly, day care may be a relatively economical alternative from a social-cost perspective but appear less desirable or more expensive because its costs are borne by government and are visible.

Cost aggregates other than total social costs, such as government costs, nonetheless are of interest and significance for public policy. These costs, however, can be calculated from fully accounted total costs, whereas the reverse is not possible. For persons with no economic resources and no family, governmental and total costs should be the same, assuming no contributions from charitable, nongovernmental sources. For other clients, governmental costs will diverge from the total costs analyzed here, and will diverge differently depending on the setting, the client's financial and family resources, and the detailed characteristics of programs.

Per person, per day costs of care can legitimately serve as the basis for comparisons across settings if the duration of needed care is independent of the setting in which care is provided. If, however, one form of care more effectively rehabilitates and thereby reduces the needed duration of care, cost comparisons based on per day costs will obviously overstate the relative total cost of the more effective form of care.

Finally, the restriction of this paper to the cost side of long-term care represents only a decision about the boundaries of this particular paper, and not that the author thinks costs are more important than other aspects of care or that a setting should be chosen because it is the least-cost setting. Other considerations, including client preferences and care impacts, obviously are important in determining the choice of an appropriate setting. Nonetheless, because costs ought to and will exert influence, a paper that clarifies their behavior is in order.

CONCEPTUAL ISSUES

The measured cost of providing care for elderly persons in any particular setting will depend, given the total social cost of care, on the cost elements that are included and on the valuations applied to inputs used in the production of care. Meaningful comparisons of the costs of providing care in different set-

tings, therefore, require consistency among settings in both the selection of included costs and the valuation of inputs.

The real social cost of providing care for an elderly person in particular settings will depend critically on (1) the client's functional impairments, (2) the family status of the individual, and (3) the quality of the care provided. Furthermore, cost differentials associated with differences in impairments, family status, and care quality will vary among settings. Statements that care in one setting costs one half, two thirds, or twice as much as care in another setting must, therefore, refer either to costs for an individual with particular but unspecified impairments and family status or to the average of care costs for a group of individuals. In either event, such statements provide no information on the influence that impairments, family status, care quality, and other variables have on the relative cost of providing care in different settings.

Identification of both the proportion of elderly most appropriately served in alternative settings and of the most appropriate setting for particular individuals requires information on the relation between costs and impairments, family status, and care quality. Assertions that on average, or for a particular unspecified individual or group of individuals, care costs in one setting bear a specified relation to care costs in another setting cannot, therefore, assist in the making of rational policy decisions.

Comprehensiveness of Cost Categories

Several categories of cost are incurred in supervising, maintaining, and caring for impaired individuals in any setting; these include housing, nutrition, supervision, environmental hygiene, personal care, transportation, recreation, medical care, and miscellaneous. To the extent that this set of cost categories is exhaustive, the total cost of providing care in any setting is the sum of these costs.

The perceived relative costs of providing care in different settings are influenced by the cost categories included in the cost comparisons. For example, if the program cost of nursing-home care is compared with the program cost of day-hospital care, nursing-home care will appear relatively expensive, because the nursing-home cost figure includes the costs from all categories except medical care and possibly miscellaneous, whereas the program cost of a day hospital includes only part of nutrition, environmental hygiene, personal care, leisure, recreation, medical care, and miscellaneous costs, and excludes all housing costs. That is, day-hospital care would appear relatively inexpensive in this naive accounting because of the volume of excluded costs. If all costs were included, the day hospital might appear the more expensive form of care.

An example of this problem arises in Sproat (1972), page 10. In that work, the cost of nursing-home care is compared to the cost of home care for 3,585 elderly persons in Connecticut who are living in institutions but who might be able to live in their own homes if home help services were available. The $6.42 per person, per day cost of nursing-home care is shown to exceed the $5.33 per person, per day cost of providing services to clients in their own homes. However, the nursing-home figure includes housing, nutrition, and other cost categories; the home care figure includes only home aide services. When a minimum figure for maintenance in the home is added to the home care figure (such as the basic Old Age Assistance payment level in Connecticut), the cost of home care rises to $8.75 per person per day and exceeds the cost of nursing-home care.

Completeness of Costs Within Categories

Since many services used by impaired elderly people are provided by philanthropic and public agencies that subsidize service, fees frequently do not reflect full costs. Thus residents of public or philanthropically supplied housing often pay rental fees that do not cover the capital costs of the housing or even the full costs of operating the housing. Yet in determining the total cost of the home care option, the total cost of housing, rather than the rental fee, should be included. Similarly, fees charged by homemaker services (and sometimes even the maximum fee under a graded-to-income fee schedule) frequently understate the total cost of service provision because service is subsidized by United Fund and other contributions. Again, regardless of the propriety of subsidization, the total, rather than after-subsidy, cost of service

should be employed in computing the total cost of providing care in a particular setting.

A related but distinct problem arises in considering foster-family and home care. Both high-quality foster-family and home care require not only the provision of particular services but also the monitoring and management of the program. These administrative costs must be included in calculating total cost.

These points are simple in concept, yet tedious in detail when one attempts to incorporate them in developing cost estimates. They nonetheless must be recognized, and cost comparisons that flagrantly neglect them are likely to be misleading.

Nonmarket or Quasi-Market Inputs

Usually, the social cost of providing a service is fairly accurately measured by the dollar costs incurred in its production. For example, the cost of providing homemaker service includes the salary paid to the homemaker, the prorated cost of administering the program, the travel costs of the homemaker, and the cost of any supplies used in the homemaker's work. If the service were not provided, these inputs could be used elsewhere. Because the prices of inputs reflect the value that the inputs would have in other uses, dollar outlays made to finance any particular service measure the value of what society must sacrifice to provide it.

However, it is apparent that this inaccurately describes the payments made for several inputs used in the production of services for impaired elderly persons. In many instances inputs are used for which no money payments are made; in other instances the money payments understate the value of the inputs in other uses. For example, when services are provided by a spouse, sibling, or other family member, no payment is made, even though the labor of the provider may be highly valued elsewhere. Similarly, when volunteers deliver meals, visit household elderly persons, or provide transportation services, labor that may be valued elsewhere receives no remuneration. Foster families also may fit this discussion. If they are paid, but paid less than the social cost of their contributions, they are analogous to other volunteers who receive payment that understates the cost of their participation.

FIGURE 1
Homemaker services are an important component of a home-care program for older people who might otherwise be insti-tutionalized. (Photo courtesy of the Administration on Aging, U.S.D.H.E.W.)

When comparing the cost of different services or the cost of providing services in different settings, it is social cost that should be the basis for comparisons. Since social costs usually correspond to dollar outlays, this imperative normally does not present a problem. However, because payments to several inputs understate the cost of using them, dollar costs of some important care services will diverge from and understate social costs. In those instances, service costs should be calculated by valuing inputs with "shadow prices" that reflect their social cost, rather than with the zero or other submarket price actually

FIGURE 2
In calculating the costs of home-delivered care, the monetary and time-related contributions of family must be considered. (Photo by Sonny Gottlieb.)

paid. One then must ask what the shadow price should be. Unfortunately, a simple or unambiguous answer cannot be supplied. In its place we offer a discussion of these issues with respect to volunteer labor, foster care of the elderly, and the provision of care services by family members.

Volunteers. The labor of volunteers should be assigned a cost lying somewhere between zero and the market price of a similar category of labor. In spite of the preceding discussion, a plausible argument can be made for the zero-cost extreme. The volunteer, by supplying his services for no remuneration is implicitly stating that the costs of voluntary participation (foregone leisure or alternative paid employment) may be equaled or exceeded by the personal benefits (enjoyment of the activity and/or satisfaction from

benefits received by clients). The net cost of using the volunteer, therefore, may be zero (or even negative!) since what the individual foregoes is compensated for by the benefits received.[2]

Against this reasonable argument for assigning a zero shadow price for voluntary labor may be set two points of particular relevance when one is comparing the costs of providing care in different settings that employ volunteers. First, assuming that volunteers find different voluntary activities equally satisfying, the use of voluntary labor in providing care in one setting (e.g., delivering meals for the homebound) prevents its use in another setting that also uses volunteers (e.g., providing recreation services in a nursing home). That is, although use of volunteer labor by the volunteer sector is "costless," use of that labor in a particular volunteer setting imposes a social cost equal to the value of the volunteer's output in the alternative volunteer activity where it has its greatest value. Since paid workers are usually available at their market price and volunteers are sometimes used in place of paid labor, it is not unreason-

FIGURE 3
Volunteers provide many useful services to older people. There is, however, a social cost to their use, which is estimated to lie somewhere between the cost of a professional service and zero cost. (Photo courtesy of the Administration on Aging, U.S.D.H.E.W.)

able to assume that the maximal value in alternative volunteer work of volunteer labor is the market wage for that class of labor. Expressed differently, unless volunteer labor is assigned such a cost, settings that use much volunteer labor will appear inexpensive even though they impose a high cost by preventing other uses of the volunteer labor. For example, the use of volunteers to deliver meals is not costless because those same volunteers could provide recreation services in a nursing home, evaluate intermediate care facilities, and transport clients to and from restaurants.

This conclusion is reinforced by a second, related issue. Many of the volunteer programs discussed here and elsewhere are programs that may grow from their present rather small scale to major programs. Day care for the elderly and chronic home care for the impaired elderly all are presently small scale but have the potential for major growth. If this does occur, the programs are likely to be increasingly forced to the market for their labor inputs. In that event, cost projections based on the use of zero-cost volunteer labor will give highly misleading impressions.

The wage received by equivalent labor in the market will be assigned to volunteer labor in the cost estimates developed later. We would also argue that this is the most appropriate cost figure to standardize on in future attempts to estimate the total costs of providing care for the elderly where volunteer labor is employed. This conclusion is important and deserves emphasis. If departed from significantly by assigning volunteers a zero or very low price, the undervaluation of volunteer labor will encourage excessive utilization of those care settings and services that now are produced by volunteers and will facilitate the allocation of volunteers to services where they yield less than their maximum value.

Foster families. A family's decision to provide foster care is generally an economic one that takes into account the income and pleasure foster care yields, the costs and pains it imposes, and the housing facilities, family status, and other work and income of the providers. It would therefore seem that payments to foster families, although lower than the market rates for equivalent labor, reflect the social cost of using families' services. This would dictate using actual foster-family payment levels, rather than

a shadow price, in comparing the cost of foster-family care with the cost of care in other settings.

Two considerations, however, suggest rejection of that conclusion. First, there is a great deal of turnover in the provision of foster-family care. This seriously impairs the quality of care provided to elderly people. It also indicates that, although payments may reflect the social cost of providing the unstable care now provided, higher payments would be required to compensate for the social cost of more stable care.

Second, it was argued previously that projections of service cost that assume volunteer inputs were risky because major program expansion was likely to force the utilization of market-priced inputs. This argument does not apply directly to foster-family care, which, by definition, will always be a family function rather than one that employs salaried persons performing narrowly defined tasks. However, if utilization of foster-family care is significantly increased, projections of foster care cost based on current payment levels are likely to err for a different but related reason. Foster care of the elderly now exists on only a small scale. If it were to be greatly expanded, increased payment levels would probably be required to induce a larger number of families to take upon themselves the burdens of caring for an impaired older person. Expansion of foster care would also encounter increased costs if brought into foster care clients whose impairments imposed greater care efforts than those now served.

Foster-family payment levels approximate the social cost of foster-family care when the quantity and stability of care are at their present levels. Current payment levels, however, are inappropriate in forecasting the future budgetary and social cost of foster care if significant expansion or improvement of foster-family care is contemplated, since increased payment levels are then likely to be required. Identification of the cost impact of program expansion requires identification of the supply curve for foster-family services, a research task that is complicated by the virtually universal minimal use of foster families in the provision of care for elderly persons.[3]

Family-provided services. The labor employed by a spouse or other family member in caring for an elderly person should be assigned a shadow price between zero and the wage of equivalent market

FIGURE 4
The senior center is a widely available service in urban areas. It provides well for social needs, but other forms of support will be required for those with health or ambulation deficiencies.

labor. If the person providing care would otherwise be employed, the individual's wages (roughly) represent the cost of the care provided and should be included in the total cost of home care. However, if the person would not otherwise be employed, the labor he or she provides should be assigned a shadow price equal to the value of the activities and enjoyment foregone and the (net) hardships endured because of the demands of caring for a family member. Although this figure is likely to be greater than zero,

it also is likely to be less than the cost of hired labor. Family thus represents an important source of low-cost labor for services, a fact reflected in the present dependence of many elderly people on services provided by relatives. It also is significant for formal programs, which consequently have important roles in training family members to provide better care and care for persons with relatively severe impairments and in supplementing the low-cost services that family can provide.

Determinants of Real Social Costs
of Care

Family status. The real cost of providing care in some settings will be significantly affected by the family status of the individual receiving care and the characteristics of the family. If a family is present, they may provide services in some settings. If services are provided, the shadow price assigned to the family effort will depend on the characteristics of the particular family.

Table 1 illustrates the influence that family status and family characteristics could have on the relative cost of care provided in different settings. The cases and cost figures for these six elderly persons who require almost full-time supervision are illustrative and are not drawn from real programs. In this example, nursing-home care costs $15 per day regardless of the client's family status; however, the cost of personal care in other settings will be significantly affected by the client's family status. If no family is present, the required extensive personal care and supervision costs $40 per day. If a day hospital is available, it may reduce those costs to $30, essentially by permitting the individual to share personal care or health aides with other people. If an employed spouse is present and can provide care during the evening and night, the personal care figure falls to $20. With a day hospital providing care during the day and the spouse providing care during the evening and night, personal care costs total $12. Finally, if a retired spouse is present, personal care costs only $4.

It must be stressed, once again, that the cost figures used here for illustrative purposes *can* demonstrate that the relative costs of providing care in different settings will vary greatly with family status. Since they are not drawn from real programs, however, they cannot accurately depict what those variations will be. If these were real figures, nursing-home care would be the least-cost form of care for an individual with no family, home care would cost more than three times as much, and home care allied with a day hospital would cost twice as much. With an employed spouse present, nursing-home care would still be the least expensive form of care, but home care allied with a day hospital would only cost 50 percent more than nursing-home care and might well possess benefits sufficient to justify the added cost. Finally, with a retired spouse present, home care is the least expensive form of care.

Impairment levels and care quality. Assume for the purposes of the following discussion that accounting problems are accurately handled and that the individual whose care costs are examined has no family and no economic resources and is dependent on public assistance for support. The preceding discussion makes it apparent that the absence of family influences care costs. However, the cost of providing care for an individual in any particular setting will additionally depend both on the individual's impairments and the quality of care provided. As a consequence, whether home care costs more or less than nursing-home care, and whether each of these costs more or less than foster care, will depend both on the

TABLE 1
Influence of Status on Cost of Care

	Costs per Day (dollars)				
	Housing	*Nutrition*	*Personal Care*	*Misc.*	*Total*
Mrs. Gable: nursing home	$3	$4	$ 6	$2	$15
Miss Butler: home, no family	3	5	40	2	50
Mr. Orlando: home/day hospital, no family	4	3	30	2	39
Mr. Chin: home, spouse employed	2	3	20	1	26
Mrs. Johnson: home/day hospital, spouse employed	3	4	12	4	23
Mrs. Davis: home, spouse retired	2	3	4	2	11

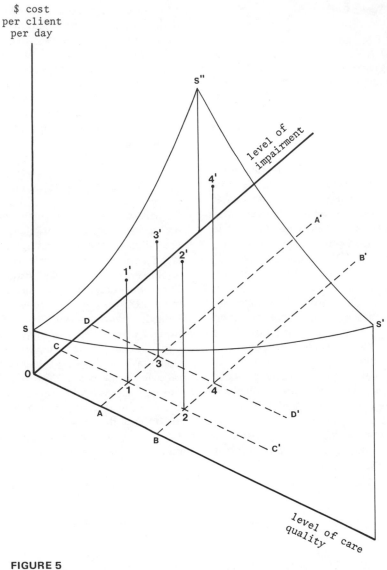

FIGURE 5
Cost of care in a particular setting.

impairment of the individual and the quality of care provided in the settings whose costs are compared. Although this logic may appear obvious, assertions that one or another form of care is "least expensive" disregard its significance when they fail to specify the quality of care provided and the level of impairments

treated. The following pages expand upon these points.

Cost of care in a particular setting. The three-dimensional graph of Figure 5 concisely illustrates the influence that impairment levels and care quality have on the cost of providing care in a particular setting and makes evident the error of speaking of *a* cost of care.[4]

The lines AA', BB', CC', and DD' are all drawn on the bottom, or floor, plane of a three-dimensional graph depicting hypothetical care costs in one setting, for example, care provided in the home. Points in that plane, such as 1, 2, 3, and 4, each represent a level of care quality and a level of impairment. Thus point 1 refers to care of quality *OA* provided to people with impairments of severity *OC*. Point 3 refers to care of the same quality provided to people with impairments of severity *OD,* and so on. The height of the "flag poles" (1, 1'; 2, 2'; etc.) indicates the cost of providing care of the quality and impairment level represented by the points in the plane from which they rise. The surface *SS'S"*, which is drawn through the tops of all the flagpoles, indicates the cost of providing care of all possible quality levels to people with varying degrees of functional impairment. By looking at the surface, it is thus possible to identify, for example, the cost of providing care of level *OA* to a person with impairment *OC* (1, 1') and to tell by how much costs would be increased if care quality were raised to *OB* (2, 2'–1, 1'), or if *OA* care were provided to individuals with *OD* impairments (3, 3'), or if higher-quality care were provided to persons with more severe impairments (4, 4').

A similar diagram could be drawn for each setting in which care can be provided. Although the precise

shape of the surface *SS'S"* would vary from setting to setting, its general character would be retained. That is, the surface would rise as impairment levels and care quality increased, reflecting the fact that both the provision of higher-quality care and the provision of care to more severely impaired persons generally increase costs.

Impairment levels and care costs in two settings. If care quality is held at a level such as *OA* in Figure 5, the relationship between care costs and impairment levels derived from that figure can be expressed as a line on a two-dimensional graph, such as that of Figure 6, where the cost of providing home care is plotted against the level of impairment of the person receiving care.[5] Such a graph is useful because it facilitates the comparison of care costs in different settings. Thus Figure 7 superimposes on the curve of Figure 6 a curve illustrating the hypothetical cost of providing care in a second setting, a nursing home.

Although the specific shapes of these curves are hypothetical, the point they illustrate is not. It is certain both that care costs vary with the impairments of clients and that the way in which they vary differs among settings. Specifically, it seems highly probable that home care costs will rise more with increasing impairments than do institutional care costs. This is likely because care services and supervision, which constitute an increasing share of costs in all settings as disabilities increase, can be shared and

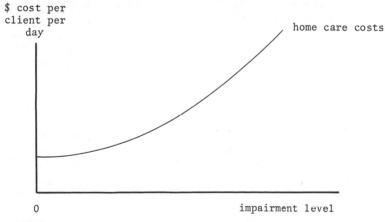

FIGURE 6
Cost of home care.

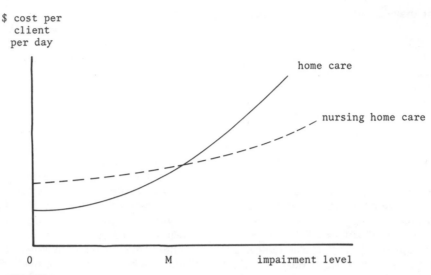

FIGURE 7
Cost of home and nursing home care.

distributed more efficiently in a group setting than when individuals reside in their own homes. As a consequence, it is very likely that home care which is relatively inexpensive over some range of impairment will be relatively expensive over a different range of impairments.[6] For example, in Figure 7 those individuals with impairments less severe than *M* can be cared for at lower cost at home than in a nursing home, whereas nursing-home care would be less costly than home care for those individuals with more severe impairments. This point is important and its implications for "deinstitutionalization" will be considered momentarily. Here it is useful to reintroduce matters lost in the transition from three to two dimensions.

Specifically, it is important to note that the nursing-home cost curve of Figure 7 is drawn on the assumption of a particular quality of nursing-home care and that the same holds for the home care cost curve. The surface *SS'S''* of Figure 5 also illustrates that, had higher-quality care been assumed for either or both settings, the corresponding cost curves on the two-dimensional graphs would have been higher, and *M* would probably have been located at a different impairment level.

In any cost comparisons based on real-world data these same points will be raised, although they may

not be raised explicitly. We have already emphasized that, because care costs vary with impairments, citation of a single care-cost figure must refer either to an assumed impairment level or an average of impairment levels. Similarly, care-cost figures must assume a quality of care, and it is instructive to consider what this is likely to be. For example, if care costs in managing Supplementary Security Income (SSI) recipients are the basis for comparisons, the care quality "assumed" for home care will be that level which is enabled by the outlay levels of the Supplemental Security Income payment and social-services program. On the other hand, the quality "assumed" for nursing homes will be the quality of care enabled by the Medicaid program reimbursement levels. If these levels are different, it is apparent that the impression of the relative costs of different forms of care would be different, and that a care form dubbed relatively inexpensive might be made to appear costly. For example, if Supplemental Security Income payment levels were higher, home care would appear more expensive at all impairment levels, and if Medicaid nursing-home reimbursement levels were lower, nursing-home care would appear less expensive at all impairment levels, even though the basic underlying facts of care costs would be unchanged.[7]

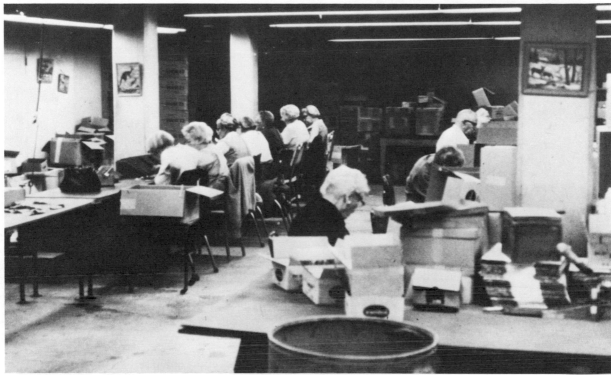

FIGURE 8
Institutional quality is difficult to define, but it clearly is enhanced by enriching programs such as this sheltered workshop. (Photo by Thomas Byerts.)

Both Supplemental Security Income payment levels and nursing-home reimbursement levels are the result of administrative decisions that vary greatly among and within states. There is little reason to expect any kind of parity in the quality of care for persons cared for in different settings under public programs. This is not to say that parity of care in different settings must be attained in the making of cost comparisons, for in fact parity of care across settings is exceedingly difficult to define. Rather, it is to stress once again that the picture given by real-world cost comparisons is heavily influenced by these relative quality matters, which, therefore, deserve explicit recognition and attention.

Readers and viewers of the mass media are familiar with the very real inhumanities and dangers of our worst nursing homes. They may, therefore, conclude that home care must be the setting of choice if it also is less expensive. That conclusion, however, neglects corresponding inhumanities that can be inflicted by inadequate housing and other basics of home care affordable under Old Age Assistance in many states. In more prosaic terms, it is likely that the housing of many Supplemental Security Income recipients would not come close to satisfying the hygienic, safety, and other standards established even in inadequate nursing-home regulations. If, in fact, examination supported this view and revealed home care to be of lower quality than nursing-home care, a comparison of costs that corrected for quality differences would be less favorable to home care than a typical cost comparison based on unadjusted program outlays.[8]

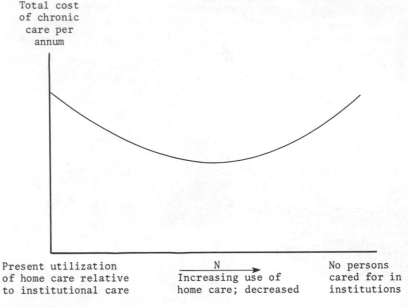

Total cost
of chronic
care per
annum

Present utilization	N	No persons
of home care relative	Increasing use of	cared for in
to institutional care	home care; decreased	institutions

FIGURE 9
Total cost of chronic care for a fixed population.

Deinstitutionalization and the total cost of chronic care. One final point can be made concisely using Figure 7 and the related graph of Figure 9. Deinstitutionalization of persons with impairments less severe than *M,* either by removing them from institutions or by diverting them to home care before institutionalization, will reduce the costs of their care. But since there are institutionalized persons with impairments more severe than *M,* a major program of deinstitutionalization would ultimately draw in persons whose care was more expensive outside than inside institutions. This point is made graphically by the curve of Figure 9, which shows how the total cost of providing chronic care to a fixed number of impaired elderly persons varies as the share of persons cared for at home increases.[9] The curve initially falls with increasing deinstitutionalization as persons who are less expensively cared for in the community are shifted out of nursing homes and mental hospitals. Deinstitutionalization beyond *N,* however, will increase total costs, because it requires the provision of community care to persons who, because of their impairments and/or family situation, are less expen-

sively served in the group setting from which they are removed.

The basic U shape of this curve is, we think, unarguable. However, in spite of the popularity of the deinstitutionalization concept, no information is available about the location of *N* to indicate the point beyond which further deinstitutionalization would raise rather than reduce total care costs. Nor is anything known about the slope of the total cost curve that shows the marginal (per client) costs (or cost reductions) associated with deinstitutionalization beyond *N,* if that is desired independent of its cost significance. These are very central concerns that should be investigated in subsequent research.

CONCLUSIONS

The cost of providing care for chronically impaired elderly people in virtually every setting will be influenced by the level of their functional impairments and the quality of care provided. The cost of care in most community settings (home, day care, and even congregate living) will additionally be influenced by the availability and cost of services that are provided by family members. Increased use of settings that use specialized inputs (e.g., foster-family care) also may increase costs to the degree that higher payment levels are required to induce greater participation. Since these cost influences act differently on the cost of providing care in different settings, it is evident both that no one setting is least expensive for all individuals and that the cost of providing care in one setting, when compared with cost in another setting, is not fixed but will depend on the following variables: client impairment levels, care quality, available family support, and utilization levels.

It is often argued that present and future chronic care costs can be reduced by providing care for persons who, under present arrangements, are or would be institutionalized. This is undoubtedly true for institutionalized persons whose impairments are not major and/or who have family to assist in the provision of community care. Efforts should obviously be made to capture these potential economies where they exist and do not conflict with the interests of clients. However, little evidence exists with which to identify the levels of functional impairments at which home care (using family and/or formally provided services, supplemented by day care and day hospitals), foster care, and congregate housing are most economical for persons with and without family support. Nor is information available about the share of presently institutionalized persons who could be served less expensively in other settings.

The policy significance to the Administration on Aging and other federal agencies of expanded and improved comparative data on chronic care costs gives immediacy to the need for cost research. Throughout, and particularly at the community care end of the spectrum, it is important that analyses explicitly include the real-cost variables discussed above: impairment levels, family support, and care quality. The measurement issues considered early in the paper also must be recognized. Substantive positions on several of these were advanced in the text. Regardless of the positions accepted, however, it is equally important that efforts be made to develop and adopt standardized criteria so that comparisons among studies are not distorted by the inclusion of different cost categories and the utilization of differ-

ent valuation procedures. The need for comparability among cost studies and the prospective application of cost data in analysis of the distribution of impaired elderly by optimal placements dictate and reinforce recommendations that a standardized classification of functional impairments be developed. In some instances, cost analyses can draw data from existing care programs, but where untried alternatives are considered, demonstrations will have to be mounted to generate data on costs and effectiveness. Obviously, when this is done, data should be collected that will enable analysis of the particular cost issues addressed in a manner consistent with normal accounting standards and the economic-accounting standards which result from the resolution of valuation and other issues addressed in this paper.

Acknowledgments

A number of people have contributed to the development of this paper. We would like to thank Jeffrey Koshel and Jerry Turem, who read and suggested improvements on earlier drafts. In addition, we are indebted to Janet Kelly, Maryland Commission on Aging; Jeannette Miller, Model City Senior Center, Washington, D.C.; Fred Ray, Intake Division, Department of Human Resources, District of Columbia; George Roby, Social Services Division, Department of Human Resources, District of Columbia; Lillian Teitelbaum and Ruby Van Croft, Visiting Nursing Association, Washington, D.C.; and Josephine Bandell, Homemaker Services of the National Capital Area, Inc., who took time from their busy schedules to discuss the services that their programs provide for the aged.

NOTES

1. Throughout the paper, "cost" refers to the per person, per day (or month) cost of care rather than the total cost of a program. The cost of a care program will obviously depend both on per person, per day costs and on the number of client days of care provided. The latter variable is important and is among the topics considered in the previous paper.
2. This discussion relates to the valuation of volunteer labor. The total cost of volunteer programs

will exceed the cost of the volunteer labor they employ because volunteers may require training and because volunteer programs generally are supervised and administered by paid workers.

3. Foster families are used on a larger scale to provide care for children, and study of supply responses in that area might be more feasible. Families providing care for children, however, may be different in their behavioral responses from those who would provide care for older people. Conclusions reached in studying foster-family supply to children may, therefore, not be transferable to the elderly.

4. This discussion neglects the influence that group-setting scale and ownership type have on costs because those are intrasetting cost issues which have been given central attention in cost studies to date (Ruchlin and Levy, 1972; Skinner and Yett, 1970). They, obviously, also must be included in cross-setting cost comparisons.

5. The line on this graph is the intersection of surface $SS'S''$ with a vertical plane through AA' in Figure 8.

6. These curves are hypothetical but reflect the likelihood that increasing impairments increase the cost of home care more than the cost of nursing-home care.

7. Although not mentioned in the text, care at any given level will use inputs in different proportions when provided in different settings. For example,

home care may use relatively more labor than nursing-home care at the same level since labor is shared more efficiently in the latter setting. Consequently, because relative input prices vary geographically, the relative cost of care in different settings will also vary geographically.

8. "Quality" here refers to the physical characteristics of settings and services rather than to the impact of the setting on the client's well-being.

9. Home care, as a share of all care provided to a fixed number of people, can be increased by removing people from institutions or, over a longer period of time, by caring for an increased share of newly impaired people in their homes.

REFERENCES

Ruchlin, H. S., and Levy, S. Nursing home cost analysis: a case study. *Inquiry,* 1972, *9,* 3–15.

Skinner, D. E., and Yett, D. E. Estimation of cost functions for health services: the nursing home case. Paper presented at the 40th annual conference of the Southern Economic Association, November 12, 1970.

Sproat, B. J. Three approaches to estimating need for personal care services. Levinson Gerontological Policy Institute, Brandeis University, Waltham, Mass., June 1972.

PART III

PROGRAMMATIC ASPECTS
OF HOUSING FOR THE ELDERLY

M. POWELL LAWTON

Introduction

M. Powell Lawton is Director of Behavioral Research at the Phildelphia Geriatric Center, Philadelphia, Pennsylvania.

In Part III the discussion on housing is continued in more specific detail. These papers are particularly relevant to local planners wishing to build for a specific elderly group in a particular location, as contrasted with the more general, policy-oriented issues discussed in Part II. The papers here accept as a basic premise that many of the housing programs discussed in Part II have been successful enough to warrant their continuation, with improvements to be sought at various stages of planning. There is, indeed, impressive evidence that the impact of such housing on the elderly is generally favorable (Carp, 1966; Lipman, 1968; Sherman, 1973; Lawton and Cohen, 1974). On the other hand, we know relatively little so far about the extent to which planned housing differs in quality and what distinguishes a good housing environment from a poor one. The material in each successive paper can be viewed as representing a rough temporal order along the path of planning housing for the elderly, raising issues that need to be considered in the search for high-quality housing.

Clearly, the first question the planner must ask is whether his area has a housing need. Many communities have accepted the need for new housing as

self-evident. In an area of great deprivation, this a priori decision is likely to be correct. One cannot be so sanguine where there has already been considerable construction of such units, where one contemplates building for a financially independent group with many options, and especially when one must make long-range plans for an entire community.

In "Estimating Housing Need," David Sears offers a method for removing some of the guesswork involved in such planning. He identifies the most basic parameters that must be considered in estimating a community's housing need and makes very clear the assumptions that must be made in applying the model. It is a working model, complete with computer software. On the other hand, Sears is just as explicit in pointing out that many key elements of a complete model are missing simply because data do not exist on such matters as personal preference, personal competence, or the extrahousing network of community social services. To anticipate, in Part IV, Glassman, Tell, Larrivee, and Helland provide a model for estimating more general service needs; they suggest the use of national sample data, where available, to fill in gaps in local data on personal factors that might be included in the model. In any case, with a baseline estimate of need such as that given by application of Sears's model, the planner should be able to provide the local housing authority or potential housing sponsor with a more accurate beginning point. Given our current minimal state of knowledge, the basic estimate of community housing need would then have to be adjusted in a rational, rather than empirical, manner to take account of such factors as the expected age range, marital status, level of health, socioeconomic status, and personal preferences of the particular subgroup that the housing might potentially serve.

Once the community's housing needs have been estimated, the planner must turn to a consideration of the personal needs, preferences, and potential sources of satisfaction in older people's housing choices.

James Mathieu draws attention to the tremendous diversity among those called "old." No amount of planning and design can create a single environment that is beneficial across the board. Kahana's concept of "person-environment congruence" reminds us that an ideal ecological niche requires the appropriate matching of personal need to an environment in which the exercise of the need is likely to be fulfilling. Options in housing types, locations, service programs, and neighbors are called for. Diversity also is a factor over time: the 65-year-old person's needs may be quite different 10 years later, and his needs may be very different following a move. Mathieu then discusses several prototypic types of communities for older people and ends with a discussion of specific aspects of housing that may enter into their preferences and satisfactions with housing.

In one way, Mathieu's paper raises more questions than it answers. In particular, we are still uncertain as to how this general information on housing satisfaction can be utilized in planning better housing; how can we hope to put such information into a revision of Sears's model, for example? And can we be certain that what people say they prefer is necessarily what is "best" for them in terms of its effect on more basic aspects of well-being? Finally, even if people prefer what is "best" for them, how do we balance the needs of older tenants with the potential effect of racial, subcultural, or age homogeneity on the larger

society? Clearly, the last word on these important issues is very distant.

The point along the planning process represented by M. Powell Lawton's paper on age homogeneity and heterogeneity is less fixed in time than some of the others. Very probably, the basic decision regarding whether one will build for the elderly alone is often made in advance of the choice of a site. On the other hand, a particular location for housing may be more suitable for an age-homogeneous than for an age-heterogeneous population. The many issues raised by Lawton relating to age mixing are clearly relevant to the personal preferences discussed by Mathieu. Although the decision about age mixing has to be made by each local sponsor, the most important point of Lawton's presentation is that the older person in fact has very little choice about whether his good new housing should include younger people. The mandate of many federally assisted programs is that old people *must* live with other old people. That is, inexpensive, good-quality, planned housing for older people has been constructed primarily in age-segregated contexts. Thus, in fact, personal needs and preferences are ignored in many localities where the *only* good inexpensive housing is in federally assisted age-segregated projects.

Once these basic planning decisions are made, the important question becomes the selection of a site for the housing from the point of view of the social and psychological needs of the tenants. Sandra Howell's paper demonstrates the sheer idiocy of the capricious manner in which many sites have been chosen. Despite the strong rationale for careful consideration of broad life-style factors, sites continue to be chosen, as Newcomer pointed out in Part II, by developers and politicians on the basis of availability alone. One hopes that some impact on such practices will be made by Howell's showing of how frequently a careful analysis of need can lead to locational decisions that are in themselves behavior-supporting.

Occasionally, the planner may have the luxury of being involved in what Alvin Zelver calls a "total neighborhood" on a scale larger than a single site or the usual suburban development. His concern is especially with the maintenance of the older population's sense of integration with the remainder of the community. Siting decisions related to those discussed by Howell are considered, but he adds concern with site plans and structural aspects of the building and dwelling unit. It is especially meaningful to see such reasoning come from one whose experience has been as a developer rather than as a social scientist. Zelver's ecological reasoning reinforces that of Howell, yet the pathway toward his conclusions is the direct experience of having seen his own concepts take form in bricks and mortar.

New communities do not represent a point on the time continuum of planning. However, if anything, they must concern themselves even more deeply with all the steps in the process. Mary Wylie deals with the very specialized situation of the new community as defined in the Housing Act of 1968. The scale of the new community may be even larger than Zelver's "total neighborhood." The complexities of such planning are correspondingly greater. Wylie rightly makes us aware that realistic limitations, both economic and human, will inevitably limit the extent to which the ideal can be attained. At the time of writing, the plans for new communities, especially those that consider the specific and shared needs of the elderly, are more impressive than the results. However, the many planning facets covered by Wylie that relate to both generation-specific and universal needs ought to constitute a major impetus to their consideration by all future planners of new communities.

These topics only sketch with broadest strokes a complete housing planning process. Although Howell mentions the desirability of involving potential elderly tenants in the process, a considerably expanded treatment of this subject is necessary to do it justice. Other basic predesign decisions must be made, such as how diverse the environment should be in terms of race, health, or economic level. Much more can be said about design of competence-inducing public spaces or dwelling units. The service package has not been discussed nor the all-important relationship between management and tenant well-being. Omission is due only to problems of space (see Gelwicks and Newcomer, 1974, and Lawton, 1975, for fuller discussions of some of these issues).

REFERENCES

Carp, F. M. *A future for the aged*. Austin, Tex.: University of Texas Press, 1966.

Gelwicks, L. E., and Newcomer, R. J. *Planning Environments for the Elderly*. Washington, D.C.: National Council on the Aging, 1974.

Lawton, M. P. *Planning and Managing Housing for the Elderly*. New York: Wiley, 1975.

_____, and Cohen, J. The generality of housing impact on the wellbeing of older people. *Journal of Gerontology*, 1974, *29*, 194–204.

Lipman, A. Public housing and attitudinal adjustment in old age: comparative study. *Journal of Geriatric Psychiatry*, 1968, *2*, 88–101.

Sherman, S. R. Housing environment for the well elderly: scope and impact. Paper presented at the annual meeting of the Gerontological Society, Miami Beach, November 1973.

DAVID W. SEARS

*David W. Sears is an Assistant Professor of Regional
Planning in the Department of Landscape Architecture and Regional Planning, the University of Massachusetts, Amherst.*

Estimating Housing Need

Housing is one of the most important problems
faced by low- and moderate-income elderly households. Part of the solution to this problem is the
provision of housing sponsored by and, in many
cases, to some extent subsidized by public agencies.
The planning, construction, and management of housing for the elderly is a rather complex process, in
which a number of alternatives should be evaluated in
terms of several relevant criteria. The focus here is
on one aspect of this process: the determination of
the need for elderly housing in a city or town.

The technique to be described was developed for
the New York State Urban Development Corporation
(UDC) and has been used to determine the need for
elderly housing in every city and town in New York
State. This technique may be useful for those involved in the planning and construction of elderly
housing.

ELDERLY HOUSING DECISION-MAKING
PROCESS

An overview of the elderly housing decision-making process is presented in Figure 1. This process may,

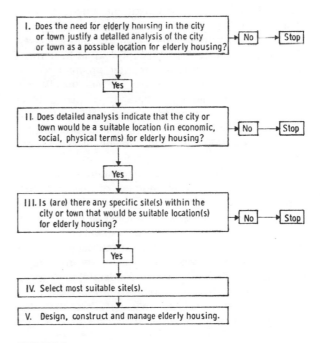

FIGURE 1
The elderly housing decision-making process: an overview.

in some cases, be carried out by a single organization, such as UDC, or it may be fragmented among several organizations, each responsible for certain parts of the process. The process would be carried out for each city and town of interest.

The need for elderly housing is first determined (step I). If the need is sufficient to justify further analysis, the city or town is examined in detail (in terms of economic, social, and physical factors) as a potential location for elderly housing (step II). If the city or town as a whole is found to be suitable, a search for one or more specific suitable sites for elderly housing is undertaken (step III). If such a site or sites are found, the most suitable are selected (step IV). Finally, the design, construction, and management of elderly housing occurs (step V).

NEED-DETERMINATION TECHNIQUE

The need-determination techniques (in conjunction with the screening procedure described later) is intended to carry out step I of the elderly housing decision-making process. The details of the technique are somewhat more complex than the following overview might indicate. In fact, complexities have made it worthwhile to write a computer program to perform the operations involved. Given the limited amount of required input data, it is then a fairly simple task to compute the need for elderly housing in each city and town of an entire state (there are more than 1,000 cities and towns in New York State).

The basic elements of the technique are outlined in Figure 2. In step I, the number of low- and moderate-income elderly households in the city or town in 1970 is determined. In step 1 and all ensuing steps the total set of low- and moderate-income elderly households is subdivided into six mutually exclusive and exhaustive subsets: the divisions are in terms of household income (low versus moderate) and household size (one, two, or three or more persons). For purposes of this analysis, an elderly household has been defined as a household where the head is aged 62 or over. The definitions of low and moderate income are designed to reflect as accurately as possible local housing authority definitions.

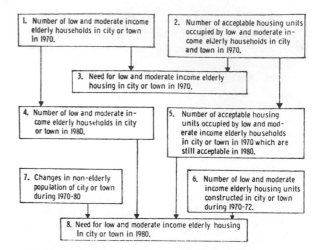

FIGURE 2
Elderly housing need-determination technique.

In step 2, the number of acceptable housing units occupied by elderly households in 1970 is determined. Acceptable housing units are defined as those with all plumbing facilities. Of course, this definition of "acceptable" is not very good (it is probably more accurate in rural areas than in urban areas). Its main virtue is that it is operationally simple. It has, however, severe drawbacks: many units with all plumbing facilities may be quite unacceptable in terms of widely accepted housing objectives, such as the provision of a healthy, secure, and satisfying living environment. In step 3, the need for low- and moderate-income elderly housing in the city or town in 1970 is computed by subtracting the results of step 2 from the results of step 1.

Steps 4 through 8 are intended to project the 1970 need to 1980. In step 4, an estimate is made of the number of low- and moderate-income elderly households in the city or town in 1980. This estimate uses, as its starting point, age-specific population projections for counties (in New York State, these projections are available from the Office of Planning Services).

The estimation procedure assumes that the 1980 population of the county which is aged 62 and over will be distributed among the cities and towns of the county in the same proportion that the population

FIGURE 3
Lack of basic plumbing facilities was the only indicator of substandard housing used in the 1970 Census. There are clearly many other features that may render a housing unit "inadequate." (Photo courtesy of Administration on Aging, U.S.D.H.E.W.)

aged 52 and over was distributed in 1970. In addition, the estimation procedure assumes that, within the town or city, the ratio of the number of elderly households of a particular type (e.g., one-person, low-income household) to the total number of elderly households is the same in 1980 as in 1970. Using the population projections and these two assumptions, the estimate can be made.

In step 5, an estimate is made of the number of acceptable housing units occupied by elderly households in 1970 that will still be acceptable in 1980. The annual rate of movement of housing units from acceptable to unacceptable is assumed to be 0.0075; using this rate, the estimate is computed. This annual rate (0.0075) is essentially "pulled out of the air." Obviously, there is room for improvement here. Also, a minor inconsistency should be noted. Although acceptable units were defined as those with all plumbing facilities, here (in applying this rate) a broader definition of "acceptable" is assumed; that is, it is not maintained that 0.0075 of all units with plumbing lose their plumbing each year. Rather, it is maintained (or hypothesized) that 0.0075 of all "healthy, secure, and satisfying" units become unhealthy and/ or insecure and/or unsatisfying annually.

In step 6, the number of low- and moderate-income elderly housing units constructed since 1970 (during 1970–1972) is determined. Data from the U.S. Department of Housing and Urban Development and the New York State Division of Housing and Community Renewal, as well as data from UDC, were used in this step.

In step 7, the change (over the 1970–1980 period) in the ratio of the elderly population to the nonelderly adult population is projected. It is assumed that this change will have an impact on the availability of housing for the elderly. (For instance, if the ratio increases over the period, i.e., if the elderly population is unchanged and the nonelderly population decreases, it is assumed that additional housing for the elderly will become available.)

Finally, in step 8, using input from steps 4 through 7, the need for low- and moderate-income elderly housing in the city or town in 1980 is computed. The basic need is computed by subtracting the results of steps 5 and 6 from the result of step 4. This basic need is then slightly modified by the result of step 7.

SCREENING PROCEDURE

The need-determination technique just described may be useful by itself. However, the determination of the need for elderly housing in each city and town of the area under consideration (e.g., state or region) does not fully complete step 1 of the elderly housing decision-making process (see Figure 1). It is not sufficient to know only the amount of elderly housing needed in each community; it also must be determined whether or not that amount is sufficient to justify a detailed analysis of that city or town.

The screening procedure has two purposes: (1) the procedure determines which cities and towns in the area have sufficient need for elderly housing to justify detailed analysis, and (2) a tentative program (number of elderly housing units) is computed for each city and town in the area. The screening procedure is presented in Figure 4.

Steps 8 through 11 are input requirements for the procedure. The community's need (N) for low- and moderate-income elderly housing in 1980 (step 8) is computed as described previously.

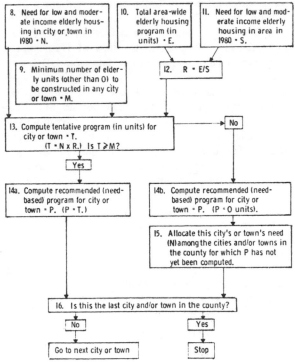

FIGURE 4
Screening procedure for the cities and towns of a county.

The screening procedure requires specification of the minimum number (M) of units (other than 0) to be constructed in any city or town (step 9). Why is there a minimum number? Certain overhead costs associated with the construction of housing (e.g., legal and architectural fees, contract administration costs) do not decrease significantly when the size of a housing project drops below 100 units (many of these overhead costs are nearly as high for a 10-unit housing project as for a 100-unit project). However, even if an agency determines (as UDC has) that its minimum-sized project is 100 units, this does not necessarily mean that the minimum number of elderly units in a project must be 100 (many of UDC's projects, for instance, contain 10 percent elderly units and 90 percent nonelderly units). Because M can be set at any value by the user, the UDC criterion of a minimum project size of 100 does not have to be accepted to use this procedure.

The screening procedure requires, in addition, specification of the total (in housing units) elderly housing program (E) to be undertaken over a specified time interval (the program period) within the area under consideration (step 10). In the case of UDC, E is the total number of elderly housing units that will be constructed by UDC within New York State over, roughly, the next 5 to 7 years. It may be difficult to determine the values of M and/or E. If so, the screening procedure can be followed more than once. For instance, for UDC the procedure was applied four separate times to the cities and towns of New York State, each time varying the values of M and/or E.

The need for low- and moderate-income elderly housing in the specified area in 1980 (S) is merely the sum of the needs of all cities and towns in the area (step 11). The areawide program–need ratio (R) is simply E/S (step 12). For UDC, S is the statewide need and R is the statewide program–need ratio.

In step 13, a tentative program (T) for the city or town is computed, stated in terms of the number of housing units to be constructed: $T = N \times R$. Were it not for the minimum project size constraint, the recommended (need-based) program in each city or town would be proportional to that community's need. For example, if the UDC statewide program–need ratio (R) was 0.10, in each city or town in the state the recommended (need-based) program would be 10 percent of the community's need. However, the minimum project size constraint does exist; thus the question "Is $T \geqslant M$?" is asked. If the answer is yes (i.e., if the tentative program is greater than or equal to the specified number of units to be constructed in any city or town) the recommended (need-based) program (P) is set equal to T (step 14a). But, if the answer is no, the recommended (need-based) program (P) is 0 units (i.e., the city or town has been screened out of further consideration in the elderly housing decision-making process) (step 14b).

The need of a city or town that is screened out in this manner is not necessarily forgotten or ignored, however. This need is, instead, reallocated among the communities in the county for which P has not yet been computed (step 15). The portion of the need reallocated to each is proportional to that community's need.

This screening procedure is flexible with respect to the reallocation of the need of a screened-out city or town. The need can be reallocated among other communities in the county (as the procedure was used in New York State for UDC), or the need can be reallocated among any other group of communities (e.g., those within a multicounty region). However, in Figure 4 it is assumed that reallocation takes place on a countywide basis.

LIMITATIONS OF THE NEED-DETERMINATION TECHNIQUE AND SCREENING PROCEDURE

The limitations of the elderly housing need-determination technique and screening procedure can be divided into three categories: (1) questions that are outside the scope of the elderly housing decision-making process, (2) questions that are within the boundaries of the process, but must be answered in steps II through V (questions of these two types are not answered, or even dealt with, by the need-determination technique and screening procedure), and (3) questions that are within the scope of step I of the elderly housing decision-making process for which the answers may be inadequate in some respect. Some of the major limitations falling into each of the three categories are discussed next.

Numerous questions are simply beyond the bound-

aries of the elderly housing decision-making process, at least as that process is described in Figure 1. For instance, should elderly housing be constructed? Should housing be viewed as a means or an end? How are the housing needs of the elderly interrelated with their health, transportation, employment, and recreation needs? How should resources be allocated among programs aimed at meeting these needs? To what extent, in what instances, could a multiple-objective program be designed for the elderly? What process should be used in the planning, construction, and management of housing? And, specifically, to what degree should residents and/or potential residents participate in this process?

In what ways might elderly housing programs of two or more agencies, operating in the same geographic area, be coordinated? Should elderly housing units be located in age-segregated projects or in age-integrated projects? To what extent should the housing that is constructed be standardized? Different two-person elderly households may have different housing needs. For instance, compare a husband–wife household with a mother–daughter household, or compare a nondisabled household with one that has a physically disabled member. Should these households all be provided essentially the same standard unit or not? Questions such as these were not considered in the need-determination technique and screening procedure.

The second category of limitations includes questions that must be considered in steps II through V of the elderly housing decision-making process. For instance, step II must include a detailed economic analysis of the city or town as a possible location for elderly housing. In step III, factors that are important in selecting a specific site for elderly housing must be considered. For example, how important is access from elderly housing to commercial, recreation, and health facilities? How important is the character of the neighborhood in which elderly housing is located?

In the third category of limitations the potential inadequacies result from the need to make certain assumptions in order to carry out the need-determination technique and screening procedure. Although it would be cumbersome to spell out each of these assumptions, the three major attributes of the assumptions are pointed out here.

First, some 1970 data required by the technique are not available for any counties, cities, or towns. In these cases, it was generally assumed that the relationships that hold for the United States as a whole will hold in specific communities.

Second, some 1970 data may be available for some cities and towns, but not for all. This was true in the case of the analysis carried out for UDC. The approach to this problem was fairly straightforward. Each community in the state was placed in one of 16 types. Data were obtained for a sample of each type. It was then assumed that the relationships that hold for the sample municipalities of a particular type hold for all communities of that type.

Third, certain 1980 estimates are required by the need-determination technique. It was generally assumed, in these cases, that the relationships which held in 1970 would hold in 1980. For instance, in New York State, age-specific 1980 population projections for each county were available. To compute the number of persons in town i aged 65 and over in 1980, it is assumed that

$$\frac{\text{number aged 55+ in town } i \text{ in 1970}}{\text{number aged 55+ in county in 1970}}$$

$$= \frac{\text{number aged 65+ in town } i \text{ in 1980}}{\text{number aged 65+ in county in 1980}}$$

The contraints of limited information have necessitated the use of several assumptions that may be, to some extent, erroneous. Nevertheless, it seems appropriate to characterize the results of the need-determination technique and screening procedure as reasonably accurate.

Three additional characteristics of the need-determination technique should be mentioned. First, the technique will encourage the location of elderly housing close to the elderly population. Thus, in general, if the location of elderly housing construction is based on the use of this technique, few elderly persons would be forced to move to another city or town in order to reside in the housing. Certainly, those who would have to move (e.g., those living in a small rural town) could move to a relatively nearby city or town.

Second, the technique ignores all household char-

acteristics except income and household size. Other characteristics could have been recognized, for instance, race or ethnicity, sex of the elderly person, age (there may be some real differences between the housing needed by a 65-year-old and that needed by an 85-year-old), and functional ability (e.g., disabled or not). However, such additional characteristics were intentionally omitted, as the small amount of additional accuracy likely to be produced did not seem warranted by the significant increase in the complexity of the technique required.

Third, the technique is designed only to compute the need for housing for the elderly with low and moderate incomes. This was an explicit decision, made with UDC's needs in mind. The technique could be modified, however, to include additional household characteristics and/or to compute middle- and upper-income elderly housing needs.

NEED FOR ELDERLY HOUSING IN NEW YORK STATE: A BRIEF ANALYSIS

The need-determination technique has been applied to every city and town in New York State. The need for low- and moderate-income elderly housing in the state in 1980 was estimated to be almost 150,000 units. By county, the need varied from rural upstate Chenango County, which needed 185 units, to Queens County in New York City, which needed 23,629 units. The need varied from several communities that needed 0 units to the city of Buffalo, which needed 3,940 units, and the town of Hempstead, which needed 5,265 units.

As might be expected, the need is generally concentrated in metropolitan areas. However, it is not necessarily true that the greater a city's elderly population the greater is its need for elderly housing. For example, some large cities, owing to considerable construction of elderly housing through 1972, had very small needs (the city of Rochester needed 0 units; the city of Albany needed 136 units). Over 80 percent of the need for low- and moderate-income elderly housing in the state was a need for low-income units. In fact, almost one half of the total need was concentrated in the low-income, one-person household category.

As indicated, the determination of need is followed by a screening procedure that (1) identifies those communities with sufficient need to justify detailed analysis, and (2) computes a tentative program for each. In the case of UDC, the necessity of the screening procedure is clear. Given a total statewide need of nearly 150,000 units, if UDC's elderly housing construction program over the next 5 to 7 years is somewhere within the range of 15,000 to 25,000 units, UDC can hope to meet considerably less than 20 percent of the state's need. Therefore, a choice is necessary: where will UDC build its elderly units?

CONCLUSIONS

The elderly housing need-determination technique and the screening procedure have certain limitations. Nevertheless, these limitations do not seem to be severe and the results obtained using the technique and procedure will be reasonably accurate. A major virtue of the technique is its simplicity. In addition, it relies completly on readily available or easily obtainable data. Yet the technique is certainly more sophisticated and useful than an extremely simple rule-of-thumb calculation of need, such as "the elderly housing need in a town = 0.10 × the elderly population of a town." The use of a computer means that the computations required by the need-determination technique and screening procedure can be carried out fairly quickly and cheaply, even for a large area such as a state.

The need-determination technique can be used for the analysis of elderly housing need in a single city or town, or for the analysis of need in each community in a geographic area such as a county, region, or state. The screening procedure can be used in any case where there is an allocation of elderly housing units to be made among two or more communities. Thus either the technique, the procedure, or both may be useful for a variety of agencies concerned about elderly housing.

Finally, it should be strongly stated that construction of elderly housing, although important, is certainly not sufficient. To improve the residential environment of the elderly, an array of programmatic approaches is needed. An overall strategy might include rehabilitation of existing housing units, housing allowances, and provision and/or improvement of neighborhood social services (e.g., police protection, recreation, garbage collection). An overall housing strategy for the elderly (whether the strategy is nationwide or communitywide in scope) should attempt to increase the range of choice of available residential environments and to provide acceptable housing for each individual elderly person.

Acknowledgments

While the author retains full responsibility for any shortcomings of this paper, he has relied heavily upon the advice and assistance of others, especially James Wiley and Maybelle Taylor Bennett, both of the New York State Urban Development Corporation (UDC). Most of this chapter was published as, "Elderly Housing: a Need Determination Technique," *Gerontologist*, 1974, *14*, 182–187.

JAMES T. MATHIEU

James T. Mathieu is an Assistant Professor of Sociology and Director of Urban Studies at Loyola Marymount University, Los Angeles, California.

Housing Preferences and Satisfactions

Housing is an indispensable essential for human life. Programs of nutrition, physical and mental health care, income maintenance, transportation, retraining for employment, involvement as a volunteer, continuing education, and leisure and recreational activities are ineffective if the "right home," in terms of location, adequacy, and safety, is not available at reasonable cost for the older adult.

Housing is unique in the degree to which its quality can enhance or diminish the well-being of individuals and families and in its impact on the structure and health of neighborhoods and communities. Unlike other essentials of living, inadequate housing cannot be hidden. Poor housing is apparent to any observer, blighting not only the individual, but the community as well. Housing, furthermore, is costly; a house is the most expensive single item most individuals ever buy, and expenditures for shelter take the largest part of the budget of most families, including the older adult. In 1973, the U.S. Department of Labor estimated that the elderly in our nation spend almost 38 percent of their budget on housing and 37 percent on food, leaving approximately 25 percent for all other needs.

The quality of housing has improved substantially in the past 10 to 20 years, yet today a high proportion of housing units for the elderly are still substandard. As Morton Leeds (1973, p. 14), Special Assistant for the Elderly to the Assistant Secretary for Housing Management, Department of Housing and Urban Development, writes:

I should like to describe the quality of the housing stock, to tell you how bad it really is. For the poor elderly who make up a large minority of the elderly, poor housing is typical. As an example: of 17 Southern states that have one half the total population on old age assistance, 68 percent of the elderly population in these States have housing with major defects. Thus, 15 percent have no running water whatever, 30 percent no inside flush toilets (the American criterion), 40 percent have no bath or shower with hot water, 46 percent have some rooms that are not heated in winter. That's a high percentage. There is an even more fascinating fact, that, among black occupants inadequacy rates are three to ten times that of white occupants.

If the definition of substandard housing were enlarged to include dwelling units with inadequate space, unsafe heating and electrical equipment, and poor and dangerous neighborhood facilities and environment, the proportion that would not meet the goal of a sound house in a suitable living environment would be considerably enlarged.

Moreover, there is little knowledge of what types of houses and what arrangements of houses in communities best serve individual needs and social demands. Isolated studies have been made of the effect of poor housing and slum conditions both upon individual physical and mental health and on the promotion of socially pathological behavior. Yet in spite of the development of more sophisticated approaches in recent years, there are great gaps in our understanding of these relationships. The effect upon the well-being of presumably normal individuals and families of different types of housing that are generally assumed to be adequate remains almost completely unexplored.

OVERVIEW OF PREFERENCES AND SATISFACTIONS

An understanding of the basic preferences and satisfactions of the living arrangements of older persons is crucial in a consideration of their general welfare. As Sheldon (1958, p. 89) notes:

The implications of low income for the widow who lives with a prosperous son-in-law, for example, are quite different from the implications for a widow without Social Security benefits, and without a home inherited from her husband. Likewise, for an isolated elderly person, problems of adequate care in case of disability and illness are quite different from similar problems of an elderly person who is part of a family group. If one is concerned with improving the living arrangements of older persons, then for those living in the homes of relatives it may become a matter of improving the general adequacy of housing; for older persons maintaining their own households, a matter of special programs for such persons; and for older people with no family connections, possibly some venture into planning ideal congregate living quarters. In short, the ways in which the needs of elderly people can be met are determined to a great extent by their living arrangements.

These living arrangements have consequences not only in terms of physical welfare, but also in regard to the older person's social and psychological well-being. Critical to this well-being is satisfaction with one's housing situation. The questions asked in this area must be centered not only around "How much housing is needed for the elderly?" and "Where is the 'best' or 'ideal' location to develop housing for older persons?" but also "Do older persons prefer or desire to live in that location? and "Does the housing of a particular older person fit or match his particular life style?"

The first set of inquiries concerns the quantity of housing (number of units and most economical location) for older adults in general; the second set is focused on the quality of life of the specific older person. It could be demonstrated that those who plan for and study the housing of the elderly are considerably more interested in dealing with the first set of factors, whereas the older people themselves are more sensitive to the latter set of concerns. An illustration of this is the language of the Post-White House Conference on Aging Reports entitled *Toward a New Attitude on Aging* (April, 1973). The lead recommendation of the delegates in the Housing Section of the 1971 White House Conference was "a call for a fixed proportion of all government funds—federal, state, and local—to be earmarked for housing for the elderly."

To this concrete, sensitive call for funds by the delegates, the majority of whom were older persons, the federal administration's response was as follows:

The President reiterated his support for this goal in his message on Community Development in March 1973: "While we believe that some of our housing programs have failed and should be replaced, we should never waiver in our commitment."

The President also stated: "In pursuing our goal of decent homes for all Americans, we know that better means are needed—that the old and wasteful programs, programs which have already obligated the taxpayer to payments between $63 billion and $95 billion during the next 40 years, are not the answer."

"One of my highest domestic priorities this year will be the development of new policies that will provide aid to the genuinely needy families and eliminate waste."

"A major housing study is now underway within the government, under the direction of my Counsellor for Community Development. Within the next six months, I intend to submit to the Congress my policy recommendations in this field, based upon the results of that study" (*Toward a New Attitude on Aging*, p. 45).

One could sense in this lead recommendation for a fixed proportion of all government funds that housing for the elderly, just as for any age group in our society, is more than "a roof over their heads." Where a person lives bespeaks his social status, which he shares with others who occupy the same neighborhood regardless of age. The neighborhood and house are the locale of informal, intimate social relations and family life. To be a neighbor, therefore, for the older person is more valued than to be a fellow member of a club or organization, or a member of a select group of retirees, or a co-volunteer. But at the same time, no one can be said to be fully independent unless he can freely choose where he will live and be satisfied with that choice. The opportunity to compete for housing of one's choice is crucial to the single most important personal attribute of the older adult, independence, and to his psychological well-being. As can be seen, this recommendation focusing on a specified proportion of money for housing addresses the issue of the quality of life of the older person.

The response to this lead recommendation needs no comment except to say that the basic philosophy of the decision makers at all levels tends to be one that "knows what is best for old people." The decision-makers' inquiries and responses continue to be oriented around the quantity of housing for older adults.

RATIONALE

No attempt will be made to treat exhaustively the infinitude of preferences in housing by the older population. These preferences and demands tend to be more varied for the older populations than for any population along the life cycle. We shall, rather, try to illuminate some of the diverse findings and proposals in the literature in regard to these housing preferences and satisfactions. The goal is less one of seeking out "ideal housing" for the elderly than of highlighting the rich diversity potentially available.

At the outset, a glaring misconception in regard to housing preferences and satisfactions of older adults must be exposed. These are not static conditions, once expressed forever to remain the same. The dynamic of change must always be kept in focus. What tends to be valid at one point in time, at one given age, or under particular circumstances may not hold for subsequent time, ages, or situations. This is so not only because of the diversity of the older adult population, but also because individuals', neighborhoods', and society's values and priorities all change. In most of the research literature, this phenomenon tends to be overlooked.

For analytical purposes, preferences and satisfactions will be examined from three perspectives: (1) goodness of fit between the individual and his housing, (2) the quality of the neighborhood environment, and (3) environmental change and attitudes toward change. We shall then describe how these three factors influence the choice of housing alternatives for older adults in indigenous communities (natural environs) and in separated communities (constructed or reconstructed retirement environs). Specific consideration of the housing options for older adults in indigenous and separated communities will form the succeeding section of this paper. Finally, we shall review the results of a number of studies in regard to the specific relative importance of various considerations in choice of housing by older people.

GOODNESS-OF-FIT FACTORS

Although the housing of 21 million older people may be considered one major national problem of the 1970s, it must also be seen in the light of 21 million individual problems. The definition of goodness of fit, for working purposes, has to do with the question, "Does the housing of a particular older person match his particular life style?"

Some persons prefer to live in retirement communities or age-segregated "projects" (see Rosow, 1967; Sherman, 1972; Hamovitch and Peterson, 1969; Jacobs, 1974). Others prefer to live in close proximity to younger families, that is, in age-integrated settings. Some prefer apartment living; others are not satisfied without a separate house with a lawn and garden to care for. Some want to live downtown with ready access to community activities and services; others would prefer to live on the edge of town or in the suburbs. Some are sufficiently vigorous and autonomous to live completely independently; others require only a small amount of help if they live in easily maintained housing. Still others require medical care and supervision in varying institutional settings.

Goodness of fit has several facets: (1) the closeness of the person's actual living situation to what he considers the ideal living situation, (2) the extent to which his living situation allows the pursuit of self-fulfilling activity, and (3) the extent to which his actual living situation is congruent with his personally

FIGURE 1
One's past experience dictates preference for living style in planned housing. These low-rise units are both beautiful and consistent with the previous life styles of many older people. (William Kessler & Associates, architects. Photo by Balthazar Korab.)

articulated needs and preferences. Goodness of fit must be examined from at least three perspectives: (1) the professional perspective, the view of planners, decision makers, and administrators, (2) the social perspective, the view of social and community workers, advocates, and the general public, and (3) the subjective perspective, the view of the elderly themselves.

The *professional perspective* considers factors like design, political desirability, cost–benefit factors, and occupancy rate as they relate to optimal matching of the older person to his housing. These are important aspects of the total housing problem, and in this light housing of the elderly must be seen as merely one aspect of the wider social problem of housing.

The *social perspective* assumes a positive value for the individual in social activity. The environment that provides for maximum individuality and privacy must at the same time be capable of fostering social relationships. This view assumes that the older person should be encouraged to keep up his former contacts in the community. If and when this is no longer

FIGURE 2
If old friendships cannot be maintained, the opportunity to make new friends must be provided. (Photo by Linz, courtesy of Leisure Technology Corporation.)

possible, opportunities must be provided to make new contacts. Preferably, the social living space and the home unit would encourage a continued, two-way relationship between the older person and the outside world. As Carp (1973, p. 409) says, "For some individuals the primary difficulty is physically substandard or inconvenient housing. For others the frustration is primarily social, involving isolation from old friends and contemporaries, or intergeneration conflict and the feeling of imposing or being imposed upon."

The *subjective perspective* considers the matching process from the view of the elderly persons themselves—their expressed preferences, needs, and demands as well as their fulfillment, satisfaction, and morale. This view stresses the dynamic that good housing results in direct enrichment of the individual's life.

The conventional wisdom of the housing professional tends to see housing for the elderly as an end in itself (good housing), rather than a means to a different end (well-being and life satisfaction). Public policy explicitly supports quality housing, "a decent home and suitable living environment for every American family," as a justifiable private and public concern. All too often this never gets translated into a "direct payoff" for the older adult. However, quality housing for the elderly can be a "win/win" situation for the public as well as the older person. The Wright Institute Report (1973, p. 6), concerning the longitudinal study of Carp's Victoria Plaza follow-up (Carp, 1966), one of the first elderly public housing sites in the country, states:

If the eight-year follow-up confirms the one-year findings, the results may show that public subsidy of housing for the aged benefits the taxpayers as well as the elderly, for she points out: "inability to locate or finance or maintain appropriate housing often results in institutional care—which the individual does not need, and which is costly to society." Moreover, the results of moving from socially isolated, decrepit housing to the public housing resulted in better physical health, less senility, more activity, sociability, self-esteem and satisfaction with life. These findings imply, if they are confirmed by the long-term follow-up, that subsidy of public housing for the elderly can be a financially rewarding investment of public funds, as well as, literally, a life-saving and life-enchancing benefit for the elderly.

It seems that two segments of our older population may have achieved a need-fulfilling match of housing and preferences: (1) affluent, high-status, activity-oriented individuals in the expensive retirement communities, and (2) the severely handicapped, chronically ill older persons in high-quality, total-care institutions. But proper matching of housing and preference has been much more difficult to achieve between these two extremes.

NEIGHBORHOOD ENVIRONMENT FACTORS

In no area of life are the housing disadvantages of the elderly more visible than in relation to the neighborhood environment. Environmental planning for the elderly, whether in urban or rural settings, often has a narrow focus upon housing itself. Emphasis has frequently been centered on the "personal life space" of the elderly rather than on the broader aspect of their "social life space." Birren (1969, p. 168) points to this when he says that

Cities are primarily social organizations and secondarily collections of concrete, steel, and wooden structures. That structure follows function can be lost sight of, and the social "creaking and cracking" now heard in cities suggests that planners thought that function was determined by structure. The concept of life space should be used in discussing the position of the aged in cities since it implies more of the functional relations of living than does the more limited structural term housing. The city should provide the largest possible life space for its residents, a life space that contains many options and the opportunity to express individual differences in needs and desires.

The neighborhood environment is crucial for the older adult. The majority live in central cities and transitional communities that represent high risk to

FIGURE 3
Despite the negative press reports they sometimes receive, the separated retirement community for the affluent elderly appears to afford a satisfying life style for its occupants. (Photo by Powell Lawton.)

property, health (air pollution, heavy traffic, etc.), and personal safety, as well as being sometimes lacking in the ability to satisfy daily needs such as for services, activities, and recreation. Carp (1970) reports that every applicant to the public housing project that she studied said that his present housing situation was "not good." Her tenants stressed the unattractive, inconvenient, and unsafe situations of their homes and the isolation or stressful interpersonal relationships of their communities.

Rainwater's (1972) interpretation of why so many persons living in substandard housing and high-risk environments tend to be satisfied is significant for us when thinking about the older person. He found that a large proportion were satisfied with their housing situations and living arrangements, even though they were substandard in the eyes of housing professionals, if the housing provided security against the most blatant threats. These persons are likely to economize on housing in order to have money available to meet other basic needs. They will make efforts to maintain the interior of the dwelling unit, but will not have much interest in improving the basic housing structure because of the cost. With respect to the immediate outside world, their main emphasis is on the availability of a satisfying peer group life, with having neighbors who are similar (Peterson et al., 1973; Rosow, 1967), and with maintaining relationships with familiar people. There is also a concern that the neighborhood be "respectable," defined mainly in the negative as an absence of "crumbs and bums"—a familiar attitude to anyone who has experienced prolonged contact or done extensive interviewing of older adults in the urban setting.

But couple substandard housing with what Rainwater calls "blatant threats from the environment" and the consequence is an astronomical rise in housing dissatisfaction (Mathieu and Sundeen, 1974). Rainwater lists the sources of danger in the home and environs as shown in Table 1. The original intent of this classification scheme was to demonstrate what standards are used by the lower class in our society to evaluate their housing. A high proportion of the elderly live in these types of areas and the enumerated dangers involve physical, mental, and interpersonal consequences for them. The table describes very pointedly the living-environment problems of many older adults.

Anthropologist Margaret Clark (1971, p. 61–62), reflecting on her own research in some of the urban settings in our society, says that

Since the average income of the vast majority of these city elderly is woefully low, we need hardly guess at the substandard housing facilities they are forced to live in. Researchers who visit the inner-city poor in their dwellings encounter the most indescribable squalor of flea-bag hotels, rodent-infested flop-houses, and filthy tenements.... The aged themselves would be the first to agree with these impressions. In fact, these deplorable housing conditions rank first in their com-

TABLE 1
Sources of Danger

Nonhuman	Human
Rats and other vermin	Violence to self and possessions
Poisons	Assault
Fire and burning	Fighting and beating
Freezing and cold	Rape
Poor plumbing	Objects thrown or dropped
Dangerous electrical wiring	Stealing
Trash (broken glass, cans, etc.)	Verbal hostility, shaming, exploitation
Insufficiently protected heights	Own family
Other aspects of poorly designed	Neighbors
or deteriorated structures	Caretakers
(e.g., thin walls)	Outsiders
Cost of dwelling	Attractive alternatives that wean oneself
	or valued others away from a stable life

Source: Rainwater (1972).

plaints about their lot (despite their equally pressing needs in nutrition), and the search for better living quarters is ceaseless. Subjects talk at length about elaborate searches and "deals"—listening for the dropped cues that might lead to a favorable move, hunting perpetually for slightly better living arrangements. Sometimes, blessedly, they come, but not without some further cost in loss of social contacts or old proximity to needed services.

As significant as these nonhuman dangers are for the elderly, the fear and anxiety generated by the human sources of danger are even more pervasive. Behavioral changes, such as not going out at night, isolation, barring doors and windows, and obtaining weapons, are significant where the threat of violence exists (Mathieu and Sundeen, 1974).

One of the most prevalent reasons for housing choice given by those moving into retirement projects and communities is that the crime, violence, and threats of the former neighborhood became more than they could cope with physically or psychologically. "We moved here because our neighborhood and community was changing and this place offered the safety and security we needed and wanted" is a frequent response to the question, "Why did you move into this place?"

ENVIRONMENTAL CHANGE AND ATTITUDES TOWARD CHANGE

Change is anxiety-producing at any age, but acutely so in old age. For the older person it requires the marshaling of his inner and outer resources in order to find a new equilibrium providing him with safety and security. He is likely to have less resilience in finding new ways of locating and using resources and dealing with unfamiliar personal and social life space. It is very important to understand the extent to which his lack of resilience interferes with his functioning in a "move" situation, which in turn leads to dissatisfaction with his new surroundings.

Some dependency is essential to personal comfort, and in old age it stems partly from a realistic appraisal of the losses, economic, physical, mental, familial and social, or from the less conscious conviction that one does not have much to lose. This has been the circumstance of a rather substantial proportion of our older adults—the destitute, blacks, chicanos, and all other deprived groups in our society (Harrington, 1962).

In addition, the elderly's anxiety may be heightened because they face rapid and monumental changes and are often deprived of satisfactions at the very time their strength is waning. When the present is frustrating, the future uncertain and frightening, realities often grim, and death a closer eventuality, a turning to immediate satisfactions is not surprising, even though a move in the long run may provide greater satisfaction.

From the research in regard to the impact of environmental change on the elderly, a rough conclusion might be that major environmental changes by the older adult can lead to physical deterioration and noxious psychological effects, but more precision is required to disentangle the conditions under which this occurs and what types of personal life styles enable more rapid adjustment.

Lieberman's (1969) review of the significant early literature on this subject points to five determinants of reactions to change: (1) whether the change is voluntary or involuntary on the part of the older person, (2) the adequacy of preparation for the change, (3) the attitudes of the elderly toward institutionalization and change in general, (4) physical and mental health, and (5) the types of environment from which and to which the change is made.

Some elderly deny feebleness and ill health and make unrealistic, sometimes hazardous, attempts at independence. Others dwell on the body and its maladies, adhere to fixed routines, or become irritable with new ways and ideas. Still others become authoritarian and competitive with children or grandchildren in desperate efforts to cling to or reassert their former status in the family.

It is important to be sensitive to the elderly person's cultural background—his uniqueness and the impact of his life style upon his immediate world view and living arrangements. As we understand the interrelatedness of his cultural background and his social, medical, and emotional preferences, we can further assess his adaptive capacity and ultimately the potential satisfactions to be gained from a move (Lowenthal et al., 1967; Clark and Anderson, 1967; Peterson et al., 1973).

It has been estimated that approximately one fourth of the elderly in the United States is foreign-born, with unique ethnic and cultural adjustment problems. Along with the majority of other older adults in our society, they tend to be clustered in the decaying cores of our cities and towns. The elderly therefore are harder hit than any other age group by urban renewal and other community redevelopment programs (Birren, 1969). Because the elderly have low incomes their concentration in such transitional communities is particularly great.

FIGURE 4
The change from a home in the indigenous community to planned housing may be the beginning of an opportunity to learn new skills or resume old interests. (Photo courtesy of Administration on Aging, U.S.D.H.E.W.)

Removal from these neighborhoods is fraught with personal, social, and cultural problems. Even if their housing is substandard, it is nevertheless situated in an area of long-standing associations, familiarity, and sometimes richness of resources, the values of which are attractive to the elderly. If the elderly must be relocated, the psychological cost must not be disregarded.

These cultural factors, if understood and dealt with by those initiating the change, might be translated into prescriptions for favorable change. As an example, the value placed on intimate, face-to-face relationships by many ethnics and cultures could be a positive, integrative force in a community for the interdependence of the elderly. The looking in on and after each other and mutual help could be encouraged and dramatically helpful.

HOUSING ALTERNATIVES AND OPTIONS IN INDIGENOUS COMMUNITIES AND IN SEPARATED COMMUNITIES

For the past 20 to 25 years we have been systematically gathering extensive data on the living arrangements and housing of the older population in our society and have endeavored to ascertain the housing and environmental preferences and satisfactions of this particular age group. One effort of investigation has sought to describe and explain the housing of the elderly in the indigenous communities where the majority dwell. A second effort has investigated alternative options of separated retirement communities. A subtype of the latter has investigated the impact of age-segregated housing projects that are not otherwise separated but embedded in indigenous communities. Carp's (1966) study of Victoria Plaza and Lawton and Cohen's (1974) investigation are examples.

This dichotomous thrust toward both indigenous and separated housing led to the following Post-White House Conference (1973, p. 49) statement:

In order to maximize the range of housing choices, the Housing Section recommended four categories of residentially oriented settings which relate to the different service requirements of elderly persons:
    —long term care facilities for the sick;
    —facilities with limited medical, food, and homemaker services;

FIGURE 5
Whatever else may be said about age-segregated housing, it is usually possible to pick up a shuffleboard game there. The wall in the background is well chosen, both to discourage the casual entry of outsiders and as wind protection. (Photo courtesy of Administration on Aging, U.S.D.H.E.W.)

—congregate housing which would provide food and personal service, but not medical care services;
—housing for wholly independent living with recreational and activity programs.

The Sections on Housing, and Facilities, Programs, and Services, and other Sections and Special Concerns Sessions recognized that another, and for many, the preferable alternative to any type of congregate living, is for older people to remain in their own homes or to live with their children or relatives.

INDIGENOUS COMMUNITIES (NATURAL ENVIRONS)

About 26 percent of older persons live alone or with nonrelatives (Weg, 1974), approximately another 5 percent are institutionalized, and about 7 percent live with their children or other adult relatives. There is pervasive evidence that many older persons who live with adult children and other relatives would prefer not to. For a great proportion of these people the arrangements cannot help but be unsatisfactory— both for the older adult himself, who has lost the independence and privacy of his own household, and for the children, who must struggle to meet the needs of the elderly parent as well as their own. This event, which risks the loss of self-esteem in return for security and safety, can be very demeaning for the older person.

This realm of independence–dependence is crucial for understanding the preferences and satisfactions of the older adult as a resident in the indigenous community and must always be seen in light of the American dream of "having your own place." "The home" serves the dual purpose of security and stability and of independence. This is reflected in the words of a middle-aged grandmother: "I've lived in an apartment all my life and I'll die in an apartment, but if I only had a home that I could call my own I could go into old age with a feeling of accomplishment, security, and independence."

There is no doubt that "having your own place" is highly functional for the healthy aged, but this does not seem to be the reality for a substantial segment of the population, according to Palmore's analysis of data (1971) from the 1968 Project FIND, the largest survey ever conducted of the needs and characteristics of the aged poor. In this investigation, 50,652 aged persons in 12 lower-income communities across the country representing three density types (urban, rural, and mixed) were interviewed. Twenty-five percent reported not having one or more of the following facilities in their dwelling: electricity, running water, hot water, toilet, indoor bath, cooking stove, or refrigerator. Very little is known concerning rural conditions alone, but one of the few coordinated reports on rural housing of the elderly (Ginzberg et al., 1954, cited in Vivrett, 1960) points out the frequent makeshift, but valiant, efforts being made in rural Iowa. Trailers, lean-to's, and small outbuildings were being used by the older people in their effort to provide separate living accommodations.

In a more recent study of rural communities in the mountain states of Idaho, Montana, and Wyoming (Mathieu, 1973), it was found that of a sample of 115 elderly persons only 31 were satisfied with their present living arrangements and their general life satisfaction was very low.

Home ownership among the elderly is rather high, but according to Clark (1971, p. 61) "Very few of the central city elderly own their own homes. The older citizen is a renter: 70 percent of households in New York City with heads 65 and older rent . . . while four-fifths of the San Francisco sample discussed here . . . were renters. In New York, nearly a fifth of all rental units are occupied by the elderly." This fact is revealing in light of the significant work by Lawton on the elderly residents of the inner city. These investigators reported findings from a sample of indigenous community residents in a slum environment of Philadelphia called Strawberry Mansion (Lawton and Kleban, 1971; Lawton et al., 1971). When compared with three other inner-city groups (a low-income urban group, somewhat less deprived than those from Strawberry Mansion, in Jersey City, a group of residents of Atlantic City who had been accepted for residence in a senior-citizen project, and a group of tenants of a public housing project for the elderly in a high-crime area of Cleveland), Strawberry Mansion residents were overwhelmingly less satisfied with their housing situation, with one exception. The exception was that the Cleveland sample was just as dissatisfied with its neighborhood location as the Strawberry Mansion residents were. The striking difference between these two was the very high degree of satisfaction (73 percent) the Cleveland group expressed with their project, in spite of the high crime locale; by contrast, only 20 percent of the Strawberry Mansion residents were similarly satisfied. Only 9 percent of these liked the neighborhood very much, 81 percent wished to move, and 39 percent had actively looked for a new place to live in the past year.

These, and other revealing findings, such as Gaynes's (1973, p. 7) "the average age of the institutionalized elderly population in public and private homes has increased very rapidly over the course of the last 15 years. The average age of such residents in 1960 was about $74\frac{1}{2}$ years, and the average age on admission was about 71. The average age of residents in homes now is about $84\frac{1}{2}$ years and the average age on admission is in excess of 81," indicate the need for fresh, new, and workable housing alternatives for the aged. An example of the possibilities is in Wilmington, Delaware, where an experimental program is under way to encourage "urban homesteading." Some proportion of the elderly up to about 80 years of age do possess the energy reserves, decision-making capacity, and the ability (with governmental support) to pay back loans for rehabilitation in such a program. The idea of homesteading is to get families to stay or to move back into houses that would be or have been abandoned because of defaulted FHA mortgages. The U.S. Department of Housing and Urban Development has ended up owning tens of thousands of abandoned city dwellings. Under urban homesteading, new owners who agree to live in the house for a period of time and bring it up to local housing codes could purchase the house for a nominal fee—the average has been a couple of dollars in Wilmington. This is the kind of imaginative thinking and planning that may help to alleviate the housing dilemma for the low-income elderly.

Another fact must be kept in mind; most elderly persons' present residence is in the place where they have lived for a major portion of their adult lives. A 1963 Social Security survey of the aged (cited by Birren, 1969) indicated that 80 percent of couples over the age of 62 had lived 10 or more years in their community at the time of the study; the median number of years in the community was 32 and the median residence in the current dwelling was 16 years.

SEPARATED COMMUNITIES

The extent to which older people move to warmer climates upon retirement is vastly overemphasized by the general public. Florida, California, Arizona, and other states with mild climates have many retirement communities, but compared to the 20 million older persons in this age category, the number in such communities is relatively small. The three most populous states, California, New York, and Pennsylvania, account for over one fourth of the older population. Add to these the states of Illinois, Ohio, and Texas, three populous "non-sunshine states," and one has well over 40 percent of the elderly population of our nation (Weg, 1974). Retirement communities tend to be highly visible in our society, but only an estimated 8 percent of elderly persons have both the financial means and the desire to spend their last years in a location other than the one in which they spent their later middle years.

From the very first, the advantages and disadvantages of age-segregated versus age-integrated housing environments for the aged have been discussed. A strong case has been made from research findings in support of age-homogeneous living arrangements (Rosow, 1967; Sherman, 1972, 1973; Peterson, 1965; Peterson et al., 1973; Hamovitch and Peterson, 1969; Carp, 1966, 1973; Jacobs, 1974; and others). The case for age-integrated living arrangements (with the

exception of the project embedded in the indigenous community) has not, on the whole, been subjected to rigorous investigative attempts.

Separated communities refer to any type of communal living arrangements composed primarily or entirely of older persons, whether or not spatially located away from centers of population. Separation in this sense can be either geographical, psychological, or both. The classificatory scheme developed by Kleemeier (cited in Webber and Osterbind, 1961, p. 4) fits this definition and is based on the degree to which communities have congregate, segregated, and institutional living arrangements. They could be classified as follows:

1. Real estate developments (developed and operated on a profit basis).
2. Supervised and planned communities:
   a. Dispersed dwelling communities (non-profit based, as in public housing projects).
   b. Mobile home parks (trailer villages).
   c. Retirement hotels (multiunit and tower apartments).
3. Full care homes and institutions (convalescent and nursing homes).

One of the first studies of the real estate community environment for the retired was by Peterson (1965), who investigated motivations for moving into a retirement community. His findings showed a number of reasons for leaving indigenous communities: loss of friends, restriction from desired activities, loss of family contact, difficulty and bother in maintaining a home, deterioration or change in the indigenous neighborhood (probably one of the strongest motivators of all), and a desire to get away from routine and responsibility were some of the most commonly mentioned.

What positive advantages are there to moving into a retirement community? Good climate and locations, minimal traffic, accessible shopping facilities, abundance of activities, and "the right kind" of neighbors have been mentioned. Along with this is housing per se. Units are proper size, maintenance is provided for, appearance is neat, and the cost is relatively low for those who can afford it. Those moving in are typically middle- to upper-class whites who lived in $30,000 to $70,000 homes that were usually paid for. In selling a home of this value and moving to a

FIGURE 6
The "separated community" is characterized by a high level of activity of its tenants, despite a low level of interaction with the nonaged community. (Photo courtesy of Administration on Aging, U.S.D.H.E.W.)

home that is approximately two thirds its cost (homes in these communities vary in price from $19,000 to $50,000 on the average), the mover is usually left with a substantial gain and now lives in a "country club" surrounding (see the case study in Jacobs, 1974).

Preference and demand for this type of housing environment is very high in the upper-income segment of the elderly population, and housing satisfaction, as reported by most studies, is also extremely high. Those dissatisfied with these housing situations tend to move within the first year (Peterson, 1965).

Carp's study (1966) of a public housing project (age-segregated housing embedded in the indigenous

FIGURE 7
The social advantages of planned housing may not always be obvious. Conversation does occur in lounges like this one, but just as important is the opportunity to observe the traffic coming through the front door. (Photo by Sam Nocella.)

community) revealed that only one resident out of 200 voluntarily moved out of the project in the first 18 months. The most serious housing criticism of the residents was the expressed feeling about the project's risk to their privacy. This shortcoming was in relation to the design of the building itself, particularly the location of large windows facing on galleries and the consequent necessity for draping of windows. Carp (1970, p. 171) relates that the "relocation was deeply and almost unanimously satisfying for the people who moved to Victoria Plaza, and they showed immediate and continuing ability to adapt to its novel geographic, architectural, physical, and social characteristics." The changes consequent to moving to this housing project were obvious in most measures of satisfaction, attitude, life style, and adjustment. They were consistently in the direction away from passivity, seclusiveness, and disengagement.

Two very significant longitudinal studies of residents at selected retirement housing facilities have been made. Peterson, Hamovitch, and Larson's cross-communities study (1973) used eight samples: (1) a coastal retirement community, (2) a desert retirement community, (3) a low-income sample drawn from a Department of Public Social Services subsample and an urban retirement local subsample, (4) denominational high-rise apartments sample comprising white, black, and life-care persons, (5) three trailer park samples, (6) a dispersed housing sample composed of retired members of one labor union,

FIGURE 8
The "separated community" for the economically secure older person typically provides active programming for the relatively independent resident. (Photos by Linz, courtesy of Leisure Technology Corporation, and Powell Lawton.)

(7) a sample of dispersed community residents matched to the retirement community subjects, and (8) those moving out of the retirement community. Sherman's (1972, 1973) analysis of the findings of a 5-year study of a cross-communities project utilized samples from a retirement hotel, a rental village, an apartment tower, a purchase village, a manor village, and a life-care community.

Some generalizations in regard to satisfaction can be made from these comparative analyses:

1. Location is an important variable in determining housing satisfaction, especially in relation to the immediate neighborhood.

2. Design of the housing situation is important, but not crucial.

3. Living in a single dwelling unit tends to be related to high housing satisfaction and morale.

FIGURE 9
This much-used coffee bar is maintained by tenants of the public housing project and open all day. (Photo by Edward Steinfeld.)

4. The higher the socioeconomic position of the tenants, the higher the housing satisfaction.

CONSIDERATIONS IN CHOICE OF HOUSING

The specific relative importance of various considerations in the choice of housing by older people should be of prime importance to anyone involved in community planning for the elderly. Morale and satisfaction, degree of independence, activities engaged in, and social patterns of the elderly are influenced by factors such as climate, transportation, location, safety, nearness to family and relatives, type of neighbors, and accessibility and availability of community facilities, such as food markets, drugstores, shops, parks and recreational centers, churches and temples, and health, medical, welfare, and counseling services.

How important are these various criteria to the older person? In answering this question we shall collate a number of investigations, such as Peterson et al. (1973), Sherman (1972, 1973), Carp (1966), Beyer and Nierstrasz (1967), and Langford (1962).

Beyer and Nierstrasz collated data from 11 West European countries and the United States. Significant similarities and differences are exhibited in considerations in choice of housing by the elderly. Langford's study reported the findings of 5,202 personal interviews supplemented by qualitative data from 39 cases in upstate New York and case records of 13 families who had recently moved to a new suburban housing development in Rochester.

In the United States, with its diverse climatological conditions, climate and weather can be decisive factors in choice of housing, where health and income allow unlimited options, as suggested by the Peterson et al. findings. But Beyer and Nierstrasz (1967, p. 104) state that

> The popular idea that all elderly people want to live in subtropical regions is not borne out by experience. However, some elderly persons want to live in such places; perhaps they belong to the categories of "the truly adventurous as well as those who need a change of climate, who seek out new places," as Mathiasen described them. However, she states that for such settlements there is a strong case for "built-in resources for social contact" (consider, for example, the possible occurrence of ill health, loneliness, homesickness).

Location of housing (urban, suburban, rural) is important, but not critically so. But coupled with socioeconomic class, locational decisions are made such that those with lower incomes choose urban housing locations. Those of middle-income status studied by Peterson et al., expressed a preference for "country living" (suburbs, mountains, or deserts). Just as important as social class is familiarity with the environment.

A strong consideration is the quality of the surrounding neighborhood. The tenants of Victoria Plaza in Carp's study strongly objected to its location near streets that were not safe; the neighborhood did not have "the right kind of people." The characteristics of "the right kind of people" in all the investigations tend to be those of the elderly respondents: similar age, socioeconomic status, religious preference, and, most important, ethnicity and race. The persons in Victoria Plaza expressed a liking for the other residents of the project, but not for the neighbors in the indigenous community. Without exception, every study found that the safety and security of the neighborhood was extremely important.

The single most important feature in choice of housing in the Hamovitch and Peterson (1969) study was proximity to shopping facilities, especially food stores, restaurants, and transportation. Carp's tenants were very critical of being isolated from food stores and inexpensive eating places, while being pleased to be only 1 mile from the downtown shopping district and having a bus stop at the project. But, as Langford suggests, for the aged proximity is a relative matter. Under certain conditions, such as high crime risk, inclement weather, or poor health, even the corner store may be too far away. This is a possible interpretation of the finding by Hamovitch and Peterson that less than one third said it was important to live near relatives or friends ("except one or two good friends"). But Langford (1962, p. 18) reports that

> Desire to be closer to facilities was found to be secondary to desire to be closer to children, with a larger proportion of women than men wanting to be closer to children. The tendency for proximity of people to be of greater concern that proximity of facilities was also found by Rosenmayr and Kockeis who reported that, although the inadequate provision of shops and other facilities in the vicinity was criticized by the aged, the complaint most often expressed was that relatives and friends lived too far away.

Those items ranking low in choice of housing tend to be proximity to libraries, movies, parks, indoor recreational facilities, religious and health facilities, traffic noise level, although noise of children in the neighborhood tends to be a strong negative factor, and privacy from others (privacy meaning to live in circumstances where one may go out of doors without having to pass by neighbors).

CONCLUSIONS

As we have seen, the quality of housing can enhance or diminish the physical, social, and psychological well-being of the older person. Housing in turn has a major impact upon the social organization and health of neighborhoods and communities. Therefore, society's plan for housing its elderly population should include (1) a variety of types of living arrangements, (2) the maximum individual freedom to choose among these options, (3) an income level sufficient to make good housing a reality, and (4) a safe, secure, and resource-rich environment.

REFERENCES

Beyer, G., and Nierstrasz, F. H. J. *Housing the Aged in Western Countries*. New York: American Elsevier, 1967.

Birren, J. E. The aged in cities. *Gerontologist*, 1969, *9*, 163–169.

Carp, F. M. *A Future for the Aged: Victoria Plaza and Its Residents*. Austin, Tex.: University of Texas Press, 1966.

____. The elderly and levels of adaptation to changed surroundings. In L. Pastalan and D. Carson (eds.), *Spatial Behavior of Older People*. Ann Arbor, Mich.: Institute of Gerontology, University of Michigan, 1970.

____. Effects of improved housing on the lives of older people. In B. L. Neugarten (ed.), *Middle Age and Aging*. Chicago: University of Chicago Press, 1973.

Clark, M. Patterns of aging among the elderly poor of the inner city. *Gerontologist*, 1971, *11*, 58–66.

____, and Anderson, B. *Culture and Aging: An Anthropological Study of Older Americans*. Springfield, Ill.: Charles C Thomas, 1967.

Davis, R. (ed.). *Housing for the Elderly*. Los Angeles: Gerontology Center, University of Southern California, 1973.

Gaynes, N. The planning process. In Davis, R. (ed.), *Housing for the Elderly*. Los Angeles: Gerontology Center, University of Southern California, 1973.

Hamovitch, M., and Peterson, J. Housing needs and satisfactions of the elderly. *Gerontologist*, 1969, *9*, 30–32.

Harrington, M. *The Other America*. New York: Macmillan, 1962.

Jacobs, J. *Fun City: An Ethnographic Study of a Retirement Community*. New York: Holt, Rinehart and Winston, 1974.

Langford, M. *Community Aspects of Housing for the Aged*. Ithaca, N.Y.: Cornell University, 1962.

Lawton, M. P., and Cohen, J. The generality of housing impact on the well-being of older people. *Journal of Gerontology*, 1974, *29*, 194–204.

____, and Kleban, M. The aged resident of the inner city. *Gerontologist*, 1971, *11*, 277–283.

____, Kleban, M., and Singer, M. The aged Jewish person and the slum environment. *Journal of Gerontology*, 1971, *26*, 231–239.

Leeds, M. Housing directions for the elderly. In Davis, R. (ed.), *Housing for the Elderly*. Los Angeles: Gerontology Center, University of Southern California, 1973.

Lieberman, M. Institutionalization of the aged: effects on behavior. *Journal of Gerontology*, 1969, *24*, 330–340.

Lowenthal, M., et al. *Aging and Mental Disorder in San Francisco*. San Francisco: Jossey-Bass, 1967.

Mathieu, J. T. Life satisfaction: a comparative analysis. Paper presented at the annual meeting of the Gerontological Society, Miami Beach, 1973.

____, and Sundeen, R. Aging and perception of law and order. Los Angeles: Loyola Marymount University, 1974 (mimeo).

Palmore, E. Variables related to needs among the aged poor. *Journal of Gerontology*, 1971, *26*, 524–531.

Peterson, J. *A Time for Work, A Time for Leisure: A Study of Retirement Community In-movers*. Los Angeles: Gerontology Center, University of Southern California, 1965.

____, Hamovitch, M., and Larson, A. *Housing Needs and Satisfactions of the Elderly*. Los Angeles: Gerontology Center, University of Southern California, 1973.

Post-White House Conference on Aging Reports, 1973. Toward a new attitude on aging. Prepared for the Subcommittee on Aging of the Committee on Labor and Public Welfare and the Special Committee on Aging, U.S. Senate. Washington, D.C.: Government Printing Office, 1973.

Rainwater, L. Fear and the house-as-a-haven in the lower class. In Palan and Flaming (eds.), *Urban America: Conflict and Change*. New York: Holt, Rinehart and Winston, 1972.

Rosow, I. *Social Integration of the Aged*. New York: Free Press, 1967.

Sheldon, H. D. *The Older Population of the United States*. New York: Wiley, 1958.

Sherman, S. R. Satisfaction with retirement housing; attitudes, recommendations and moves. *Aging and Human Development*, 1972, *3*, 339–366.

____. Methodology in a study of residents of retirement housing. *Journal of Gerontology*, 1973. *28*, 351–358.

Vivrett, W. Housing and community settings for older people. In C. Tibbits (ed.), *Handbook of Social Gerontology*. Chicago: University of Chicago Press, 1960.

Webber, I., and Osterbind, C. Types of retirement villages. In E. W. Burgess (ed.), *Retirement Villages*. Ann Arbor, Mich.: Division of Gerontology, University of Michigan, 1961.

Weg, R. The aged: who, where, how well, health care, and mortality. Los Angeles: Gerontology Center, University of Southern California, 1974 (mimeo).

Wright Institute Report. Does better housing for the aged mean a longer, happier life? Wright Institute, Berkeley, Calif., Fall 1973, p. 6.

M. POWELL LAWTON

M. Powell Lawton is Director of Behavioral Research at the Philadelphia Geriatric Center, Philadelphia, Pennsylvania.

Homogeneity and Heterogeneity in Housing for the Elderly

Specialized planned environments for older people are being created in great variety. In contrast to the rural poor farms or urban charity homes of the past, our day is spawning environments with all types of architecture, geographic location, sponsorship, clientele, and onsite resources. Animated debate exists about the merits of high-rise versus garden-apartment versus detached-housing living; central-city versus suburban site location; proprietary versus governmental versus nonprofit sponsorship; integration versus segregation, based not only on age, but also health, mental status, or national origin; and housing alone versus medical, meal, social, recreational, or housekeeping services. The existence of stimulating controversy about these issues is evidence of a healthy attempt to deal with widely varying needs. While we may eventually hope to demonstrate the superiority of one member of each of these pairs of alternatives for the majority of older people, research should ideally give us the ability to predict who will fare best under which condition. Thus the major task would seem to be to optimize the congruence of personal characteristics and environmental resources.

Perfect person—environment congruence might theoretically be viewed as a situation in which en-vironmental press never exceeds the indivdual's capacity to respond competently. Some utopias have been so constructed, and one gets the impression that the benevolent eleemosynary institution could take the extreme form of an asylum where all needs are anticipated. In fact, an ethologist has tried to do this very thing with a colony of self-sufficient birds by suddenly providing limitless food and freedom from any threat to their existence. This intrusion of the welfare state was devastating to their society, to the point of markedly reducing their population.

Much recent research has been devoted to the demonstration of a need to explore, to create variety, or to alter a constant stimulus field. White (1959) has termed this need "effectance"—"what the neuromuscular system wants to do when otherwise unoccupied or gently stimulated by the environment." Effectance has long been neglected in favor of sex, aggression, power, and dependency, all of which in tranditional psychodynamic thinking have propelled the individual from within. Only recently have scientists demonstrated what was long ago obvious to everyone else, that under conditions of sensory, affective, or cognitive boredom, both animals and people will create stress, problems, or conflict for themselves

(Berlyne, 1960; Calhoun, 1963; Fiske and Maddi, 1961).

Although we are just beginning to learn what the conditions and limits of tolerable stimulation levels are, evidence for the existence of a need for variety is clear. Therefore, we must reject any attempt to populate an environment with people who are so much alike that a single environmental plan becomes sufficient to meet all needs. Note that this negative model requires both the human population and the environmental structuring to be homogeneous. That is, even if we should succeed in selecting a remarkably homogeneous population, an environment with a great deal of diversity would still provide the possibility of differential activation for different people. At least people would still have the option of choosing which aspects of the environment to react to. Or, a monotonic institutional environment, if it had a heterogeneous resident population, would at least provide differing social stimuli to the residents. As Goffman (1961) has suggested, the "total" mental institution or prison strives for a homogeneous environmental stimulus field. Similarly, the physical wasteland of the ghetto and the exploitative white society provide stimulus fields for the black resident that are relatively unvarying compared to the variety available to the middle-class white. Conversely, exclusive admission policies to country clubs, fraternities, boards of directors, or even housing sites for the elderly produce homogeneity that may severely restrict the stimulus input to the member. These personal and environmental homogeneities reinforce each other so that diversity becomes more difficult to obtain.

Living situations for the elderly have the potential of narrowing their admission policies to the point where gray sameness characterizes both resident and environment. The old-age home typically used to have residents who were healthy enough at least to resist the leveling pressure of the institution. Now that our national economic and welfare situation permits the healthy people to stay in the community, it is the sick who enter such institutions, and even, to some extent, the special housing environments that provide on-site services (Lawton, 1969). It is common for these group living facilities to attempt to define minimum levels of competence that prospective members must exhibit to qualify for admission.

It will require only a brief statement to justify the insistence on some minimum standard: the patient's physical and mental well-being depend on his not being challenged beyond his resources. This is the whole rational basis for the search for assessment instruments that will screen applicants or provide favorable placement decisions. On the other hand, there are irrational bases for this search, also. A homogeneous environment is easier to provide than a pluralistic one, and once you have a homogeneous environment, diversity among people is a nuisance. Thus, for the sake of administrative ease, more efficient nursing care, or more clear-cut admission decisions, living areas may be endlessly divided and subdivided, from the gross distinction between a skilled nursing care area and an intermediate care area to such finely differentiated areas as having patients with moderate brain syndrome and major physical illness housed separately from those with mild brain syndrome and moderate physical illness.

Research evidence on integration has just begun to accumulate. The importance of the characteristics of other individuals was illustrated in studies by Kahana and Kahana (1970a, 1970b), where elderly admissions to a state hospital were assigned randomly to either a ward for older people only or to an age-integrated ward. In measures of both cognitive and social functioning, those in the age-integrated ward were superior after 2 to 3 weeks.

Bennett has suggested that the provision of many kinds of socially differentiating textures in an environment may stimulate the individual to respond in a way which extends his competence. Weinstock and Bennett (1971) found enhancement of cognitive functioning as a consequence of admission to a home for aged; newcomers remained relatively stable and oldtimers appeared to decline over the two occasions of testing. Thus, although this environment was relatively homogeneous for age, the new personal and social demands of the setting may have provided stimulation for newly admitted residents, while the same setting was ineffective in stimulating oldtimers.

When given a choice, people are frequently likely to choose homogeneity. We have found that blacks and whites living together in planned housing environments tend to choose friends of their own color (Nash et al., 1968), and that German-born Jews tend to choose each other as friends (Simon and Lawton,

FIGURE 1
In age-homogeneous housing, people of different backgrounds are particularly likely to live with mutual enrichment. (Photo courtesy of Administration on Aging, U.S.D. H.E.W.)

1967). Certainly, preference will always be a powerful and legitimate factor in planning living facilities and their personal composition. However, where competence is somewhat limited, whether through personal, social, or environmental factors, the planner may have to consider whether other considerations should enter into a decision about building in homogeneity, even to the point of overruling personal preference. If we can learn better what the conditions are under which diversity is beneficial, we may be able through planning to provide measured doses of the kind of diversity with which we deal normally in earlier life: racial, ethnic, or economic heterogeneity, for example.

The ethical considerations involved in the problem of homogeneity are implied in the foregoing discussion. Do we have the right, on the one hand, to deprive older people of low competence of the stimulation and exercise of their residual capacities that would arise as a consequence of steadily interacting with those somewhat more competent than they? One can just as easily look in the opposite direction from the point of view of the more competent. Segre-

gation deprives them of the full range of exercise of their social skills, such as helping, or empathic behavior, or simply adapting to different types of people. These are essentially the reasons the Supreme Court used in ruling that racial segregation in schools was illegal. In short, the comfort of the segregated group, whether expressed in terms of morale or heightened social activity, is not necessarily the only factor to be considered.

The critical issue is undoubtedly a matter of how much stress is tolerable. Many older people lack the resources necessary to resolve major confrontations, such as those facing them in urban slums; it may be that relocation of those who wish it is the only solution. Where the range of health is very wide, the sight of grossly deteriorated patients is very disturbing to more competent residents of homes. In this instance, a relative degree of segregation may be the only answer. It would be highly useful to be able to define the "safe limits" of variation that older people with different types and degrees of competences could tolerate in the people in their proximate social environments. One aspect of this question is the degree of competence of the individual. Elsewhere I have phrased the "environmental docility hypothesis," stating that the individual is more susceptible to environmental influence as his competence diminishes (Lawton, 1970). According to this hypothesis, people of higher competence should be able to tolerate greater diversity; those of lowered competence (poor physical health, low morale, involuntary isolation) perhaps require a more homogeneous environment. Research can do much to elucidate what the acceptable limits are for different people and situations.

Is it true that older people are being herded together against their will? Research data show that about 80 percent of those living in age-segregated housing are satisfied with that type of environment; they are more accepting of the idea of having younger adults without children living near them than they are about having either teen-agers or children. As far as we have been able to tell, the very great majority of older people who move into age-segregated housing environments do so of their own free will. In fact, the people who have the most choice—the well-to-do elderly—are those who seem especially likely to choose age-segregated living.

FIGURE 2
Most people living in senior citizen housing are competent
enough to tolerate the presence of some tenants with visible
handicaps. (Photo by Thomas Byerts.)

On the other hand, among all older people now living in the community, about two thirds say they would prefer to remain living among people of all ages. My interpretation of this set of facts is that people differ greatly in their preferences for living with people their own age. If you are a person who cannot stand the idea, you will probably never apply for such housing. Unfortunately, good housing, at a reasonable rent, is scattered in the community and not as available as good, new age-segregated housing. Thus it is probable that a certain percentage of people with really major housing problems are going against their preference into age-segregated housing because there is no alternative. The policy implications are clear: develop federal programs to help those who wish to stay in a normal age environment.

Before implementing such a policy, however, we must ask, "What is the effect of age segregation or age integration?" The verdict thus far supports those who choose to live with age equals. Very briefly, the research of Rosow (1967) shows that elderly apartment dwellers are likely to have more friends as the number of people their own age living in their apartment buildings increases. This effect is especially marked for women, for working-class as opposed to middle-class people, and for people living alone. Other research has shown that living in public housing limited to older people makes the morale of these tenants less dependent on a high level of social interaction than is true for tenants living in projects with people of all ages (Messer, 1967). Recent data from the Philadelphia Geriatric Center's national survey of 100 public housing sites show favorable effects of age segregation on amount of participation in activities, neighborhood mobility, amount of satisfaction with housing, and amount of interaction with families (Teaff et al., 1973). Our data are particularly compelling because this heightened well-being occurs even after a number of other possible influences were ruled out, such as age, sex, race, socioeconomic status of tenants, size of town in which projects were located, number of apartments in the project, and building type.

Research on older people living in scattered homes

in the community is not nearly so clear in showing a positive effect from living in neighborhoods with high concentrations of older people (the studies previously mentioned were limited to apartments or projects). We cannot firmly conclude that an effort should be made to encourage the development of "old people's neighborhoods" as a way of meeting the needs of people who do not want to move to specialized housing projects for the elderly.

We thus must accept the tentative generalization that the well-being of the elderly who voluntarily choose multiunit housing with high concentrations of older people is likely to be better than those who live interspersed with younger families.

The major question remaining is "Why is age segregation better in these situations?" Research tells us

pretty clearly that one reason is that the tenant has the opportunity for social contact with others who have lived through similar experiences, who share the same attitudes and values, and whose standards for acceptable behavior are compatible with his. However strong this effect is, it does not explain all the favorable results, especially the greater freedom of movement, the higher level of contact with family, and the generally higher satisfaction with their housing that older people have when living with age peers only.

Knowing as we do that freedom from fear of crime is one of the highest-priority needs of all people, and especially the elderly, it is natural to suggest that personal safety may be another gain of age-segregated housing. The data are few, although our national survey should ultimately provide a definitive test of

FIGURE 3
Social interaction and activity participation are greater in housing limited to older people. (Photo by Carol Rosenberg.)

the extent to which people's constructive behavior and feeling of inner security are related to the fear of crime. Is the fear of crime, or the actual risk, greater in age-integrated than in age-segregated projects? Both casual observation and statistics such as those reported by Newman (1972) tell us that the answer is very clearly yes. We have visited and observed at great length several hundred projects and spoken to large numbers of administrators and tenants. The consensus is very strong that older people and the teen-aged children of problem families constitute a lethal mix. Younger children from such families are frequently a source of stress, although more for their nuisance value than for serious criminal behavior.

How do we improve the situation in the present age-integrated projects and plan better age-integrated projects for the future? When thinking about these problems, we must remind ourselves that solutions will involve the tenants, the administrator, the housing authority and its policies, the physical housing environment, and the neighborhood context of the housing.

The most drastic solution in some instances may be the best one: high-rise public housing buildings where both elderly and problem younger people live should be converted into more homogeneous environments by whatever remodeling is necessary, so as to house only the aged and handicapped or only families. We do not know how many there are in the country as a whole, probably relatively few, but those that do exist are notorious.

More usually a project is integrated by having a building or set of units limited to older people embedded in a larger project housing families. Improvements may be sought in these instances through both administrative and structural limitations on the access of nonelderly tenants to areas expected to be used by the elderly. In addition to the usual desirable security measures, strong effort should be made to divert pedestrian traffic from family units and the wider neighborhood away from the elderly site. Sometimes fences are the only solution. Separate indoor and outdoor senior-citizen recreation areas should be provided. There may, of course, be considerable entertainment value in watching the behavior of people other than elderly tenants. Where there is adequate surveillance, outdoor seating near the sidewalk but with the protection of an unobtrusive fence may

strike the best balance between safety and stimulation.

The administrator can help greatly by taking the time to teach caution to tenants concerning strangers. There is no substitute for an on-site manager and one or more full-time, on-site employees. Physical remodeling should be considered to allow the office of an employee to have a view of the front door and entrance lobby and, ideally, a direct view of the outdoor areas where security might be questionable.

The administrator should also take the initiative in assisting self-help efforts by tenants. He can further increase tenants' sense of confidence by arranging for regular contact between tenants' patrols and the city or housing authority security personnel.

We have as yet little specific information on whether tenants in high-rise buildings feel any less or more secure than those in other types.

For future housing environments for the elderly, it is easy to recommend that most such projects be limited to elderly people and, if possible, not even border on a project serving families with young children. However, I imagine all of us will be somewhat

FIGURE 4
Tenant patrols have provided an effective security measure to complement housing guards and local police. (Photo by Jonathan Harris.)

be deprived of the stimulation of the real world if they never see youth in action.

It is very important that virtually the only instances of mixing families and elderly to have been examined in our research and in the observations of others have been projects where the worst possible conditions existed: vulnerable elderly people, welfare families with problems beyond their ability to cope with, and often a housing site embedded in a neighborhood having even greater problems that the families in the housing do.

Thus we are in no position to recommend that all federally assisted project housing be age-segregated. I have spoken as strongly as I could to policy makers and legislators suggesting that we must try to determine through demonstration projects with evaluation whether there are conditions under which the generations may live together with mutual enrichment.

The critical factor that might make an age-integrated environment work is the attainment of a situation where the amount and type of exposure of

FIGURE 5
Contact between the generations is essential. We need to know more about how to plan housing so that it allows such contact for those who wish it, as well as providing age-dense environments for those who prefer living with those of their own age. (Photo courtesy of Administration on Aging, U.S.D. H.E.W.)

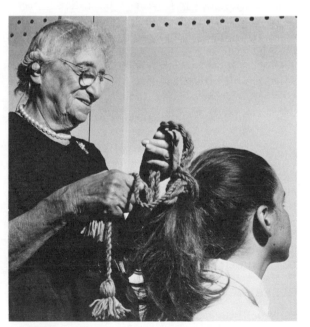

FIGURE 6
Where intergenerational contact is desired and its amount controllable by the older person, satisfying roles are provided for both. (Photo by Lindelle Studios.)

uncomfortable with the seemingly absolute barrier to contact between the generations. Our children will be deprived of appropriate role models and of the raw material out of which their conceptions of old age can be constructed if such segregation became the only pattern available. Older people themselves will older people to youth is regulated and within the control of the older person. The regulation needs to have both architectural and administrative aspects. It is possible to build living units for the elderly and families side by side where access and traffic paths are controlled. An especially useful interface would be a children's play yard visible from indoor and outdoor sitting areas of the senior housing, but with no physical access between the two, as has been designed by Los Angeles architect Louis Gelwicks.

The single most important feature, however, is the commitment of the housing authority or sponsor to making intergenerational relationships work. Such a commitment would be evidenced by a willingness (1) to seek social science consultation in the design of a new project, (2) to provide full-time, professional-level management, (3) to provide security by means of physical and administrative solutions as well as personal surveillance, and (4) to provide activity programs for young and old under the direction of trained people with realistic expectations regarding how much intergenerational contact is constructive.

In conclusion, I feel that age segregation is necessary under two conditions: (1) where the older individual actively chooses to live this way, and (2) where age segregation is the only way to ensure freedom from anxiety about personal safety. In the latter instance, however, age segregation may limit the richness of life for both young and old. Thus we should continue to seek alternatives other than total segregation.

Acknowledgments

Part of this chapter originally appeared as "Assessment, Integration, and Environments for Older People," *Gerontologist*, 1970, *10*, 43–46. Some of the work reported was supported by grants from the National Institute of Mental Health and the Administration on Aging, U.S. Department of Health, Education, and Welfare.

REFERENCES

Berlyne, D. E. *Conflict, Arousal, and Curiosity*. New York: McGraw-Hill, 1960.

Calhoun, J. Population density and social pathology. In L. Duhl (ed.), *The Urban Condition*. New York: Basic Books, 1963.

Fiske, D. W., and Maddi, S. (eds.). *The Functions of Varied Experience*. Homewood, Ill.: Dorsey Press, 1961.

Goffman, E. *Asylums*. Garden City, N.Y.: Doubleday, 1961.

Kahana, B., and Kahana, E. Changes in mental status of elderly patients in age-integrated and age-segregated hospital milieus. *Jouranl of Abnormal Psychology*, 1970a, *75*, 177–181.

Kahana, E., and Kahana, B. The therapeutic potential of age-segregated and age-integrated patient environments for elderly psychiatric patients. *Archives of General Psychiatry*, 1970b, *23*, 20–29.

Lawton, M. P. Supportive services in housing for the elderly. *Gerontologist*, 1969, *9*, 15–19.

_____. Ecology and aging. In L. Pastalan and D. H. Carson (eds.), *The Spatial Behavior of Older People*. Ann Arbor, Mich.: Institute of Gerontology, University of Michigan, 1970.

Messer, M. The possibility of an age-concentrated environment becoming a normative system. *Gerontologist*, 1967, *7*, 247–251.

Nash, G., Lawton, M. P., and Simon, B. Blacks and whites in housing for the elderly. Paper presented at the annual meeting of the Gerontological Society, Denver, October 1968.

Newman, O. *Defensible space*. New York: Macmillan, 1972.

Rosow, I. *Social Integration of the Aged*. New York: Free Press, 1967.

Simon, B., and Lawton, M. P. Proximity and some other determinants of friendship formation in housing for the elderly. Paper presented at the annual meeting of the Eastern Psychological Association, Boston, April 1967.

Teaff, J. D., Lawton, M. P., and Carlson, D. Impact of age integration of public housing projects upon elderly tenant wellbeing. Paper presented at annual meeting of the Gerontological Society, Miami Beach, November 1973.

Weinstock, C., and Bennett, R. From "waiting on the list" to becoming a "newcomer" and an "old-timer" in a home for the aged. *International Journal of Aging and Human Development*, 1971, *2*, 46–58.

White, R. W. Motivation reconsidered: the concept of competence. *Psychological Review*, 1959, *66*, 297–333.

SANDRA C. HOWELL

Sandra C. Howell is an Associate Professor in the Department of Architecture at the Massachusetts Institute of Technology, Cambridge, Massachusetts.

Site Selection and the Elderly

If all consumers of housing were alike in their needs or if there existed a wide choice of settings economically available for residential construction or conversion, there would be little necessity for discussing criteria for selecting sites particularily appropriate to the aging or the socially and physically disabled.

Elderly people are not substantially different from other housing consumers. A greater proportion of them, however, bear economic and social burdens that are both different from and more severe than those borne by other groups. In addition, associated with the process of chronological aging are various physical disabilities that make the choice of terrain, climate, exposure, and man-made surroundings more critical than for younger age groups.

Site-selection criteria currently used by housing planners rarely attend to the particular needs of aging residents, nor do they provide guidelines that are easy for architects and developers to interpret. An attempt will be made in this paper to offer reasons, based on user needs, for suggesting certain criteria. In addition, the implications for the decision-making parties of one or another site decision will be described.

SITE-SELECTION CRITERIA

No residential site will be ideal for all potential residents. However, some particular needs that elderly residents have can assist in the determination, by a community or developer, of the relative quality of one site compared to others. Based upon the available knowledge of social and personal life styles among the elderly, these special needs can be listed as follows:

1. Familiarity of neighborhood (and/or its characteristics).
2. Pedestrian accessibility to key services.
3. Safety and security in relation to the surrounding social or physical environment.
4. Modifiability of major environmental barriers.
5. Proximity to middle-aged and older neighbors.

Familiarity of Neighborhood

Older people move less than younger families. When they move voluntarily, they tend to try to remain as close as possible to the neighborhood where they have spent the greater part of their adult lives. Unless there are significant social or physical reasons for changing neighborhood (e.g., renewal programs, major increases in crime, substantial loss of neighbors, or medical necessity), older people are loathe to give up customary shopkeepers, streets, and neighbors and, above all, to go to the trouble of transporting their accumulated belongings a great distance. In addition, the security they believe they have in a relatively fixed rental relationship or ownership of property makes alternatives appear quite unpredictable.

Any residential move outside of a familiar neighborhood involves adjustments in daily living. A new grocery store, drug store or cleaner has to be identified. The bus route is different and the day and night habits of new neighbors are strange and interfere with established living patterns. Even older people whose mobility has been and continues to be great find the efforts loaded with anxiety and very energy depleting. A new neighborhood that closely resembles an earlier familiar neighborhood in service and commercial amenities is probably preferable for elderly. Thus a site that is on the periphery of the same community, overlaps another town, or lies in an industrial area would not be as good as a site within the heart of a neighboring town of high-density, middle-aged to elderly residents and shopping activities. Familiarity also relates to the way streets are laid out, the types of shops and signs that typify a neighborhood, and the choice of activity alternatives within a neighborhood.

To consider the "quality of life" in the selection of sites for elderly housing, it is therefore important to assess, by sample survey, the types of neighborhood experiences potential tenants have had and, by reason of these experiences, wish to preserve. The format suggested as a brief survey instrument (see Appendix 1) attempts to draw out such consumer interests and preferences.

Familiarity also has to do with the way a site relates to the cycles of day and night, days of the week, and seasons of the year (e.g., office neighborhoods barren of people at night).

What makes a neighborhood "familiar"? The characteristics of a setting that contribute a sense of familiarity to potential elderly tenants of a housing site will vary with the tenants' geographic history. In general, older people remember cities by landmarks that they have seen or used over the course of their lives. For this reason it seems incompatible with the need of elderly for continuity of place to select sites for elderly housing in areas of major land clearance, industrial parks, or new superhighways. "However fast most parts of the environment may change, we are at least in some contact with well-remembered yesterdays. We deal successfully with change only where we can simultaneously preserve some partial continuity—whether of people, things, or places" (Lynch, 1972, p. 199).

Sounds, as well as sights, make neighborhoods familiar. People used to the traffic sounds of a busy city street are not likely to feel comfortable in a pastoral environment, and the sound of a railroad, fire engine, or factory whistle may provide auditory security to people whose vision and mobility are waning.

Pedestrian Accessibility to Key Services

A community of elderly or of housing planners has to consider how accessible a proposed site is to key services required by residents and must deal with certain related issues.

Although they may not like it, as people grow older, they become more dependent on pedestrian access to facilities (Carp, 1971). Site-selection criteria that have been used by states and local authorities often list a collection of services to which a site should be proximate (i.e., within $\frac{1}{2}$ mile).

Shops and services that exist when a site is selected may not continue to exist without support, subsidy, or incentive to replace. Thus the closeness of a grocery store at the time of site selection may not be relevant even 1 to 2 years after occupancy. Necessary services become more easily accessible when door-to-door transportation is provided. Residents of elderly housing have been known to give up their local market when a competitor has provided a weekly minibus to a supermarket as far as 2 to 4 miles away.

Amenity criteria also typically include a library and church. Since it is not likely that sites can be found that are this close to public libraries, an alternative of choice which a number of housing managers and tenants have developed is on-site library space serviced by a mobile unit from the local library. In the case of church proximity, it is very improbable that the church closest to a site would meet the religious needs of a majority of tenants, except within a distinctly ethnic neighborhood. Of far greater importance to the elderly, whose frequency of church attendance appears to wane in later years, is the accessibility of public transportation within one or

FIGURE 1
Shoppers returning from a weekly trip from their housing site in Worcester, Massachusetts. The site is nested among resi- dences housing older as well as younger families. (Photo by Graham Rowles.)

two blocks of the site. Criteria should require the developer to specify the routes and destinations provided by public transportation close to the site. Obviously, transportation that does not operate regularly on Saturday and Sunday or which requires one or more transfers to arrive at service and commercial centers would severely restrict the mobility of tenants and their accessibility to a wide range of places and activities.

The most frequently demanded services and facilities close to or on sites are those which can meet the daily needs of tenants, such as groceries and drugs, and those which might be needed in emergencies, such as a hospital emergency room (Lawton, 1969). Although the elderly frequently request medical facilities, there are no good data on tenants' actual or potential use of medical offices located on the premises or nearby. It is probable that the scheduled presence of a registered nurse and a 24-hour on-call

system are the true need and a more economical way of delivering health services.

Since most elderly people remain ambulatory for the major portion of their later lives, a site that allows them to walk to such facilities as beauty and barber shops, a notions store, a post office, and a bank would seem the most desirable.

Safety and Security

Recent studies of crime in metropolitan areas indicate that the elderly, regardless of race, are particularly vulnerable to the onslaughts of petty burglars and street vandals. The implications of such information for site selection strongly indicate removing the vulnerable population to a neighborhood with fewer such hazards. However, many inner-city elderly do not wish to move from familiar surroundings. Thus the sites selected within densely populated or hazard-

FIGURE 2
Within two blocks of the elderly site in Augusta, Georgia, is a
church heavily used by tenants, a private nursing home, and a
public library. (Photo by Karen Ouzts.)

ous areas must minimize the existing, but not necessarily permanent, hazards of the neighborhood. A site
of concentrated elderly directly opposite or within
the movement path of a junior high or a high school
population is probably undesirable within a high-
crime area.

Decision makers must deal with certain specific
issues in regard to inner-city sites for elderly housing:
Where, within the area, are the most stable residential
sections with the lowest crime rate? How will the
site's protection be reinforced by other structural or
social features of the area? For example, a site surrounded by a three-block area that contains owner-
occupied residential buildings and established, long-

term merchants is probably more desirable than one
in which the commercial and residential vacancy rates
are high and the residential tenants are heavily tran-
sient. The presence of rental units within low-income
inner-city areas is by no means indicative of transiency. The renting individuals and families may be
long-term residents in the neighborhood. Thus the
degree of transiency in the neighborhood needs to be
measured by planners in terms of unit turnover rather
than home ownership. The stage in the life cycle of
residents of a neighborhood also needs to be assessed
in site-selection decisions (Sclar, this volume; Golant,
1972). A neighborhood in which the dominant residents are families with children aged 8 to 18 and with

a high turnover rate is not likely to be a safe and supportive one for elderly housing.

Environmental Barriers

Certain physical characteristics of a site or its immediate neighborhood constitute special barriers to the freedom of movement of an aging population. Some barriers can be overcome by careful site development, given that architects and engineers are aware of their potential impact. Others, however, may be generic to a locality (e.g., the hills of San Francisco or Seattle) or be relatively permanent land-use patterns that are not likely to be changed (e.g., the presence of a busy highway between a site and a shopping center or park, or the presence of railroad tracks that prevent access to shopping). The development of many suburban areas in the United States virtually ignored the eventual needs of aging homeowners and non-drivers.

In certain urban neighborhoods, the presence of alleyways and abandoned structures constitute essentially psychological barriers to free neighborhood mobility by elderly since they may conceal potential attackers.

The condition of sidewalks and streets (or their absence) can be a danger particular inconvenience to elderly. In climates where rain and snow prevail many months of a year, a location that requires tenants to walk in an unpaved street en route to shopping areas is a safety hazard.

Sidewalks and streets that are poorly maintained, uneven and pocked with holes, or have irregular paving surfaces are major accident hazards to the elderly, whose balance or vision may be somewhat impaired.

Proximity to Middle-Aged and Older Neighbors

Research into the social relations among older people indicate that, like most distinguishable age groups, they tend to make friends more easily with their age peers and to have sustained friendships and neighboring habits with adults with whom they have shared child rearing, shopping, or work relationships for many years. Such information indicates that community criteria for site selection should be related to the age distributions of a neighborhood. Sites sur-rounded by children and young adults in heavy concentrations might well be given low priority. Sites that border on behavior settings in which children and adolescents congregate should also be reviewed very carefully by a community and compared to the pros and cons of alternative sites.

These admonitions should not be taken either as a recommendation to isolate elderly people from the possibility of moderate daily contact with other age groups or to support consistent selection of sites within neighborhoods that are already predominantly and densely populated by other older people (Nahemow and Lawton, 1975).

Preference for age-peer affiliation does not mean that young and middle-aged adults should be regarded as poor potential neighbors, friends, or helpers. In fact, in evaluating the age characteristics of a neighborhood, the presence of middle-aged residents should be considered a positive site-selection criterion.

ESTIMATING NEED FOR ELDERLY HOUSING UNITS

Studies of interurban residential patterns show that over a 30- to 40-year period, older populations tend to become concentrated in definable neighborhoods. The processes by which this occurs may include (1) the retention of owned residences throughout the adult life span by people who purchased homes 30 years earlier, when they started their families, (2) the migration of younger families to more suburban settings, and (3) the selection of newer neighborhoods by newly formed families. In the studies of both Golant (1972) in Toronto and Sclar (this volume) in Boston, there appears to be a definite correlation between the age of a neighborhood and the age of the residents, as one moves out from the core inner city.

This information can be put into the planning context to guide local housing authorities and community developers. Local housing authorities should provide would-be developers and potential community group sponsors with area maps based upon decennial census data to indicate those blocks in which there tend to be concentrations of particular age groups. It then becomes possible for the inter-

FIGURE 3
On-site seating brings the elderly tenants in contact with other age groups and other life styles in New Jersey. Note the children's murals on the wall to right. Where elderly are a minority (less than 25–30 percent) such peer groupings may not occur. (Photo by Behrooz Modarai.)

ested parties to seek out potential sites in blocks where the middle-aged and elderly are neither excessively concentrated nor extremely sparse.

In addition, such maps provide a basis for studying the residential and service needs of the existing elderly populations and of verifying their expectations, attitudes, and preferences for neighborhood and sites.

Site Selection
and the Availability of Land

One major limitation to free selection of sites for multifamily residences (including those specifically for the elderly) is the value of land in terms of alternative possible uses. Locations close to urban service centers are often the most in demand for commercial uses that are seen to be more profitable than residential use to both developers and city officials.

186   As it becomes more apparent that a desirable plan-

FIGURE 4
A center for youth and an area for active child play may prevent the cautious elderly from walking one block to stores and services in this Ohio neighborhood. (Photo by George Gardner.)

FIGURE 5
A "familiar" neighborhood invites tenants to bring their social world out into the neighborhood in Hoboken, New Jersey. (Photo by Behrooz Modarai.)

ning goal for a community is to mix residential with commercial and service facilities, it will perhaps be easier to persuade businessmen and officials to incorporate certain types of residential settings, more or less on a systematic basis, in order to provide life-cycle housing for local citizens.

Local zoning ordinances have, as well, restricted site choices for multiunit dwellings (especially high-rise) within single-family residential neighborhoods. It is probably neither feasible nor appropriate to recommend the construction of a 200- to 300-unit high-rise structure for such residentially defined zones. It should, however, be possible to convince a community that there are few disadvantages and a number of positive advantages to the construction or conversion of housing in a family neighborhood for use by 20 to 50 middle-aged to elderly people of mixed incomes

(Ryan et al., 1974). Some arguments in favor of such zoning and appropriate to community discussions have been based upon the following:

1. The actual need by the residents of a neighborhood for smaller residential units for themselves or older members of their own families who they wish to have living closer to them.

2. The absence of additional children in the area, where neighborhood parents are concerned with the possible overcrowding of local schools.

3. The possibilities inherent in such tenancy for additional consumership for small businesses and contribution to local taxes.

4. The possibility of on-site provision of community spaces and services for use by neighbors living in their own homes.

Local housing authorities and state agencies should

become aware of a growing tendency in suburban communities to vote negatively on zoning decisions regarding elderly housing. Apparently based on a fear of economic or racial integration, the attitudes are often masked by arguments about the effect of zoning waivers on property values, overloading of sewer or trash services, or exacerbation of traffic problems. The housing needs of low-income families and elderly are so great in the United States that community education efforts, supported by the documented experiences of communities that have successfully integrated racial, income, and age groups, should be mounted by state agencies and local authorities in advance of site selection. Developers who contemplate providing subsidizable housing need particularly to attend to the expressed concerns of the community in presenting their plans, in other words, to document ways in which sewage, trash handling, and potential traffic problems will be resolved.

Social Cost of Poorly Chosen Sites

It may well be argued that the actual production of new units for elderly is more important than site selection and that, therefore, it is better to build on a less desirable site than not to build at all. Studies of populations relocated from their familiar residences indicate that severe social and psychological effects can often result. The most extreme cases concern elderly people moved involuntarily from one nursing home to another. Developers who are contemplating the removal of a nursing facility or elderly residences in clearing a site for new construction should be advised of the literal mortal danger to inhabitants of making this decision. If at all possible, an alternative site or a site plan that permits the retention or slow phasing out of the existing residential—nursing structure should be proposed.

Many elderly have particular problems in reorienting themselves in new and strange environments and in resocializing in new neighborhoods where the population is alien to them. The result of radical forced relocations is often depression and withdrawal of the individuals involved, culminating in higher health and social-service costs. Not so incidentally, there is growing social science evidence that families with young people who are moved too abruptly or too frequently

also suffer from the break with human networks, producing social and personal pathologies that, in turn, have impacts on their elderly neighbors.

Exceptional management efforts, which require specific expenditures of money, are often necessary to support the losses felt by mislocated elderly and families. Real costs of poor siting and improperly conducted tenant selection and premove preparation can be measured in terms of increased hospitalization and service needs for distressed movers. Modification of the worst effects of relocation can probably be accomplished by site selection based upon locational preferences of potential future tenants and by tenant-selection criteria that consider friendship and neighboring groups rather than the individual applicant in isolation from his premove social contacts.

New construction is costly. Inappropriate siting, particularly within large urban communities, has sometimes resulted in chronic underoccupancy, even in buildings designed expressly for the elderly. In addition, cases have been reported where housing authorities have unthinkingly agreed to convert poorly used public housing for families into elderly units without realizing that elderly, low-income citizens would refuse to move to the site. The reasons for refusal may be both rational and irrational. Elderly, long-time residents of a community may be perfectly aware of the distance of the converted site from the center of activity and of the lack of amenities in the site neighborhood. They may well sense that the isolated nature of the site will make it difficult for them to maintain an independent household or that such physical barriers as railroad tracks and super-highways will prevent them from meeting their most ordinary shopping needs. Disruptive noise and pedestrian safety are potential problems about which the elderly express particular concern.

Site-Related Issues—
Density of Residential Units

The typical site-selection process rarely considers how many residents of the same age group should properly be housed in a single structure. ("Over 60" is *not* an age group. It is now clear that from middle age on rather distinct characteristics differentiate decades among the elderly.) In addition, the issue of the age densities of the surrounding neighborhood rarely receives proper consideration in selecting sites for elderly housing.

These two related subjects are increasingly important to the elderly. In addition, it is necessary to take a broader social view of what it may mean in the long run for a society to set a particular group apart from other groups and to concentrate them heavily in one location. In the case of all aging people, current research indicates that at least 60 to 70 percent of older people apparently wish to continue living in integrated communities with people of all ages. To isolate them from visual or physical interaction with other generations may mean a loss of meaningful contact with the real world as it changes around them. Isolation may force them to depend predominantly on radio and television as media for selective information about the happenings of the society and accentuate a tendency to turn inward and become rigid in their ideas and behaviors. For the middle aged and youth of a society, who must mold policy with regard to their own future aging, an image of old age as representing isolation may result from their loss of meaningful contact with the older generation. This negative image, in turn, can lead to personal and public denial of the fact of aging and of the variety of ways in which individuals or societies may cope with growing old (Mead, 1972). Since approximately one third of surveyed elderly actually express strong preference for living in a building with people "their own age," these situations should be provided, but not to the exclusion of younger adults and children being visible or physically present in the immediate neighborhood.

All these issues are important to site selection, but they should not blind the planner to the possible discomforts and hazards to older people in locating their residences in the middle of a high-youth-density, high-crime location. Such sites, which represent a sizable proportion of existing public housing units in large cities, virtually invite disaster for elderly pedestrians and force restrictions on their off-site movement that most older people would not wish to give up.

A population of healthy people 65 to 70 years of age who constitute the initial tenants of a site become older, and, as they do, the variations in their health

states become greater. Some of the country's elderly housing projects are now 15 or more years old and contain populations whose average age is in the late seventies. Such a population shows behavioral and functional changes that make the residence more institutional in certain key ways:

1. Fewer residents participate in established social programs on site.

2. Residents make fewer trips outside the structure; thus on-site spaces take on greater meaning.

3. More services need to be introduced into the site; thus original site-planning criteria might consider expansion potentials.

FIGURE 6
On-site path which leads down to laundry and recreation area may become unusable by tenants of this Georgia elderly housing project as they grow older. (Photo by Gerald Falls.)

4. Site characteristics that were of little concern to the healthy earlier population become physical barriers to the older residents (e.g., steeply graded paths from one building to another or from site to shopping).

Site Selection and Local Politics

The reality of how sites are often chosen for housing elderly and low-income people is that a parcel of land with few immediate alternative uses and already owned by a developer is offered to a housing authority. Furthermore, developers and real estate operators who are most familiar with local city officials and the business community often obtain preferential treatment in the selection of sites.

Since these widely known practices are not likely to disappear, incentives must be provided, probably at state and federal levels, to encourage the use of site-selection criteria and the simultaneous consideration by local authorities of two or more alternative sites in any decision about provision of housing for elderly.

The following general rules on site selection and the suggested forms (see Appendixes 1, 2, and 3) are designed to minimize subjectivity in siting housing for the elderly.

GENERAL RULES FOR DEVELOPING SITE-SELECTION CRITERIA

1. Site-selection criteria for elderly housing should be interpreted as preliminary and flexible and thus be able to be modified in light of the particular needs and values of the community and potential user population.

2. The site-selection process should be coordinated with the service delivery planning for elderly residents of the total community. Planners of physical facilities should be working closely with program planners to maintain a continuous and evolving model for meeting changing needs.

3. Site-selection criteria should be used to evaluate various feasible sites simultaneously rather than a single site at a time. Commitment to a single site may lead to loss of alternative, superior sites.

4. Sites that conform to criteria and to program goals also should be reviewed in terms of possible community support or opposition.

5. Alternative available sites should be compared on the basis of *complete criteria* rather than individual standards; such evaluation will allow for qualitative trade-offs to be made in relation to program needs (see Appendixes 2 and 3).

APPENDIX 1

Community Survey: Housing Preferences

1. If you were thinking of moving from your present housing, which type of housing would you prefer? (Please check the appropriate box.)

☐ A house
☐ An apartment with bedroom, bathroom, kitchen, and living room in which I could live independently.
☐ An apartment, but with the opportunity to take my meals in a dining room with the other residents.
☐ Hotel style with my own bedroom and bath with all services (such as meals and cleaning) provided for me.
☐ Other_____
a. Is this the *same* or *different* from your present housing? (circle)
b. How long have you lived at your present address?_____Yrs._____Mos.

2. Where would you prefer that your housing be? (Please check as many answers as you wish.)
a. ☐ In downtown city
   ☐ In _____ neighborhood
   ☐ In _____ suburb
   ☐ Outside of city but in county
   ☐ Other _____
b. ☐ Near a shopping center
   ☐ Near churches
   ☐ Near a hospital or other medical facility
   ☐ Near parks and recreation facilities
   ☐ Other _____
c. ☐ Near people my own age
   ☐ Near people of all ages
   ☐ Near my friends or relatives

3. What services would you like provided within the actual building where yo live? (You may check more than one answer.)
   ☐ Shopping (drugs and grocery)
   ☐ Restaurant
   ☐ Library
   ☐ Chapel
   ☐ Other _____
   ☐ Barber and beauty shop
   ☐ Recreation and hobby rooms
   ☐ Gardening plots, greenhouse

4. Would you like health services provided?
   ☐ Yes   ☐ No
   If yes, what health services would you like?
   ☐ Nurse on call or scheduled 1/week.
   ☐ Doctor on call or scheduled 1/month.
   ☐ Nurse on duty and available at all times.
   ☐ Physical therapy or exercise program.
   ☐ Clinic that provides daily medicine.
   ☐ Small hospital bed area for residents who become ill.
   ☐ Other _____

5. What features would you use in selecting a new neighborhood?
   ☐ Closer to shopping
   ☐ Quieter
   ☐ Less traffic
   ☐ Closer to friends or relatives
   ☐ Less crime
   ☐ Other

6. What features would you consider in selecting another home now?
   ☐ Smaller kitchen
   ☐ Fewer bedrooms
   ☐ All on one floor
   ☐ Building with elevator
   ☐ Patio or balcony
   ☐ Central laundry
   ☐ Newer, less maintenance and repair
   ☐ Other

7. If services such as health care, meals, and cleaning assistance could be provided to you in this home, would you prefer to remain here rather than move?
   ☐ Yes   ☐ No

8. Are you planning on moving?
   Within the next year   ☐ Yes ☐ No
   Within the next two to three years ☐ Yes ☐ No
   Within the next three to five years ☐ Yes ☐ No

9. If you are planning to move within the next five years and if housing is developed at _____ site, _____ site, _____ site, would you consider moving in?
   _____ site:
   ☐ Very likely
   ☐ Possibly yes
   ☐ Perhaps
   ☐ Probably no
   ☐ Very unlikely
   _____ site:
   ☐ Very likely
   ☐ Possibly yes
   ☐ Perhaps
   ☐ Probably no
   ☐ Very unlikely
   _____ site:
   ☐ Very likely
   ☐ Possibly yes
   ☐ Perhaps
   ☐ Probably no
   ☐ Very unlikely

10. What events that might occur in the future would cause you to consider moving? (List in order of response.)

    _____

    _____

    _____

    _____

    _____

    _____

11. What type of housing do you live in now?
    ☐ I own my own home.
    ☐ I live in a rented house.
    ☐ I live in an apartment.
    ☐ I rent a room.

12. How many people live with you in that housing?
    ☐ Myself only
    ☐ One other (specify spouse, child, sibling, non-related)
    ☐ Two others (specify)
    ☐ More than two (specify)

13. How much money per month do you currently spend on housing? _____ dollars per month, on utilities _____

14. What type of transportation do you use most often?
    ☐ Car
    ☐ Taxi
    ☐ Other _____
    ☐ Bus
    ☐ Walk

APPENDIX 2

Site-Selection Planning Questionnaire

A. Population 55 years of age and over for whom community claims current housing need:
   Low (under $3,000) _____
   Moderate ($3,000–6,000) _____
   High (over $6,000) _____

B. Method(s) used in estimating current and future need in community for units 55± populations:

   _____

   _____

   _____

   _____

C. Community participation:
   1. Have adult residents of total community been consulted on sites and proposed housing?

      Describe method of consultation and relate to proposed site(s).

      on neighborhood preferences?

Describe survey and relate results to characteristics of proposed site(s) and surroundings.

D. Sites potentially available for new or converted construction of elderly housing (provide a minimum of three sites by map). Map should include major cross streets and average traffic flow, permanent structures now on or within two-block radius, current use to which structures are being put, age distribution of population in census tract containing site, number of elderly units proposed for site.

E. Do any of the sites require (specify):
   1. Zoning variance (under what conditions; check off issue):
      Height limit _____
      Number of units _____
      Land use _____
      Other (specify) _____
   2. Extraordinary site development costs (e.g., grading, demolition, piling, etc.).
   3. Modification of immediate neighborhood (e.g., removal of off-site vacant buildings, promotion of off-site services such as grocery or drugstore, changes in traffic patterns or controls, sidewalks, improved street lighting).

F. For each proposed site, describe and map the primary settings in which people tend to congregate within two blocks of proposed site. Specify the particular age groups and time of day or night of their congregating. Examples:
   High school, 1 block south, weekdays 8–4
   _____

   Street corner ice cream parlor, 1 block north, preteen and teen-agers, weekdays 4–10 P.M., Saturdays 10 A.M.–11 P.M.
   _____

   Parking lot, $\frac{1}{2}$ block east, teen-agers, young adults, late night _____
   Launderette, $\frac{1}{2}$ block east _____
   Elementary school _____
   Park and playground _____

G. Characteristics of surrounding neighborhood:
   1. Census tract(s) considered part of neighborhood (by community consensus).

2. Presence of health facilities within 2 miles of site:
   (a) Hospital (general or specialized)
   (b) Clinic (specify services)
   (c) M.D. offices
   (d) Licensed nursing homes
   (e) Other
3. Presence of open space (specify use).

4. Presence of industrial firms in site neighborhood. Number and nature of product.
5. Average age of residential structures in containing census tract.
6. Median value of property—census tract.
7. Ratio of residential to nonresidential structural use in census tract.

APPENDIX 3

Suggested Site Evaluation Summary

Evaluation Factors	Site		
	1	2	3
1. Accessibility to:			
Shopping	2[a]	2	1
Public Transportation	1	1	1
Churches	1		
Recreation	1		
Parking	−1		
Medical care	−1		
Personal service: beauty shop, cleaner, etc.			
2. Compatibility with other plans:			
Hospital master plan; regional medical plan			
Land use and zoning			
Social-service delivery			
3. Utilities and services:			
Gas			
Electricity			
Water			
Sanitary sewer			
Storm sewer			
Trash pickup			
Sidewalks			
Crosswalks			
4. Natural features:			
Topography			
Vegetation			
5. Incompatible surrounding land use:			
Industrial			
Juvenile			
Recreation or school			
Vacancies			
6. Vehicular traffic			
7. Expansion potential			
8. Economies:			
Land costs			
Existing structures demolition			
Potential for sharing facilities			
Totals			

[a]Scoring: 2, advantage; 1, acceptable; −1, disadvantage; −2, serious problem.
Source: Adapted from L. Pastalan, "Retirement Housing Study," Methodist Hospital of Madison, Wisc., July, 1972.

NOTE

1. Derived from L. Pastalan, "Retirement Housing Study," Methodist Hospital of Madison, Wisc., July, 1972.

REFERENCES

Carp, F. M. Walking or driving in the older years. *Gerontologist,* 1971, *11,* part I, 101–111.

Golant, S. M. *The Residential Location and Spatial Behavior of the Elderly*. Chicago: Department of Geography, University of Chicago, 1972.

Lawton, M. P. Supportive services in the context of the housing environment. *Gerontologist*, 1969, *9*, 15–19.

Lynch, K, *What Time Is This Place*. Cambridge, Mass.: MIT Press, 1972.

Mead, M. Long living in cross-cultural perspective, paper presented to the Gerontological Society Annual Meeting, San Juan, Puerto Rico, December 1972.

Nahemow, L., and Lawton, M. P. Similarity and propinquity in friendship formation. *Journal of Personality and Social Psychology,* 1975, *32*, 205–213.

Ryan, W., Sloan, A., Seferi, M., and Werby, E. *Audit of mixed income housing*. Boston: Massachusetts Housing Finance Agency, 1974.

ALVIN ZELVER

Alvin Zelver is a city planning and urban development consultant with offices in San Mateo, California.

Model for Planning a Special Neighborhood

There is, of course, no one model for planning housing and social centers for the elderly. The need is for choices in housing scattered throughout the community, as well as grouped housing, and choices in supportive services and in the level of service desired—to be determined by the elderly themselves. An older person with a slight infirmity should not be assigned to a nursing home to live confined as a patient; conversely, no one should languish in isolation, cut off by lack of transportation if his or her needs are for continuing and immediate medical care, meals, social life, or opportunities for recreation.

If community leaders have the courage of utopian thinking, they may imagine a model, an ideal of how the elderly might live, given the opportunity. Such a model begins with the community (whether central city, suburb, small town, or rural county) perceived as a "service area," much in the same way as a school, recreation, or utility district is primarily intended as an area of specialized service. Planning begins with the question, what are the conditions of the elderly within the community? Are there *other* elderly who might live within the service area, attracted by the proximity of family and friends, climate or community amenities, if their particular needs can be served?

What are the gaps in service? Is there a single-purpose public or private organization dedicated to the needs of the elderly, as a school board concerns itself with the education of the young within its district?

In this paper we deal with the concept of a "special neighborhood" for the elderly within the larger context of a community's comprehensive general plan. The special neighborhood attempts to recognize both the unique needs for special services for older people, the advantages of living close to age peers, and simultaneously the need to retain some solidarity with the people and the resources of a "normal" community with a wide age spectrum.

Often, a concentration of housing in its own small special neighborhood (Figure 1) with its own social center can be the focal point for the service area, with the special neighborhood for the elderly designated as a unique land use on the community's general plan. The special neighborhood for the elderly may have its own standards for densities, housing types, automobile parking, public buildings, and architectural design, since the residential needs of the elderly are different from younger age groups.

Planners of service areas and special neighborhoods for the elderly will recognize the conditions of those

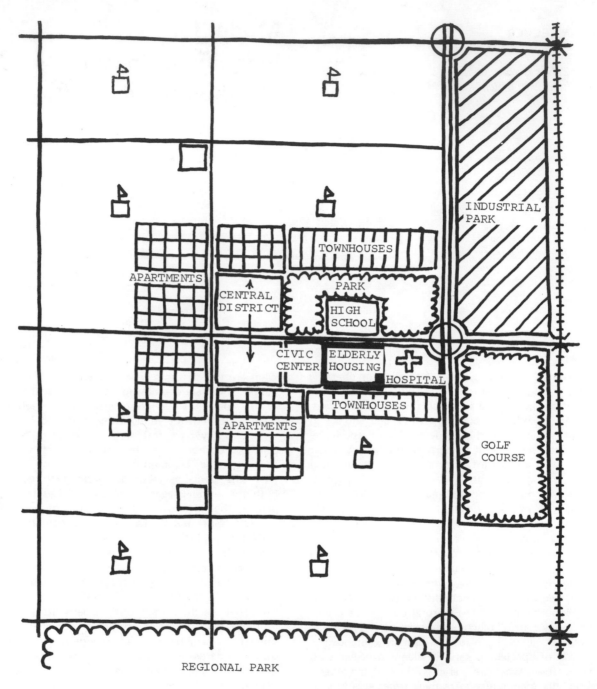

FIGURE 1

In the general plan for this hypothetical town, a neighborhood for the elderly is designated as a special land use. It is centrally located, linked by public transportation or its own minibus service along major thoroughfares with the central district and civic center, the hospital, the golf course. The neighborhood center also may serve the older population who live outside the neighborhood, scattered throughout the community in apartments, townhouses, and single-family houses.

over 60: their ratio in the population, their demographic changes, the greater number of women than men, the greater probability that the surviving spouse in a household will be a widow, not a widower, the uneven distribution of elderly between city and suburb and small towns and farms, the prevailing pattern of independent living for the elderly in their own households, the continuing need for significant roles whether in work or in leisure and the need for organization and assistance in assuming those roles, the need for careful management of fixed incomes, the need for regular, routine preventive health care, and, despite the changing role of the family, the continuing importance of family ties.

GUIDELINES

In developing a special neighborhood for an older population, the planning team must find physical solutions for social, economic, and health-care problems. It is necessary to translate an ideal into an environment.

What size should the neighborhood be; what area and how many housing units should it contain? What type of housing units should they be, with how many of each? At what density should the housing be concentrated? Where should the neighborhood be located within the community? What are preferred site characteristics and standards for site design? How should the housing, neighborhood center, and streets and pedestrian paths be linked for coherent, attractive, safe circulation? How much parking space should be provided, considering that the elderly drive less, and what other transportation modes, such as a neighborhood minibus or electric cards, may be available? What share of the parking space should be covered? What should be provided at the neighborhood center in the way of facilities and services?

Finally, what architectural details should be considered as peculiarly desirable for creating a barrier-free environment for residents who may suffer sensory impairment or other physical handicaps with aging?

The following discussion is offered as a guide to planning a special neighborhood. Judgment, experience, local customs, and the budget, rather than rigid standards, should determine the final plan.

For example, a nearly flat site is easier to work

with than a dead flat site, which may be difficult to drain, or a steeply sloping site, which will be difficult to grade for gently sloping walks. But in a hillside town there may be no choice if the neighborhood is to be close to other important existing community amenities. Special hardware, often cited as desirable in the architectural literature in building for the elderly, may not always be worth what it costs. To be sure, handles rather than doorknobs are easier for arthritic fingers to manage, but if nonstandard, they may be too expensive. Hardware normally specified for hospitals may offend those independent-spirited elderly who do not want architectural appurtenances to appear institutional, albeit sensible.

Several hundred housing units may be required to absorb the costs of providing a complete range of services for lower and middle-income elderly. But where there is not a strong enough demand to fill several hundred housing units, certain services may be cut back or modified. Rather than a special minibus for the neighborhood, the community may find it less expensive to subsidize taxi fares (at least for emergencies) for those elderly who would otherwise be immobilized.

Reduced parking space is the concession granted most frequently to developers of senior-citizen housing. Many jurisdictions make only this adjustment. Ratios range from one parking space per dwelling unit to one per 10.

Demand for parking for residents' cars in any particular project for the elderly will depend on the "mix" of components in each project, that is, the age, sex, and income of residents, as well as the climate, the availability of alternative transportation modes, and local traffic in the community. Often, determining the proper number of parking spaces is more accurate if approached empirically rather than by theory or assumption.

It would seem better economy to provide minimum parking for residents, with an area to be held in reserve in the event of demand, rather than budget for maximum possible demand from the start. However, such ideas are not always easy to carry out. Converting reserved space (especially if it has been landscaped) to parking after a project is built may be more expensive than including the parking stalls as a part of the original construction contract.

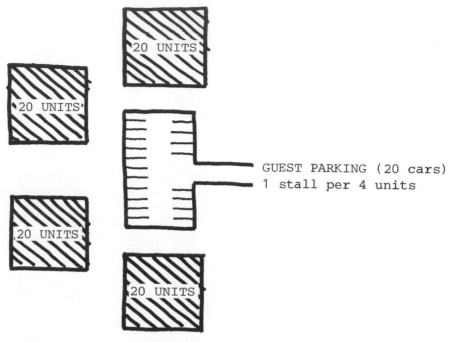

FIGURE 2
Guest parking should be spaced more or less equally between the housing units it is intended to serve. Spaces do overlapping duty to serve different housing units, since all residents do not have guests at the same time.

Experience shows that reducing parking ratios (even if permitted or encouraged by local public agencies) should be considered with great caution in areas where there is little public transportation and the auto is the dominant transportation mode. Giving up the car is, for many elderly, giving up independence, and ranks high with other traumatic experiences of aging. True, the elderly may drive less, but unless parking space is available in their neighborhood, younger couples in their sixties will not be attracted to move in. The population will be limited from the start, by de facto design, to the very old who are unable or cannot afford to drive. Riders to participate in car pools are a valuable transportation resource to the neighborhood.

The number of guest parking spaces required will—like the need for resident and staff parking—depend upon automobile use in each community. In middle-income suburbia, one guest parking space for each four housing units will generally prove adequate.

Population

A special neighborhood is intended as one option for those elderly in the community who choose grouped housing, but the neighborhood should be a size that does not create isolation. It should be large enough to provide economy of scale in building and services, yet small enough to serve the community's elderly without creating an isolated community of elderly.

Also, the population should be large enough in the neighborhood to permit residents to have a choice of friends from among their age peers. As one ages, he may develop narrower interests. Unless there is a variety among the contemporaries at hand, it will not

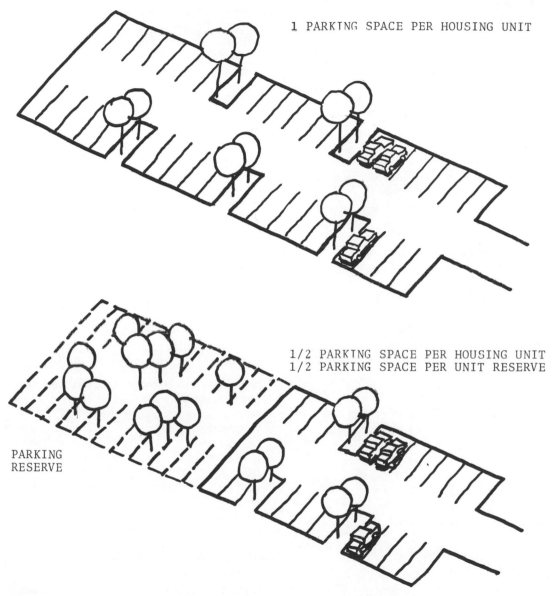

1 PARKING SPACE PER HOUSING UNIT

1/2 PARKING SPACE PER HOUSING UNIT
1/2 PARKING SPACE PER UNIT RESERVE

PARKING
RESERVE

FIGURE 3

In the illustration, a ratio of 0.5 parking space per housing unit is provided with an equal landscaped space for a parking reserve. The rationale for a reserve is to allow the actual demand (rather than an arbitrary standard) to dictate the supply of parking stalls. If unneeded, the reserve space can be put to better use, such as for permanent landscaping.

be easy to make new friends when old ones move or die. But the neighborhood population must not be so large that residents feel redundant or suffer a loss of identity.

Although there is divided opinion as to the number of elderly who may be concentrated in their own neighborhood (as there is not always general agreement as to the optimum population for an urban settlement of all ages), up to 500 housing units divided into clusters of 30 to 50 is a scale to which most residents can comfortably relate. With less than two persons per household, the neighborhood will house a population of under 1,000. Residents from each housing cluster may select leaders so as to have a direct voice in managing their own local affairs. If costs of construction and services are not divided among enough households, middle- and lower-income elderly will not be able to afford living in their own neighborhoods, unless housing and services are subsidized.

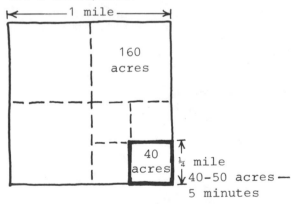

Walking time:
1 mile—20 minutes
(at 3 miles/hour)

1 mile
160 acres
40 acres   ¼ mile
40-50 acres —
5 minutes

o   1-mile square (640 acres)—
    1 hour 20 minutes to walk around

o   ¼-mile square (40 acres)—
    20 minutes to walk around

FIGURE 4
Within 40 to 50 acres, about the size of a high school campus, it is possible to create a park-like setting with destinations accessible on foot.

Area

The neighborhood area will depend upon the exact number of housing units for which there is a demand and the number of housing units per acre that is appropriate for the community's general plan and housing design. Rules of thumb to determine area are (1) over 40 to 50 acres is beyond the size of an enclave for comfortable walking (Figure 4), (2) less than 10 acres may not provide enough space to create an inviting atmosphere, and (3) for 500 units of housing, a density of 10 units per acre is the minimum possible if the neighborhood is to be kept within walking bounds (Figure 4). Inasmuch as housing for the elderly is generally smaller than normal family housing (Figure 5), contains fewer persons per household, and generates less traffic, 10 housing units per acre for the elderly can fit into a community's general plan for lower-density, single-family housing of less than five units to the acre (Figure 5). Tall buildings, requiring steel frame or reinforced concrete, will generally cost more than one- to three-story wood-frame construction (Figure 6).

Site Planning

Although a square-shaped site gives the shortest distances for walking, with a shorter perimeter than a rectangle or an irregularly shaped site enclosing an equal area, nonsquare site shape may be better related to specific land uses and also produce less sense of an isolated enclave. The site should have its own clearly marked entry (Figure 7) and be free from crossings by public streets that interrupt the neighborhood with through traffic not serving the residents.

Up to 50 units grouped around a court or other focal point allow residents to identify with their own housing cluster (Figure 8).

The site should be planned for walking; walking can be both a healthful activity and a useful transportation mode for many elderly. Ironically, most urban and suburban development patterns discourage walking. In city centers, where 50 percent of the elderly residents may walk somewhere every day, it is not always safe. To encourage walking, the design must be at pedestrian scale, separated from the harassment of high-volume vehicular traffic, and with clearly de-

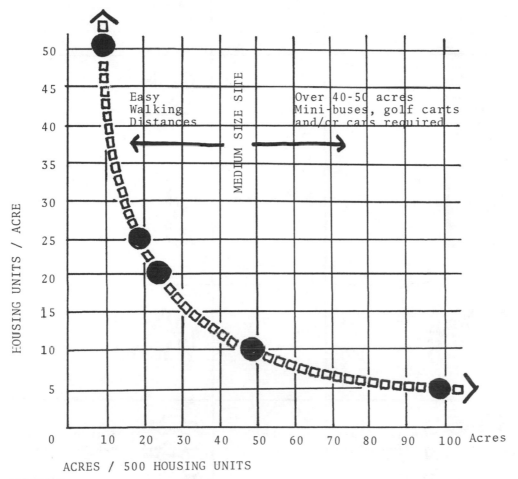

FIGURE 5

When sites are more than 40 to 50 acres, they begin to generate their own internal vehicular traffic. For 500 housing units, densities must be more than 10 units to the acre to create a "walking" neighborhood for many of the elderly.

lineated, safe crosswalks, with origins and destinations no more than 5 to 10 minutes apart.

If heavily guarded walls or fences are required as more than a symbol of security, second thoughts may be in order as to the suitability of the community for the elderly.

A fixed guard station that must be manned around the clock will add to costs and also offers less incentive for the community to enter the elderly's neighborhood. It will make the residents seem more institutionalized and segregated.

Bright lights, a sign, or a "bottleneck" in the entry road will slow traffic and discourage the entry of unwanted guests, while still providing easy access to those whom the residents want to encourage to visit.

Level sites are easier to plan for the elderly, but, where unavailable, a complete architectural vocabulary of ramps, elevators, and bridges may be required

5 FAMILY HOUSING UNITS PER ACRE			10 ELDERLY HOUSING UNITS PER ACRE	
	1000-2000 sq. ft. 2-3 Bedrooms	COVERAGE		500-1000 sq. ft. 0-2 Bedrooms
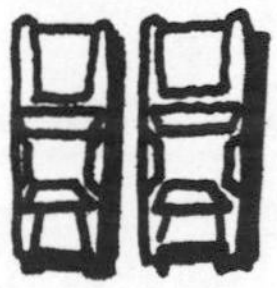	1-2	AUTOS		0-1
	3-4	PERSONS		1-2
	6-12 Trips per week day	TRAFFIC	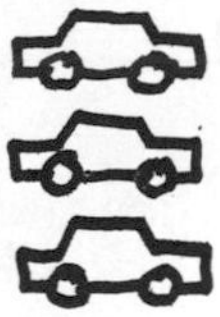	3 Trips per week day
	2 Spaces	PARKING		Less than 1 (average)

FIGURE 6

Compared by "land-use intensity," rather than housing units per acre, housing for the elderly may have twice as many units as normal single-family residential developments and be approximately equal or less in basic measurements of population, coverage, and traffic per unit of land.

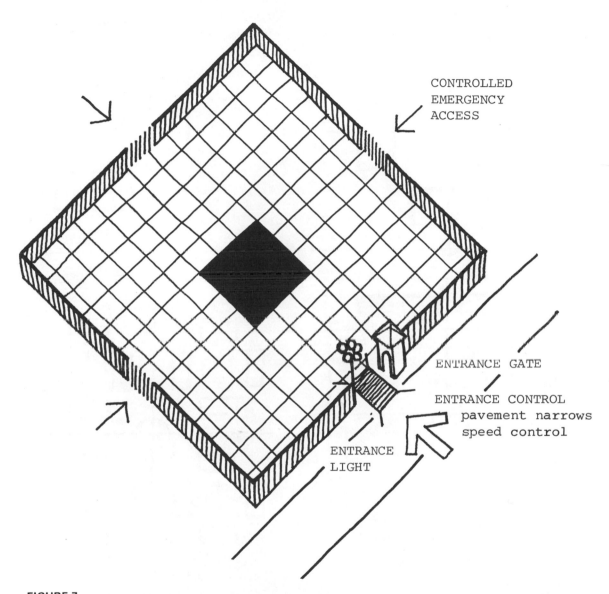

CONTROLLED
EMERGENCY
ACCESS

ENTRANCE GATE

ENTRANCE CONTROL
pavement narrows
speed control

ENTRANCE
LIGHT

FIGURE 7
One clearly identified entry will add to the feeling of security of residents. Other access points may be controlled by electronic gates, operated for emergencies only or, if required for convenience of residents, by plastic, magnetically coded key cards. Boundaries may or may not be walled or fenced—depending on the need for protection from harassment or vandalism in each community.

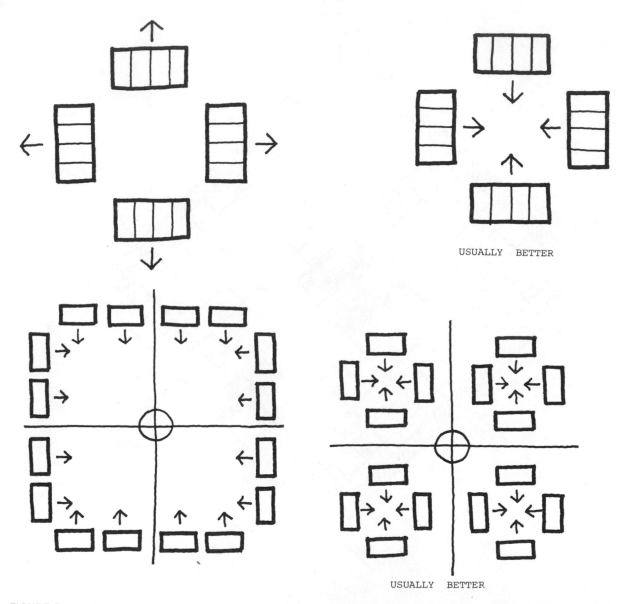

USUALLY   BETTER

USUALLY   BETTER

FIGURE 8
Orientation of housing units toward or away from each other may determine the extent of interaction between residents of housing clusters. Housing units opening out will usually create a "dead" inner court; opening in, they will create the opportunity for chance meetings—if only for nodding acquaintances—so that residents of the same housing cluster will at least recognize each other rather than only faceless neighbors.

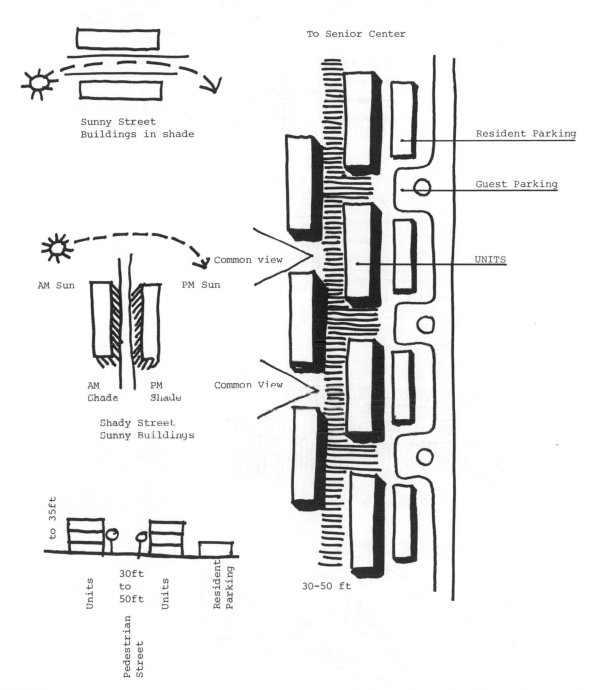

Sunny Street
Buildings in shade

AM Sun

PM Sun

AM
Shade

PM
Shade

Shady Street
Sunny Buildings

to 35ft

Units

30ft
to
50ft

Pedestrian
Street

Units

Resident
Parking

To Senior Center

Resident Parking

Guest Parking

UNITS

Common view

Common View

30-50 ft

FIGURE 9
Buildings three stories high or more may appear bulky and overbearing if scattered. In orderly rows, they relate to a pedestrian street, where, as in a village, residents may observe the pedestrian scene. Orientation to street and sun will determine whether rooms are sunny or shady.

205

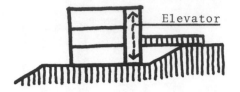

BRIDGES FROM PARKING
TO BUILDINGS

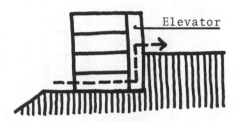

BUILDINGS AT GRADE
CHANGE USING ELEVATORS
FOR EASY ACCESS

BRIDGES AND RAMPS FOR
MAJOR CHANGE IN LEVELS

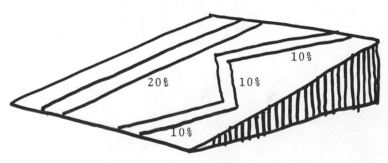

LONG RAMP, GENTLE
SLOPE

FIGURE 10
A barrier-free environment means no steps that the elderly *must* use. Ramps are the usual tools for changing levels in an environment for the elderly. Bridges over streets can be attractive and functional but may be too expensive to design and build on most sites. Some well-lighted, not-too-steep steps can be therapeutic for the active elderly.

to allow pedestrians or residents in wheelchairs to change levels without climbing stairs (Figure 10).

Neighborhood Center

The neighborhood center (Figure 11) should be a strong symbol of communal activity, visible throughout the neighborhood—not unlike a church in a village (Figure 12). Buildings and activities at the center can revolve around an outdoor sheltered place where residents may go for no other reason than the chance opportunity of meeting a friend, making a friend, or watching activities (Figure 13).

Areas and elements of a senior center will depend on the budget to build and operate and the number of users. Depending upon climate, an outdoor space sheltered from direct sun and buffered from the prevailing wind may serve as a "village square" where some play shuffleboard while others watch.

Architectural details of the neighborhood center may include a few especially wide parking spaces near the entry reserved for those who use wheelchairs or walkers, a covered carriage entry for weather protection, no threshold, a wide front door that opens at a touch, and a reception desk just inside to suggest an immediate welcome.

The purpose of elderly housing with supportive activities is, like other urban functions, to provide choice and maximize the opportunities for interaction. Activities should be concentrated, not segregated in isolated locations, even though activities are not directly related, to make a lively center. Opportunity for social interaction jumps dramatically with the addition of each activity at the center.

Housing Units

Units must be designed to fit the needs of an unstable population. In the event of the death of a spouse or of a serious disability, will the housing unit still work? There should be a wide enough variety of housing types—studio apartments and one- and two-bedroom apartments or attached cottages—to satisfy single persons as well as couples. The mixtures of units and sizes of units are tied to demand, but planners must keep an eye to the future. Will the housing unit sizes and types attract a mixture of ages within the 60-and-over group of couples and single

persons? The active recreation facilities planned for those in their sixties may not be needed a decade later, when residents are in their seventies. A concentration of studio units will attract single, unrelated individuals who will probably be predominantly women over age 75. Couples in their sixties who are active enough to provide local leadership may not be attracted to grouped housing where they will be outnumbered by the very old.

SERVICES

Meal Service

Those who live alone may not relish taking all their meals alone. Still, unless eating in a communal dining room is a choice rather than an obligation, some elderly may decline grouped housing as seeming more institutional than they care for. The option of meals should be available even to those who wish to maintain their own kitchens; they may wish to lighten their housekeeping loads or to eat with friends, but not necessarily in a commercial restaurant setting.

Transportation

Within the neighborhood, walking can be the chief mode of transportation on campus-like sites. When destinations are too far, weather is heavy, or the residents themselves do not walk easily, other transportation must be made available (especially for those who can no longer own or drive automobiles). A minibus (with low steps and wide doors) with flexible routing and schedules can circulate throughout and beyond the neighborhood.

Health Care

Health care can be provided for the neighborhood by a health-maintenance organization with its own small clinic for routine examinations, medication, monitoring chronic infirmities, and the processing of Medicare forms. In the event of a short-term minor illness, a homemaker should be available to aid with cooking and cleaning, if the patient does not choose to recuperate in an infirmary where nurses are on 24-hour duty. Those in the neighborhood may sum-o The Neighborhood Center is also a symbol of the programs and services it offers

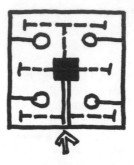

o Center visible from entry

o Center should also be visible and accessible for pedestrian paths

o Architectural symbols of public use:

o Clocktowers

o Flags

o Entrance gates

o Graphics, colors and designs should make functions and locations and directions clear

FIGURE 11

The neighborhood center, as an architectural symbol of community services, should be visible from the entry, as well as from walkways and housing units throughout the neighborhood. In addition, such devices as clock towers, flags, or gateways may identify the architecture for public use, with color, design, and graphics clearly marking functions.

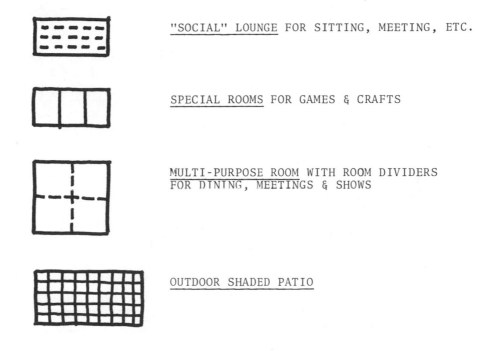

"SOCIAL" LOUNGE FOR SITTING, MEETING, ETC.

SPECIAL ROOMS FOR GAMES & CRAFTS

MULTI-PURPOSE ROOM WITH ROOM DIVIDERS
FOR DINING, MEETINGS & SHOWS

OUTDOOR SHADED PATIO

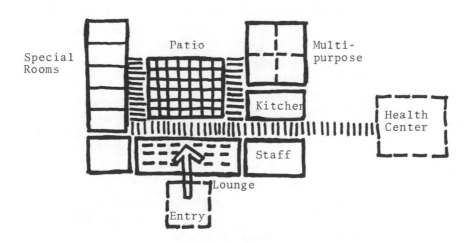

Spacial relationships for traffic flow and
separation of activities in Senior Center.

FIGURE 12
Basic space for a small center will start with a multipurpose room for dining, dancing, talks, and shows. It can
be divided to make private space for separate activities, cards and sewing, and so on. With an increase in
budget, space may be added; it should include a small lounge for nothing special except meeting to say hello
(it is the center's parlor), and smaller rooms for crafts and games. Traffic flow should permit maximum
interaction between activities.

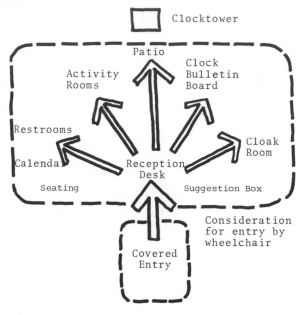

Clocktower

Patio

Activity
Rooms

Clock
Bulletin
Board

Restrooms

Cloak
Room

Calendar

Reception
Desk

Seating

Suggestion Box

Consideration
for entry by
wheelchair

Covered
Entry

FIGURE 13
Entry to a center for the elderly should permit easy access,
allow orientation at a glance to a clock, a calendar, notice of
events of the day, location of rest and cloak rooms, drinking
fountain, and comfortable seating.

mon help from the health center in emergencies by
the press of a button; those outside the neighborhood
but within the service area can be linked to the health
center through a telephone reassurance program, that
is, with a volunteer calling daily those who live alone
to be sure all is well. Those with lingering illnesses or
serious disorders may require longer stays in nursing
homes or hospitals outside the neighborhood but still
within the service area.

Security

A roaming guard, like a village constable walking a
beat, will offer closer contact with residents and be

better able to help in the event of emergency than a
guard assigned only to check traffic at the gate. In the
event of an emergency, the roaming guard can be
quickly summoned by an electronic paging device
that he carries. Recent developments in electronic
emergency call systems are improvements over the
typical push buttons in the bathroom and by the bed.
For example, it is possible to carry a button that
operates a radio signal (like an automatic garage-door
opener). Emergency call systems can also be clock-
activated to set off a prerecorded announcement by
phone to a doctor in the event it is not reset at
predetermined intervals of time.

Service Area Center

The service area is a one-stop center, including a
transportation terminal point, health center, and
buildings and grounds for social and recreation services.

Architectural Standards and Details

Design details should be sensitive to needs for a
barrier-free environment, not only for the infirm but
also for those who without warning become infirm
and whom the environment must then not fail. Architects must be aware of the hardship of climbing stairs
for one who has suffered a stroke or of turning
doorknobs rather than levers for one with arthritic
fingers, of the older person's sensitivity to drafts and
sudden changes of temperature, and his frequent sensory impairment.

Grade changes between pedestrian and vehicular
territory must be designed with sensitivity to the
elderly's difficulty in negotiating curbs, especially for
those using walkers or wheelchairs. The conventional
approach to channeling drainage by curbs and gutters
does not create a barrier-free environment.

FIGURE 14
Pedestrian paths should be at least wide enough for two persons to walk abreast. They should have flat grades, have a nonskid,
glare-free surface, and not be obstructed by curbs, edges, or uneven surfaces. They should be well lighted for both visibility and
security, and rest stops should be located at least every 200 to 300 feet. Seating at rest stops should have backs with high seats
and arms. Those who must stop for rests will need seating designed to be easy to get up from. Rest stops should be at least
partially shaded from the heat of the day. A nearby fountain or bird bath offers something to look at; for many elderly, observing is an "activity."

o   WIDE ENOUGH FOR SMALL
    WHEELED VEHICLES AND
    TWO PERSONS

o   WELL LIGHTED

o   SMOOTH NON-SKID SURFACE
    FLUSH HEADER

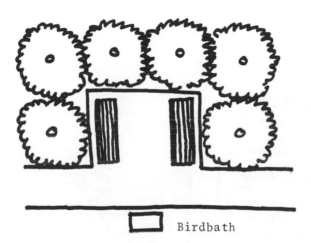

Birdbath

o   REST STOPS 200-300 FEET

o   BENCHES, TREES AND
    BIRDBATH

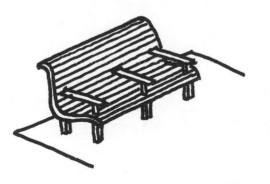

o   COMFORTABLE WOOD BENCHES
    WITH ARMS AND HIGH BACKS

FIGURE 14

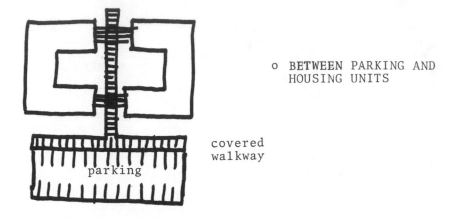

o **BETWEEN** PARKING AND
   HOUSING UNITS

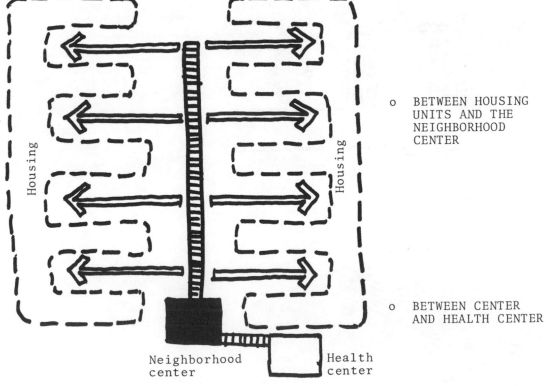

o **BETWEEN** HOUSING
   UNITS AND THE
   NEIGHBORHOOD
   CENTER

o **BETWEEN** CENTER
   AND HEALTH CENTER

FIGURE 15
Covered walkways protect most frequently used segments of the pedestrian system from heavy weather.

Details should include oversized graphics, balanced lighting, nonskid and glare-free surfaces, rest areas related to activity areas, and shelter from sun and wind. Elevators should be large enough to accommodate stretchers and have controls that are easy to see and operate. Design should be flexible and able to be revised or added to inexpensively in the event of disability. Grab bars may be added to sides of toilets (Figure 24); toilets may need to be raised; bathrooms require space for therapy devices; showers may include ledges for sitting; kitchen counters may need to be lowered to be managed from a wheelchair; doors should be wide and free from thresholds. Public seating should be high enough to support thighs; chair backs should support shoulders; chair arms must be sturdy enough to offer support when rising and chair bottoms firm yet resilient enough to prevent discomfort that may result from long periods of sitting.

If automobile parking must be separated from the housing unit to which it is assigned, a roofed-over passenger and unloading zone located near each building's entry will overcome the inconvenience of long walks with packages. Carts stored at the entry help when carrying packages into elevators and down corridors. A loading zone must be designed and marked clearly to discourage permanent parking.

CONCLUSIONS

No community leader, institution, or real estate developer should embark on the planning and development of a special neighborhood for the elderly without being prepared to grapple with a wide variety of surprising problems whose solutions may come only with experience rather than through rational analysis.

Our own experiences have taught us the following:

1. Market research is not easy. Respondents do not easily visualize what is meant by "a special neighborhood for the elderly," and therefore their expressed preferences cannot always be helpful in making decisions.

2. The housing units and amenities should be planned to attract a spectrum of age groups. If the majority of residents are over 75, there will be a heavy demand on services from those least able to afford them. If the majority of residents are in their early sixties, there will be a more even balance between men and women, but they may be unwilling to support the services that the older residents need immediately and which the younger residents will, themselves, need in a few short years.

3. In neighborhoods with condominium ownership of the housing, there may, of course, be no restriction that interferes with anyone's right to buy. Restrictions on occupancy, however, should be considered. A provision in the deed which requires that residents be capable of living independently *at the time of occupancy* will ensure that the residents do not arrive with the need for a level of care beyond the capacity of the neighborhood to provide it. Once a social fabric has been established, those living in the neighborhood who, with age, become incapable of independent care may be helped by the neighborly concern of the more capable.

4. There seems to be strong resistance among many of the heartier elderly to the location of a long-term nursing home close to their residences. To be sure, it would be a convenience for a husband or wife to visit his or her infirm spouse in such a facility set aside on a corner of a special neighborhood for the elderly, and others may feel more secure knowing that such a resource is available. We need more information in order to be able to plan the ideal physical relationship between housing and long-term-care facilities.

5. There is little demand for special facilities for visiting grandchildren, such as playgrounds or extra bedrooms, that would stimulate them to visit any more often than they are asked.

6. Exactly what to call a special neighborhood for the elderly is a puzzle. The terms "elderly," "retirement," and "senior citizens" all have connotations that will offend some of the intended population.

Acknowledgment

The artwork in this chapter is by Howard Altman.

MARY L. WYLIE

Mary L. Wylie is a Professor at the School of Social Work, the University of Wisconsin–Madison.

New Communities

Investigators in the field of aging are only now beginning to document suspicions that community environment bears an important relationship to the health and happiness of elderly persons. The damaging effects of social isolation, inappropriate or substandard housing, economic and physical insecurity, and reduced mobility, conditions to which the elderly are especially prone and which can be addressed through environmental interventions, are now of national concern.

At the same time, widespread attention is being given to the living areas of all citizens, not just the elderly. The broader problems of controlling urban growth and preventing urban decay have resulted in a set of programs and strategies designed to improve the quality of community life. Included among the programs is the "planned new community," a relatively new form of urban development in this country, which holds promise of extending the range of the living choices traditionally available to the elderly (Downs, 1970).

New communities offer a major advantage for designing alternative choices that can be tested, since planning and allocation of resources begin with a relatively clean slate. Ideally, wasteful competition, duplication, gaps in service coverage, and the rigidities of existing bureaucratic systems need not hamper the vision of the developer. Novel arrangements become possible in such areas as building codes, public and private programs of all types, governance structures and relationships, and uses of urban technology on a mass scale. Indeed, much of the literature in America conceptualizes the "new town" as a pilot plant, or laboratory, where innovative social and physical urban systems can be developed and tested (Minnesota Experimental City, 1969).

There are very real constraints, however, on the amount and kind of change that can be implanted in new communities. How much innovation can man tolerate? Are radically changed city systems tolerable (such as a unique educational system) when many must operate within state and federal regulations and guidelines? These are unanswered questions. There is an inevitable loss of control over community design and activity as new residents press their wishes. Additionally, planning and design efforts for an age-balanced new locality will encounter competing claims for resources when age-specific needs surface (e.g., prenatal health services versus geriatric facilities, playgrounds versus open spaces without noise). Furthermore, new-city development in the United States usually proceeds through private, profit-making corporations. As a consequence, decisions must be made within a framework that assures profit on financial investment. The developer must be concerned with attracting a population that can assume the costs of development for dwelling units, will constitute an attractive labor pool for industrial operations, and can afford to consume the commercial products and services any community demands. This leads to an emphasis on the "productive members" of our society who are employable or otherwise have sufficient financial resources to meet the demands of a changing market. Except in the special instance of the "new retirement community," developers will tend, understandably, to give low priority to the needs of the aged in planning deliberations.

With the passage of the Housing and Urban Development Act of 1968, the federal government responded to the growing demand for governmental stimulation of new-city development, and a public—private partnership in the planning, financing, and development of new communities was launched (U.S. Department of Housing and Urban Development, 1968). Under Title IV, the New Communities Act, the government guarantees loans to private developers and supplements local and state public funds for the expensive "front end" requirements—water, sewer, and open-space projects essential to the development. The developer's plans must be economically feasible and include a proper balance of low- and moderate-income housing. The act mandates the federal government to place primary emphasis on establishing the *financial* soundness of the developer's plan before loan guarantees can be made. Much less emphasis is placed on planning for the social, educational, cultural, political, and health systems of the new community.

To receive the mortgage guarantees provided under the New Communities Act, special consideration must be devoted to "low-income" residents. The emphasis is on minority ethnic groups, but where the developer chooses to interpret the elderly as a "low-income" group eligible for housing, the elderly will receive special planning attention. Thus even with this legislation, the creation of an environment responsive to the unique needs of the elderly must await policy

changes that will either provide incentives to the developer to design for older persons or provide more of the aged population with sufficient incomes to contribute to the profits of the new community.

PLANNING FOR THE LIFE CYCLE

Improved environments for the elderly can, however, be achieved despite the very real financial constraints placed upon the developer. The challenge becomes to prepare a master plan that gives highest priority to the needs and preferences of younger residents and concurrently addresses important priorities of the elderly. It is from that stance, the common needs throughout the life cycle, that one can begin to identify community features which may represent an advance in urban living and, at the same time, be tested for their effectiveness in reducing some of the damaging consequences of the aging process. Decisions incorporated into the original master plan stand the best chance of being realized since many will be executed before the developer loses control to residents or to societal forces beyond the geographic boundaries of the new community that impinge upon and influence original goals.

The objectives and philosophy of the new-cities concept find full expression in the publications of the Minnesota Experimental City (MXC), now in its planning phase (Minnesota Experimental City, 1969). The city is conceptualized as developing through a joint public—private effort to improve significantly the human condition, to respond to human needs throughout life, and to serve as a national proving ground for political, economic, social, and physical innovations. This is a unique social policy goal by its very elaboration of all age groups. Perhaps because the MXC planners examined human needs across the life cycle, not just the needs of a particular population group, their deliberations anticipated, by some three years, many of the 1971 White House Conference on Aging recommendations (Toward a National Policy on Aging, 1973). Illustrative examples drawn from MXC publications that directly relate to the White House conference recommendations demonstrate that, when social systems achieve parity with physical and economic systems in planning, the yield can be very high indeed for elderly residents.

FIGURE 1
The new community of Reston, Virginia. There is a clear village center convenient to the elderly housing in the lower right corner of the photograph. (Photo by Blue Ridge Aerial Surveys, courtesy of Gulf Reston, Inc.)

Education. Expanded to provide lifetime learning rather than limited to occupational and vocational training through early adulthood. "Open" programs support a concept of students as all those who wish to take advantage of learning activities in the home, in schools, on the job, in recreational facilities, and in other community settings.

Employment. An alternating work participation—withdrawal cycle throughout the life span to be ter-minated when the employee chooses to retire, with assurance of income through periods of withdrawal and retirement.

Health care. Franchised under a public authority that conceptualizes health care as a right of all residents and specifically recognizes the value of consumer input in the evaluation of quality.

Housing. Included are (1) the home as a "communication center" made possible through the co-

FIGURE 2
Educational programs for older people are an essential ingredient of the new-community service package. (Photo by Linz, courtesy of Leisure Technology Corporation.)

axial cable, (2) housing constructed in accord with performance codes, (3) diverse housing types and sizes to accommodate the full life cycle, and (4) residential communities neither integrated nor segregated but seeking an appropriate intermix of population types.

Transportation. An integrated movement system under single management (as opposed to today's dominant private model) with linkages between places of residence and shopping centers, recreational and cultural centers, industries and airports. Special attention is given, in a review of candidate systems, to a choice appropriate for children, the handicapped, and the aged.

Communications. Coaxial cable to provide home links to physician, hospital, and educational and cultural outputs, surveillance of physical threats to security, participation in governance, and for ordering of goods and services from the home.

Social services. Consumer oriented; based on a determination of common and age-specific needs throughout the life cycle.

Although systematically derived findings on the elderly who now live in new communities are sparse, a few investigations do give us some knowledge about the features of existing new communities that the elderly find attractive. The 1972–1974 project conducted by Weiss et al. (1974) draws together the most comprehensive set of information ever collected for new communities in this country. This is also one of the first efforts to match household responses to objective characteristics of the environment. An outstanding finding from this study is that elderly residents place highest value on the physical environment. Housing, community facilities, social environment, work and transportation opportunities, and living costs were less important as reasons for moving there. Such qualities as appearance of the neighborhood, climate, nearness to natural surroundings, and overall planning were most important reasons for

FIGURE 3
The fully planned community can offer a variety of options, from the combined recreational–shopping transportation fa- cility shown here to highly supportive services for the home- bound. (Photo by Arvil Daniels, courtesy of Gulf Reston, Inc.)

moving and received the highest marks as appreciated community features in comparison to previous residential locations.

These data suggest that planning attention to the physical design of the new community, features over which control can be exercised, is quite properly placed. Generally speaking, the elderly do not see amenities addressed to improved health services or social and convenience needs to be compelling in their search for a new home, although they become highly valued once the elderly person has moved to the new community.

SOME DIVERSE MEANS OF IMPLEMENTING THE CONCEPT

The financial status of the elderly is a crucial issue throughout the White House Conference report. Income problems will be beyond the scope of any single new-town developer to resolve, as evidenced by the fact that the elderly residents in existing new communities have median incomes of well over $10,000. Nonetheless, the concepts set forth by the Minnesota Experimental City planning group are instructive in regard to a proposed development which may indeed have a positive, direct effect on income, and an indirect effect in terms of making available alternatives that are now closed because of limited purchasing power, health care as a right, life-cycle education, and so on.

Technology

Serious questions surround the intrusion of the technological world on man's destiny. However, the MXC consideration of alternative social and physical system concepts could not have been forged without knowledge and acceptance of technological capabilities. From the available inventory of technology, items were chosen on the basis of their potential contribution to the social systems of the city (e.g., the coaxial cable and transportation systems that can be used by the handicapped). For persons with a lessened ability to negotiate their environments, characteristic of many elderly, the MXC list demonstrates that compensation can be effected through technological supports. The new-community planning team will find it can create new options for elderly residents when it operates from a full knowledge of available technologies.

Housing, Land Use, and Transportation

In the absence of clear design criteria to accommodate the needs and aspirations of a vastly heterogeneous elderly population segment, two planning concepts assume real importance:

1. The design of alternative arrangements (e.g., housing) wherever possible so that choice may be exercised by the residents.

2. Major system designs (e.g., transportation and education) that can be comfortably used by persons with conditions or aspirations requiring special consideration.

Adherence to these two concepts moves the planner beyond the customary caveat coming from the social scientist to engage in less planning in the face of uncertainty. In the real world of new-community planning and development, many irrevocable decisions must be made quite early in the game—decisions regarding land use, transportation systems, industrial bases, and the like. Such decisions will have an enormous influence on the character and nature of the developing community. By looking to alternative designs and expanded usage of major systems, the planner can, at the very least, improve urban environments for the elderly by providing options not now available.

If the elderly, and particularly those who have physical handicaps, can move through the community to service, commercial, and cultural facilities, then neighborhood and area concepts regarding the pedestrian proximity of residence to amenities can be reexamined. Innovative transportation systems hold promise of providing the elderly with a level of accessibility that many do not now have. Compact, or one-stop, service and commercial facilities could then be placed close to the transportation system's exit points with supplemental short-range modes of transportation available. Just as the multiservice center is gaining favor in urban areas as an appropriate way to improve accessibility, the new-town planner might well consider the multicommercial establishment rather than a series of shops that may extend over a

FIGURE 4

A compact shopping area close to housing for the elderly offers not only amenities, but a destination for walks and social occasions. The seating arrangements could clearly stand improvement for the older user. (Photo by Arvil Daniels, courtesy of Gulf Reston, Inc.)

considerable distance. Prescriptions, groceries, sundries, post-office services, for example, could be centrally housed.

Undoubtedly, the new community's elderly persons will select a variety of dwelling arrangements. Many elderly will prefer to locate near other older persons; others will prefer to locate in a heterogeneous area. Sales staff can assist prospective residents in their location decisions with a demographic description of households within walking distance.

Many elderly may eventually require a host of supportive services to be delivered within the home as an alternative to institutionalization—health and personal care, dwelling-unit maintenance, grocery or meal delivery, and opportunities to "visit" with other community residents. Most of these services will, at one time or another, be useful to younger residents also. The planner might well consider establishing a proprietary multiservice organization offering such services to community residents. Such an organization could be an employer for elderly persons. Importantly, a well-organized service program operating as soon as possible in the developing new community would provide valuable information on the need for and design of a long-term, health-care facility in the community.

Testing the Market

A repeated suggestion in the literature on aging is that the elderly fare best when their world is a familiar one. One interpretation is that they would then be loathe to move to a new, quite different environment, which is explicit in the objectives of new-community developers. There are suggestions, however, that familiarity with the environment may be less important in voluntary migration decisions than whether the environment is perceived as one that meets the individual's needs. The success of retirement communities, specifically designed as a departure from the characteristics of existing population centers, is established. Approximately 18 percent of the population in the 13 age-balanced new communities examined in the North Carolina project is 55 years or older. The elderly are among the new communities' most satisfied residents, with 90 percent rating their new locality as an "excellent" or "good" place to live. These preliminary observations suggest that there are elderly citizens who for a variety of reasons wish to participate in the new-community alternative. If the public–private partnership is successful in achieving the quality human settlements for all population groups to which it is committed, the nation's future elderly citizens will have an exciting community environment to ponder.

REFERENCES

Delbecq, A., and Van De Ven, A. A group process model for problem identification and program planning. *Journal of Applied Behavioral Science*, 1971, *7*, 466–490.

Downs, A. Alternative forms of future urban growth in the United States. *Journal of the American Institute of Planners*, 1970, *36*, 3–11.

Minnesota Experimental City: Progress Report, May, 1969 (Vol. I, II, III, IV). Minneapolis: School of Architecture, University of Minnesota, 1969.

Status Report I: Research and development goals in social gerontology. *Gerontologist*, 1971, *11*, part II, 1–98.

Status Report II: Research proposals in applied social gerontology. *Gerontologist*, 1971, *11*, part II, 1–98.

Status Report III: Research designs and proposals in applied social gerontology. *Gerontologist*, 1971, *11*, part II, 1–108.

Toward a National Policy on Aging, Final Report. Proceedings of the 1971 White House Conference on Aging, Vol. II. Washington, D.C.: Government Printing Office, 1973.

U.S. Department of Housing and Urban Development. Housing and Urban Development Act of 1968 (Summaries) (Public Law 90-448), August 1968, Washington, D.C.

Weiss, S. F., Burby, J., III, and Zehner, B. *Performance Criteria for New Community Development: Evaluation and Prognosis, NSF/RANN/SSHR Research Grant G1-34285, Evaluation of New Communities, Selected Preliminary Findings*. Chapel Hill, N.C.: Center for Urban and Regional Studies, University of North Carolina. 1974.

ROBERT J. NEWCOMER

Introduction

Robert J. Newcomer is Senior Research Analyst for the County of San Diego Human Resources Agency, Senior Citizens Affairs, San Diego, California.

Successful social-service delivery programs do not just happen; they must be carefully developed through a planning process. This process is composed of inter-related steps: goal identification, needs assessment, priority setting, alternative evaluation, program implementation, and program monitoring.

The paper included here are intended to provide an extensive overview of issues relating to goal identification and alternative evaluation, particularly in matching service locations to their community context. Additionally, there is an explicit guideline for service-need estimation. The major planning steps are briefly reviewed here to put this section's material into a broad context.

Goal identification. The first step in planning recognizes that general goals are necessary direction setters for action. Goals may originate from an organization's statement of purpose, a generalized concern of some community group, or a mandated policy or regulation. Whatever the source, a goal-setting review facilitates effective social-service development by keeping eventual programs within regulations and identifying target populations, the problems to be served, the course of action to be taken, and geographic areas to be served.

For many persons now involved in program planning for the elderly, Title III of the Older Americans Act is seen as the shaper of goals. While these goal statements may define broad program areas, they leave many goals unspecified and questions relating to the size, scope, and configuration of services to be provided unanswered. What should be the spatial distribution of services in terms of access for target groups and economies of scale? How should formal programs be used in relation to informal service networks? What are the factors within the community that are subject to change and which affect service need and utilization?

Kahana, Felton, and Fairchild examine these and many more questions as they discuss the factors potentially affecting service use and modes of delivery. Their paper, in the breadth of issues it addresses, provides the frame of reference for the other papers in Part IV. The orientation of their paper and the subsequent papers is to identify and utilize the links between physical and social phenomena in the provision of services.

Victor Regnier directly complements Kahana, Felton, and Fairchild by providing empirical data on the importance of neighborhoods as service systems.

While summarizing his own work in this area, Regnier also outlines alternative methodologies for the measurement of neighborhoods and for the incorporation of these techniques into environmental design decisions. An overview of cognitive mapping theory, as it applies to this process, is a further bonus.

Needs assessment. The choice of methods for studying needs is limited by the skill, manpower, time, and funds available. Five approaches are commonly used: community surveys, staff surveys, use of available data, monitoring rates of inquiry or service requests, and consumer participation. It is the expectation of the Administration on Aging that information and referral systems will ultimately produce substantial information on the number of services requested, services provided, and unmet service needs. Such a system may function well as a social indicator system, but it lacks the capacity for estimating the actual number (as opposed to relative number) of service units needed within a community.

The paper by Glassman, Tell, Larrivee, and Helland illustrates one technique that is readily adaptable and which can provide this needed information at low cost. Essentially, their approach is to develop service-need estimators from available research findings. National, state, or local data can be used as applicable to the problem in question. In their application, frequently quoted functional ability measures are used to predict the potential population at risk regarding the need for home help services. A subtraction of estimated need from available resources yields an estimate of unmet need.

Many refinements need to be made to this technique, particularly in the areas of applying service-cost estimates and the likely duration of service need, but it is a good beginning for discussion and thought.

Needs assessment, especially as presented here, using census-tract or other geographically aggregated data, has both target-population and target-area connotations, since needs will be based on static population profiles. Effective planning requires an ability not only to react to current problems and spatial distributions, but to expected future problems. Elliott Sclar, in examining aging and residential locations, underscores the importance of migration and population aging in shaping the geographic distribution of the older population. The prediction of these densi-

ties as a requisite for the localization of service-need estimates and service delivery systems over time. The discussion of these issues in the context of urban economic theory further enhances their interest.

Priority setting. The third phase of social-service planning is simply a process of ranking concerns according to given criteria or values so that the order in which the unmet needs will be attacked through program development can be established.

Priority setting is largely a judgmental rather than a technical operation, but a number of techniques have been developed to aid in the judgment. The severity of unmet need, defined as either the absolute number of persons affected or how seriously each need endangers those affected, is one criterion. Additional techniques include ranking according to the availability of resources, administratively establishing a ranking, and a process of participation by the consumers and providers affected.

None of the papers included here specifically addresses the priority-setting issue. However, many issues have been raised that might be incorporated into priority-setting criteria.

Alternative evaluation. The fourth phase begins with an attempt to designate all possible methods of attaining priority objectives. In most cases only a relatively small number of options may be available, but attempts should be made to be exhaustive. One alternative is eventually selected from among the group of feasible alternatives for implementation. This selection process ideally considers such tangible factors as cost, staffing, number served, and resources needed.

Stephen Golant in his review of intraurban transportation needs and problems of the elderly provides an excellent illustration of the background material needed to make such decisions as applied to transportation systems. Golant identifies the extent of the incongruity between elderly consumers and urban transportation systems as he examines underlying causes and attempts to evaluate societal responses, such as reduced fears, special vehicle designs, and minibus services. In the course of his discussion, transportation use patterns, car ownership, trip purposes, and travel time data are presented.

Program implementation. The fifth step is the movilization of resources to generate actions arising from the preceding planning steps. In general, established service organizations implement programs through at least one of the following processes: reallocation of staff and funds or the use of new staff or funds from outside the agency. If no established service agency is involved, implementation requires applications for grants from governmental or foundation sources or the use of voluntary contributions. Grantsman, community organizer, public relations specialist, politician, and salesman are but some of the roles required to develop and activate any program effectively. These multiple roles within one agency by necessity must interact with a similar set of roles within a variety of other agencies. Herein lies the basis for many of the "political" problems in program planning. C. L. Estes, using a case study of three planning organizations for the elderly, documents a pervasive tendency toward goal displacement, which diverted attention away from service to agency image building. Estes concludes that this problem is great enough to threaten the meaningful implementation of comprehensive planning for elderly services. Thus, although case study material on specific program implementation is unavailable, her paper has broad salience for identifying likely problems that can befall attempts at program coordination.

Program monitoring. The last step in planning provides feedback about program operation, permitting the service delivery system to grow and function as a self-correcting system.

Monitoring is basically the process of checking a program's performance relative to program objectives and is accomplished by a routine flow of information. The minimum kinds of information required include the number of eligible consumers requesting service, number receiving service, length of service need, number not receiving service, number and type of unmet need, and number and type of services delivered. These measures should be adequate indicators of how well program objectives are being met. Such other

measures as units of manpower expended, type of staff activity, and cost outlay can indicate the rate and effectiveness of resource consumption.

A third type of monitoring is concerned with a program's effectiveness in solving the problems or meeting the needs of those for whom it was originally implemented. Included in this type of evaluation research are attempts to discover the causal factors that produce problems and the factors operating to reduce the effectiveness of a program intervention strategy. The papers by Newcomer and Baer in Part II, which criticized housing programs for the elderly, provide illustrations of the complexity of issues and measurement that may arise in service program evaluation.

Sophisticated evaluation of major programs is essential if we are to learn from both our mistakes and successes. Recent evaluations of information and referral systems, such as those conducted by Nicholas Long in Wisconsin, and comparisons of home helps and nursing-home service efficiencies, as provided by Pfeiffer in North Carolina, are examples of efforts having national significance.

Not all evaluation need be extensive or of long duration to be effective. Thomas Byerts's paper is an example of how inexpensive evaluative research can be used to produce appropriate design and policy decisions. In this case both questionnaires and behavior observation were used to monitor park equipment usage.

Although the papers in this section provide less than a complete guideline to the planning of community services for older people, they do raise important questions and even suggest some answers about goals, site selection, service accessibility, needs estimation, mobility patterns, program coordination, and program monitoring. Of equal importance, they reiterate the theme that social-service planning must be done within the context of the physical environments in which people reside.

E. KAHANA, B. FELTON, AND T. FAIRCHILD

Eva Kahana is an Associate Professor at the Elderly Care Research Center of the Department of Sociology, Wayne State University, Detroit, Michigan. Barbara Felton is a graduate student at the University of Michigan and is affiliated with the Elderly Care Research Center at Wayne State University. Thomas J. Fairchild is a graduate student at Wayne State University and is affiliated with the Elderly Care Research Center.

Community Services and Facilities Planning

Elderly persons undergo many and varied role losses and are often burdened by health, financial, and emotional problems that render them especially vulnerable to adverse environmental circumstances. Due to social changes the family, friends, or neighbors no longer provide sufficient supports to the older person to help him cope with problems of old age or incapacity. Organized supports are needed to maintain many aged persons in their independent community living arrangements and to prevent or delay the need for institutional care.

Numerous surveys show that older people, when given a choice, would overwhelmingly prefer to stay in their own homes or live in settings offering maximum independence and privacy, even when faced with incapacity (Riley and Foner, 1968). Even older adults who are capable of continued independent living in the community encounter many special problems in coping with social role changes and limited resources. Concern with maintaining and improving the quality of life for older people involves a wide array of approaches, ranging from basic life supports and treatments to deal with incapacity through provisions of facilities and resources to promote interaction, high morale, and continued high levels of functioning.

In the following discussion issues related to the planning and delivery of a spectrum of services for older people will be presented. The need for organized, formal, community-sponsored services will be considered in the light of existing informal resources. Research evidence relevant to determining service needs, the planning of alternative service typologies, service priorities, and cost effectiveness will be reviewed. Of necessity, the review of research evidence will be illustrative rather than exhaustive; emphasis will be placed on the delineation of critical issues. A discussion of the nature and types of formal services will be followed by a discussion of the relevance of informal social supports and the community context of services including housing. Factors affecting needs for services, service utilization, and service effectiveness will be raised and the discussion will conclude with a consideration of alternative strategies in service delivery.

NATURE AND TYPES OF FORMAL SERVICES

Proper functions of community services may include varying degrees of support. Thus *preventive or facilitative services* help the competent elderly utilize and retain their existing capacities and provide ameni-

FIGURE 1
A major preventive service is the senior center, which tends
to be utilized by healthier-than-average older people. (Photo
courtesy of Administration on Aging, U.S.D.H.E.W.)

ties for productive, fulfilled living past retirement.
Supportive services help those with incapacity to remain in their own homes. *Rehabilitative services* help
to restore a level of functioning consistent with inde-

pendent or semi-independent living. Finally, *sheltered
care* provides congregate, semi-institutional facilities
for those who cannot cope with community living
owing to physical or mental problems. Services may
also be classified as "prosthetic" or "therapeutic"
(Lawton, 1970). A prosthetic approach assumes the
existence of disability and provides environmental
supports. In contrast, the therapeutic approach seeks
to alter the disability, striving for improvement in the
individual rather than in the environment.

The large majority of older people show needs for
certain basic programs. facilities, and services to promote customary life styles and standard of living and
to improve the quality of life. Such services range
from transportation, shopping, and provision of
safety, which are essential to daily living, through
amenities such as parks, recreational services, senior
centers, and adult education programs, which promote social interaction and well-being of older people
and become especially significant after retirement.
Such services are especially important for those
whose impairment is greater and resources more limited.

The older people who have special needs for service supports to enable them to maintain independent
existences in the community often require special
health, social, institutional, and couseling services.
The more acute nature of the needs in this group has
focused the attention of planners on the provision of
environmental supports primarily for this relatively
small but needy group.

Many programs could potentially fulfill two sets of
functions. They may serve preventive and enrichment
functions for those aged with minimal incapacity and
supportive functions for those whose impairment is
greater and resources more limited. Because of the
generally fragmented system of service delivery and
the lack of coordinated approaches, numerous community agencies have undertaken the development of
individual programs in selected areas that are available
only to special target populations.

Once different levels of functional ability and individual need are specified and different types of services existing in the community identified, those people requiring maintenance or supportive services may
be guided to the appropriate source. The individual
would also be able to move between different levels
of service. For example, special bus or transportation

service may be sufficient during the summer for a given older person but home-delivered meals may be required during winter months. A survey of the literature on actual services reveals that service consumers have different needs, characteristics, and utilization patterns. It is therefore important to focus on the variety of needs for noninstitutional services for the aged.

In developing estimates of the extent of needed services per unit of population, the total population of elderly minus about 5 percent residing in institutions is often used. When social services aimed at prevention are considered, potential users of such services may come from the entire noninstitutionalized aged population. In contrast, the need for supportive functions such as social or nutritional programs has been estimated at about 20 percent of the noninstitutionalized age population.

Classification of services in terms of objectives and content at least partially describes their sponsorship, location, and service delivery pattern. Thus public sponsorship of welfare services and recreational programs is typical. Supportive services that provide alternatives to institutional care are often sponsored by

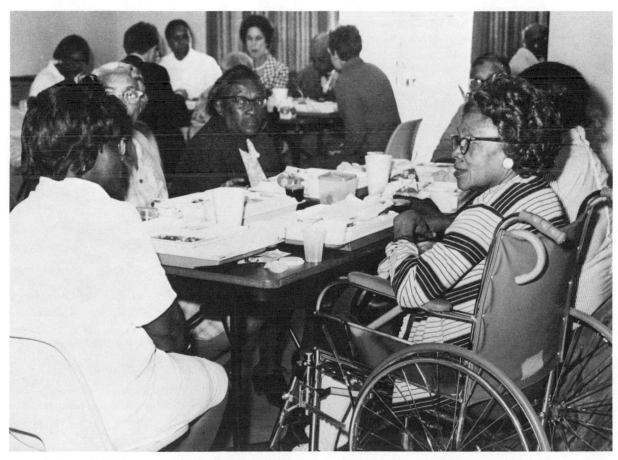

FIGURE 2
Nutrition programs serve not only those whose diets would be otherwise unsatisfactory, but those who enjoy a social occasion or the occasional relief from having to prepare their own meals. (Photo courtesy of Administration on Aging, U.S.D.H.E.W.)

voluntary agencies. Many sheltered care programs are operated on a commercial basis. Supportive services often develop out of a medical model of service delivery and are administered by or located in health-care facilities. Similarly, counseling programs may develop as part of a community mental health facility, whereas recreational or adult education programs tend to grow out of community center activities. There is some controversy about the relative merit of institution-based versus community-based comprehensive service programs. The medical model of services that attempts to "cure ills" is at times seen as creating dependency, whereas the community-based model, which attempts to prevent these ills, is criticized for the inadequacy of its resources and the unavailability of trained personnel. On balance, both appear to be viable and potentially productive alternative models in service delivery.

Few elderly avail themselves of traditional social services and those who do are not the most needy. Even the operation of a community-based action program may find that its major impact is on the relatively small number of able and aggressive elderly who made their way to an agency (Ehrlich, 1969). Similarly, Storey (1962) suggested after studying users and nonusers of a multiservice senior center that such centers may be "mainly attracting a large group of energetic, outgoing older people who especially enjoy group associations." The notion that senior-citizen centers serve a rather elite group of older people was also supported by Tissue's (1971) study showing participants in a California senior-citizen center to be of higher socioeconomic status, healthier, and more sociable than nonparticipants.

Community outreach represents one potentially useful method for overcoming the reluctance of the aged to ask for help and for developing demand for services that are not available. Such outreach programs also represent a preventive orientation in contrast to traditional service programs, which are usually aimed toward ameliorating already existing programs. At present, very few preventive or case-finding programs seek out people with medical and psychosocial needs before their condition deteriorates and institutionalization is required. In addition, in those programs which provide supports there is usually little concern with the total problem of the individual

FIGURE 3
Energetic behavior is required for some senior-center activities, but onlookers also get their shares of enjoyment.

client. Instead, services are often developed to fit a single presumed need and individuals must translate their total needs into the scheme of the single service provided. Such lack of comprehensive, problem-oriented services results in frequent referral of individuals from agency to agency, with resulting confusion and discouragement. In this context, Kaplan

(1967) urged that we recognize the importance of individualization of essential services and argued that community services must be organized to provide alternatives for the older individual.

INFORMAL SERVICE SUPPORTS

A very important but often overlooked source of services to the aged is "the significant others," that is, friends, family, and neighbors. The family often is the major informal resource providing needed supportive services, especially in crisis situations (Shanas, 1962). In assessing the informal social networks of older people with any accuracy, one must consider its multidimensional nature:

1. Interaction patterns, visiting, phone calls, and the like, represent one important aspect of that network.

2. Helping patterns represent a related but distinct area for understanding the relationships of the older person with his significant others.

3. In addition to looking at problems of interaction or helping patterns, one must also consider the emotional significance of various people for the aged.

In planning for *formal* services for older people, a consideration of the *informal* social network may be helpful in several ways. Knowledge of areas where informal helping patterns are insufficient to meet needs provides a logical starting point for setting service priorities. Members of the informal social network should be involved and utilized as much as possible in planning and implementing services, for example, in volunteer and advocacy capacities. Providing services to those individuals who are interested and involved in giving supports to the older person may also represent a valuable shortcut in the delivery of formal services. For example, providing babysitting services to a young mother may permit her to care periodically for her older parents. Thus in a very real sense planners and providers of services to the aged can utilize the helping potential of the family and neighbors.

COMMUNITY CONTEXT OF NEEDS FOR SERVICES

The neighborhood and community are additional important influences in determining needs for formal services. In this context, neighborhoods may be conceptualized as stressors or facilitators. Thus there is evidence that neighborhoods characterized by high socioenvironmental stresses affect the physical and mental health of their residents (Goering and Coe, 1970). The physical characteristics and social fabric of the neighborhood may affect the older person and influence the aggregate need for services. On the one hand, the community may be seen as a potential service in and of itself and, on the other hand, as a context within which formal services are required and delivered.

Thus behavior settings that in one community are congenial and encouraging of participation may in another be crime-ridden or alien, discouraging older people from congregating. Local stores that are familiar and stable such as the corner grocery store may represent an important informal social resource to older residents in one community but be threatening as a kids' corner "hangout" in another neighborhood. Larger new shopping centers may be difficult for older people to navigate in but once familiar may afford stimulation to a suburban elderly group.

Studies relating environmental features to needs for services have traditionally focused on institutional settings (Turner et al., 1972). A few investigators have turned to the broader context of the community, where the majority of aged in fact reside, in considering service needs (Kent and Hirsch, 1971; Kahana, 1974).

HOUSING CONTEXT OF SERVICES

The majority of people over 65 are homeowners who maintain independent life styles in a community setting (Vivrett, 1960). Because of current demographic trends, the number and proportions of elderly community residents will continue to increase; however, little if any planning has dealt adequately with the present and future problems and needs of these people. Too often programs are developed for the minority of the aged population who require sheltered care; the vast majority of community residents who also require assistance are overlooked.

On the one hand, adequacy of housing is an important determinant of needs for various community services; on the other hand, housing may represent or include services that contribute to the satisfaction of social and psychological needs of the older person. The familiar residential environment, when supportive of customary living habits and combined with an adequate standard of living, provides the older person with a sense of security and reduces anxiety (Donahue and Ashley, 1959). Residential stability that also ensures continuity of important social contacts within the older adult's life space is similarly facilitative.

The older person's housing arrangements, like his larger environment, can be viewed as a stressor or a facilitator. Demands for upkeep made by the housing unit constitute a common form of environmental stress. Furthermore, psychosocial losses and reductions in the individual's functional ability may exacerbate the amount of stress imposed by a particular housing arrangement. Evidence of service needs in terms of repairs, yard work, and home maintenance was found in a recent survey of relatively intact and independent aged living in the community (Kahana, 1974). Planners and service providers may thus be faced with a trade-off between providing special services versus relocating the individual in a relatively maintenance free environment. Reductions in environmental demands must here be weighed against the stresses of relocation.

The individual with a more dependent life style, resulting from declining health, bereavement, or psychosocial losses, may require more extensive home-based services. Many of these older adults seek special or sheltered housing. They may no longer seek out community services away from their home but rather rely on the ability of the protective environment to satisfy their needs. Thus there is an increasing demand for special housing for the aged that provides such services as the preparation and serving of meals, housekeeping, and medical care.

FACTORS AFFECTING SERVICE UTILIZATION

For services to be utilized, especially by those aged or disabled who are suffering from impairments, they msut be accessible. Accessibility is not only a geographic but also a social issue. The aged person must perceive services as within his usual life space and hence accessible. It is generally agreed that proximity of residence to the service facility is a key factor in utilization. Yet provision of several different services in one location (centralization of services) may also help increase use (Vivrett, 1960). Few older people actually live within walking distance of all needed services. Therefore, location of residence and accessibility of services must take into account the transportation routes and systems within the community. It would appear that utilization of a service is less a function of actual distance to service than of the time it takes to reach these services or the transportation route to them. Factors such as the familiarity of cultural or ethnic symbols and real and perceived safety in reaching the services also contribute to accessibility. The particular type of social interaction with peers that is incidental to the provision of a service may also facilitate or hinder utilization of formal services, thereby encouraging or thwarting efforts at service delivery (Frederick, 1971).

The relation of residential density to delivery of services raises some important issues. Older adults living in rural areas are often more physically, though not less socially, isolated than their urban counterparts. Special services to meet the needs of rural aged must rely more heavily on approaching the target groups in their natural habitat, for example, by providing nutritional, cultural, and recreational services in mobile units, rather than developing centralized services that are not readily accessible to the older person in a rural setting. On the other hand, the high residential density that characterizes many urban settings dictates a different strategy for service delivery. Satellite service centers may be located within walking distance of large numbers of older people, or transportation may be provided to utilize already existing services.

Older, central-city neighborhoods often constitute the residential context of older people. The age of the community itself may influence the presence or absence of services and the need for new facilities as perceived by planners and politicians (Vivrett, 1960). High concentrations of older people are often found in such older areas along with urban renewal and frequent resultant relocation of older residents. Because of their weakened tax base, such neighborhoods often offer few facilities and suffer from a decay of their social fabric.

FIGURE 4
If satisfactory public transportation is not available, specialized transport systems will be necessary to provide access to services. (Photo by Richard Mowrey, U.S.D.H.U.D.)

Public housing projects, which are characterized by congregate living arrangements, offer still another challenge to delivery of services. Some of the more pressing issues in this setting are crime and physical security (*Housing for the Elderly*, 1973).

Two approaches may be taken to combat problems of crime. First, services may be provided that themselves curb crime. For example, instruction may be given in ways to secure one's household and person, when to go out, how to cash checks, or how to use a checking account. In addition, physical settings with architectural features that reduce the potential for crime and better police protection may help to protect the elderly from victimization. The concept of "defensible space" (Newman, 1972) may be espe-

cially useful to planners in this regard. Such protection may be best secured by integrating service delivery to the aged into the larger context of communitywide social action and planning. Second, special services may be needed to make other services more accessible. These include escort services to shopping, the location of senior centers in facilities familiar and safe to older people, and the bringing of mobile services to the homes of the elderly. Crime affects both the providers and recipients of services, creating staffing problems in high-crime areas.

Attempts to upgrade residential areas and to provide preventive aid to older residents in the upkeep and stabilizing of neighborhoods represent genuine community services. Yet urban-renewal programs,

FIGURE 5
Independent housing units may be located in proximity to an institution, but linked loosely enough so that tenants do not feel like part of the institution. Shown here is the Community Housing Branch of the Philadelphia Geriatric Center, which has utilized existing row houses. (Photo by Lindelle Studios.)

which on the surface appear to improve or upgrade neighborhoods, in the past have often served to displace older people and destroy the quality of life in the neighborhood. Recently, successful efforts have been made to relocate older people from communities that no longer provided needed services and which threatened their life styles to more supportive communities (Sherwood, et al., 1971).

The important role of the community as a context of service needs suggests that service planning for the urban aged must use the *community* as a basic unit of analysis.

FACTORS AFFECTING NEEDS FOR DEVELOPMENT OF SERVICES AND SERVICE EFFECTIVENESS

Based on the foregoing discussion and a review of the literature, an outline of factors related to service delivery can be provided.

1. Development of new services may be seen as a function of the needs of significant numbers of older people. The level of self-sufficiency and expressed preferences of the potential consumers determine, in part, the need for new services.

2. The nature and availability of existing services within the community likewise affect the need for service development. The extent of this need is a function of both the availability of adequate informal social supports and the capabilities of existing formal services.

3. The need for the development of new services is also affected by the potential resources available in the community for such activities. The accessibility of local, state, and federal funds and the local priority system will determine the scope of service development.

The determinants of service needs comprise a dynamic rather than a static system, because the needs of the aged change over time. Consequently, models of service delivery must be flexible. The availability, accessibility, and quality of existing services must be continuously evaluated. The cost of expanding or modifying existing services must be weighed against the advantages of developing new services. In this regard, the utility of expanding services in existing hospitals and institutions to serve the needs of older people outside their walls may be noted. Successful examples of this approach are reflected in work of the Philadelphia Geriatric Center (Brody, 1974) and the British day hospitals in Oxford (Cosin, 1956).

A review of program planning in the area of services to the aged reveals that the above criteria are in fact seldom used as the basis for creating services (Binstock, 1967). New services have in fact largely been developed in response to political pressures and under the impetus of available funding. The norm has too often been short-term, uncoordinated planning of unidimensional services, resulting in duplication of efforts in some areas and wide gaps in services in others.

ALTERNATIVE STRATEGIES IN SERVICE DELIVERY

The strategy by which services are delivered may have an impact on whether or not the services are utilized and whether they are effective in improving the well-being of older people. In choosing a strategy for delivering community services, the planner must determine the appropriateness of various locations, the different recipients, and the various types of service.

One crucial issue in determining appropriate location is that of accessibility versus choice. Older peo-

FIGURE 6
Freedom of choice for the older person may be provided in many settings. The high activity level of the senior center should not preclude the possibility of intimate contacts or solitary activity. (Photo by Sam Nocella.)

ple are often victims of immobility. If services are located close to the residences of older people, the potential for service utilization and for meeting service needs will certainly be enhanced. The older person, however, may thus be denied freedom of choice in selecting different types of services or service personnel. The current concern for consumer choice and self-determination of needs underlines the necessity for providing the aged individual with the opportunity to select specific service agents as well as the types of services that he feels he needs. Blenkner et al. (1971) point out our excessive dependence on experts in deciding how service needs of the older person are met.

In view of the generally poor financial status of the elderly population, a crucial issue in service delivery revolves areound the manner of providing aid to the aged in defraying service costs. Options include provision of cash so that older adults may purchase services, direct provision of service to the aged at no cost, or third-party payments for existing services. Financial assistance provides the greatest freedom of choice to the older adult among these options. However, it presupposes judgmental capacity, the availability of low-cost services that the individual could purchase, and his familiarity with such services. Direct service provision may secure services at a lower cost to the aged recipient than privately purchased

FIGURE 7
Options should include the opportunity to engage in activities with people of all ages or with people of one's own age group. (Photo courtesy of Administration on Aging, U.S.D. H.E.W.)

comparable services but may also eliminate consumer control. Third-party payment for commercial services, although currently most available, leaves older people with little recourse if they receive inadequate services, especially in institutional settings.

Although the cost-effectiveness implications of different service programs are not clear, it has been argued that programs aimed at prevention are more economical than those whose object is support or rehabilitation. Although this may be true when the target population is easily identified, the cost of locating the needy, isolated older person is high.

The question of the social integration of the aged has been a major issue underlying program planning for the elderly. Most studies on the effects of age segregation have focused on institutional and group housing. Whereas Rosow's (1967) studies of housing suggested age segregation to be beneficial in promoting social interaction, Kahana and Kahana (1970) found that placement of psychiatric patients in age-integrated mental hospital wards led to signficantly greater improvement in interactivity and cognitive functioning than placement in a completely age segregated setting. Results of studies considering leisure programs for older people (Goodman et al., 1974) suggest that older adults are often reluctant to utilize leisure activities which are primarily designated for older people.

The relative desirability of homogeneity or heterogeneity of groupings with respect to age, sex, common cultural and ethnic background, or functional ability is as much of an unsettled issue in serving the aged as it is in serving other sectors of our society. Sterne and Woolf (1971) have recently described a successful community-based pilot program to test the mutual benefits derived from an integration of both well and sick elderly in an activity and service program. Extensive interviews held with both sick and well groups indicated that after program participation the psychological and social well-being of both had improved.

On balance, further work is needed to specify the conditions under which relative homogeneity or heterogeneity are desirable. At the same time, services should be planned so as to give the option of participating in either age-segregated or age-integrated programs.

FIGURE 8
If a setting for the elderly is age-homogeneous, extra effort should be made to encourage other forms of contact among generations.

CONCLUSIONS

Adequate funding is necessary if optimal use is to be made of the ideas presented in this paper. In view of federal cutbacks in many welfare expenditures, financially efficient, as well as maximally effective, approaches to the development of new services and to the delivery of existing services are required. The need to rely on existing services is more pressing than ever before. Retraining staff and developing new forms of services within established structures may be necessary. Private service delivery programs may have to be expanded, and cooperation between public and private agencies will be essential if we are to meet the ever-increasing needs of our elderly population. The burden of care for the elderly would thus rest upon such comprehensive service delivery networks. State financing of personal care to older people may represent a promising prospect to planners (Morris and Harris, 1972).

In practical terms, then, services may be planned using a framework that takes into account individual as well as community needs, supportive systems already available, and prevalent cultural attitudes. A multidimensional system model also makes it possible to enter the system with equal effectiveness at any service level, that is, the community, the informal social organization, the family, or the individual.

The abilities of older people themselves, both as consumers and as service providers, must not be devalued. The importance of older people as a resource has been overlooked in past planning. The attitudes and opinions of older people and their capacity to assist in the provision of help must be utilized for optimal planning.

REFERENCES

Binstock, R. H. What sets the goals of community planning for the aging? *Gerontologist*, 1967, *7*, 44–46.

Blenkner, M., Bloom, M., and Nielsen, M. A research and demonstration project of protective services. *Social Casework*, 1971, *52*, 483–499.

Brody, E. M. Service-supported independent living in an urban setting. In T. O. Byerts (ed.), *Housing and Environment for the Elderly: A Working Conference on Behavioral Research Utilization and Environmental Policy*. Washington, D.C.: Gerontological Society, 1974.

Butler, R. Proposals for changes at St. Elizabeth's Hospital: with special reference to the care of elderly patients. Mimeographed. Washington, D.C.: St. Elizabeth's Hospital, 1969.

Cosin, L. Z. The organization of a day hospital for psychiatric patients. *Proceedings of the Royal Society of Medicine*, 1956, *49*, 237–239.

Donahue, W., and Ashley, E. E., III. Housing and the social health of older people. In C. Tibbitts (ed.), *Aging and Social Health in the United States and Europe*. Ann Arbor, Mich.: University of Michigan, Division of Gerontology, 1959.

Ehrlich, P. Report on the older adult community action project. Mimeographed. St. Louis, Mo.: Jewish Federation of St. Louis, 1969.

Frederick, K. L. Interaction among the aged and role of the user of services: implications for planning services for the aged. Paper presented at the annual meeting of the Gerontological Society, Houston, Tex., October 1971.

Goering, J. M., and Coe, R. M. Cultural and situational influences on the medical adaptations of the poor. *Social Science Quarterly*, 1970, *51*, 269–319.

Golant, S. M. *The Residential Location and Spatial Behavior of the Elderly: A Canadian Example*. University of Chicago, Department of Geography Research Monograph, no. 143. Chicago: University of Chicago, 1972.

Goodman, M., Bley, N., and Dye, D. The adjustment of aged users of leisure programs. *American Journal of Orthopsychiatry*, 1974, *44*, 142–149.

Herz, K. Community resources and services to help independent living. *Gerontologist*, 1969, *9*, part 2, 75–86.

Housing for the Elderly. Report of the Senate Subcommittee on Aging, 1973. Washington, D.C.: Government Printing Office, 1973.

Kahana, E. Service needs of urban aged in two ethnic communities. Paper presented at the annual meeting of the Gerontological Society, Portland, Ore., October 1974.

_____, and Kahana, B. Therapeutic potential of age integration. *Archives of General Psychiatry*, 1970, *23*, 20–29.

Kaplan, J. Appraising the traditional organizational

basis of providing gerontological services. *Gerontologist*, 1967, *7*, part 1, 200–203.

Kent, D., and Hirsch, C. Needs and use of services among negro and white aged. Vol. 1. Social and economic conditions of negro and white aged residents of urban neighborhoods of low socioeconomic status: final report. University Park, Pa.: Pennsylvania State University, Department of Sociology and Anthropology, 1971.

Lawton, M. P. Planner's notebook: planning environments for older people. *Journal of the American Institute of Planners*, 1970, *36*, 124–129.

Morris, R., and Harris, E. Home health services in Massachusetts, 1971: their role in the care of the long-term sick. *American Journal of Public Health*, 1972, *62*, 1088–1093.

Newman, O. *Defensible Space.* New York: Macmillan, 1972.

Ogle, T., Kahana, E., Harel, Z., and Clack, C. A multitrait, multimethod analysis of preferences of aged in three residential homes. Paper presented at the annual meeting of the Gerontological Society, Houston, Tex., October 1971.

Riley, M. S., and Foner, A. (eds.). *Aging and Society. Vol. 1: An Inventory of Research Findings.* New York: Russell Sage Foundation, 1968.

Rosow, L. *Social Integration of the Aged.* New York: Free Press, 1967.

Shanas, E. *The Health of Older People.* Cambridge, Mass.: Harvard University Press, 1962.

Sherwood, S., Grier, D. S., Morris, J. N., and Sherwood, C. C. *The Highland Heights Experiment.* Washington, D.C.: Government Printing Office, 1971.

Sterne, R., and Woolf, L. Centralizing a program for sick and healthy senior citizens. Paper presented at the annual meeting of the Gerontological Society, Houston, Tex., October 1971.

Storey, R. T. Who attends a senior activity center? *Gerontologist*, 1962, *2*, 216–222.

Tissue, T. Social class and the senior citizen center. *Gerontologist*, 1971, *11*, 196–200.

Turner, B. F., Tobin, S. S., and Lieberman, M. A. Personality traits as predictors of institutional adaptation among the aged. *Journal of Gerontology*, 1972, *27*, 61–68.

Vivrett, W. K. Housing and community settings for older people. In C. Tibbitts (ed.), *Handbook of Social Gerontology.* Chicago: University of Chicago Press, 1960.

VICTOR REGNIER

Victor Regnier is Preceptor, Urban and Regional Planning, Ethel Percy Andrus Gerontology Center, University of Southern California, Los Angeles.

Neighborhoods as Service Systems

The measurement of neighborhood use and comprehension is of critical importance in the evaluation of how areas of the city should be altered or preserved to match best the needs and preferences of user groups. To date much of the renewing of our cities has been performed with economic and political motivations, which show little sensitivity toward the subpopulations that are most affected by the planning of services and the reconstruction of the physical environment.

The objective of renewal and reconstruction is generally to precipitate a positive change in the total environment. However, most often the change is positive only for a small select group and sometimes has negative outcomes for all persons involved.

Traumatic change, typified by large-scale renewal, represents a fundamentally different process from that of incremental change. Furthermore, the persons most affected by the loss of a familiar, well-delineated physical neighborhood, the rerouting of bus lines, and the delivery of services in poorly selected locations are the elderly.

Clearly, a methodology is needed that will communicate to decision makers and planners the values that the elderly place on existing areas and resources within a neighborhood so that efforts to improve the neighborhood context will not result in the destruction of identifiable key elements.

This paper introduces "cognitive mapping" as an applied tool for evaluating the use and perception of local neighborhood areas. Two empirical case studies that employ substantially different research designs are reviewed and their implications for planners and decision makers discussed.

Cognitive Mapping

Cognitive maps are the mental result of the everyday coping process that requires the individual to learn where in the environment a certain valued object is located and how one navigates from a given location to that object (Downs and Stea, 1973).

The formation of cognitive maps is motivated by the need to order the elements of the physical environment so as to facilitate navigation. For example, we have all found ourselves on the telephone being given instructions to a particular place and tracing our position along an imaginary route in our minds. Later, as the trip is negotiated, this internalized guidance map is used constantly to reinforce the correctness or incorrectness of navigation decisions based on a comparison of the actual environment with an imagined cognitive representation.

Use of an internalized "imaginary map" in navigation was documented early by geographers (Trowbridge, 1913). Trowbridge discovered that people orient themselves in cities and elsewhere by relying on a mental map that dictates the direction in which things lie from a given point of reference.

Psychologists did not begin grappling seriously with this notion until Tolman (1948) hypothesized that rats actually did build in their brains neuropsychological representations of the pathways that led them from a starting point through a maze to a food box at the end. His belief was that rats developed over time an internal comprehensive representation of the pathway. Rather than merely reacting to immediate external stimuli such as sight, sound, or smell, the rats were thought to use cognitive maps to help learn the food-box location.

Since Tolman's early experiments, the notion of cognitive mapping has been given multidisciplinary application. Currently, researchers in the fields of geography, education, psychology, urban planning, and architecture have all become interested in discovering more about the process through which information is acquired, coded, stored, recalled, and decoded so as to comprehend the locations and attributes of phenomena in the everyday spatial environment (Downs and Stea, 1973).

Few current research efforts in cognitive mapping have dealt specifically with the elderly as a subpopulation group, although they possess great potential for study. Children have often been the subjects of various cognitive mapping research efforts because of their restricted view of the surrounding environment and their ability to discuss or represent with ease their perceptions of the surrounding environment.

The elderly are similar to children in that they often relate to a much smaller geographical area than the more mobile age cohorts between childhood and old age. The importance of a locally defined neighborhood setting to the elderly is well recognized. It has generally been accepted by most that the loss of the spouse or worker roles, a decrease in general physical competence, and low fixed incomes all contribute to a lessening of mobility that constricts life

space. These events, in part or together, increase both dependence on a local environment and the ability to define with relative precision a local neighborhood. It is this ability to define a local neighborhood that gives cognitive mapping methodologies in elderly subjects great promise. Most cognitive mapping methods to date have not been satisfactory in explaining neighborhood use and behavior patterns in middle-aged, middle-class individuals precisely because their financial independence and high mobility free them from depending on a local neighborhood for a majority of goods and services.

Translating the Cognitive Image to Paper

Understanding the simplistic notion of the cognitive map and attempting to operationalize a methodology for eliciting, measuring, and comparing cognitive images are two very different tasks. The research presented here has chosen to measure, compare, and analyze the geographic areas outlined by respondents as being included in their local neighborhood. To facilitate this comparative analysis, respondents were given a special large-scale map of the city and asked to outline their neighborhood. An inherent drawback to this chosen methodology is the fact that individual cognitive maps may deviate significantly from accurate cartographic reality. Cognitive maps may include, exclude, or create elements of the familiar environment (Ladd, 1970; Appleyard, 1970). Furthermore, the encoding and decoding process involved in the creation of cognitive maps may organize and categorize various elements of the environment in substantially different ways (Weisman, 1974).

Other researchers have attempted to deal more accurately with cognitive representations by using a blank sheet of paper to elicit the neighborhood cognitive map. Although this method provides the best representation of that individual's unique neighborhood, the results from this approach are often impossible to compare because of the highly diverse manner in which respondents reconstruct their cognitive maps on paper. Often the neighborhood representation is abstract and consists of inaccurately related parts of the actual environment.

The chosen methodology in the research to be reported here facilitated the comparison of results because it forced respondents to relate their particular image of the neighborhood to a common base map. Thus a reliable composite map was created.

Social and Environmental Delimiters and Incentives

Cognitive maps can be affected by a broad range of delimiters and incentives, each of which may exert a force of different strength so as to limit or enhance the cognition of the surrounding neighborhood. Incentives encourage the use, and thus the cognition, of surrounding areas. Within this category, factors such as low crime rates and flat surrounding streets could be included. Delimiters act to discourage use and thus limit the use and cognition of surrounding areas. Within this category could be included factors such as high crime rates and major topographic changes. The strength and relationship of delimiters to incentives have a great effect on the relative importance each may possess. For example, if the topography surrounding a site is extremely varied it may be a strong delimiter, canceling the positive effect of a resource such as a convenience store. Likewise, the strength of an incentive such as public transportation can cancel the negative effect of a topographic delimiter.

Delimiters and incentives can be separated into two categories: environmental factors and social factors. Environmental factors include variables such as street traffic, topography, bus routes, retail goods, or social services. These variables are both natural and man-created factors that affect the use and accessibility of the surrounding neighborhood. Social factors may include crime, elderly population density, ethnic mix, or incidence of pathology. These variables are defined by the sociological and pathological characteristics of surrounding neighbors. Social and environmental factors are defined by the composition of the surrounding environment, but each subject's ability to use neighborhood resources is contingent on that respondent's personal characteristics.

Effect of Personal Characteristics

Personal characteristics such as health, neighborhood familiarity, physical capability, automobile ownership, and the individual's perceptions of his own capability monitor each respondent's ability to cope with incentives and delimiters. For example, a slight topographic change between a residence and an important retail service will be negotiated more easily by a person in good physical shape than the person with an acute arthritic condition.

Each subject's individual characteristics lend a uniqueness to the perceived neighborhood, but the basic set of given environmental and social factors creates the context within which this perception is exercised.

Delimiters and incentives have a collective effect on the amount, direction, and shape of the area claimed to be part of the neighborhood. For example, if a number of individuals perceive the shape and direction of the neighborhood similarly, then patterns of spatial reinforcement begin to define those areas most often claimed as belonging to a local, familiar "home range."

Delimiters and incentives are defined as that set of environmental and social factors that tend to direct the use of the physical environment. The continuing reinforcing source of stimulation for the formation and maintenance of cognitive maps is the actual manner in which the individual establishes an interface with the environment to provide himself with a minimum level of "life support." Creating and maintaining cognitive maps is a continuous dynamic process, and sustained daily use of the surrounding environment enhances that image, making it more easily decoded. The activities involved are shopping, browsing, and imagining the surrounding environment are the primary stimulants for the growth, maintenance, and renewal of a neighborhood cognitive image.

Use of Neighborhood Goods and Services

The most powerful incentive and the variable that is of greatest consequence in determining the shape and direction of the perceived neighborhood is access to critical goods and services. These services vary slightly from individual to individual but normally include grocery store, supermarket, drugstore, bank, variety store, department store, post office, doctor's office, cleaners, library, church, and restaurant.

External delimiters such as crime and topography discourage the use of certain poorly located services, and generally reduce the area within which individuals can comfortably shop for needed goods and services.

ENVIRONMENTAL CASE STUDIES

The following two case studies report on the findings of research conducted in Los Angeles and San Francisco. Although the research designs in each case are substantially different, their purpose is to further refine the methodology of cognitive mapping.

The Los Angeles study made the basic assertion that, although each individual's perceived neighborhood is unique, a composite neighborhood does exist that contains the most viable community elements.

The San Francisco study asserted that the size and direction of cognitive neighborhoods is highly dependent on the quality, location, and characteristics of surrounding neighborhood goods and services. Furthermore, the environmental and social conditions of the surrounding neighborhood mediate access to these goods and services.

Both studies provide information regarding the makeup and structure of the neighborhood for older persons and have important implications for the design of service delivery systems.

These case studies are exploratory in nature and their implications and results should be verified by further research before policy decisions are made. The research was carried out with the purpose of uncovering salient facts about the nature of cognitive mapping strategies rather than attempting to verify and test a particular theoretical approach.

Los Angeles Study

Research design. The Westlake district of Los Angeles is an older part of the city that was developed in the 1920s directly west of the downtown area along Wilshire Boulevard. The housing stock consists primarily of low-cost, small-sized apartment units or converted hotel rooms, and these accommodations have attracted the city's highest concentration of elderly. The elderly living here are primarily

from blue-collar backgrounds and many exist solely on fixed-income pensions or Social Security.

The close proximity to the rapidly developing downtown has had spillover effects. Planning projections to 1980 predict that large sections of Westlake will eventually succumb to the bulldozer of modernization as the downtown continues to expand.

The elderly have selected this area of the city for a number of good reasons, including the inexpensive housing stock, the neighborhood working-class atmosphere, the mix of convenient commercial goods and services, and the fact that many other people like themselves live here. The sample was selected by a review of census-tract data, which identified a two-square-mile area within the district that had the highest concentration of older persons. This area was stratified into three sectors and a random selection of six blocks was made from each sector. A quota sample from each selected block averaged between five and seven elderly respondents and resulted in a total sample size of 107.

Figure 1 pinpoints the locations of apartment buildings and retirement hotels where interviewing took place. Each dot represents a location where from one to seven persons may have been interviewed.

Eliciting and combining cognitive maps. The survey instrument consisted of a questionnaire and a scale map of the district large enough so that streets and landmarks could be read easily. Respondents were instructed to "draw a line around your neighborhood"; only five respondets could not conceive of a neighborhood area (n = 102). A synagraphic counter program was developed (Regnier et al., 1973) that enabled the separate maps to be geographically coded and combined into a final map representing differing degrees of neighborhood consensus. The edges of each neighborhood were defined by a series of coordinate points. A two-dimensional array was created to document each map configuration and a three-dimensional array was used to sum the total number of respondents that chose certain areas of the district to be within their neighborhood.

Figure 2 documents the final collection of neighborhood consensus rings. A core area of high consensus is centralized within a series of larger areas repre-

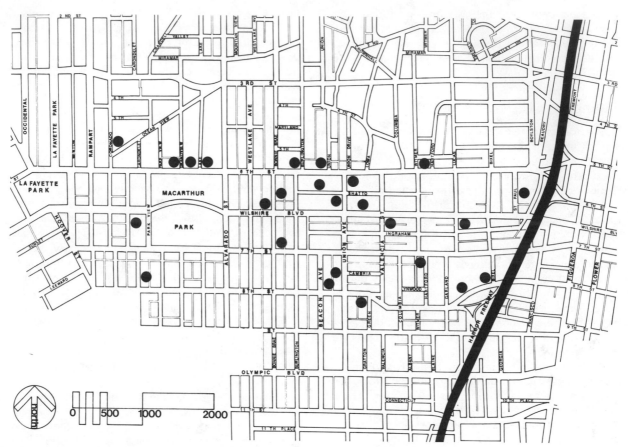

FIGURE 1
Sample distribution, Westlake study.

sents successively lower levels of consensus. The final recommendations to decision makers suggested that the optimal location for place-bound services in this district would be within zone 1 or zone 2 of the consensus map.

Neighborhood configuration characteristics. Although the traditional assumption is that residents will place themselves in the center of their neighborhood (Lee, 1968), this conclusion was not supported in this research. Data suggest that many individuals' neighborhoods are oriented toward supportive services and that neighborhood areas are not necessarily distributed in a concentric manner about one's housing location.

Examination of the relationship between individual neighborhood configurations and the location of the respondent's apartment created three neighborhood–housing location typologies. Figure 3 provides a schematic representation of the three relationships. Fifty percent of the sample chose a neighborhood boundary that was approximately equidistant in all directions from their housing location (Figure 3a).

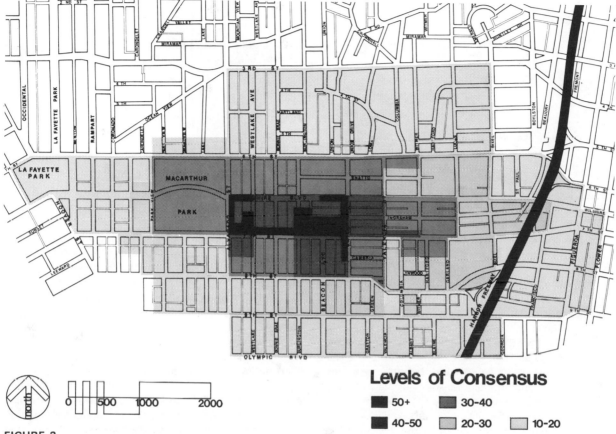

FIGURE 2
Consensus rings, Westlake study.

Levels of Consensus

■ 50+   ■ 30-40
■ 40-50   ▨ 20-30   ▢ 10-20

Thirty-five percent of the sample chose to place one of the neighborhood boundaries adjacent to their housing location (Figure 3b). The remainder, 15 percent, conceived of a neighborhood area that did not include their housing location (Figure 3c). Although these results should be confirmed by a larger and better distributed sample, it appears that the conceptual notion of a neighborhood as always surrounding in an equidistant manner the residential location of an individual does not have universal applicability.

The size and shape of each individual cognitive map was distinct, even though many chose to include the same core areas of the neighborhood. The size

range varied from 4.2 acres to 1,414.0 acres. Obviously, use of an ambiguous descriptor such as "neighborhood" was one reason for the range in size. Theoretically, it is argued that the cognition of the local environment can occur on several different scale levels and that "our neighborhood," "my neighborhood," and "the neighborhood" may define distinctly different geographic areas (Suttles, 1972). Because of this lack of a precise neighborhood definition, correlations between neighborhood size and other social and behavioral variables are difficult to measure. Trends, however, were discovered indicating that large perceived neighborhood size was correlated

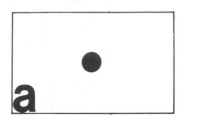 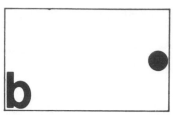 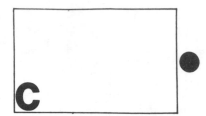

FIGURE 3
Positional typologies, Westlake study.

with increased automobile use, high socioeconomic status, length of residence, increased activity, and good health. These correlations between neighborhood size and behavioral variables generally agree with the work of other researchers attempting to measure the same phenomena (Lee, 1968; Everitt and Cadwallader, 1972).

Implications for service delivery. The implications for the use of this method are greatest in terms of location theory. It is particularly noteworthy to mention that, although a great deal of energy has been expanded to identify the "needs" of older persons, less attention has been paid to where and how these "most needed" services should be delivered. For example, the selection of meal sites in the Title VII nutrition program and of locations for senior-citizen centers in many cities has been accomplished in a much less systematic manner than the identification of the needed services. The result of this unsystematic approach to site selection has been to identify target locations where services reach only a small proportion of those in the community in need of services.

San Francisco Study

Research design. This study centered on an investigation of the similarities between neighborhood cognitive maps and the location of surrounding neighborhood goods and services. Older persons ($n = 94$) living in two public housing projects in San Francisco that were located in substantially different neighborhood settings were surveyed. Rather than establishing a consensus neighborhood that defined the dominant elements from a sample whose residences were diversely distributed, this study controlled for housing location. The size and orientation of cognitive maps were analyzed in relation to elements of the surrounding environment that provided positive or negative incentives.

Figure 4 pinpoints those two locations within the city of San Francisco. The easternmost site was located in the Yerba Buena Redevelopment district surrounded by industrial and manufacturing land uses. The closest retail store was three blocks from the site. However, Market Street, which acts as a major shopping district, was only six blocks away. Before redevelopment the area was the hub of the famous Skid Row, which housed primarily derelicts, alcoholics, and drug addicts. Clementina Towers was constructed during the initial phase of the redevelopment. Subsequent legal battles, however, involving the total project's environmental impact halted additional construction for nearly four years. During that time the towers stood amid demolished and abandoned buildings.

The second site was located near the southern edge of the Pacific Heights district in the Western Addition. The surrounding neighborhood was rich in services but oriented to a younger age and higher income group, which effectively canceled the utility of many of the surrounding retail shops for older people. This building, John F. Kennedy Towers, was one of the first publicly subsidized structures within San Francisco that was open only to elderly residents. Although the neighborhood offered many convenience goods and services, it lacked larger-scale retail services.

Eliciting, combining, and comparing cognitive maps. The cognitive mapping procedure and analysis was similar to that performed in the Westlake study,

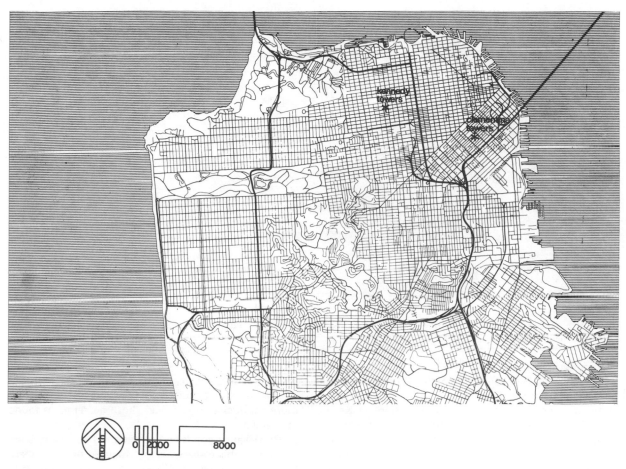

FIGURE 4
Housing locations, San Francisco study.

with two exceptions. The first was the basic set of instructions given to the respondent when eliciting map configurations. The Westlake respondents were asked to define "their neighborhood"; in San Francisco they were asked, "When thinking of the local neighborhood area that surrounds your apartment, what area do you use?". This more explicit definition provided a measure of neighborhood in terms of use.

The second difference was that the cognitive representations from each site were synthesized separately so that their relative sizes and configurations could be compared.

Respondents were presented with large-scale maps from which the boundaries of their cognitive representations were elicited. Some respondents used the map to orient themselves; other spoke by name of the surrounding streets that formed the border to their local neighborhood. In both cases, every respondent could identify a local area that he used.

Figures 6 and 7 display the final consensus maps of respondents from Clementina and Kennedy Towers, respectively. Each consensus map has been categorized into four zones, each one representing 25 percent of the sample. Zone 1, for example, includes

FIGURE 5
Clementina Towers was an early addition to the Yerba Buena Redevelopment Project and therefore had been located in a primarily industrial neighborhood surrounded by vacant property. (Photo by Victor Regnier.)

75 to 100 percent of the sample; each successive lighter zone represents 25 percent fewer respondents. Note that the consensus map configurations at Kennedy Towers are much smaller than those at Clementina. The smaller map configurations found at Kennedy Towers reflect a more centralized pattern of spatial service use. The Kennedy neighborhood area provided residents with a more compact, convenient geographic concentration of goods and services, even though these resources probably did not meet their needs as well as did the more distant ones for Clementina. Additionally, the topographic conditions and social pathology that plagued adjacent areas were perceived as threatening to many elderly residents and thus further restricted their use space.

At Clementina the lack of nearby convenient services forced respondents to venture farther into adjacent areas for goods and services. Respondents were attracted to areas that contained an abundance of supportive goods and services. The neighborhood area east of the Clementina project containing primarily industrial type activity was ignored by all respon-dents. Fortunately, the physical and social conditions of the somewhat more distant supportive areas were more conducive to use than those nearer areas found at Kennedy.

Retrieval of goods and services. The primary comparison in this research effort focused on a comparison between *where* and *how often* respondents go to receive goods, on the one hand, and, on the other, the configurations of cognitive consensus maps. Some information has been gathered by various researchers regarding the "home range" and "activity" patterns of older adults (Gelwicks, 1970; Pastalan and Carson, 1970; Cantilli and Smeltzer, 1970); other studies have focused on the identification of specific services that are used on a local level (Foley, 1950). Very little effort, however, has been spent on investigating the similarities or differences between cognitive maps and patterns of service use. The location and use of various goods and services have a direct bearing on the formation of cognitive maps. A detailed explanation of the distribution of service-use patterns is available elsewhere (Regnier, 1974a).

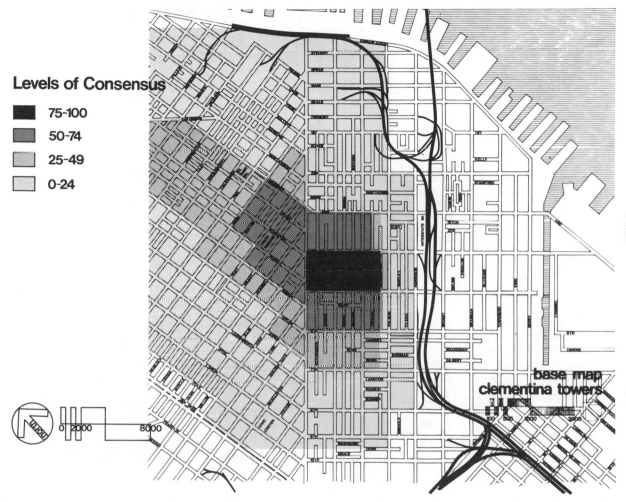

FIGURE 6
Consensus neighborhoods, San Francisco study: base map, Clementina Towers.

Three factors determined the activity patterns behind the selection of goods and services: physical proximity, ties to services in previous neighborhoods, and the relative cost of goods and services. Even if nearby general merchandise stores contained only a limited inventory, residents tended to shop there rather than to travel to more distant stores with more complete inventories. For the less physically capable this meant that nonnecessary items were often omitted.

Ties to services in previous neighborhoods were maintained when merchants or their merchandise had special importance to residents. The use of Chinatown by the Chinese, of Richmond District by first-generation Russians, and of the Western Addition by blacks were all examples of strong ties to previous neighborhoods created by the bond of ethnic identification. Although service use in other neighborhoods was generally limited to shopping for special foods, personal services, and events like churchgoing, the

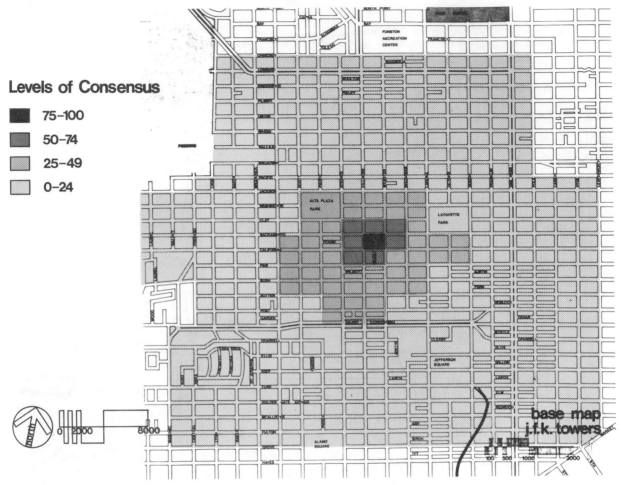

FIGURE 7
Consensus neighborhoods, San Francisco study: base map,
J.F.K. Towers.

effort to revisit older familiar areas of town was made by a majority of the respondents. The Chinese in particular depended a great deal on goods and services provided in Chinatown. On the average each Chinese respondent would make two trips to Chinatown every three days in search of a particular good or service.

Older respondents necessarily had to be conscious of the price of goods and services. They would capitalize on special sales and shop at stores that discounted items. The downtown area along Market Street was the most popular district for this kind of shopping activity. At Clementina, the lack of a convenient supermarket forced a sizable contingent to travel nearly 12 blocks to a large discount food store.

These three factors were instrumental in providing an explanation for different patterns of goods and service retrieval. Although some goods and services attracted respondents to shop in other parts of the city, the local neighborhood provided the primary source of support. Only about 18 percent of shopping trips were mady beyond a 12-block radius from each site.

FIGURE 8
Although Market Street was a number of blocks from Clementina Towers, the variety of appealing goods and services offered here was much greater than at Kennedy. Generally, Clementina residents were more active in neighborhood window-shopping and park use than were Kennedy residents. (Photo by Victor Regnier.)

Comparing the conceptual and functional neighborhood. Responses to a list of 29 service-use questions were coded and given a value in accordance with their frequency of use. A system was established that assigned one "day-use unit" to a geographic location where a service was used by one person once per month. Day-use units were accumulated for each service location by frequency of use and the number of persons from each location using the service. For example, a particular service used by one person four times per month (or once per week) would receive four day-use units. Likewise, another service used once per week by four people would receive 16 day-use units.

The spatial distribution of day-use units from respondents at each site created a consensus functional neighborhood documenting the areas and particular stores in the surrounding neighborhood that are used

by elderly residents. When this functional consensus neighborhood was compared to the cognitive consensus neighborhood, it showed amazing congruence.

The four geographic concentric zones created by the cognitive mapping procedure were used to form the basis of a comparison illustrated by Figure 9. The number of day-use units within each consensus zone was summed and the percentage of the total generated by each zone was calculated. Both location and intensity of day-use units were linked with the size and configuration of consensus cognitive maps. For example, if a store provided a major source of day-use units, it was generally included within the first or second consensus zone.

The first zone of the consensus map for the two housing projects differed in area by nearly 800 percent. However, the first zone in both locations accounted for 39 percent of the total day-use units. In other words, the centralization of cognitive representations at Kennedy Towers was tailored to the centralization of goods and service retrieval. Conversely, the larger consensus cognitive maps at Clementina

	Clementina		Kennedy	
	P*	DUU*	P*	DUU*
Zone One	39	662	39	510
Cumulative Total	39		39	
Zone Two	18	310	29	378
Cumulative Total	57		68	
Zone Three	22	374	5	69
Cumulative Total	79		73	
Zone Four	5	79	7	91
Cumulative Total	84		80	
Outside	16	265	20	259
Total	100	1690	100	1307

* **percentage**
* **day-use units**

FIGURE 9
Distribution of day-use units in consensus neighborhood zones, San Francisco study.

responded to the much wider distribution of services in the local neighborhood.

Figure 9 shows the percentages of day-use units devoted to each consensus zone at Kennedy and Clementina. Comparing zones 2 through 4, the largest day-use difference between sites occurs in zone 2 (11 percent); zones 3 and 4 have a 6 and 4 percent difference, respectively. In other words, the relationship that ties the size of the consensus neighborhood to the location of day-use unit concentrations remains valid as the zones become much larger and further removed.

If further research confirms the relationship between use patterns and composite cognitive maps, it might be feasible to use specifically directed cognitive mapping procedures to measure life space, home range, and neighborhood use of older people. This appraoch could aid in generating neighborhood service areas without the costly and time-consuming effort of assembling trip destination information on respondents.

Neighborhood delimiters and incentives. The role of environmental delimiters and incentives as introduced in the first portion of this paper was investigated by a procedure that compared maps of block census variables and other aggregate data with cognitive consensus maps from each site (a more detailed account appears in Regnier, 1974b). Although use patterns provide accurate information regarding the locations where goods and services may be purchased, they do not delineate positive locations that are used but involve no actual purchase of goods. For example, window shopping, walking, and sitting activities are difficult to quantify in day-use units. Furthermore, areas with negative connotations are not easily established except by conspicuous lack of day-use units. It is important that within the vehicle of the cognitive map each individual can weight the importance of factors such as topography, health, car ownership, or fear of crime.

The Kennedy neighborhood, for example, is made up of a collection of positive and negative features that limit both neighborhood use and cognition. To the north and east, sharp topographic changes effectively limit the use of two medium-sized parks; to the south and west, perceived crime frightens many residents from using those areas. Cognitive consensus

maps reflect the lack of use, which in the one case is the result of an environmental delimiter and in the other a result of a social delimiter. The following summary outlines the effects that nine social and environmental variables have on the size and configuration of consensus cognitive maps.

Topography. The portions of the neighborhood area surrounding each project that are characterized by steep grades are avoided and excluded from cognitive maps. Kennedy Towers is sited on the edge of a

FIGURE 10
The use of goods and services in surrounding areas was lessened or completely absent when these areas were typified by a large change in topography. (Photo by Victor Regnier.)

hill. Not only do use patterns here reflect the avoidance of two nearby neighborhood parks that are a substantial climb uphill from the housing project, but cognitive representations also do not include these areas. Clementina Towers is located in a relatively flat part of the city, but an abrupt change to topography is clearly delineated by the edge of zone 2 of the composite cognitive map.

Traffic patterns. Indications are that busy streets do not become barriers to respondents except at the outer reaches of their use patterns. In other words, if a busy street separates the respondent from a basic life-supportive service such as a grocery store, it does not create an effective barrier to that good or service. A busy street may, however, affect the direction or area in which respondents choose to take walks.

Land use. The land-use patterns in the neighbor-

hood provide the strongest determinant of use and cognition. The retail commercial shops that provide life-supportive goods and services from the basic core elements of the cognitive map. Industrial areas that have no attractive land uses, such as those south and east of the Clementina site, are neither used nor included in cognitive maps of the surrounding neighborhood. Park areas such as Union Square are relatively accessible and attract residents from Clementina Towers. The high correlation between cognitive maps and use patterns reinforces the notion that land use is a major influence on how respondents use and "image" the surrounding environment.

Bus routes. The well-developed San Francisco bus system provides important links with other parts of the city. Bus routes correlate highly with areas outside of the immediate neighborhood where residents

FIGURE 11
Busy streets such as this one began to act as significant borders to cognitive neighborhoods and use patterns in the second and third consensus zones. (Photo by Victor Regnier.)

go to shop for goods and services. Direct bus routes to Golden Gate Park, the Mission district, and Chinatown are used by Clementina residents. At Kennedy Towers the Marina, Richmond, and Chinatown are visited frequently because of such routes.

District designations. Because the districts in San Francisco have no set formal boundaries, respondents can claim residence in bordering districts. At both sites respondents had the opportunity to identify with bordering districts of high or low status. Respondents used this flexibility to emphasize the positive and negative qualities and the geographic extent of the surrounding neighborhood. The cognitive maps of Clementina residents were affected strongly by the historically perceived edge of the "South of Market" district boundaries. An attempt to control this phenomenon, however, was initiated by the instructions that directed respondents to define areas that they *used* rather than areas of historic or emotional value.

Percentage of elderly residents. Elderly that live in age-dense neighborhoods frequently experience greater life satisfaction (Rosow, 1967; Peterson et al., 1972). Therefore, the percentage of elderly living within a neighborhood may be one index of the quality of life for older people living in the area. Not only is neighboring enhanced, but social services and retail shops that are oriented to the older individual are more common in neighborhoods with a higher concentration of elderly. Kennedy Towers is located in an area that has a low concentration of elderly. This has limited the kind of retail services provided and the opportunities available for older persons to meet others of similar interests and backgrounds. At Clementina Towers the high concentration of elderly within the surrounding area has encouraged the development of shops and stores that cater to the older individual. In addition, the increased visibility of older persons on the street may stimulate or encourage other older persons to use the neighborhood. At Clementina the number of persons who windowshop often and eat lunch in cafes in the neighborhood is much greater than at Kennedy, where the resources are available but not as attractive to older residents.

Ethnic identity. Ethnic identification had a noticeable effect on the formation of cognitive maps. Kennedy Towers is located on the edge of a predominantly black area of the city. Although neither white,

black, nor Chinese residents used the higher-income neighborhood directly to the north, whites and Chinese were much more reluctant to use goods and services in predominantly black areas to the south than were black tenants. All respondents, however, were reluctant to use the areas south of Geary, where redevelopment left many abandoned buildings. The Chinese had a very strong identification with Chinatown. Use patterns at both sites reflected a similarly heavy intensity of goods and service retrieval for Chinese residents in Chinatown.

Population density. Low population densities generally connote either vacant property, underdevelopment, or high concentrations of commercial, manufacturing, or industrial land use. Although the low population density of industrial areas does not attract individuals, areas with a high concentration of commerical activities (and an accompanying low population density) provide considerable attraction. Therefore, population density is a poor indicator of neighborhood use.

Average contract rent. Used as a proxy for income, this factor also varied with topography. Use of higher-rent neighborhoods was limited because of the generally accompanying change in elevation. Both sets of cognitive maps were oriented toward lower-rent areas.

These delimiters and incentives were not as precisely related to the shape and orientation of composite cognitive maps as use patterns. However, they did show a rough correspondence to the size and configurations of cognitive maps.

Implications for Environmental Designers

In the spirit of exploratory research, the case studies presented seem to pose more questions than they answer. It is possible, however, to formulate a few directives to help improve planning efforts in behalf of older persons.

1. Individual cognitive maps and the resulting consensus maps can be used to identify areas of the neighborhood where services should be delivered to reach the greatest number of older persons. A cognitive mapping question can be included in a survey whose purpose is to identify the needs of people living in the area, thus providing information about

FIGURE 12

A centralized collection of supportive stores near Kennedy Towers focused the distribution of use patterns. Many of the convenience stores, however, did not cater to the social class or age cohorts present within Kennedy Towers and therefore were of marginal value. (Photo by Victor Regnier.)

what services are desired and where they should be located.

2. Cognitive mapping can be used to identify district neighborhood areas so that future planning efforts will not disturb or destroy strong existing centers of cognitive relevance. Using this approach, incremental planning efforts such as rehabilitation or site selection for elderly housing can be made without harming areas that currently have important value to older persons. Particularly, viable neighborhood cen-

ters could be reinforced by a selective process of adding urban design elements, such as street furniture, police patrols, or retail stores.

3. Cognitive mapping can be used in transportation planning to identify the street networks of a particular neighborhood that should be serviced by special bus transit or streets where traffic lights should be timed so as to create pedestrian districts while discouraging vehicular access. The results of mapping might also be used to minimize the disturbance a freeway or large artery would have on the integrity of a neighborhood.

4. Cognitive mapping could be used partially or wholly as a proxy to service-use questions. This would minimize the size of questionnaires focused toward identifying neighborhood activity patterns. It could also be combined with a service identification questionnaire to provide the best answer to where in the neighborhood needed services should be located.

The future implications for the applied use of cognitive mapping are great. Some environmentalists believe that the missing link between the relationship of man to his environment rests in the process through which the mind selectively encodes and decodes information provided by the environment.

Clearly, cognitive mapping methodologies have special promise for the planner and environmental designer in helping him understand more about the needs and limitations of older persons. Understanding more about how older people use and perceive the surrounding environment can allow decision makers to reinforce the positive and minimize the negative elements of both the physical and social environment that act as barriers to the freedom of choice.

REFERENCES

Appleyard, D. Styles and methods of structuring a city. *Environment and Behavior*, 1970, *2*, 100–117.

Cantilli, E., and Smeltzer, J. *Transportation and Aging: Selected Issues*. Proceedings of the Interdisciplinary Workshop on Aging and Transportation. Washington, D.C.: Government Printing Office, 1970.

Downs, R. M., and Stea, D. *Image and Environment: Cognitive Mapping and Spatial Behavior*. Chicago: Aldine, 1973.

Eribes, D., and Regnier, V. Neighborhood service delivery: a cognitive mapping approach. Paper presented at the American Society of Planning Officials (ASPO) annual meeting, Los Angeles, 1973.

Everitt, J., and Cadwallader, M. The home area concept in urban analysis: the use of cognitive mapping and computer procedures as methodological tools. In W. J. Mitchell (ed.), *Environmental Design: Research and Practice*, Proceedings of the EDRA 3/ AR 8 Conference. Los Angeles: University of California at Los Angeles, 1972.

Foley, D. J. The use of local facilities in a metropolis, *American Journal of Sociology*, 1950, *3*.

Gelwicks, L. E. Home range and the use of space by an aging population. In L. A. Pastalan and D. H. Carson (eds.), *Spatial Behavior of Older People*. Ann Arbor, Mich.: Institute of Gerontology, University of Michigan, 1970.

Ladd, F. C. Black youths view their environment. *Environment and Behavior*, 1970, *2*, 74–99.

Lawton, M. P., and Nahemow, L. Toward an ecological theory of adaptation and aging. In W. Preiser (ed.), *Environmental Design Research, Volume 1*. Stroudsburg, Pa.: Dowden, Hutchinson & Ross, 1973.

Lee, T. Urban neighborhood as a socio-spatial schema. *Human Relations*, 1968, *21*, 241–267.

Pastalan, L., and Carson, D. (eds.). *Spatial Behavior of Older People*. Ann Arbor, Mich.: Institute of Gerontology, University of Michigan, 1970.

Peterson, J., Hadwen, T., and Larson, A. *A Time for Work, a Time for Leisure: A Study of Retirement Community In-movers*. Los Angeles: Ethel Percy Andrus Gerontology Center, University of Southern California, 1972.

Regnier, V. Matching older person's cognition with their use of neighborhood areas. In D. Carson (ed.), *Proceedings of EDRA 5*, Milwaukee, Wisc., 1974a, in press.

_____. The effect of environmental incentives and delimiters on the use and cognition of local neighborhood areas by the elderly. Paper presented at the annual meeting of the Gerontological Society, Portland, Ore., 1974b.

_____, Eribes, D., and Hanson, W. Cognitive mapping as a concept for establishing neighborhood service delivery locations for older people: the use of synagraphics as methodological tools. In J. Highland (ed.), *Eighth Annual Association for Computing Machinery Urban Symposium*, New York, 1973.

Rosow, I. *Social Integration of the Aged*. New York: Free Press, 1967.

Suttles, G. *The Social Construction of Communities*. Chicago: University of Chicago Press, 1972.

Tolman, E. C. Cognitive maps in rats and men. *Psychological Review*, 1948, *55*, 189–208.

Trowbridge, C. C. On fundamental methods of orientation and "imaginary maps." *Science*, 1913, *38*, 888–897.

Weisman, J. Environmental legibility and architectural design. Mimeographed. Institute of Gerontology, University of Michigan, 1974.

J. J. GLASSMAN, RICHARD L. TELL,
JOHN P. LARRIVEE, AND ROBERT HELLAND

*J. J. Glassman is Senior Planner, the Los Angeles
County Department of Senior Citizens Affairs, Area
Agency on Aging Division, Los Angeles, California.
Richard L. Tell and Robert Helland are affiliated with
the Ethel Percy Andrus Gerontology Center, University of Southern California. John P. Larrivee is with
the Council on Aging of Santa Clara County (California), Inc.*

Toward an Estimation of Service Need

As a response to the special considerations required in the planning and delivery of social services
for older people, state commissions and bureaus on
aging have been established. These have been charged
by the 1973 Amendments to Title III (Comprehensive Services) of the Older Americans Act to develop
state plans that identify the status and needs of the
elderly population. The state units on aging have also
designated Area Agencies on Aging to implement
state mandates at the local community level and to
ensure the coordination of all local efforts in the
provision of social services for the aging. Central to
those tasks is a need for reliable social indicators and
other methods for predicting the levels of unmet
service need.

Many attempts at needs assessment for health care
and social services may be described as "epidemiological," that is, concerned with the distribution of disease, defects, and disabilities in populations and the
various personal and environmental factors that affect
the manifestation of such conditions. Service delivery
systems may also be analyzed under this term, insofar
as such systems affect the occurrence and distribution
of disease.

This paper presents one such epidemiological approach that focuses on the rate of functional disability for noninstitutionalized older persons, that is, the
inability to perform some basic tasks of daily living.
To the extent that this target population fails to use
existing services in the community, or if such services
are not available, a latent demand may be said to
exist. To quantify this latent demand requires social
and health indicator analysis, community surveys of
needs and resources, and nonsurvey citizen and consumer input. We present a method for estimating the
need for long-term community or institutional care
by that segment of the aging population with chronic
functional disabilities.

This procedure, with some modifications, has been
used in California and elsewhere. Essentially, the
technique derives from previous studies of older persons and their ability to perform daily activities. One
such study reported findings from a national sample
of noninstitutionalized older persons showing that 2
percent were "bedbound," 6 percent "homebound,"
and 6 percent needed "help in getting around"
(Shanas, 1968).

The total of 14 percent who need some self-maintenance assistance has been used extensively as a planning benchmark. In application, however, little attempt has been made to properly weight the relative contributions of age, sex, and income that contributed to the total. This concept of differential weighting allows one to adjust the importance of certain variables. Not all communities have demographic characteristics identical to a national sample. A procedure is required that disaggregates the service-need estimator by each of these dimensions. The technique presented here enables this, and in so doing, permits substantial estimator refinement for local application.

FUNCTIONAL ABILITY— AN APPLIED THEORY

The ability of older persons to perform daily activities and care for themselves has been used by many researchers (Katz et al., 1963; Rosow, 1966; Sokolow and Taylor, 1967; Lawton and Brody, 1969) as an indicator for assessing functional competence for a prescription of services to meet an individual's health needs. When these health estimates are combined with local-level demographic data, it is possible to derive the size of the elderly population at risk or potentially in need of supportive services. The principal source of data to be used here comes from the National Senior Citizens Survey, as presented by the Institute for Interdisciplinary Studies of Minnesota (Administration on Aging, 1972) for the Administration on Aging. The survey was administered in 1968 under the direction of Kermit Schooler to 4,000 noninstitutionalized persons aged 65 and over. Self-maintenance and self-care, the major components defining functional competence, were operationalized in terms of the individual's ability to carry out the following tasks[1]:

1. Go out of doors.
2. Walk up and down stairs.
3. Get about the house
4. Wash and bathe without help.
5. Dress and put on shoes.

Respondents were asked to rate the degree of difficulty they experienced in performing each of these tasks in terms of "never," "occasionally," "frequently," or "always."

FUNCTIONAL ABILITY COEFFICIENT

A function ability coefficient (FAC) was derived by aggregating the responses to these questions. The percentages of respondents reporting frequent or continual difficulty with each task were summed and an average computed. This process was repeated for four age cohorts (60–64,[2] 65–69, 70–74, and 75 and over), sex, income, and living arrangement. These averages (coefficients) represent the expected disability among the older population. In other words the FAC is a surrogate for the percentage of individuals who, because of their chronic dysfunctions in either self-maintenance or self-care, need social-service supports to maintain themselves in a home setting. A listing of FAC's computed by these population characteristics is shown in Table 1.

DEMOGRAPHIC INDICATORS

Variance in population composition among geographic areas argues in favor of an elastic estimation technique. However, such an approach is constrained by the availability and accuracy of data. Demographic indicators readily available in the *U.S. Census Reports* provide descriptors of the local aged population in terms of age, sex, income, and living arrangement. By considering some or all of these factors in conjunction with the appropriate FAC, planners can estimate the need for services among a wide variety of population status groups, and quantify the number of older persons in the total elderly population at the greatest risk.

APPLICATION

To illustrate the estimation technique, it is applied with population data from the state of California. As shown in Figure 1, the aging population, 60 and over, is disaggregated by age cohorts. The number of persons in each category is first multiplied by its respective FAC and then modified by the percentage of individuals living alone.[3] Living alone, which in itself

TABLE 1
Functional Ability Coefficients (FAC)

	FAC
Age analysis	
65+	11.77
Male	8.95
Female	13.77
60+	8.67
Male	6.35
Female	10.41
Income less than $2,000	12.19
Income greater than $2,000	6.25
Cohort analysis	
60–64	1.72[a]
Male	1.29
Female	2.15
Income less than $2,000	3.67
Income greater than $2,000	1.63
65–69	5.25
Male	4.13
Female	6.15
Income less than $2,000	9.26
Income greater than $2,000	5.42
70–74	11.85
Male	9.81
Female	13.33
Income less than $2,000	12.58
Income greater than $2,000	9.37
75+	17.54
Male	13.35
Female	21.10
Income less than $2,000	21.10
Income greater than $2,000	12.12

[a]The 1968 National Senior Citizens Survey, which provided the sample from which the coefficients are derived, included only persons 65 and over. For this reason the FAC for individuals 60–64 is an extrapolation by rate of change.

does not define need, has been identified as a decisive indicator of need when it occurs in conjunction with a functional disability. Family support is assumed to be a significant factor in overcoming barriers that block an individual's access to social services. Thus those persons with functional disabilities who live alone are presumed to represent a high priority for social-service intervention.

When these calculations are applied to the aggre-
gate population of persons 60 and over and to the percentage living alone, a substantial underestimation of the high-risk population is obtained. The total population 60 and over multiplied by an FAC of 8.67 percent yields 223,824 persons needing some help. Multiplying this number by the percentage living alone, the population at risk is 57,970.

Using age-cohort analysis and repeating the same computation process of multiplying first by the cohort's FAC and then by the percentage living alone, the total population risk is 69,094. These calculations diverge by a factor of 1.19 or almost 20 percent.

An assumption has been made that the percentage distribution of those older persons living alone corresponds to that of the total elderly age cohort.

A further refinement in the procedure is the disaggregation of age cohorts by sex. The methodology is identical, but applied to age–sex cohorts. As shown in Figure 2, this disaggregation yields an at-risk population of 72,986, with a preponderance of older females 70 and over in the at-risk target group.

An alternative application that may be more appropriate for some planning efforts would substitute an income criterion for sex. If we employ cohort analysis by age and living arrangement, and reported income of less than $2,000, an at-risk population of 44,506 is revealed for California (see Figure 3). Because the published *U.S. Census Reports* (U.S. Department of Commerce, 1971) do not cross-tabulate age cohorts by sex by income, the planner using the FAC estimation procedure must select either the cross-tabluation age by sex or age by income.

It is to the advantage of state and local planners to utilize all these population status descriptors so that a more precise estimation of the at-risk population is made possible.

POLICY IMPLICATIONS

Although the functional ability scales reported in the literature have been applied in institutional settings with success, state and local planning applications have not yet received detailed attention. In the absence of more precise local information, it would appear that the FAC–Census technique can fill an important function. To date, this procedure has been

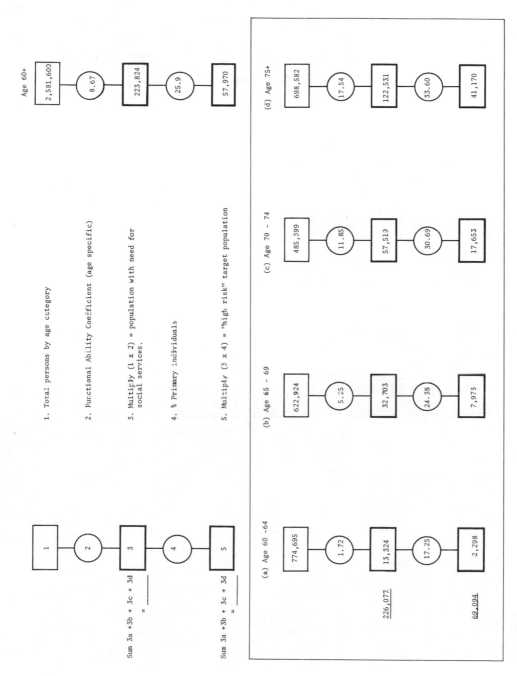

Age 60+

2,581,600 — 8.67 — 223,824 — 25.9 — 57,970

1. Total persons by age category

2. Functional Ability Coefficient (age specific)

3. Multiply (1 x 2) = population with need for social services.

4. % Primary individuals

5. Multiply (3 x 4) = "high risk" target population

1 — 2 — 3 — 4 — 5

Sum 3a +3b + 3c + 3d =

Sum 3a +3b + 3c + 3d =

(a) Age 60 -64

774,695 — 1.72 — 13,324 — 17.25 — 2,298

226,077.

69,094

(b) Age 65 - 69

622,924 — 5.25 — 32,703 — 24.38 — 7,973

(c) Age 70 - 74

485,399 — 11.85 — 57,519 — 30.69 — 17,653

(d) Age 75+

698,582 — 17.54 — 122,531 — 33.60 — 41,170

FIGURE 1
Estimation of service need disaggregating by age.

261

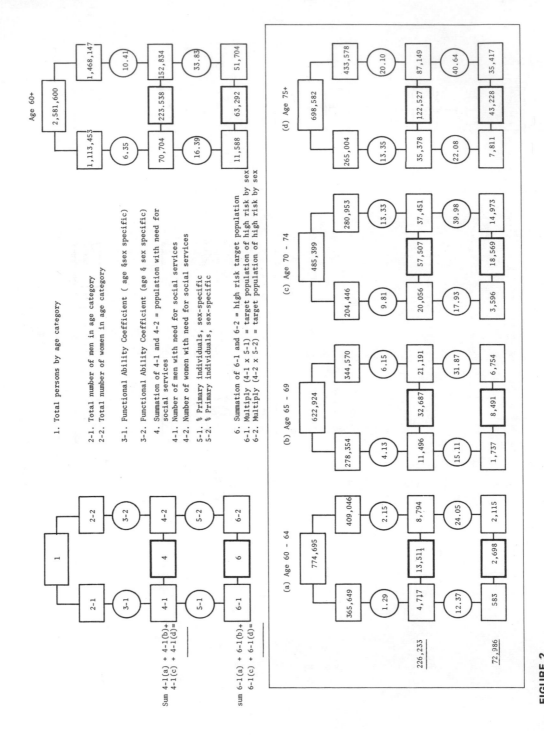

FIGURE 2
Estimation of service need disaggregating by age and sex.

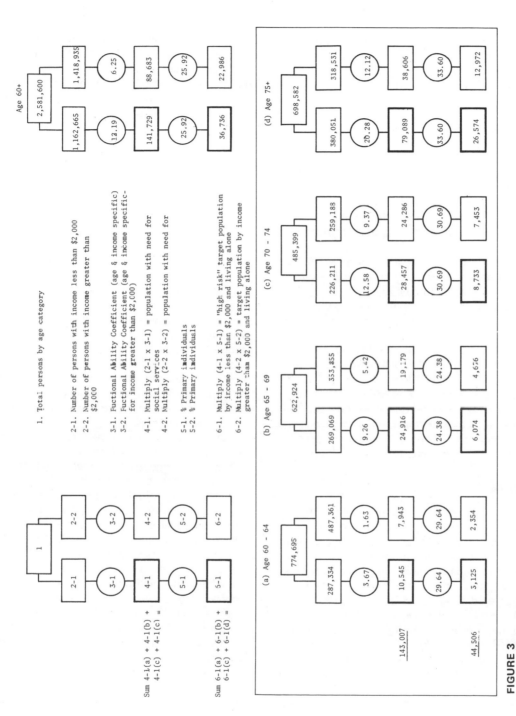

FIGURE 3
Estimation of service need disaggregating by age and income.

applied to census tract and block-level comparisons among intrastate and intracity geographical areas with respect to the following:

1. Determining eligibility criteria for general areas of service programs. For example, the level of need among the older age cohorts is indicated by their numerical preponderence in all three tables.

2. State allocations based on the proportion of the high-risk population in each planning and service area. This technique can be further refined by utilizing population projections and migration patterns. It then becomes possible to predict changes in the characteristics and location of the elderly population and monitor these changes with updated demographic data.

3. The designation of local target areas and the setting of priorities for allocation of local resources.

4. As a means of estimating the need among alternative modes of delivery; the high-risk target group would require a more intense mode, such as portal-to-portal, demand-activated service delivery.

The planning tool explicated here combines a snapshot representation of the functional ability of older persons with current demographic data to generate an estimation of the number of people in the target group of greatest need. We caution the local planner that it is only a *first* step; a more rigorous analysis of local conditions is essential for program development and implementation.

DISCUSSION

The actual category of support required by the individual may be any number of services; the FAC does not reveal the needed service. But the development of global techniques for needs assessment, of which the FAC is an example, suggests a new, emergent form of intervention predictors for social services. Rather than predicting a population's aggregate need for health care, for example, our intervention strategies and tools should identify the target group in greatest need who are likely to require multiple social-service supports. These tools would enable us to design multicategory social-service programs. The comprehensive services strategy of the Title III Amendments is an initial step in this direction, em-

phasizing the role of community-based services in meeting the chronic care needs of the aging.

That the acute care medical model cannot fit the problems of long-term care remains an obvious fact this society has been tardy in accepting. For long-term care, the social needs of the patient are primary while medical needs remain secondary; success is measured in terms of the patient's maintained functioning, not in terms of a cure (Weiler, 1974). Needs-assessment procedures should not reflect the bias of the acute care model found in our current national health programs, Medicare and Medicaid. The level of service delivered to an individual should be appropriate to that individual's functioning; the setting for that service is another distinct variable which has nonservice impacts on that individual (see the chapter by Pollak, page 106).

Functional assessment is only the beginning of this intervention process, but it is essential for policy decisions on services and settings for those services. We must develop our abilities to assess a community's functional status in terms of environmental, psychological, and social functioning, as well as health. A promising forecast of national studies to come may be indicated by a recent federal classification scheme that attempts to standardize patient-assessment procedures (Jones, 1973).

One may concede some weaknesses in the technique described here. The survey is "old," from 1968, the methodology used in the design of the survey instrument has been refined, and the findings are based on data self-reported by the subjects. Thus it is a *prevalence* study reporting the number of persons with functional impairments at a single point in time. However, these findings are linked with the demographic indicators of the decennial U.S. Census. Although it might be better for individual communities to administer methodologically sound longitudinal surveys, these are expensive, complicated, and time-consuming undertakings. The combinatorial process of the FAC—Census method allows the survey task to be completed nationally by researchers whose resources are presumed to be greater.

The FAC—Census technique satisfies various constraints that hinder the policy planner seeking a methodology to identify the high-risk target population in local areas. The data requirements are simple; moreover, the technique is applicable in a variety of contexts and is adaptive to varying levels of expertise. The FAC–Census technique is sensitive to this variation, and yet enables comparisons among disparate geographic areas.

NOTES

1. This list was originally developed by Peter Townsend and Ethel Shanas as a component of an index of incapacity. See Shanas et al. (1968).
2. The 1968 National Senior Citizens Survey included persons 65 and over. For this reason the FAC for the age cohort 60–64 is derived through extrapolation.
3. Number of persons living alone is approximated by the census category "primary individuals."

REFERENCES

Administration on Aging, Office on Human Development, Department of Health, Education, and Welfare. *Indicators of the Status of the Elderly in the United States*. Minneapolis: Interstudy (formerly Institute for Interdisciplinary Studies), 1972.

Bloom, M., and Blenkner, M. Assessing functioning of older persons living in the community. *Gerontologist*, 1970, *10*, 31–37.

Jones, E. W. *Patient Classification for Long Term Care: User's Manual*. Washington, D.C.: Department of Health, Education, and Welfare, Health Resources Administration, Bureau of Health Services Research and Evaluation (HRA 74-3107), 1973.

Katz, S., Ford, A. B., Moskowitz, R. W., Jackson, B. A., and Jaffe, M. W. Studies of illness in the aged. *Journal of the American Medical Association*, 1963, *185*, 914–919.

Lawton, M. P., and Brody, E. M. Assessment of older people: self-maintaining and instrumental activities of daily living. *Gerontologist*, 1969, *9*, 179–186.

National Center for Health Statistics. *Chronic Conditions and Limitations of Activity and Mobility, United States, July, 1965–June, 1967*, Vital and Health Statistics, Series 10, no. 61. 1969, Washington, D.C.

Rosow, I., and Breslau, N. A Guttman health scale for the aged. *Journal of Gerontology*, 1966, *21*, 556–559.

Shanas, E., Townsend, P., Wedderburn, D., Friis, H., Milhøj, P., and Stehouwer, J. *Old People in Three Industrial Societies*. New York: Atherton, 1968.

Sokolow, J., and Taylor, E. J. A method for functional disability evaluation. *Journal of Chronic Disease*, 1967, *20*, 896–909.

Townsend, P. Measuring incapacity for self-care. In R. Williams, C. Tibbits, and W. Donahue (eds.). *Processes of Aging: Social and Psychological Perspectives*, Vol. II. New York: Atherton, 1963.

U.S. Department of Commerce, Bureau of the Census. *Census Reports*, Detailed Characteristics (California), PC (1)-D, Washington, D.C., Government Printing Office. 1971.

Weiler, P. G. Cost-effective analysis: a quandry for geriatric health care systems. *Gerontologist*, 1974, *14*, 414–417.

ELLIOTT D. SCLAR

with the assistance of
S. DONNA LIND

Elliott Sclar is an Assistant Professor of Political Economy at the Florence Heller Graduate School for Advanced Studies in Social Welfare, Brandeis University, Waltham, Massachusetts. S. Donna Lind is a Ph.D. student at the Heller School, presently working at Portland State University.

Aging and Residential Location

Perhaps the most important element in the process of planning services for any group is a solid understanding of their residential patterns. The U.S. Census gives us information about the present location of the elderly, but we know little about the factors that shaped these location patterns. The purpose of this paper is to review existing knowledge with respect to one metropolitan area and to explore the relationships among aging, metropolitan growth, and residence. This work is directly applicable to many current planning tasks and also useful in identifying the gaps in our present understanding of the relationship between aging and urbanization.

In 1950, 64 percent of the population over the age of 65 resided in metropolitan areas. By 1960 that figure had risen to 70 percent, and by 1970 the figure was 75 percent. No evidence suggests that the growth in that population has begun to stabilize. A 1968 report of the National Commission on Urban Problems has projected a 75.5 percent increase in the elderly population of metropolitan areas between 1960 and 1985. Since the proportion of elderly within the total U.S. population has remained fairly steady,[1] this increasing proportion of elderly metropolitan residents is the outcome of spatial shifts in population location. Thus planning for the needs of the elderly must involve, at minimum, an increase in the quantity of service within metropolitan areas.

If location patterns within the metropolitan area also are shifting, qualitative service changes may be necessary. When we look at aggregate data for regions such as "urban places," "metropolitan areas," or "SMSA's," we tend to overlook the fact that these are not spatially homogeneous areas clearly distinct from "rural areas." Within any metropolitan area one can readily find living arrangements ranging from almost unbearable crowding at some urban center locations to almost rural spaciousness at the suburban fringe. Although the implications of such variation with respect to income maintenance programs may be slight (i.e., variations in rents), they can be significant for service programs. Walk-in centers for meals and recreation that may be very effective in highly dense areas could be virtually useless in low-density suburbs. The effectiveness of such programs in suburbs will depend upon the ability of individuals to drive. Thus not only may the quality of service deteriorate, but suburban isolation may engender a need for an increased quantity of service. To the extent that we understand the relationship between spatial context and service quantity and quality, we can better plan services for the elderly.

In addition to problems of density, other aspects of differential residential location also imply differing service needs. Location by neighborhoods and communities greatly reflects differences in socioeconomic class, no less for the elderly than for the rest of the population. Such class differences reflect very different social structures and thus suggest different needs for services from the larger society. For example, some communities (like the West End of Gans's *Urban Villagers*, 1962) may have strong built-in social networks that provide from within the community itself many of the services needed by the elderly. Provision of some of these services from outside might duplicate such community functions. Approached from another perspective, the elderly in such a community might have special needs if the "natural" service networks should be broken down, as they were for West Enders when their community was destroyed by urban renewal. If we are to develop services that meet the real and differential needs of the various groups of elderly, while making efficient use of scarce social resources, we must begin to include in the planning and implementation process some understanding of the complex interaction among spatial location, socioeconomic class, and the need for social services.

The need for modeling such variables in the planning and implementation process can be seen more clearly if we consider the relationship between metropolitan growth and aging as it has occurred to date. The process of urbanization in the United States has been one of physical expansion. Cities have grown, over the past century, from small walking cities with radii of between 1 and 2 miles to large metropolitan areas with radii of from 50 to 75 miles. The most rapid phase of this growth process has occurred in the past 50 years. In this period transportation availability went from scarcity to almost overabundance. Much of this growth has been due to the development of the automobile. Some growth of residential suburbs occurred prior to World War II, but it was in the period after that that growth truly accelerated.

The rapid postwar suburbanization was partly an unintended outcome of postwar social policy. The creation of the VA and FHA mortgage guarantee programs and the development of massive highway aid programs made it possible to turn much of the farm and wilderness acreage around cities into suburban bedroom communities. The original settlers of these new postwar suburbs are today's middle-aged generation; within the next 10 to 20 years, these suburbanites will comprise a large portion of the elderly population. Will that middle aged-generation still be living in the suburbs when they become elderly? Will they move back to the central city or to someplace in between? Will such migration patterns, if they occur, vary with respect to socioeconomic status? The answers have important implications for the development of effective and efficient service delivery programs for the elderly.

The 1960s saw the enactment of much new federal and state legislation designed to provide both income and services to the elderly. An often unstated assumption was that the urban elderly could be found in residence clusters, mostly located around central-city areas, to which services could be easily provided. Although there is some empirical support for such an assumption about today's elderly, there is evidence too that residential shifts are beginning to undermine program effectiveness.

An important sign of that shift is the rapid expansion of transport service for the elderly, which suggests that ease of access, an indication of central-city location, is less and less available to the elderly. Those concerned with the development of services for the elderly should view such need as symptomatic of a more serious underlying problem. It may be that the isolation and immobility of the elderly should be treated by the development of policies that encourage more supportive surrounding communities rather than more vehicles on the road. Whatever the answer, policies that are designed to meet long-run needs should be based upon a firmer foundation than the current assumption (implied if not explicitly stated) that the elderly in the next 30 years will live where they do now.

LOCATION OF THE BOSTON ELDERLY DURING THE PAST 40 YEARS

According to the 1960 Census definition of Boston's standard metropolitan statistical area (SMSA), there were 78 cities and towns in metropolitan Boston. Using that definition, the locations of residential concentrations of the elderly from 1930 until 1970 were plotted with regard to city and/or town of residence. The following measure was used:

$$P_i = \frac{E_i/T_i}{E/T}$$

where $E = \sum_1^{78} E_i$

$$T = \left| \sum_1^{78} \right.$$

P_i = ratio of proportion of population over 65 in community i to proportion of SMSA population over 65

E_i = number of people over 65 in community i

T_i = total number of people in community i

E = total number of people over 65 in SMSA

T = total number of people in SMSA

i = 1–78 because there are 78 cities and towns in the SMSA

Note that when P_i is greater than 1, the ith community has a larger proportion of its population in the 65+ category than has the metropolitan area as a whole. When P_i just equals 1, the proportion of 65+ population is just equal to that in the metropolitan area, and when P_i is below 1, the proportion of community i population over 65 is less than that of the metropolitan area as a whole. Using P_i, we can identify those communities which, at any point in time or over time, have a disproportionately large elderly population.

If age were not a factor in metropolitan location, we presumably would find that most communities exhibited a ratio of about 1. Where there appeared to be a smaller or larger ratio at any point in time, we would expect that such variation was random and not indicative of any pattern. However, if in fact the value of the ratio departed from 1 and appeared to follow a pattern over time, it would be clear that some systematic factors were affecting the location of the elderly. A value for P_i was calculated for each city and town in the Boston SMSA for each of the census years from 1930 through 1970. The results of these calculations are presented in maps 1 through 5. Communities with P_i greater than 1.10 were considered disproportionately elderly. Those with P_i between 0.90 and 1.10 were considered proportionately. elderly, and those with P_i below 0.90 were listed as less than proportionately elderly.

In 1930 a large number of the cities and towns (45) had a disproportionately large elderly population. These communities were mainly concentrated at the northern and southern edges of what, in 1960, would become the SMSA. In addition, there was a distinct, if somewhat less pronounced, grouping of communities with disproportionately elderly populations out to the west. By 1940 the number of cities and towns with a disproportionately elderly population had decreased significantly to 30. The pattern to the west had all but disappeared; however, the concentrations in the north and south were still quite distinct. During this period, with the exception of the town of Brookline, the inner-ring and central-city areas of the SMSA tended to be proportionately and even less than proportionately elderly.

The 1950 was the first census year after World War II. In that year the number of communities with a disproportionately elderly population had declined to 18. The north–south pattern had begun to disappear. Almost half the 78 cities and towns (38 to be exact) had a proportionate elderly population. By 1960, postwar suburbanization was reflected in the census, and it is not surprising to find that the newly created bedroom suburbs had a very small proportion of elderly. The number of communities that had a proportionate population had declined from 38 to 21. At the same time, the number of cities and towns with a disproportionately elderly population had continued to decline, reaching 11 by 1960. The pattern was quite pronounced in the entire ring of suburban communities where not one disproportionately elderly community could be found. The disproportionately elderly communities were now found in the inner-ring and central-city areas. By 1970 the age segregation pattern that was emerging in 1960 had become even sharper. The number of proportionate communities dropped to 10, its lowest number in five census years. The inner ring and central city became more pronouncedly elderly, and suburbia even more strictly followed the opposite trend.[2]

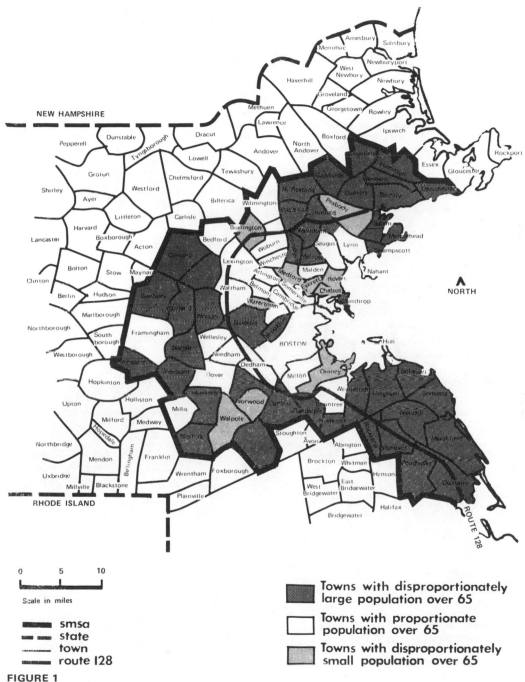

FIGURE 1
Proportion of population over age 65: Boston SMSA, 1930.

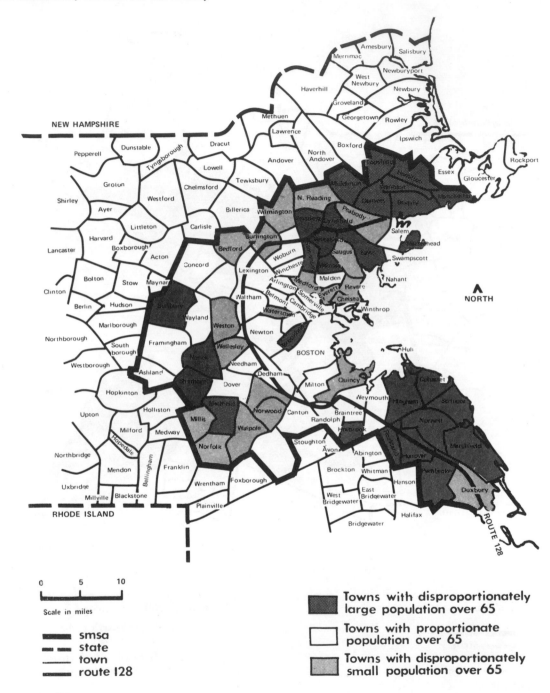

Scale in miles

▬▬ smsa
▬ ▬ state
──── town
▬▬ route 128

■ Towns with disproportionately large population over 65
□ Towns with proportionate population over 65
▨ Towns with disproportionately small population over 65

FIGURE 2
Proportion of population over age 65: Boston SMSA, 1940.

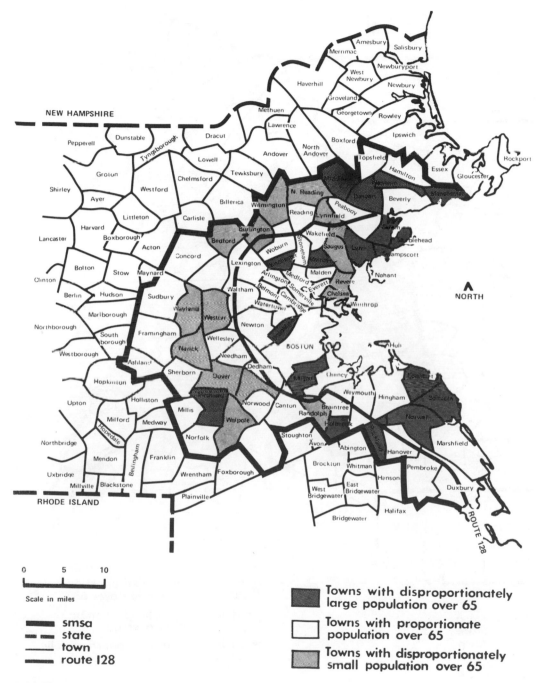

FIGURE 3
Proportion of population over age 65: Boston SMSA, 1950.

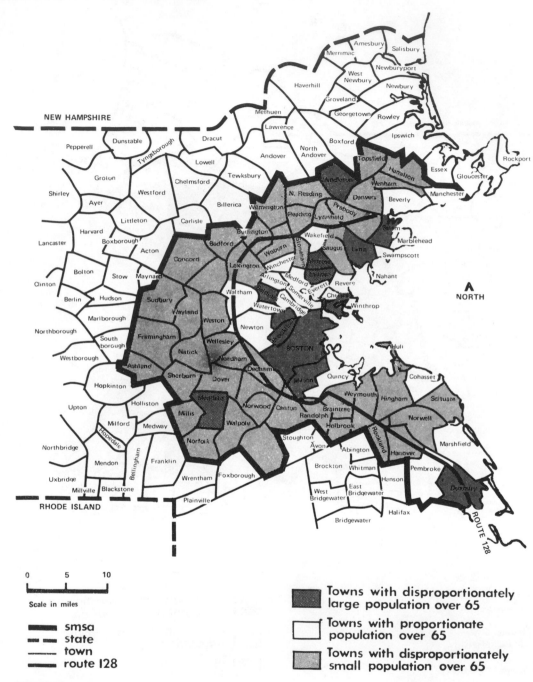

Scale in miles

━━━ smsa
- - - state
----- town
━━━ route 128

FIGURE 4
Proportion of population over age 65: Boston SMSA, 1960.

Towns with disproportionately large population over 65

Towns with proportionate population over 65

Towns with disproportionately small population over 65

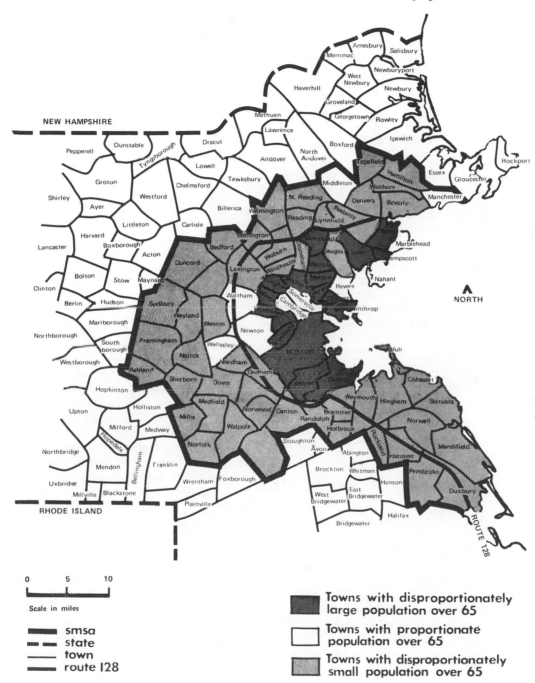

FIGURE 5
Proportion of population over age 65: Boston SMSA, 1970.

TABLE 1
Number of Communities with Various
Proportions of Population over 65

Year	Total	Proportion		
		High	Average	Low
1930	78	45	23	10
1940	78	30	28	20
1950	72[a]	18	38	16
1960	78	11	21	46
1970	78	17	10	51

[a]The 1950 census used a more limited definition of metropolitan area. The U.S. Census did not publish sufficient data to derive as large a sample for 1950 as for the other years.

The maps and Table 1 make two things clear. First, a pattern of age segregation does exist in the Boston area. This pattern has become especially pronounced in the past 20 years, during which time the combination of mortgage guarantee programs and automobile travel has permitted the spread of nuclear families and the geographic dispersion of their housing. Second, communities with disproportionately elderly populations have shifted toward the center of the metropolitan area for the past 40 years. What the maps and table do not tell us is why these patterns have occurred; nor do they tell us whether the patterns are likely to continue or to change in the future.

URBAN GROWTH THEORIES AND AGE SEGREGATION

To understand the particular patterns of age segregation that occurred in the metropolitan area, it is necessary to look at urban growth theories and their empirical applications. Theories of urban growth usually have some element of land-use economics and rent theory built into them to explain the spatial specialization of activity that accompanies urban development. Theories which explain the residential behavior of individuals within that broader context can be divided into two general classes. The first we can call pure income-theory models; the second, although they contain an element of income theory, are more appropriately called life-cycle models.

The income-theory models posit the view that where individuals and families locate in a metropolitan area is almost purely a function of their income. The work of Kain (1967) is typical of this class of models. Using an Alonso-type model of the urban land market, Kain argues that the higher a family's income, the more likely the family is to move to a suburb where it can consume more space. In the type of world postulated by models in this class, income and wealth variables alone would explain where in the suburbs a family or individual would be found once their preference for space was understood. Although this class of model is not very good at explaining the role of other variables, such as race and ethnicity, let alone age, it has been used as a basis from which to advocate suburbanization strategies to overcome racial segregation. A similar extension of the model could be made to explain residential location by age, to the extent that income is an age-linked variable. Since the elderly as a group tend to be low-income, one would expect to find them wherever low-income groups tend to reside in the metropolitan area. Models of this type are especially useful during times when the metropolitan area is growing. They posit a continued path of real income growth and of consumption of physical space. When transport technology reaches a plateau and continued metropolitan growth begins to slow down and even halt, such models explain far less. This is especially true when the end to transport expansion is accompanied by a slowdown in the rate of overall real income growth and by higher fuel costs. In such a world, other factors explaining location, such as the point in its life cycle that a family has reached and even the life-cycle stage of a whole community, become far more important.

Models and theories that give such life-cycle variables more credit have begun to appear recently. Typical and principal in this group of models is the work of Birch (1972). His "stage theory" of urban growth suggests that the character of neighborhoods and communities changes over time following well-defined patterns. The stages he distinguishes are (1) rural, (2) first-wave development, (3) fully developed, (4) packing, (5) thinning, and (6) recapture. Thinning is defined as the stage in which buildings in stage 4 have deteriorated and the children of the original residents leave. Population declines absolutely, leaving older couples behind in what Birch calls old slums. The displaced residents usually find locations in areas that are in stage 3 or 4 of the process. Birch tested this model using Italians and blacks. Although he found considerable support for this hypothesis, it is still far from an age theory of urbanization. Since ethnic and racial groups present an assortment of problems that differ from those of aging per se, the findings of Birch are far from directly transferable to our needs.

Nonetheless, there are some important links between such life-cycle theories of spatial areas and those of people. Let us consider the family life-cycle model and its adaption of space to family needs. The family life-cycle stages are marked off by events. These events are marriage, birth of the first child, birth of the last child, first child leaving home, last child leaving home (empty nest), and the death of spouse (widowhood). Such a model not only has implications for spatial location but also for other variables, such as expenditure patterns, savings patterns, and the interrelated variable of family size itself. Spatially, assuming that families had adequate income and/or savings at each stage, they could move from small, centrally located quarters to larger locations in the direction of the periphery, reaching the largest location and farthest distance when family size is maximum. After that the family would tend to move back toward the center into smaller and smaller quarters. Of course, for a variety of reasons, the model does not work that simply. First, family income does not adjust automatically to meet increased spatial needs for all families at about the same age. Second, it does not follow that all with rising incomes will want to consume more suburban space; there may be ties to ethnic neighborhoods or to extended family. Finally, when the family reaches maximum size, at about middle age of the parents, they may not move anymore. Given the cost of renting with a limited income versus the cost of being overhoused in the suburbs, in a mortgage-free home with little maintenance need (thanks to automatic furnaces and the like), older families and individuals may continue to age in the "wrong" place despite declining income and family size. Thus, although we may find some overlap between patterns of neighborhood aging and

person aging, it is not clear that the patterns will always coincide.

Indeed both hypotheses, (1) that the elderly continue to adapt their spatial context to life cycle and (2) that they tend to stay fixed beyond middle age, find some support in existing statistics. The first hypothesis is supported by statistics which show that 30 percent of the population over 65 years of age changed their place of residence between 1955 and 1960. Of this group, 19 percent moved to a residence within the same county as their previous location (Riley and Foner, 1968). Furthermore, the general trend of this movement was toward the city. Overall, it is young adults who exhibit the greatest amount of residential mobility. Individuals become less likely to move as their age increases. This tendency levels off after the age of 60 when movement occurs again. There is another slight increase in movement in the age group beyond 80. When these older age groups move, they are more likely to remain within the same state (9 times out of 10) (Birren, 1959). Older women appear to be more geographically mobile than men.

On the other hand, there is also a body of statistics to support the notion that the elderly tend to remain in their residence of middle age. Most older people, 77 percent in 1970, lived in owner-occupied homes (U.S. Department of Housing and Urban Development, 1971). Approximately 33 percent of the residents over 60 years of age had lived in their present residence 20 years or more. In the rest of the population only 13 percent had lived in a home for that long. The concentration of old people appeared to be high in the older suburbs, reflecting a possible tendency for the population to age as the suburb ages (1960 census of population).

Long (1972) has studied the influence of the age of children on family residential mobility. The younger age group was eight times as likely to move as the oldest age group (55 to 65 years of age). "This range of variation is not to be found for any other social, economic or family characteristics." Unfortunately, the age group beyond 65, which is our primary concern, was not included in this study. Whether another set of factors occurs in the 65+ group or whether a simple projection of the data to that group would be accurate is an open question.

TABLE 2
Regression Results Testing Urbanization Hypotheses[a] (Figures shown are regression coefficients significant at least at 5 percent level)

Equation	Proportion of Pop. 65+ for Year	Constant	Tax Rate	Per Pupil Education Expenditure	Proportion of Pop. Under 21	Distance from Center	Distance Squared	Distance Cubed	Zone
1	1930	0.076	NS	NS	−0.087	NS	NS	NS	NS
2	1940	−0.19	NS	NS	0.67	NS	NS	NS	NS
3	1950	0.14	NS	0.0000031	−0.16	NS	NS	NS	NS
4	1960	21.96	NS	NS	−0.31	NS	NS	0.0011	NS
5	1970	0.32	NS	NS	−0.57	NS	NS	NS	NS
6	1950	0.077				NS	NS	NS	NS
7	1970	0.14				NS	NS	0.000015	NS
8	1960	18.65			−0.27				
9	1970	0.12			−0.23				
10	1950	NS							
11	1950	NS	NS						
12	1950	0.10				−0.002			
13	1960	8.48				−0.17			
14	1970	NS				−0.003			

[a]NS, value not significant; Blank spaces indicate that a variable was not included in the regression equation.

The preceding models and evidence are not necessarily contradictory. The question for our purposes is one of degree of validity. To develop a model that relates socioeconomic class, residential location, and age to issues of service delivery, the question of the degree to which each of the effects operates must be examined. It is indeed true that the consumption of residential space is positively related to income and wealth level. However, it is also true that families will become more reluctant to move as they age. Furthermore, the relationship is somewhat complicated by the fact that as families age their incomes tend to fall at retirement time. If we wish to relate these shifts in residence to the need for services, we must also take into account the fact that families and individuals with higher incomes, irrespective of residence, may require fewer services from public sources. For example, it could be that the elderly who are beginning to relocate to the center city are financially better off than the elderly who remain in their own homes in the suburbs. This view would run counter to the picture that emerged from the 1950s and 1960s of old and poor couples and individuals living in squalor at or near the center city. It may also be that, because of ethnic and class ties, some elderly living in the inner

suburbs may enjoy a network of family and community that lessens the need for the provision of public services, despite their qualification for those services in income terms.

In any case, the first step in developing a model of aging and residential location that can be useful for planning service needs requires testing the existing theories against existing data.

AN EMPIRICAL LOOK AT URBANIZATION

To statistically test existing theory, it is necessary to place the theory in a format that allows for its quantification. As a first step, we can think of urban migration theory in a dichotomous manner. Individuals remain or move either because of income or life-cycle considerations. If the patterns of residence observed in the previous mappings were solely the result of life-cycle considerations, we would expect our statistical tests on quantitative measures of life cycle to yield significant results. But if income and wealth affect location, measures of these factors should yield significant results. Finally, and most likely, if each of these factors affects intraurban location and/or migration to some extent at each point in

TABLE 2 (*continued*)

Median Family Income	Prop. of Pop. 55–65 One Decade Earlier	Prop. of Pop. 21–45 Two Decades Earlier	Prop. of Pop. of Foreign Stock	Prop. of Owner-Occupied Housing	Prop. of Housing Built Before 1940	Population Density	Median House Value	R^2
								0.62
								0.66
								0.90
								0.54
								0.86
0.016								0.42
								0.52
NS	NS	NS	NS	NS	6.17			0.59
	0.58	NS	NS	−0.21	0.00043			0.94
		NS		NS	0.0008			0.14
NS						NS		0.39
NS							NS	0.21
							0.0001	0.22
							0.000005	0.45

time, we seek to know the extent and shift over time.

The statistical technique employed to carry out this examination was regression analysis.[3] The independent variables used in the 14 regressions represent an attempt to test life-cycle and income and wealth effects upon intraurban location patterns through five census periods. Median family income, median house value, population density, distance from the center city, and zone are variables that in one way or another reflect income and wealth considerations in choice of residential location. Distance is specified in three different ways—as distance, distance squared, and distance cubed. The purpose of the latter two forms of the distance variable is to allow for the possibility that the relationship between distance and age-specific residential location may not be a linear relationship. The variable labeled "zone" is included because it has been found in previous research that suburbanization in the Boston area proceeded in two very distinct zones for higher- and lower-income groups. Higher-income groups moved to the west, as a rule, and lower-income groups tended to move along a north–south axis (Edel and Sclar, 1971).

The life-cycle variables are tax rate, per pupil educational expenditures, proportion of population under 21, proportion of population 55 to 65 one decade earlier, proportion of population 21 to 45 two decades earlier, proportion of population of foreign stock, proportion of owner-occupied housing, and proportion of housing stock built prior to 1940. Since a major share of the property tax in Massachusetts goes for educational expenditures, presumably tax rate and educational expenditures would be higher in communities where families at the younger ends of the life cycle reside. Hence these two variables have been included with the group of life-cycle variables.

Table 2 shows the significant regression coefficients for a series of tests of these hypotheses. The first five regression equations are an attempt to test the two approaches with the same variables for each of the five census years. These regressions are particularly interesting because they employ sets of variables for which we have comparable data for that long a period of time. An important finding is that for each year proportion of population under 21 is significant. Furthermore, for four of the five years, the relationship is negative. This suggests that younger and older families have tended to reside in different parts of the metropolitan area since before World War II. The year

1940 presents an interesting contrast. The proportion of population under 21 variable is also significant but the sign is positive. The negative sign on the other four coefficients implies that the relationship is inverse. The positive sign on the 1940 coefficient implies that communities with a larger proportion of young people also had a higher proportion of older people. This is perhaps a reflection of the impact of the great depression. During the 1930s older and younger relatives would have been more likely to live together. Thus equation 2 suggests that the depression acted to retard the development of the trend toward residential age segregation for a while. The correlations presented in Table 3 provide another measure of these findings.

Although only one distance measure for one year (1960) proved significant, some of the other specifications for distance were almost significant for the 1960 and 1970 equations. Furthermore, in equation 7 one of the distance variables for 1970 was significant. This suggests that it was not until the postwar period that distinct distance and age-segregation patterns began to develop. The fact that the significant variable was distance cubed suggests that the relationship between age and distance is nonlinear. Thus concentrations of elderly increase for a while, then drop off, and then increase again. While this finding needs further confirmation, it does suggest that, should the trend continue, the elderly will be found in a bimodal distribution at the center and at the periphery of the metropolitan area in very low and very high density living situations at some point in the not too distant future.

The public finance variables included in the regression equations proved to be insignificant overall. This is not to say that older and younger families have similar desires with regard to major local expenditures

such as education; rather it suggests that the impact of differences in this area is masked by other more important issues in the metropolitan environment. The impact of younger families moving to low-tax suburbs and expanding school expenditures there was offset by the fact that increasing numbers of elderly were located in the inner portion of the metropolitan area, which inherited a higher expenditure and hence tax structure as a result of earlier development. This is also borne out to some extent by equation 3, the only equation in which the tax rate coefficient is significant at least at the 5 percent level. The positive sign on the 1950 equation suggests that tax rates were higher in the communities with a higher proportion of older people. It should also be noted, however, that the coefficient was of a very low value. The year 1950 was quite early in the postwar period of automobile suburbanization. As a result, the expansion of school and other expenditures in the suburbs had not yet occurred, even though out-migration had already begun.

The two variables most clearly reflective of income and wealth considerations are median family income and median house value. The only year in which median family income is a significant variable with respect to the proportion of population 65+ is for the year 1950 (equations 6 and 11). The relationship is positive, indicating that communities with higher income tended to have a larger proportion of their population over 65 years of age. This inference is at first glance at odds with the well-known fact that the elderly as a group tend to be among the poorest members of society. The paradox is resolved if we remember once again that in 1950 postwar suburbanization was just beginning. The central city is a relatively large place containing not just older people but a goodly proportion of the more affluent. Consequently, the rich and the elderly, regardless of income, could be found in the same vicinity in 1950. More importantly, the fact that the income variable was not significant in either 1960 or 1970 suggests that the process of intraurban migration responds to a complex of factors other than merely income and wealth. If we assume that distance from the center city to the suburbs is a continuum along which higher and higher incomes can be found as we move out (as postulated by Kain-type models), and we also know

TABLE 3
Correlations Between Proportion of Population 65+ and Proportion Under 21 for Years 1930–1960

Year	Value	Year	Value
1930	−0.45	1950	−0.93
1940	0.76	1960	−0.66

that the elderly have low incomes by and large, we would expect to find significant and negative coefficients for income variables, especially in the 1960 and 1970 regressions when automobile suburbanization was at its peak. This suggests that suburbs have not been and are even less likely to be (in light of the end to automobile suburbanization) the homogeneous units suggested by such theories.

The house value coefficients provide further confirmation of this fact. Equations 12, 13, and 14 demonstrate that median house value varies positively with the proportion of 65+ population. Furthermore, that variation was significant in 1960 and 1970, but not in 1950. Since newer houses are usually worth more than older houses and the elderly tend to live in the portions of the region with the older housing stock (see equations 8, 9, and 10), the fact that median house values are higher where the concentrations of elderly are larger indicates further than the continuum from poor center to rich suburb is not a simple straight line.

If income and wealth are poor predictors of location, it does not automatically follow that life-cycle considerations are much better. Consider equations 9, 10, and 11. In each the percentage of owner-occupied housing was used as an independent variable. It was assumed that, if older people tended to remain located in the communities in which they spent their middle years, we would find a higher proportion of owner-occupied housing in those communities with a higher proportion of population past 65 years of age. Yet for the years 1950 and 1960 the sign is negative. Only the 1960 regression is significant. This result suggests that the elderly live in those communities in which most people are not owner occupiers. In 1970 the sign is positive but the result not significant. This paradox can be reconciled if we consider that, to the extent that the elderly live nearer the center, they live in areas in which a larger percentage of the dwellings are rental units. Thus, even if they are by and large owner occupiers, the heavy domination by renters would mask that fact in the regression.

One of the most direct and best tests of life-cycle considerations is the relationship between age change over time and location. If people aged in the location in which they spent their middle years and population size did not change drastically over the decade,

we would expect to find a strong direct relationship between the proportion of the population 55 to 65 in one decade and the population over 65 in the next. For the year 1950 the relationship was negative, although not significant. This reflects the fact that postwar suburbanization was causing drastic changes in the population size and composition in suburban communities. Ten years later the relationship had the hypothesized positive sign, but it was not statistically significant. This reflects the fact that outward population movements were still destabilizing the area and hence the underlying relationship between life cycle and location could not be discerned in the statistics. The year 1970 is the first time that a positive and statistically significant relationship exists between the two population proportions. Thus overall we must conclude that, while there is some evidence for a relationship between life cycle and location, the evidence is not conclusive.

CONCLUSIONS

The evidence investigated thus far reveals that age-segregation patterns exist and are becoming more acute. Furthermore, existing urban development models do not appear to explain the observed patterns. This may be due in part to the inadequacies in the data base used to test the theories, the problems inherent in the statistical techniques employed, and the particular specifications of the variables used. However, the theories were not designed to explain age–residence patterns. Thus we must conclude that both the existing evidence and shortcomings in the conceptual basis of existing urban development theory are such as to suggest the need for further development of age-specific theories of urban change. The evidence does suggest, however, that existing theory provides a foundation upon which such further conceptualization may be developed.

In developing new theory in empirically testable form and hence in a form usable by service planners, there are two important tasks. The first concerns improvement in the data base and the second pertains to the specification of variables for use in statistical modeling of the theory. One major obstacle to the more widespread application of knowledge generated by the social sciences is the inadequacy of the data base. Statistical technique and theoretical modeling have run far ahead of an adequate data base upon which to put such knowledge to work. Those of us concerned about planning services for the elderly will not be able to solve that problem, but we can be aware of it in our own work. It is important that we seek far more disaggregate and specific measures of the various social and economic phenomena which generate the problems that we seek to solve. Regardless of whether we use existing data bases or improved ones, it is important to identify as clearly as possible those variables which best predict the location patterns of the elderly over time. Consequently, the specification of the variables used in the statistical modeling needs to be reworked in many more forms than they have been to date.[4]

Once the migration patterns of the elderly are better understood, the next task is to develop links between these patterns and the generation of demand for services. Methodologically, this will involve finding measures that go beyond using existing service levels as indicators of service need. Since existing levels of service provision only indicate what is being provided, such conceptualization and subsequent measurement may require the generation of data not now available in existing sources.

The importance and urgency in the further development of age-specific theories of urbanization lie in the fact that service programs for the elderly have grown considerably in the recent past and are expected to grow at rapid rates in the foreseeable future. However, the fact that age, residence, and urban development do have systematic patterns which underlie them suggests that, even in the absence of more definitive research, planners must take such relationships into account in planning services. As this paper has shown, it is a poor assumption, implicit or explicit, to think that the elderly of the future will locate where the elderly of the past did.

Location is too often taken as a "given" by those who plan services. Location patterns respond to the same social and economic environments that create the need for services in the first place. Since location interacts with social and economic factors and affects the quantity and type of service needed, planners must be mindful of the effect of their service intervention not only on the social and economic context of the elderly but the spatial one as well.

The links between service need and location must also be introduced into the service planning process. At present, service need is usually estimated by estimating the size of the population to be served and using some proportion, however derived, as the estimate of service need. This paper suggests that in estimating the proportion the entire population of elderly should be disaggregated, not only by social and economic variables but by locational ones too.

The introduction of locational factors into the planning process will help to create the kinds of effectiveness and efficiency in service delivery that are called for by times such as the present when scarce social resources become even more precious.

Acknowledgments

This paper presents some of the preliminary results of an inquiry into the interrelationships of social class, residence, and occupation in the process of economic growth in the Boston metropolitan area during the past century. It was supported by Grant MH22407 from the Center for the Study of Metropolitan Problems, National Institute of Mental Health, to the Florence Heller Graduate School for Advanced Studies in Social Welfare, Brandeis University, and Grant GS 36880 from the National Science Foundation to Queens College, City University of New York. The principal investigators were Elliott Sclar (Brandeis University) and Matthew Edel (Queens College). Opinions expressed are not necessarily those of the funding organizations.

NOTES

1. In 1960 just over 9 percent of the population was over 65. By the 1970 census this figure had risen only slightly to just under 10 percent. Furthermore, the highest projection places the 1990 proportion at about 11 percent. The lowest projection is 10 percent (*Statistical Abstract of the United States, 1971*).
2. When a similar analysis was done using the proportion of population under 21, the result, while not symmetrically opposite, was close enough to allow the description of the elderly population distribution to serve as a proxy for all age segregation in the SMSA.

3. The reader unfamiliar with this technique is urged to consult a standard text in statistical analysis.
4. The approach being developed here can also be used to develop similar models of service need for different population groups.

REFERENCES

Birch, D. Toward a wage theory of urban growth. In S. Yin (ed.), *City in the Seventies.* New York: Rand Institute, F. E. Peacock Publishing Co., 1972.

Birren, J. E. (ed.). *Handbook of Aging and the Individual.* Chicago: University of Chicago Press, 1959.

Edel, M., and Sclar, E. Differential taxation, transportation and land values in a metropolitan area. Working paper 1 in *Boston: Studies in Urban Political Economy*. Presented at the Econometric Society Meeting, New Orleans, December 1971.

Gans, H. *The Urban Villagers*. New York: Free Press, 1962.

Kain, J. F. Post-war metropolitan development: housing preferences and automobile ownership. *American Economic Review*, 1967, *57*, 223–234.

Long, L. The influence of number and ages of children in residential mobility. *Demography*, 1972, *9*, 371.

Riley, M. W., and Foner, A. *Aging and Society*, Vol. 1. New York: Russell Sage Foundation, 1968.

U.S. Department of Housing and Urban Development. *Housing*. Prepared for the 1971 White House Conference on Aging, 1971.

STEPHEN M. GOLANT

Stephen M. Golant is an Assistant Professor in the Departments of Geography and Behavioral Sciences at the University of Chicago.

Intraurban Transportation Needs and Problems of the Elderly

The avilability of high-quality transportation is a factor that increasingly is considered by researchers and professionals in their evaluation of the suitability of residential locations occupied by the elderly. It is now well documented that for many elderly the quality of their transportation is far from optimum (for overviews see U.S. Senate, 1970; Revis, 1971; Cantilli and Shmelzer, 1971). At least one research investigation, moreover, has suggested a direct relationship between the quality of transportation services and the psychological well-being of older persons (Cutler, 1972). Research on the transportation needs of the elderly has been remarkably sparse (Carp, 1971c) and only in the last six years have both pure and applied research efforts been intensified. This greater research interest has coincided with and been stimulated by increased concern on the part of legislators (and reflected by greater funding) for the well-being of the elderly population in general, and in particular with the importance of transportation to this group (U.S. Senate, 1973b).

There has been increasing emphasis on measuring "quality" of transportation services from the perspective of the consumer utilizing (or not utilizing) a system, with the recognition that such evaluative judgments may likely provide more meaningful insights as to how well the transportation system is functioning. "Quality," however, when measured in this subjective fashion becomes a relative concept. A transportation service in a neighborhood that is considered adequate or very good from the point of view of one consumer group may be considered entirely inadequate and as constituting a barrier to activity by another group. An urban population of actual or potential transportation consumers, accordingly, cannot be treated as an undifferentiated mass with similar needs and resources.

"Quality" used in this context therefore implies congruity between the user and the transportation service. This congruity can be maintained or achieved by changing the needs and resources of the consumer and/or changing the structure and operating characteristics of the transportation system.

The decision as to what strategies will best accomplish this congruity must be based on an understanding of the consequences of changing either or both of these demand and supply components. The purpose of this paper is to identify the extent of the incongruity between the elderly consumer and his urban transportation system, to examine underlying causes, and to evaluate societal responses.

SPECIAL IMPORTANCE
OF ADEQUATE TRANSPORTATION

Adequate transportation is obviously important for all age groups, but for the older person the inability to reach required destinations can restrict his style of living. Transportation difficulties may represent the first concrete signs that he is becoming old and will no longer be able to carry on his accustomed way of life. Considerable discontinuity and anxiety may be experienced by the older person who finds that he can no longer use his car. If in fact this loss of mobility threatens his ability to maintain his independent living arrangements, the deleterious psychological impact may be even greater.

Growing old necessarily involves adaptation to various types of problems, such as lower income or poorer health. As a result, the impact of unavailable or inadequate transportation services may in combination with other problems prove to be far more serious for the older person because of its cumulative effect.

The loss of the work role, of old friends, of a spouse, represent activities and relationships that the older person may wish to replace. The need for good transportation services may be particularly important, giving him the mobility to find substitutes for these losses. Expressed in a more positive sense, retirement is usually accompanied by a large increase in leisure time and there will be greater opportunities for the older person to engage in activities for which previously he did not have time.

The physiological and psychological changes associated with growing old may result in a decline in either physical strength or motivation to engage in new activities. Trips to destinations accessible only by public transportation may be curtailed because of the physical exertion and fatigue experienced when using this transportation mode. The older person may fear leaving his familiar neighborhood to engage in activities located at some distance from his residence, irrespective of the potential benefits. The energy or

effort that many elderly persons are willing or have the capacity to expend on an activity in return for some benefit may be less than that of a younger person. Poor-quality service and inconveniences of various kinds may represent to some older persons far more significant barriers than they might for younger population groups.

Finally, the elderly person often faces considerable difficulty when seeking new residential accommodation because of the cost, type, and size of dwelling units available. The poor accessibility of some dwelling units to required services and facilities adds another restraint in the selection of adequate housing.

TRANSPORTATION BEHAVIOR
OF THE AGING AND THE AGED

Interpreting Previous Findings

The findings of studies reporting on the actual or observed transportation behavior of older persons should be interpreted with care. In particular, the assumption cannot automatically be made that overt behavior patterns accurately reflect the demands or the preferences of this population group, since their transportation needs often are not satisfied. A latent demand for transportation services often cannot be fully realized because of a number of constraints caused by the poor health and low income of the older person and because of the structural and operating characteristics of the transportation system. Accordingly, the observed transportation behavior of older persons and consequently their level of activity may reflect less their preferences or wants than their capability of utilizing the existing transportation facilities.

That such latent demand does exist will be illustrated by two types of evidence. First, the transportation problems experienced by older persons have now been well documented, providing cogent evidence that travel barriers prevent the satisfaction of their needs. Second, there is now sufficient evidence to demonstrate that by increasing the income of the older person (albeit indirectly through reduced transit fare programs), or by providing special-purpose transportation systems (e.g., dial-a-bus), one will increase the older person's use of transportation facilities and level of activity.

In reporting on the transportation behavior of older persons, it is also necessary to distinguish between two types of studies: (1) origin–destination, home-interview studies initiated by urban municipalities that focus primarily on vehicular trip activity of a representative sample of the total population, of whom the over age 65 has been a subgroup; (2) studies that focus specifically on the transportation behavior of older persons who may or may not be representative of the total elderly population in the area sampled. Studies in the second group also differ from those in the first group in that they analyze both vehicular and pedestrian transportation trips, they provide a more detailed typology of trip purposes, and the transportation behavior of older subjects often is not directly compared with younger population groups. Also, studies in the second group very often restrict their analysis to a particular subgroup of older persons, for example, the retired or applicants for reduced-fare transit programs who are primarily dependent on mass transit. Unfortunately, the findings in these two groups of studies often are not directly comparable, thus influencing the organization of the following review.

Vehicular Transportation Modes

The dependency of elderly persons on either mass transit service or on automobile transportation supplied by others is reflected by car ownership rates (Table 1 and Figures 1 and 2). At every income level, older persons have a considerably lower rate of automobile ownership than other age groups. There is also considerable and systematic variation in car ownership rates among elderly households with different income levels. Over 91 percent of elderly headed households with annual incomes of over $15,000 own at least one car, a figure that is higher than for most low-income households headed by younger persons. Low-income households headed by elderly have the lowest rate of car ownership of any low-income group in any age group.

These car ownership statistics may overestimate the *actual* availability of the automobile as a transportation mode. As will be emphasized, a number of

TABLE 1

Percentage of Households Owning Automobiles by Age of Head and (Household) Income, 1971

Age and Income ($) of Household Head	No Car (%)	At Least One Car (%)	Total (%)
Under 25			
Under 5,000	28.3	71.7	100.0
5,000–9,999	9.4	90.6	100.0
10,000–14,999	5.0	95.0	100.0
15,000 and over	r	r	r
25–34			
Under 5,000	35.2	64.8	100.0
5,000–9,999	11.5	88.5	100.0
10,000–14,999	3.2	96.8	100.0
15,000 and over	3.4	96.6	100.0
35–44			
Under 5,000	36.0	64.0	100.0
5,000–9,999	10.0	90.0	100.0
10,000–14,999	4.8	95.2	100.0
15,000 and over	3.4	96.6	100.0
45–54			
Under 5,000	34.5	65.5	100.0
5,000–9,999	11.6	88.4	100.0
10,000–14,999	4.3	95.7	100.0
15,000 and over	2.0	98.0	100.0
55–64			
Under 5,000	38.8	61.2	100.0
5,000–9,999	11.7	88.3	100.0
10,000–14,999	6.2	93.8	100.0
15,000 and over	4.2	95.8	100.0
65 and over			
Under 5,000	55.5	44.5	100.0
5,000–9,999	20.8	79.2	100.0
10,000–14,999	18.6	81.4	100.0
15,000 and over	8.4	91.6	100.0
All income classes			
Under 25	16.9	83.1	100.0
25–29	12.4	87.6	100.0
30–34	12.5	87.5	100.0
35–44	11.9	88.1	100.0
45–54	12.1	87.9	100.0
55–64	18.6	81.4	100.0
65 and over	45.4	54.6	100.0

Source: U.S. Department of Commerce, Bureau of the Census, *Consumer Buying Indicators, Current Population Reports*, Series P-65, No. 40, 1972, Table 1.

r = poor sampling reliability.

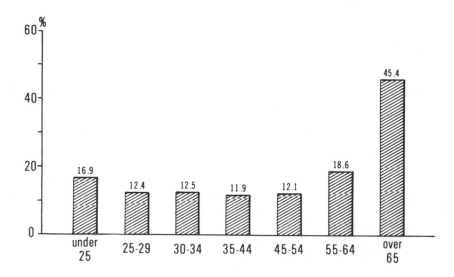

Source: See Table 1. Graphics by C. Muller-Wille,
Dept. of Geography, University of Chicago

FIGURE 1
Percent of households in United States not owning an automobile, by age of head, 1971.

factors may restrict the older person's use of his automobile.

An analysis of driver license statistics of persons (as opposed to households) in different age groups reveals a similar trend. Of additional significance is the much lower proportion of persons over age 70 possessing a license than the age 65 to 69 group. Also, there is large sex differential in license possession particularly for the age 65 to 69 and over age 70 groups. Over 60 percent of over age 70 males compared with just over 20 percent of over age 70 females were licensed as drivers (Table 2). Although the statistics in Tables 1 and 2 are not directly comparable, evidence by Markovitz (1971) would suggest that the percentage of elderly who own automobiles is greater than the percentage licensed as drivers, owing in part to license renewal difficulties.

Total Vehicular Trip Generation Related to Automobile Availability and License Possession

The positive or direct relationship between automobile availability or license possession and the generation of vehicular trips of older persons has been well documented (Carnegie-Mellon University, 1968;

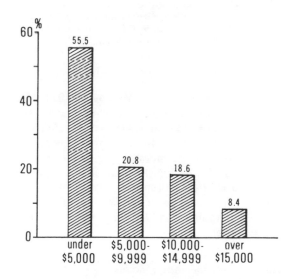

Source: See Table 1. Graphics by C. Muller-Wille, Dept. of Geography, University of Chicago

FIGURE 2
Percent of households in United States headed by persons 65 years and over not owning an automobile, by household income, 1971.

285

TABLE 2
Percentages of Total Population in Each Age–Sex Group Licensed as Drivers, 1969–1970

Age	Male	Female	Both Sexes
16–19	70.1	53.6	61.9
20–24	90.6	76.5	83.3
25–29	96.1	79.4	87.6
30–34.	93.2	77.4	85.1
35–39	94.9	75.8	85.1
40–44	94.6	74.5	84.3
45–49	94.0	72.9	83.1
50–54	92.6	62.6	77.0
55–59	90.5	53.4	71.1
60–64	87.4	45.6	65.1
65–69	74.0	38.9	54.6
70+	61.8	20.2	37.0
All ages	87.0	61.5	73.6
Number of licensed drivers	57,987,494	44,998,820	102,986,314

Source: U.S. Department of Transportation, Federal Highway Administration, *Nationwide Personal Transportation Survey. Report No. 6, Characteristics of Licensed Drivers*, by Robert E. Gish. Table 4, Apr. 1973.

Carp, 1971c; Golant, 1972; Markovitz, 1971; Marsh, 1960; Wynn and Levinson, 1967). The most comprehensive analysis of this relationship (Markovitz, 1971), using data from the home interview survey of the Tri-State Transportation Region (New York, New Jersey, and Connecticut), revealed that "drivers" (possessing a driver's license) made as many as four times as many trips as "nondrivers" (Table 3). This relationship applied to elderly in both high- and low-income households.

Vehicular Transportation Modes Used for Trip Making

The lower proportion of elderly persons owning an automobile or possessing a driver's license is reflected in the greater relative importance of trips by mass transit modes (bus, rail, streetcar, etc.) in contrast to younger age groups (Ashford and Holloway, 1971; Carnegie-Mellon University, 1968; Golant, 1972; Mar-

TABLE 3
Weekday Trips per Elderly Person by Income and Area of Residence: Drivers Versus Nondrivers

Area of Residence	Household Income[a]								All Income Groups	
	$0–2,999		$3,000–5,999		$6,000–9,999		$10,000+			
	Drivers	Nondrivers	Drivers	Nondrivers	Drivers	Nondrivers	Drivers	Nondrivers	Drivers	Nondrivers
New York City	0.83	0.36	1.34	0.53	1.65	0.48	2.03	0.69	1.49	0.47
New York suburbs	1.54	0.41	2.08	0.52	2.13	0.48	2.43	0.66	2.11	0.52
New York State	1.08	0.36	1.61	0.53	1.85	0.48	2.20	0.68	1.73	0.48
New Jersey	1.56	0.38	1.71	0.45	2.24	0.51	2.68	0.47	1.96	0.44
Connecticut	1.27	0.43	2.02	0.50	2.63	0.54	2.47	0.62	2.03	0.49
Study area	1.30	0.37	1.69	0.51	2.04	0.49	2.37	0.62	1.85	0.47

Source: Markovitz (1971), p. 245.
[a]Income of household of which an elderly person is a member.

ble et al., 1973; Markovitz, 1971; Wynn and Levinson, 1967). In particular, the relative importance of mass transit for social and recreational trips by elderly persons is much greater than for younger persons (Golant, 1972). This increase in the relative importance of mass transit usage by older persons occurs, however, because trips by automobile have decreased at a greater rate than trips by mass transit. Consequently, the increase in the relative importance of mass transit does not imply an increase in the absolute number of trips by mass transit, only a decrease in the absolute number of trips by automobile. Elderly persons still make the majority of their vehicular trips by automobile, either as drivers or passengers. In all studies the relative importance of the taxi is reported to be very small.

The frequency of trips utilizing the automobile rather than mass transit is related to income levels and whether the older person is licensed to drive. High-income elderly are more likely than low-income elderly to make their trips by automobile. Licensed older persons are more likely than nonlicensed persons to use automobile transportation (as drivers or passengers). Controlling simultaneously for income level and the possession of a driver's license, Marko-

vitz (1971) reported that auto trips (as passengers) by low-income, nonlicensed elderly drivers were lower than for high-income, nonlicensed elderly drivers. She also showed that the level of mass transit trips by low-income, nonlicensed drivers was very similar to high-income, nonlicensed drivers, and that high-income elderly persons, even if they did not possess a license, were more likely to make their trips by auto (as passengers) than by mass transit.

An examination of the relative importance of transportation modes by Golant (1972) emphasized the considerable variability of vehicle usage by different subgroups of elderly defined by their personal attributes and household status (Table 4).

Vehicular Trip Generation and Trip Purpose

On the average weekday the elderly tend to make fewer total vehicular trips per person than the total population. This relationship also tends to exist at all income levels (Golant, 1972; Markovitz, 1971; Wynn and Levinson, 1967). However, this disparity is largely a function of the considerable importance of work trips in the activity pattern of younger age groups, and when only nonwork vehicular trip pur-

TABLE 4
Relative Importance in Percentages of Transportation Modes for Trips by Persons Aged over 65

Population Group	Total	Auto Driver	Auto–Truck Passenger	Taxi	Public Transportation	Other[a]	Sample Size
Total persons	100.0	38.2	19.9	1.4	38.5	2.1	3,628
Total heads[b]	100.0	50.0	8.6	1.3	36.6	2.4	1,847
Total nonheads	100.0	13.2	41.8	1.5	42.4	1.2	1,781
Male nonheads	100.0	41.5	17.6	2.5	34.0	4.4	328
Male heads	100.0	59.8	6.6	0.9	29.8	2.9	1,212
Female heads	100.0	21.1	18.3	2.7	56.5	1.3	635
High-income heads[c]	100.0	70.2	6.9	2.9	18.4	1.6	106
Low-income heads[d]	100.0	35.6	13.3	1.1	46.4	3.6	637
Retired heads	100.0	51.6	11.4	1.3	34.8	1.0	1,229
Nonretired heads	100.0	48.3	7.7	1.3	38.6	4.1	618
Retired male heads	100.0	60.8	8.2	0.9	29.1	1.0	886
Retired female heads	100.0	25.3	20.3	2.5	51.1	0.7	343

Source: Golant (1972), p. 159.
[a] Railway, school bus, walk between home and work.
[b] Refers to head of household.
[c] Household annual income greater than $8,000.
[d] Household annual income less than $4,000.

poses (excluding also trips for "school" purposes) are analyzed, the differential between the elderly and the total population becomes very small and may be nonapparent in the lower-income strata (Golant, 1972; Markovitz, 1971).

A comparison of the nonwork vehicular trip generation of the over age 65 population with the population aged 56 to 65 in metropolitan Toronto by Golant (1972)[1] revealed very small differences. The pattern of variation in the generation of nonwork vehicular trips became more complex when comparable subgroups identified by retirement status, household status, income, and sex were examined in each of the two age groups (Table 5). For example, the

TABLE 5
Trips per Person by Trip Purpose for Average 24-Hour Period

Population Group	TT[a] No.	NW[b] No.	Work[c] No.	Personal Business[d] No.	Shopping No.	Social No.	Recreation No.	Other[e] No.	Home No.
Age 56–65									
Total persons	1.49	0.36	0.45	0.08	0.14	0.09	0.03	0.02	0.67
Total heads[f]	1.98	0.38	0.72	0.10	0.12	0.09	0.04	0.03	0.89
Total nonheads	0.99	0.37	0.17	0.07	0.15	0.10	0.03	0.04	0.44
Male nonheads	0.97	0.12	0.39	0.04	0.03	0.03	0.00	0.02	0.46
Male heads	2.14	0.33	0.84	0.09	0.10	0.06	0.04	0.04	0.96
Female heads	1.40	0.49	0.27	0.11	0.17	0.18	0.03	0.00	0.64
High-income heads[g]	2.63	0.40	1.08	0.10	0.10	0.10	0.04	0.06	1.14
Low-income heads[h]	1.45	0.37	0.41	0.11	0.15	0.09	0.01	0.01	0.65
Retired heads	1.14	0.61	0.04	0.16	0.23	0.11	0.06	0.05	0.49
Nonretired heads	2.11	0.35	0.82	0.09	0.10	0.09	0.04	0.03	0.95
Retired male heads	1.32	0.72	0.03	0.22	0.25	0.10	0.07	0.08	0.56
Retired female heads	0.80	0.40	0.04	0.04	0.20	0.13	0.03	0.00	0.36
Age over 65									
Total persons	0.83	0.33	0.12	0.07	0.13	0.09	0.03	0.01	0.36
Total heads[f]	1.11	0.43	0.19	0.10	0.16	0.11	0.04	0.02	0.49
Total nonheads	0.54	0.25	0.04	0.04	0.11	0.07	0.03	0.00	0.24
Male nonheads	0.48	0.16	0.11	0.04	0.06	0.03	0.02	0.01	0.22
Male heads	1.26	0.44	0.27	0.11	0.15	0.11	0.04	0.03	0.55
Female heads	0.82	0.41	0.04	0.07	0.18	0.11	0.04	0.01	0.37
High-income heads[g]	2.32	0.73	0.61	0.12	0.27	0.20	0.12	0.02	0.96
Low-income heads[h]	0.83	0.34	0.10	0.07	0.12	0.11	0.04	0.00	0.38
Retired heads	0.86	0.46	0.01	0.11	0.17	0.12	0.04	0.02	0.38
Nonretired heads	1.60	0.35	0.55	0.07	0.13	0.10	0.03	0.02	0.70
Retired male heads	0.88	0.48	0.02	0.12	0.17	0.12	0.04	0.03	0.39
Retired female heads	0.80	0.44	0.01	0.09	0.18	0.12	0.04	0.01	0.36

Source: Golant (1972), p. 146.
[a]Total trips per person. Includes trips to nonwork, work, and home destinations. Small discrepancies in totals due to rounding.
[b]Total nonwork trip destinations (excluding return trips to "home").
[c]Includes work-to-work trips.
[d]Refers to trips made to complete transactions not considered part of a person's regular employment. Examples include trips to the dentist or doctor, to the post office, or to an office to pay a bill.
[e]This category includes primarily "serve passenger" trip purposes and applies to trips made in an automobile to pick up or deliver someone at a specific location.
[f]Refers to head of household.
[g]Household annual income greater than $8,000.
[h]Household annual income less than $4,000.

nonwork vehicular trip activity of high-income, over age 65 household heads was considerable greater than the nonwork trip activity of high-income household heads aged 56 to 65. It is significant that several older population subgroups made a greater number of nonwork vehicular trips than comparable younger population subgroups. In particular, social (visits to friends or relatives) and shopping trips are made more frequently by some over age 65 subgroups than comparable younger subgroups (Ashford and Holloway, 1971; Golant, 1972; Marble et al., 1973).

Not surprisingly, if different subgroups of older persons are examined, there is considerable variation in the level of their nonwork vehicular trip generation. Particularly dramatic are the differences in the nonwork vehicular trip activity of high- and low-income elderly. On the average weekday, the former group made twice as many nonwork vehicular trips per person as the latter group (Table 5). Markovitz (1971) described comparable variations in the nonwork trip activity of elderly with different levels of income as did Carp (1970), who examined a variety of mobility correlates. It is important to emphasize that an elderly person's level of vehicular trip activity reflects not only his ability to successfully use a car or a mass transit system but also his preferences or motivation to do so. Low vehicular trip activity may only indicate that most of the older person's needs are within walking distance.

The *relative* importance of vehicular trips for different purposes taken by the elderly have been documented in several studies (Ashford and Holloway, 1971; Carnegie-Mellon University, 1968; Golant, 1972). Interestingly, several studies reveal that for the elderly group as a whole, the work trip still has the greatest relative importance, followed by shopping trips. These are followed by personal business trips and social trips, which sometimes alternate in relative importance. Recreational vehicular trips, relatively, are of least importance. This finding may reflect interviews administered primarily on weekdays. There is need to emphasize again that the relative importance of vehicular trips for different purposes will vary considerably among elderly subgroups (Table 6 and Figure 3).

Vehicular Trip Travel Times

The length of time taken by older persons to complete a trip (i.e., from origin "door" to destination "door") will vary depending on the transportation mode. The average trip duration time will vary

TABLE 6
Relative Importance in Percentages of Trip Purposes for Persons over Age 65

Population Group	Total	Work	Personal Business	Shopping	Social	Recreation	Other
Total persons	100.0	27.4	15.3	27.9	18.6	8.4	2.6
Total heads[a]	100.0	32.5	15.8	24.7	16.6	7.4	2.9
Total nonheads	100.0	16.6	14.1	34.6	22.8	10.4	1.6
Male nonheads	100.0	45.2	13.7	20.5	9.6	8.2	2.7
Male heads	100.0	39.9	15.8	19.4	15.0	6.5	3.4
Female heads	100.0	11.4	16.0	39.7	21.1	10.1	1.7
High-income heads[b]	100.0	41.5	11.3	19.8	13.2	12.3	1.9
Low-income heads[c]	100.0	25.5	17.3	25.9	20.6	8.6	2.1
Retired heads	100.0	2.8	23.8	35.7	22.7	10.4	4.7
Nonretired heads	100.0	64.0	7.4	13.0	10.1	4.3	1.1
Retired male heads	100.0	3.2	24.6	33.2	23.2	10.3	5.4
Retired female heads	100.0	1.6	21.3	42.6	21.3	10.7	2.4

Source: Golant (1972), p. 150.
[a]Refers to head of household.
[b]Household annual income greater than $8,000.
[c]Household annual income less than $4,000.

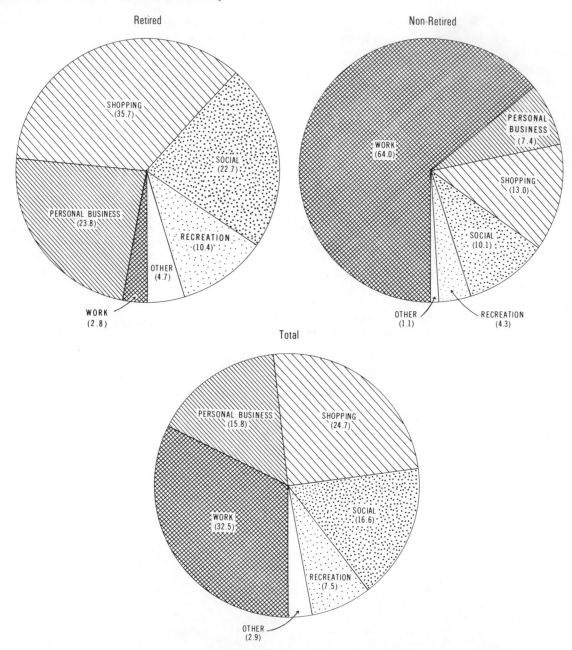

Source: Golant (1972). Graphics by C. Muller-Wille,
        Dept. of Geography, University of Chicago

FIGURE 3
Percentage distribution of trips taken by retired and non-retired persons over age 65 heading their own households.

TABLE 7
Travel Times of Trips from Home to Destination Taken by Persons over Age 65, by Purpose and Mode (Figures in percents)

Travel Time (minutes)	Work		Personal Business and Shopping		Social and Recreation		Total Trips	
	Auto	PT[a]	Auto	PT	Auto	PT	Auto	PT
0–10	21.6	2.4	42.5	8.0	22.1	4.1	32.1	5.5
11–20	35.1	9.1	31.9	27.3	27.7	23.1	31.4	21.0
21–30	28.1	40.0	19.1	32.9	24.4	22.4	22.3	32.1
31–40	5.3	16.4	2.2	4.8	2.3	4.8	3.0	8.2
Over 40	10.0	32.1	4.3	26.9	23.5	45.5	11.1	33.2
Total	100.0	100.0	100.0	100.0	100.0	100.0	100.0	100.0
Average	24.6	37.5	17.8	32.1	35.5	44.8	24.4	36.9

Source: Golant (1972), p. 169.
[a]PT, public transportation.

also among different urban centers, reflecting the spatial structure of their transportation systems. Golant (1972) has reported that, irrespective of trip purpose, the travel time to reach a destination by older persons was considerably longer by mass transit than by automobile (Table 7). This travel time reflects the physical location of the destination relative to the origin as well as the operating characteristics of the transportation system. Controlling for transportation mode and examining travel times for three major groups of trip purposes, he found that on the average the longest trips were for social—recreational purposes, followed by work trips, and then by personal business and shopping trips, which were of shortest time duration. Irrespective of transportation mode, however, the large majority of trips by older persons were less than 30 minutes in duration. Nahemow and Kogan (1971) in their New York study emphasized that trips requiring subway modes or both bus and subway modes were of considerably longer duration. There are no significant differences in the travel times of vehicular trips by older and younger (but over age 25) age groups, if vehicular mode and trip purpose are controlled (Ashford and Holloway, 1971; Golant, 1972; Marble et al., 1973).

Time of Departure of Home-Based Vehicular Trips

Work-trip departures by the older population tend to be more dispersed throughout the day than for a younger labor force population (Golant, 1972). The greater relative importance of nonwork vehicular trips by older persons influences considerably the temporal pattern of their trip making. Older persons are most likely to depart between the morning and evening traffic rush-hour periods (Table 8). In comparing the nonwork vehicular trip activity of the age 56 to 65 and over age 65 groups, the latter were more likely to avoid starting both automobile and transit trips during the early morning rush-hour periods and were less likely to depart on nonwork trips, particularly by automobile, during the evening hours (after 6 P.M.);

Vehicular and Pedestrian Transportation Modes Used for Trip Making

The most comprehensive analysis of both vehicular and pedestrian transportation behavior, focusing specifically on older persons, has been by Carp (1971c), who examined a sample of 709 retired older persons

TABLE 8
Time of Departure by Trips from Home Taken by Persons Age 56–65 and over Age 65, by Purpose and Mode (Figures in percents)

Departure Time	Work		Personal Business and Shopping		Social and Recreation		Total Trips	
	Auto	PT[a]	Auto	PT	Auto	PT	Auto	PT
Total Persons Age 56–65								
6 A.M.–9 A.M.	75.0	71.8	6.2	12.5	4.0	6.9	43.1	50.7
9 A.M.–4 P.M.	14.0	14.8	59.5	79.5	31.8	60.2	28.8	35.2
4 P.M.–6 P.M.	3.5	2.3	8.2	2.0	11.8	8.2	5.6	2.8
6 P.M.–12 midnight	3.9	3.6	25.7	6.0	51.6	24.7	19.4	6.2
Total[b]	96.4	92.5	99.6	100.0	99.2	100.0	96.9	94.9
Total Persons over Age 65								
6 A.M.–9 A.M.	61.4	70.3	4.4	7.6	3.7	6.1	18.1	25.6
9 A.M.–4 P.M.	29.9	19.2	77.9	84.7	47.5	57.9	56.0	58.6
4 P.M.–6 P.M.	0.6	1.8	6.5	4.8	8.9	8.9	6.3	5.0
6 P.M.–12 midnight	7.6	1.8	10.1	2.8	39.4	27.2	19.2	8.9
Total[b]	99.5	93.1	98.9	100.0	99.5	100.0	99.6	98.1

Source: Golant (1971), p. 165.
[a]PT, public transportation.
[b]The percentages may not add up to 100 due to a small number of trips occurring outside these time periods.

in San Antonio in 1968 and 1969. The following sections emphasize her research findings.

An analysis of transportation modes used in trip making reemphasizes the greater relative importance of the automobile for the elderly person either as driver or passenger (Table 9). Of added significance is the considerable importance of walking as a mode of transportation. Forty-four percent of the sample made walking trips at least two or three times a week. Similar findings have been reported by Bourg (1973), Marble et al. (1973), and Nahemow and Kogan (1971).

Trip Purposes

The more detailed pattern of vehicular pedestrian trips (Table 10) is similar to the trip pattern reported for vehicular transportation alone. Because Carp's sample comprised only retired persons, the work trip was of no significance. Shopping trips had the greatest

relative importance, followed closely by social trips to visit friends and children. Trips to friends were more frequent than trips to children. Visits to other relatives, however, were made much less frequently. Over 50 percent of the elderly sample visited their church at least twice a month. Trips to a doctor were relatively infrequent with just over 25 percent making a trip at least once a month. Other trips, particularly those for recreation purposes, were made relatively infrequently. This pattern of trip activity is very similar to findings provided by Nahemow and Kogan (1971) and Shmelzer (1971).

Purpose and Duration of Trips by Vehicular and Pedestrian Transportation Modes

The automobile was used most frequently for trips to children, other kin, doctors, groceries, meetings, and sports. For trips to children, the elderly person was more frequently an automobile passenger than

TABLE 9
Percentages of Older People Using Certain Modes of Transportation by Frequency

	Frequency					
Transportation Mode	Daily or 2–3 Times per Week	2–4 Times per Month	Once per Month	Several Times per Year	Infrequently or Never	Total[a]
Drive	29	3	1	1	66	100
Driven	32	31	8	17	12	100
Bus	13	16	9	10	51	99
Walk	44	12	3	2	39	100
Taxi	1	6	6	15	72	100

Source: Modified from Carp (1971b), p. 36.
[a]May not add exactly to 100 percent because of rounding.

driver. The bus was used more frequently for trips to other kin, doctors, nonfood shopping facilities, sporting events, and recreation places than for other trip purposes. Walking was used more frequently for trips to friends, churches, grocery stores, entertainment places, senior centers, and libraries than for other trip purposes (Table 11). Bourg (1973) and Nahemow and Kogan (1971) have reported similar findings. Because Nahemow and Kogan's sample was overrepresented by reduced-fare transit applicants, mass transit in general was used more frequently than the automobile for most trip purposes. Of special significance is Nahemow and Kogan's finding that "walking" was important for the nonpurposive trip, that is, in order to "get out" (p. 32).

Both Carp (1971c) and Nahemow and Kogan

TABLE 10
Percentages of Older People Visiting Specific Destinations by Frequency of Trips

	Frequency					
Destination	Daily or 2–3 Times per Week	2–4 Times per Month	Once per Month	Several Times per Year	Infrequently or Never	Total[a]
Friends	23	20	8	8	42	100
Children	13	17	6	9	54	100
Other kin	9	16	8	10	57	100
Doctor	1	12	15	34	39	100
Church	9	45	4	5	36	100
Grocery	33	44	5	0	18	100
Other stores	4	21	20	26	29	100
Meetings	4	10	12	2	72	100
Entertainment	1	4	5	8	81	100
Senior center	3	3	1	2	91	100
Library	3	4	2	2	88	100
Sports	0	2	1	5	91	100
Travel	0	1	4	20	75	100

Source: Modified from Carp (1971b), p. 29.
[a]May not add exactly to 100 percent because of rounding.

TABLE 11
Percentages of Older People Visiting Specific Destinations by Mode of Transportation

Destination	Transportation Mode							
	Automobile							
	Total	Driver	Passenger	Bus	Walk	Taxi	Train, Plane	Total[a]
Friends	50	29	21	8	42	0	1	100
Children	69	24	45	8	16	0	7	100
Other kin	61	30	31	15	16	1	7	100
Doctor	60	28	32	20	16	4	0	100
Church	58	26	32	7	34	1	0	100
Grocery	62	31	31	4	31	3	0	100
Other stores	53	29	24	23	23	0	0	100
Meetings	66	32	34	6	25	2	0	100
Entertainment	58	26	32	10	31	1	0	100
Senior center	54	16	38	1	45	0	0	100
Library	25	19	6	6	67	1	0	100
Sports	73	37	36	16	8	1	1	100
Travel	54	22	32	22	0	0	23	100

Source: Modified from Carp (1971b), p. 29.
[a]May not add exactly to 100 percent because of rounding.

(1971) found that walking trips were of very short duration, averaging less than 15 minutes; however, Nahemow and Kogan reported that in their sample about 5 percent of walking trips were over 1 hour in duration and the average older person said ". . . that he could walk at least nine blocks without becoming tired" (p. 30).

Since a large proportion of trips to friends are by walking, these trips were of the shortest travel duration, along with trips to church, grocery and other stores, senior centers, and libraries. In contrast, trips to relatives, doctors, and recreation centers were often over 30 minutes in duration (Bourg, 1973; Carp, 1971c; Nahemow and Kogan, 1971).

EVALUATION OF EXISTING TRANSPORTATION MODES

Walking

Walking achieves two distinctive purposes: as the primary means of transportation when overcoming the distance between the residence and a selected destination, and as a secondary means, when used in conjunction with vehicular transportation to reach a destination. The latter purpose is exemplified by the walk from the residence to the bus stop or to the automobile, or after departure from the vehicle, the walk to the destination. The inability of the older person to utilize walking as a secondary means of transportation correspondingly limits the utility of vehicular transportation. As Gelwicks (U.S. Senate, 1970, p. 21) has expressed the problem:

Of what use is it to bring an elderly person . . . to the corner of the shopping center if there is no internal transportation system to assist him in transversing the several acres of parked cars or moving from area to area within the center.

Three major types of problems are experienced by older persons when walking is used either as a primary or secondary means of transportation (U.S. Department of Health, Education, and Welfare, 1969; Carp, 1971a; Carp, 1972): (1) many destinations are too far to be reached by walking especially if bundles or packages must be carried on the return trip; (2) there are realistic fears that walking may result in

FIGURE 4
Locomotion in a wheelchair is facilitated by curb cuts at important facilities or intersections. (Photo courtesy of Administration on Aging, U.S.D.H.E.W.)

from the perspective of the older person (in contrast to younger persons) may be less than optimum. The quality of the walking environment is poorer when walking surfaces are unavailable, poorly constructed, or slippery or icy, when steep slopes must be negotiated (Priest, 1970), when pedestrian traffic control signals are absent, confusing, or change too quickly to allow safe crossing, when there is poor separation between vehicular and pedestrian traffic flows, when public rest facilities (e.g., benches or shelters) are absent, when paths are particularly crowded or occupied by activities (e.g., children playing) that interfere with walking, when weather conditions make walking hazardous, and when streets are poorly lighted.

FIGURE 5
The long pedestrian walkway may pose difficulties for older people with ambulation problems. (Photo courtesy of Chicago Department of Public Works.)

injuries from falling, vehicular accidents, or from being attacked or mugged; and (3) walking can cause considerable fatigue, physical soreness, and general weariness.

These potential problems originate partly as a result of physiological changes accompanying aging, including, for example, decreasing agility, endurance, and strength, declining visual acuity and peripheral vision, reduced ability to see in the dark, changes in color perception, and decreasing hearing acuity (Libow, 1971). However, they are a function also of the quality of the "walking environment," which

FIGURE 6
The "moving sidewalk" may alleviate problems of older people having difficulty with ambulation or who must carry large packages. (Photo courtesy of Chicago Department of Public Works.)

Because there are problems associated with walking, the automatic assumption that a "short" distance between a dwelling unit and a required facility or service does not represent a barrier to some older persons is often invalid. Older persons who depend heavily on walking have frequently expressed considerable dissatisfaction with it as a transportation mode (Carp, 1971a). The over age 65 population has the highest death rate from pedestrian accidents of any age group (National Safety Council, 1973). This fact alone is compelling testimony for the need to evaluate carefully this mode of transportation before assuming its positive utility.

Mass Transit

Older persons attempting to use mass transit experience problems related to (1) the frequency, flexibility, and complexity of service, (2) the physical design and operating characteristics of the system, (3) the completeness and accuracy of the elderly consumer's knowledge of mass transit system operation, and (4) the cost of service (Abt Associates, 1968, 1969; Bell and Olsen, 1971; Carnegie-Mellon University, 1968; Carp, 1971b; Kinley, 1971; Nahemow and Kogan, 1971; National Old People's Welfare Council, 1971; Neilson and Fowler, 1972; Ohio Department of Mental Hygiene and Correction, 1970; U.S. Senate, 1970, 1973b).

Frequency, flexibility, and complexity of service. The elderly person using mass transit in major urban centers is generally disadvantaged because he is using the system at non-rush-hour periods for non-work purposes. The optimum transit service, however, is available during rush-hour periods and for routes oriented to major employment concentrations. Very often, posted schedules are not followed with any reliability. Service to desired destinations is often infrequent or entirely absent. Varying types of difficulties are experienced by older persons because of long waits for transit service, including fatigue, fear of crime, loneliness, and discomforts caused by extreme weather conditions. The older person must often transfer several times to finally reach his destination. He often experiences a great deal of inconvenience and difficulty in reaching these transfer points (Carp, 1971b; Nahemow and Kogan, 1971).

Physical design and operating characteristics of the system. If bus stops are located at considerable dis-

FIGURE 7
Rush hour is no time for some older people to try to negotiate public transit vehicles. (Photo by Photo-Art.)

tance from either the residence and/or the final destination, walking problems will be more likely to be experienced. The problem of waiting for long periods for bus service, especially in bad weather, is often accentuated by the absence of shelters or benches. These are not usually provided except on a limited basis because of cost constraints. Entering and departing from buses result in a number of difficulties. The necessity of climbing high bus steps, insufficient time

to reach exit doors, the fear and reality of doors closing too soon, and the stopping of vehicles at unsafe points of street exit are examples. Some difficulties could be alleviated by the bus driver or preferably by personnel hired to provide assistance to the older person when he enters or exits from the bus. Various "moving" characteristics of buses also create problems, including the rapid acceleration and deceleration of stop-and-go driving, insufficient time to get seated after the bus is entered, and poorly placed or insufficient hand grips. The negotiation of crowded moving vehicles can be very stressful; if seats are not available and it is necessary to stand, these difficulties will be accentuated.

Completeness and accuracy of knowledge of mass transit system operation by the elderly consumer. Many elderly persons experience difficulty understanding the operation of the mass transit system. Specifically, they have problems interpreting bus and rail schedules, locating transfer points, and finding entrance and exit (subway) gates (Carnegie-Mellon University, 1968). They also may have difficulty seeing or hearing information communicated by signs and loudspeakers.

Cost of service. Transportation costs are sufficiently high to represent the third largest item (after housing and food) in the household budget of older persons (U.S. Senate, 1970, p. 4). Rising transit fares and the need for two or three separate fares on multizone tips, in combination with low incomes of elderly persons, have made transit cost one of the most serious barriers to full transit utilization.

Automobiles

Older persons who own and are licensed to drive an automobile have the greatest potential of fully realizing their transportation needs. However, such factors as physiological changes resulting in a decline in driver's skills, institutional barriers preventing the license renewal or the continuation of automobile insurance coverage, or operating and maintenance costs too great for the small household budget may singularly or collectively force the older person to restrict either spatially and/or temporally his automobile driving.

It has been shown that older persons make many trips as passengers in automobiles. In these arrangements they can realize most of the advantages of the automobile without experiencing many of its potential problems. However, as Carp (1972, p. 66) summarizes, there are also negative aspects:

Accepting rides may be distasteful because it represents a loss of autonomy and self-sufficiency. Acceptance may involve indebtedness which becomes burdensome and demeaning when reciprocation is impossible. The schedule, route or destination of the driver may not conform to the needs of

the passenger. The older person may be nervous about the driving skill of the person who offers a ride.

A number of physiological changes impair the older person's ability to operate an automobile skillfully (Freeman, 1972; Libow, 1971; McFarland et al., 1964; Marsh, 1960; Planek et al., 1968). Difficulties are accentuated by the use of the automobile in the large urban center. Driving has become more hazardous for the older person because of increased traffic flows, higher speeds related to expressway and freeway driving, and more complex traffic patterns. Although he may possess considerable driving experience, if declines occur in his sensory and perceptual processes and motor skills, his reaction times may be slowed, increasing the probability of an accident in demanding urban driving situations. As a result of a decline in visual acuity and peripheral vision, the elderly driver has more difficulty interpreting traffic lights and signs and in seeing cars approaching from the side. Consequently, he may have to restrict his driving to daytime hours or to less demanding traffic situations.

Some older persons have difficulty renewing their driver's license or its legal use may be restricted to daytime hours (Carp, 1971c). Auto insurance companies also have a discriminatory attitude toward the older driver. Some companies arbitrarily cancel insurance policies of clients over age 65 or they may be relegated to the "assigned risk" category, which results in higher insurance rates and the loss of the premium financing options (U.S. Senate, 1970).

There is some justification for these licensing and insurance policies. Although there are conflicts in empirical evidence, Planek et al. (1968), after reviewing the literature, suggest that based on an index "accidents per mile traveled" elderly auto drivers appear to be more accident-prone than younger age groups. It has been shown that accidents by the older driver are more likely to occur when he is involved in such maneuvers as changing lanes, turning, passing, or backing up, as opposed to simply maintaining his position within the traffic flow of his lane (Planek et al., 1968). Older persons (particularly aged 75 and over) have one of the highest death rates from collisions between motor vehicles when compared with younger age groups (National Safety Council, 1973).

Nevertheless, a general policy of license and insurance discrimination applied to all elderly drivers would appear both unfair and unnecessary. A more selective evaluation procedure to identify the high-risk elderly driver is required to avoid penalizing the competent.

GENERAL TRENDS IN THE SOCIETAL RESPONSE TO TRANSPORTATION NEEDS

One major consequence of urbanization has been a spatial organization of facilities and services that has increasingly favored the automobile driver. For those population groups without automobile transportation, an increasingly larger proportion of metropolitan opportunities have become inaccessible or accessible only with an expenditure of a great deal of energy required because of the inconvenience, inflexibility, and discomfort associated with mass transit transportation. Persons living close to the central business district (CBD) have experienced fewer difficulties but sometimes at the expense of living in older, often poorer quality housing in a community environment that is less safe and less responsive to their other needs.

Unfortunately, mass transit has not proved to be very competitive with the automobile. For persons requiring transportation service in off-peak hours to non-CBD destinations, the system has been particularly inadequate. The decline of the mass transit system has been succinctly characterized by a 1971 report produced by the U.S. Urban Mass Transportation Administration (p. 10): "... reduced ridership, curtailment of services, increased costs, growing deficits, failure of firms, and the increased public acquisition of systems to prevent the abandonment of service."

However, there are some indications that future trends will be more positive. The passage of the Urban Mass Transportation Act of 1970 marked a significant increase in the fiscal role of the federal government in urban mass transportation and a rapid expansion of all aspects of the Urban Mass Transportation Administration's (UMTA) program of capital grants, technical studies, research and development, and demonstration projects.

The inclusion of the Biaggi amendment in the 1970 act marked the first time legislation declared as national policy that the planning, design, and operation of urban mass transportation services should specifically meet the needs of the elderly and handicapped. It authorized 1½ percent of the total funding of UMTA programs to assist state and local public bodies and agencies to provide loans and grants to modify mass transit systems to meet the needs of the elderly and handicapped. The Biaggi amendment is particularly significant in that the underlying assumption characterizing urban mass transit planning and policy has been that the travel characteristics and needs of all users were the same and "policy changes have been evaluated on the basis of the total benefit they would bring to the whole system, and not to any one group of users" (Toronto Bureau of Municipal Research, 1970, p. 7).

With the recent passage of the Federal Aid Highway Act of 1973, states will be allowed under certain conditions to transfer funds from unwanted interstate system routes for an equal amount of public mass transit aid from general funds. Urbanized areas in 1975 and 1976 will also be allowed under certain conditions to use revenues from the Highway Trust Fund for rail and bus mass transit capital improvements. For the first time also, UMTA capital grants and loans will be made available to private nonprofit corporations.

Beginning July 1, 1974, about $20 million will be made available under the 1973 act (on a matching ratio of 80 percent federal and 20 percent nonfederal funds) to state governments to provide transportation to meet the special needs of the elderly and handicapped. It is expected that these capital funds will be used in conjunction with Title III and Title VII funds of the Older Americans Act, which will be used to meet operating expenses of transportation projects.

Associated with the three-year extension of the Title VII nutrition program, in July, 1974, $35 million were authorized under Title III to support operating costs of transportation services especially related to elderly nutrition projects. The actual funding appropriation awaits further congressional action.

This recent federal legislation should have a positive impact on the quality of mass transit service for the elderly. The actual funding appropriation for elderly special transportation projects, however, has been very small, and there is no certainty at what level it will be continued in the future. There has also been no specific legislative requirement at the federal level to ensure that projects receiving transit capital grants will provide accessibility features in their systems for the elderly and handicapped.

ALLEVIATING TRANSPORTATION PROBLEMS: MAJOR PROGRAM DEVELOPMENTS

The Administration on Aging of the U.S. Department of Health, Education, and Welfare has been the principal source of funds for research and demonstration transportation projects oriented exclusively toward the elderly. However, other important projects benefiting the elderly have been funded by the Urban Mass Transportation Administration (UMTA) of the U.S. Department of Transportation, the Office of Economic Opportunity through its Community Action Services, and by the Model Cities Administration of the Department of Housing and Urban Development.

Three major categories of response are described and evaluated in the following sections: reduced-fare programs and the West Virginia experiment; the physical redesign of mass transit systems; and specialized transportation services.

Reduced-Fare Programs and the West Virginia Experiment

The rationale behind reduced-fare programs is that older persons often have had to restrict their use of mass transit facilities because of lower incomes. Over 100 communities have implemented reduced transit fare schedules on their local transit systems for persons aged 65 and over (U.S. Senate, 1973a, p. 81). The amount of reduction is generally between 35 and 50 percent of the regular fare and is usually applicable only during the off-peak nonwork hours of weekdays and during weekends. Recently, Chicago extended its half-fare program to a full 24 hours; it is possible that other communities will adopt a similar policy. At present there are significant variations among urban communities both in the "income" eligibility requirements of the older person and the amount of fare reduction.

Studies that have assessed the impact of reduced-fare programs on elderly ridership show consistently an increase in transit use (Cantor, 1971; Hoel and Roszner, 1972; Nahemow and Kogan, 1971).

Evaluation methodologies employed in these studies have varied considerably in their conceptual and statistical sophistication (see Morlok et al., 1971, for a discussion on methodology). One of the more rigorous analyses evaluated the impact of reduced fares on elderly in Allegheny County (Hoel and Roszner, 1972). In total, elderly ridership increased from 5.73 to 6.95 monthly round trips per person, or by 21.2 percent (p. 354). Of the newly generated trips associated with the reduced fare, 61.5 percent were shopping trips, 26.2 percent were social trips, and 6.8 percent were for medical purposes.

Poor cost-evaluation estimates were exemplified by the initial criticism of the reduced-fare program concept. The generation of greater trip activity in off-peak periods helps to compensate for losses in fares during peak periods, and therefore the amount of revenue lost to a system is not simply the amount of fare reduction multiplied by the number of elderly transit trips taken at new fare rate. Nevertheless, there are revenue losses from reduced-fare programs that must be subsidized from some source. In return many older persons experience increased mobility and realize significant savings.

Since the reduced-fare program in effect increases the economic resources of the older person, a fundamental issue is whether income maintenance should be provided in this indirect manner. Rather, should not a guaranteed minimum annual income for older persons be sufficiently large that a service like transportation can be purchased at its market price? In response, it can be argued that large numbers of elderly are neither dependent on mass transit nor poor, and therefore only those requiring these indirect income subsidies should actually receive them. Accordingly, the reduced-fare program may represent a less expensive and more efficient strategy to ensure that low-income carless elderly are not deprived of public transportation because of its cost.

An alternative strategy to ensure that low income does not restrict transportation use is exemplified by West Virginia's new experiment of distributing "transportation stamps" to low-income elderly and handicapped persons in a similar manner as food stamps. In this program the emphasis is on ensuring that the *consumer* at least for *one specific service* (transportation) has sufficient income resources to pay the regular "market price," as opposed to the suppliers reducing the price of his service (as is the case in the reduced-fare program or in low-income public housing programs) to accommodate the lower income of the consumer. (There are interesting similarities between this program and the experimental housing allowance program of the U.S. Department of Housing and Urban Development.) This program if successful will help increase the demand for bus service, thereby increasing the revenues of the financially depressed bus lines in the area (U.S. Senate, 1973a, p. 179).

Physical Redesign of Mass Transit Systems

As emphasized, the design of mass transit facilities can create barriers that can restrict elderly persons with ambulatory difficulties, especially those using walking devices or wheelchairs, from fully utilizing the transit system.[2] Two major approaches have been used to eliminate design barriers. First, special design features have been incorporated in new mass transit vehicles and systems to be used by the total population, and vehicles already in service along selected routes have been modified in design. Second, new special-purpose transportation systems (such as dial-a-bus) have been developed with design features enabling the elderly and handicapped to effectively use them.

Several projects involving the design of a prototype bus intended to eventually replace existing buses on regularly scheduled routes have been funded (e.g., Transbus). Design features have included wider doors, extended hand rails, public address systems for waiting passengers, large destination signs in front, side, and back of vehicle, fewer steps, a lower floor for bus entry and egress, and driver-operated doors (U.S. Senate, 1972, p. 203).

FIGURE 8
The "dial-a-bus" is particularly useful in providing transportation for people living out of walking distance from regular lines and those requiring assistance.

FIGURE 9 (*above and right*)
Another form of specialized transportation service. (Photos by Linz, courtesy of Leisure Technology Corporation; Dr. Paul Dudley White, courtesy of Administration on Aging, U.S.D.H.E.W.)

Some local transit authorities have also purchased regular buses and have altered them so as to incorporate such design features. They have had limited use on routes serving housing projects containing elderly and handicapped persons (U.S. Senate, 1973a, p. 195).

The most important example of a specially designed new transit system is the San Francisco Bay Area Rapid Transit (BART). A similarly designed system is planned for the Washington Metropolitan Area Transit system. In 1964, BART incorporated the "American Standards Specification for Making Buildings and Facilities Accessible to and Usable by the Physically Handicapped" (1961) into all design

elements of its system. This required the allocation of $10 million by the state government.

The BART system provides at considerable expense special design features intended to eliminate utilization barriers experienced by the elderly but, at least in the short run, may provide fewer benefits than expected. The BART system is chiefly a center city—suburban service and lacks the areal flexibility to serve such groups as the elderly whose origins and/or destinations for nonwork purposes are not located along existing routes. The success of this system will depend on the adequacy of bus feeder lines to serve the elderly. If connecting bus services cannot be easily used by elderly persons, the utility of BART

will be substantially reduced. Even if there is a commitment by the major urban transit authorities to provide specially designed transit vehicles, the deficiencies in their older systems will prevent maximum mobility of such groups as the elderly, since the replacement process will take a considerable time to complete. In economic terms, replacement represents the only feasible strategy, since the costs of redesign-

ing an existing system except on a piecemeal basis are very great.

Specialized Transportation Services

Because the regular service provided by the fixed-route transit system is inadequate and because some older persons have difficulties when using it, several communities throughout the United States have initiated demand-responsive transportation services on an experimental basis (Lundberg and Lustig, 1972). Specially designed passenger vehicles generally carrying fewer than 35 older or handicapped persons have been placed in operation to service communities containing high concentrations of elderly persons. They have often but not always provided access to specific destinations, such as medical districts or senior centers. Providing door-to-door service, this personalized transportation service has overcome the scheduling and routing difficulties associated with regular bus service. This type of service has utilized regular transit or school bus vehicles rather than smaller, specially designed vehicles.

This special bus service has been described by various names—minibus, dial-a-ride, dial-a-bus, etc. The older person telephones a central office and conveys his trip needs. To varying degrees the scheduling and routing aspects of the system have been computerized, significantly increasing efficiency. Service comparable in quality to a taxi is offered at significantly lower costs to the passenger. In a similar type of bus service the potential rider does not specify his route needs. Rather, minibuses or jitneys serving local communities make stops at key points along established routes that are widely publicized. The routing is often revised to meet the changing needs of the community's elderly population.

Few formal studies have evaluated the benefits and costs of these systems. However, they appear successful since they have given mobility to those elderly without other viable transportation alternatives (see Cantilli and Shmelzer, 1971, pp. 138–168). New social relationships facilitated by the assemblage of isolated older persons in these transportation vehicles have provided unexpected benefits (Gywnn, 1972). Many of these systems have operated, however, only with significant economic deficits, particularly when the cost of transportation trip fares has been subsidized by the local municipality. Most important, it is unclear whether federal, state, or local governments will be willing or able to assume permanent responsibility for the subsidization of these programs, particularly their operating costs. Also unclear is whether the social benefits provided by these systems justify their

FIGURE 10
A tightly organized system of housing and services to community residents may make a fleet of special vehicles cost-effective. (Photo courtesy of Administration on Aging, U.S.D.H.E.W.)

costs or, alternatively, whether there are better means of ensuring spatial accessibility.

Car pools organized by drawing on the services of older drivers or younger volunteers (Wendkos et al., 1972; Breslau and Haug, 1972) have been developed on an informal basis, although there has been no systematic evaluation of the benefits and costs of this potentially very significant transportation alternative.

Professional planners and bureaucrats disagree as to whether groups such as the elderly should be singled out for special treatment with respect to transportation services. Typical are the following comments by Kanwit (1972, pp. 87–88):

Serving the unmet needs of all the people would be a fantastically costly undertaking; it might be cheaper to build more convenient housing near shopping, medical service, and recreation areas than to provide regular public transportation in sparsely populated areas. It might be even more effective to break down the institutional barriers and set up self-help projects.

There must be some determination of priority in relation to per capita cost. We must become more realistic and less sentimental on this issue, because the rising operating costs of transit in relation to passenger revenues are rapidly driving both public and private transit into a narrow area of service restricted largely to that of carrying rush-hour patrons in densely occupied urban corridors.

These types of argument are frequently cited in opposition to federal and state funding of special transportation systems for the elderly. However, given the existing operating and service characteristics of urban mass transit systems and the utilization problems experienced by many elderly, even if special vehicle or station design features were to be incorporated, there would still be a need for special-purpose transportation services. Supplementary services, such as dial-a-bus, would be helpful even if they were only available in neighborhoods with large concentrations of older persons or if they provided transportation only to *one* specific destination. While of particular utility to the elderly, to improve their economic viability such systems could serve the transportation needs of other "captive" transit riders such as the poor, the housewife, the physically handicapped, the young, and the part-time worker. When deciding in what areas in the city to implement such systems, special efforts should be made to identify the locations of those elderly who are presently restricting

their activities because of transportation user difficulties.

Under existing federal policy, special transportation services have been provided only on a random basis, usually in the form of demonstration projects, so that continuous funding has always been in doubt. The lack of participation of county and state governments in demonstration grant programs may reflect uncertainty about their ability to fund in part or in whole a program after the demonstration period ends (McKelvey and Dueker, 1974). There has been little governmental coordination at any level to ensure that new services are being initiated where they are needed the most or that existing services are being utilized in the most effective way. Testimony to the waste of mass transit capital equipment is the large number of buses that stand idle during daily non-rush-hour periods. Bell and Olsen (1973) have emphasized the weaknesses underlying programs for special-purpose systems:

They rarely reflect a high degree of advance planning, they tend to be discrete and relatively simple solutions to complex problems which require comprehensive planning, coordination and control. Special purpose systems may drain off pressure on local authorities responsible for public transit developments, and thereby deter or divert the comprehensive, more lasting and efficient solution. Moreover, knowledge derived from these experiments which could be profitably shared by transit planners is generally unavailable due to lack of thorough documentation, or test results may or may not be disseminated.

The costs cited to develop and operate special transportation services or better-designed vehicles are based on static measurements that do not take into account a variety of direct or indirect benefits that could be achieved with such programs. For example, the consequences of improved transit services in reducing the need for special housing programs, home-delivery systems, and institutional or quasi-institutional accommodations, or in reducing the psychological and economic burden of elderly on their families, should be given greater consideration.

NOTES

1. The data source for this analysis was the Metropolitan Toronto Area Region Transportation Study (MTARTS), a home-interview, origin–destination transportation study undertaken in 1964. The

study sample included 3,394 persons aged 56 to 65 and 3,628 persons aged 65 and over.

2. According to the National Center for Health Statistics the number of persons 65 and over in the United States with transportation dysfunctions included visually impaired, 1,430,000; hearing impaired, other mobility limitations, 1,510,000; acute conditions, 100,000; total, 6,060,000 (U.S. Department of Transportation, 1973).

REFERENCES

Abt Associates, Inc. *Qualitative aspects of urban personal travel demand.* Springfield, Va.: National Technical Information Service, 1968.

_____. *Travel barriers: transportation needs of the handicapped.* Springfield, Va.: National Technical Information Service, 1969.

American Standards Association (now U.S.A. Standards Institute). *American Standard Specifications for Making Buildings and Facilities Accessible To And Useable By, The Physically Handicapped.* New York, American Standards Association, 1961.

Ashford, N., and Holloway, F. M. The effect of age on urban travel behavior. *Traffic Engineering,* 1971, *41,* 46–49.

Bell, J. H. Senior citizens mobile service. In E. J. Cantilli and J. L. Shmelzer (eds.), *Transportation and Aging.* Washington, D.C.: Government Printing Office, 1971.

Bell, W. G., and Olsen, W. T. *Public transportation and the elderly in Florida.* Research Report I. Prepared for Florida Department of Transportation, Department of Urban and Regional Planning, Florida State University, Tallahassee, 1971.

_____. An overview of public transportation and the elderly: new directions for social policy. Paper delivered at 3rd Annual Transportation Conference, St. Petersburg, Fla., November 29, 1973.

Bourg, C. J. Elderly in the central sections of Nashville. Paper presented at annual meeting of the Gerontological Society, Miami Beach, November 8, 1973.

Breslau, N., and Haug, M. R. The elderly aid the elderly. *Social Security Bulletin,* 1972, *35,* 9–15.

Cantilli, E. J., and Shmelzer, J. L. (eds.). *Transportation and Aging.* Washington, D.C.: Government Printing Office, 1971.

Cantor, M. H. The reduced fare program for older New Yorkers. In E. J. Cantilli and J. L. Shmelzer (eds.), *Transportation and Aging.* Washington, D.C.: Government Printing Office, 1971.

Carnegie-Mellon University, Transportation Research Institute. *Latent demand for urban transportation.* Springfield, Mass.: National Technical Information Service, 1968.

Carp, F. M. Correlates of mobility among retired persons. In J. Archea and C. Eastman (eds.), *EDRA 2, Proceedings of the Second Annual Environmental Design Research Conference.* Pittsburgh: Carnegie-Mellon University Press, 1970.

_____. Walking as a means of transportation for retired people. *Gerontologist,* 1971, *11,* part I, 104–111 (a).

_____. Public transit and retired people. In E. J. Cantilli and J. L. Shmelzer (eds.), *Transportation and Aging.* Washington, D.C.: Government Printing Office, 1971 (b).

_____. The mobility of retired people. In E. J. Cantilli and J. L. Shmelzer (eds.), *Transportation and Aging.* Washington, D.C.: Government Printing Office, 1971 (c).

_____. Retired people as automobile passengers. *Gerontologist,* 1972, *12,* part I, 66–72.

Cutler, S. J. The availability of personal transportation, residential location, and life satisfaction among the aged. *Journal of Gerontology,* 1972, *27,* 383–389.

Freeman, J. T. Elderly drivers; growing number and growing problems. *Geriatrics,* 1972, *27,* 46–56.

Golant, S. M. *The Residential Location and Spatial Behavior of the Elderly: A Canadian Example.* Department of Geography Research Paper no. 143. Chicago: Department of Geography, University of Chicago, 1972.

Gwynn, D. W. Dial-a-ride demonstration project in Haddonfield. *Traffic Engineering,* 1972, *42,* 68–74.

Hoel, L. A., and Roszner, E. S. Impact of reduced transit fares for the elderly. *Traffic Quarterly,* 1972, *26,* 341–358.

Kanwit, E. L. The Urban Mass Transportation Administration: its problems and promise. In D. R. Miller (ed.), *Urban transportation policy: new perspectives.* Lexington, Mass.: D. C. Heath, 1972.

Kinley, H. J. Latent travel demands of the aging and handicapped and barriers to travel. In E. J. Cantilli and J. L. Shmelzer (eds.), *Transportation and Aging.* Washington, D.C.: Government Printing Office, 1971.

Libow, L. S. Older people's medical and physiological characteristics. In E. J. Cantilli and J. L. Shmelzer (eds.), *Transportation and Aging.* Washington, D.C.: Government Printing Office, 1971.

Lundberg, B. D., and Lustig, C. W. Demand responsive transit service: a new transportation tool. *Planning Advisory Service,* American Society of Planning Officials, 1972, *286,* 1–14.

Marble, D., Hanson, P. O., and Hanson, S. E. Intra-urban mobility patterns of elderly households: a Swedish example. *Household Travel Behavior Study, Report no. 6.* Evanston, Ill.: The Transportation Center, Northwestern University, 1973.

Markovitz, J. Transportation needs of the elderly. *Traffic Quarterly,* 1971, *25,* 237–253.

Marsh, B. Aging and driving. *Traffic Engineering,* 1960, *31,* 11–29.

McFarland, R. A., Tune, G. S., and Welford, A. T. On the driving of automobiles by older people. *Journal of Gerontology,* 1964, *19,* 190–197.

McKelvey, D. J., and Dueker, K. J. *Transportation Planning: the Urban and Rural Interface and Transit Needs of the Rural Elderly.* Technical Report 26. Iowa City, Iowa: Center for Urban Transportation Studies, Institute of Urban and Regional Research, University of Iowa, 1974.

Morlok, E. K., Kulash, W. M., and Vandersypen, H. L. Reduced fares for the elderly, effects on a transit system. *Welfare in Review,* 1971, *9,* 17–24.

Myers, S. Turning transit subsidies into compensatory transportation. *City,* 1972, *6.*

Nahemow, L., and Kogan, L. S. *Reduced fare for the elderly.* Report submitted to Mayor's Office for the Aging, City of New York. New York: Center for Social Research, City University of New York, 1971.

National Old People's Welfare Council. *Age Concern on Transport.* London: The Council, 1971.

National Safety Council. *Accident facts.* Chicago: The Council, 1973.

Neilson, G. E., and Fowler, W. F. Relation between transit ridership and walking distances in a low-density Florida retirement area. *Highway Research Record,* 1972, *403,* 26–34.

Ohio Department of Mental Hygiene and Correction, Division of Administration on Aging. *Transportation needs of older people in Ohio.* Columbus, Ohio, 1970.

Pignataro, L. J. Recommendations of the Workshop Committees. In E. J. Cantilli and J. L. Shmelzer (eds.), *Transportation and Aging.* Washington, D.C.: Government Printing Office, 1971.

Planek, T. W., Condon, M. C., and Fowler, R. C. *An investigation of the problems and opinions of aged drivers.* Springfield, Va.: National Technical Information Service, 1968.

Priest, G. E. *An investigation of the elderly in the urban environment with special reference to their housing.* Unpublished masters thesis, Department of Geography, Simon Fraser University, Burnaby, British Columbia, 1970.

Revis, J. J. *Transportation.* Background paper, 1971 White House Conference on Aging. White House Conference on Aging, Washington, D.C., 1971.

Shmelzer, J. L. Elderly ridership and reduced transit fares: the Chicago experience. In E. J. Cantilli and J. L. Shmelzer (eds.), *Transportation and Aging.* Washington, D.C.: Government Printing Office, 1971.

Toronto Bureau of Municipal Research. Transportation. Who plans? Who pays? *Civic Affairs,* 1970, Autumn, 1–24.

U.S. Department of Health, Education, and Welfare, Administration on Aging. *The older pedestrian: a social gerontological view.* By J. L. Shmelzer and M. L. Taves. AOA Position Paper. Washington, D.C., 1969 (mimeographed).

U.S. Department of Transportation, Transportation Systems Center. *The handicapped and elderly market for urban mass transit.* UMTA-MA-06-0039-73(1-3), 1973.

U.S. Senate, Special Committee on Aging. *Older Americans and transportation: a crisis in mobil-*

ity. 91st Cong., 2d Sess. Washington, D.C.: Government Printing Office, 1970.

_____. *Developments in aging, 1971 and January–March, 1972.* 92nd Cong., 2d Sess. Washington, D.C.: Government Printing Office, 1972.

_____. *Developments in aging, 1972 and January–March, 1973.* 93d Cong., 1st Sess. Washington, D.C.: Government Printing Office, 1973a.

_____. *Post-White House Conference on Aging reports, 1973.* 93d Cong., 1st Sess. Washington, D.C.: Government Printing Office, 1973b.

U.S. Urban Mass Transportation Administration.

Feasibility of federal assistance for urban mass transportation operating costs. Springfield, Va.: National Technical Information Service, 1971.

Wendkos, M. H., Soudack, M., and Fischer, G. A novel rehabilitation program for the non-institutionalized disadvantaged elderly residing in an urban community. *Journal of American Geriatrics Society,* 1972, *20,* 116–120.

Wynn, F. H., and Levinson, H. S. Some considerations in appraising bus transit potentials. *Highway Research Record,* 1967, *197,* 1–24.

C. L. ESTES

C. L. Estes is an Assistant Professor of Sociology at the University of California, San Francisco.

Goal Displacement in Community Planning for the Elderly

Community planning in the field of aging is a relatively new phenomenon, although an important one. Until recently, programs and planning for the elderly have been developed primarily by informal networks of interested professionals representing social agencies at the community level. With the new 1973 Comprehensive Services Amendments to the Older Americans Act of 1965, social agencies and planning bodies can be expected to play a progressively more significant role in determining official aging policy—both in terms of the problems of aging that the community will recognize and the strategies and services that will be made available to deal with them.

Research was undertaken to study the planning organizations that claim to deal specifically with problems of the elderly in one community. In this research, organization and conflict theories were found useful in explaining significant aspects of the "politics of planning"—organization theory for its emphasis on the primacy of activities devoted to organizational survival, maintenance, and enhancement (Blau and Scott, 1962; Selznick, 1966), and conflict theory for its emphasis on the inevitability of human struggle over the distribution of prized re-

sources (Collins, 1968; Dahrendorf, 1958; Weber, 1946).

If we add another perspective, which emphasizes that reality is socially constructed (Berger and Luckmann, 1966), that it is negotiated and renegotiated, we would anticipate struggles between and among members in the determination of acceptable reality and in the construction of planning as an activity. Also, we would hypothesize that such struggles would be intensified by the lack of a technology of planning, the ambiguity of which encourages power struggles among members and leaders over definitions of the task of planning.

At this point, it may be useful to review the concept of "goal displacement" and the factors that have been found to contribute to the phenomenon. The term "goal displacement" was first applied by sociologist Robert K. Merton (1940) in his classic article on the bureaucratic personality, in which he used the concept to describe the process whereby organizational means replace organization ends or goals. An example of such displacement would be when bureaucratic rules, initially established to better enable the organization to reach its goal of serving clients, come to take first priority. The procedures (originally the means) become the ends, replacing the initial goal of serving the clients. Goal displacement now refers to more than the simple means—end inversion just described; it includes other types of goal changes in which major organizational goals are replaced or altered.

Some major types of factors that may influence goal outcome in the direction of attainment or displacement are (1) the *characteristics of the organization,* in this case, the planning organization (the organizational task, structure, legitimacy, division of labor, etc.) (Thompson, 1966); (2) the *Individual members* of the organization and their interest and needs (Gouldner, 1959; Haire, 1959; Selznick, 1948, 1957); (3) the *environmental context* in which the organization operates and the degree of dependence of the organization on other organizations or institutions in that environment for resources requisite to its survival (Cyert and March, 1963; Selznick, 1966; Thompson and McEwen, 1958); (4) the *institutional character of the organization* (its value orientation and character as represented by its distinctive aims, methods, and role in the community) (Selznick, 1957); and, finally, (5) the *general culture of the society* in which the organization operates (Bendix, 1947) and historical factors relevant to it (including legislation and broad societal approaches for solving social problems) (Selznick, 1966).

STUDY OBJECTIVES

The widespread implementation of area planning for the elderly as a result of the 1973 Comprehensive Services Amendments suggested the need for an examination of planning organizations similar to the current Area Agencies on Aging in order to assess their potential for the achievement of goals. This was one of the major purposes of the study reported here.

The focus of this study was on (1) the activities of the planning organizations and (2) the contributions of economic, status, or power interests in explaining planning activities (i.e., the extent to which outcomes resulted from competition and/or conflict over economic, prestige, or power resources).

PROCEDURE

Two years of fieldwork were spent (between April 1970 and 1972) in observing activities in three organizations that claimed to deal specifically with problems of the elderly in one community. Two planning organizations were studied from their inception and one had been in existence for 5 years prior to the study.

Observations were focused primarily on the monthly meetings of each of the planning organizations, the majority of which this researcher attended. These observations accounted for 42 of 67 planning meetings (62.6 percent) held in the 2-year study period. Interviews were conducted with the population of 43 officers, staff, and members of the three organizations. Minutes of organizational meetings were analyzed to obtain information on the historical background and issues of these planning organizations.

FINDINGS

The organizational structure of the three planning organizations was modeled after the community welfare council concept; that is, all three planning bodies were essentially federative or collegial. They were ostensibly partnerships among equals.

One planning organization was composed of 27 members, 26 (96.3 percent) of whom represented organizations; another planning group had 26 members, with 23 (88.5 percent) from organizations; the third group had only 12 members, with 10 (83.3 percent) representing organizations. Thus the predominant membership in these planning bodies was held by persons who were *employed by and represented other organizations* in the community, most of which were social agencies. Of particular importance is the fact that many of these organizational members shared *similar domains* in terms of the services they provided and the functions and goals they claimed, as determined by measures of organizational interdependency developed by the author.

Interdependency among member organizations was measured in terms of overlapping goals and functions, overlapping organizational domains (services, problems, and client population), and dependency on the field of aging for resources. Of the 29 member organizations, 17 were determined to have "overlapping domains" with one or more other member organizations (in terms of the combination of services provided, population served, and problems covered);

and 20 of the 28 member organizations for which complete data were available were determined to share overlapping goals and functions with one or more other member organizations (Estes, 1972).

As described by Levine et al. (1963), organizations occupying similar domains can be expected to compete for scarce resources. Competition among members engendered by overlapping domains was intensified by the fact that 14 (51.9 percent) of the 29 service delivery organizations who were members of one or more of the planning bodies claimed to be survival-threatened; that is, they were only temporarily funded and indicated they were facing crises in this regard. In addition, a core of nine leaders (representing organizations) were members of all three planning bodies, assuring that rivalry among members would be a major factor in each of these planning settings.

In regard to the three planning organizations themselves, their goals and functions overlapped extensively with one another, inviting competition between and among these organizations as well as between and among their members. All three organizations claimed both planning and coordination as major goals, and two of the three also claimed research and education as goals. Furthermore, between 75 and 100 percent of the chairmen and members of each of the planning organizations reported problems of competition, duplication, and coordination among planning groups. When asked with an open-ended question to describe how the planning organizations functioned, the members indicated that the major activities were coordinating their respective programs through information sharing, providing information regarding referrals to one another, and identifying gaps in services by finding out from other members what services were available or unavailable through programs of fellow members. The validity of these descriptions was substantiated in the extensive field observations conducted by the researcher.

In addition, the activities of the planning organizations studied were observed to consist of (1) passing resolutions and sending letters regarding current issues, (2) encouraging individual members to apply for their own grants, or (3) organizing groups in areas of interest to individual members (retirement and legislation). Actual problem solving was rare.

When asked to describe the accomplishments of the planning organizations, again with an open-ended question, members were most likely either to report the "implementation of programs" (primarily the founding of new planning organizations) *or* to state that there were "no accomplishments." In one planning organization, 58 percent of the members reported they could recall no accomplishments.

Planning organization chairmen consistently indicated the value of communication among members as a major accomplishment while the members stressed bringing agencies together as being important. Given the positive view of communication among member agencies, maintaining harmony among members was a premium value.

Significantly, activities usually requisite to planning (e.g., systematic needs and resources analyses) were not reported either in terms of functions or accomplishments. Although research was given lip service, being listed among organization goals and functions, it never materialized as an ongoing activity of the planning bodies. Nor was it a part of committee work on different issues.

GOAL ATTAINMENT AND DISPLACEMENT

The primary *goal attainment*, then, was the achievement of informal coordination through regular communication among members. *Goal displacement* was in the direction of maintenance and enhancement activities benefiting the member organizations in the planning bodies, with these activities overshadowing the more central goals of planning, research, and education.

The major factor contributing to goal displacement is found in the basic *organizational structure* of the planning bodies themselves and in the central task of these organizations—planning and the ambiguity of the work required to accomplish it.

In terms of organizational structure, goal attainment was hampered in all three planning organizations first because of their collegial-type structure, which made compliance from organization members especially problematic (Warren, 1971). Composed of members who are technically equal in status, the collegial or federative organization lacks hierarchical authority.

Given the equal status among members, relationships among them tended to be personalized and conflictful, and external pressures unrelated to the needs of the planning organizations influenced organization outcomes more than they would have if relations among members had been dictated impersonally, according to prescribed authority patterns.

In addition, there was no central authority in any of the planning organizations who could enforce ground rules or the decisions that members made. The chairmen were limited in this respect because the membership was voluntary. The planning organizations were unable to take either decisive or controversial action lest the members resign. Hence the organizational and professional rivalries constituted within the planning groups had to be minimized. Emphasis was placed on the values of harmony, consensus, communication, and nonthreatening topics of discussion. Consequently, the major activity of the planning organizations was "talk" (as exemplified in their self-reported functioning as sources of information, referral, and communication among agencies).

Furthermore, the delegation of tasks among members was based on voluntary self-selection rather than according to the objective requirements of the job to be done and particular competencies of the members. Thus the principles of specialization and competence in the division of labor, which are essential means to task accomplishment in the modern organization, were lacking.

Another problem contributing to goal displacement was the fact that the activity of "planning" as practiced by the organizations studied was neither uniformly nor consistently defined in any sense of the word, nor standardized in terms of the tasks required to plan. This ambiguity opened broad areas of uncertainty, which encouraged members to conflict over what planning should include and over actual planning outcomes.

For planning members, the positive aspect of the lack of task specificity was that its uncertainty enhanced the potential control and domination of this activity by self-proclaimed experts in the membership. As Crozier (1964) has shown, lack of predictability arising from the task itself provides a potential source of power to organization members if they choose to use it, for those who can control the area of uncertainty can claim expertise in situations that no one else can really evaluate. Planning appears

highly complex and, as a result, planning performance is difficult for outsiders to evaluate. Precisely because the occupation of community planning is not highly predictable, professionals can argue that they are the only ones qualified to validate their own performance. The consequent potential for social agency planners to professionalize their planning work, and thereby keep out "nonprofessionals" (or at least, minimize their input), offers them a great source of power. Furthermore, external pressures for accomplishment are diminished as a result of the claimed expertise and resultant autonomy. In addition, the influence of experts so designated can be expected to move beyond the initial specific areas of acclaim to other areas, about which the experts may know very little. As Wilensky has shown, if an expert "is successful within his sphere of technical competence . . . he is likely to be chosen for tasks outside that sphere of competence, where his specialized knowledge may be irrelevant" (Wilensky, 1956).

In the current instance, becoming intensively involved and invested in planning activities was a major strategy employed by social agency directors (who were planning members) in negotiating the contingencies associated with the basic insecurity regarding the continued operation of their individual and independent programs.

A heavy concentration of an agency director's energies in this area may have had several advantages. First, planning may be a means of demonstrating to the community that there are almost unlimited areas of need for the elderly, thereby legitimating the essential nature of their current ongoing service programs. Second, participating in community planning, if successful, may create new job opportunities for the directors of financially insecure, short-term, grant-based programs. Finally, such activities may contribute to the development of a subculture of "experts" in the field of aging, thereby enhancing the marketability of such designated "experts" as consultants and future policy makers.

In essence, then, the work (and goal attainment) of the planning organizations was limited by the organizational and professional rivalries constituted within the planning organizations.

The needs and interests of the members of the planning groups contributed heavily to the goal displacement observed. An example of how such interests hampered the planning organizations is that none of the planning bodies was incorporated; therefore, they were technically *ineligible* to apply for or receive grants. Planning members insisted incorporation was unnecessary since they could individually apply for grants through the organizations that employed them. This is evidence that the primary loyalty of planning members was to their own organizations.

Additional evidence of this "secondary" type of membership support is that all three planning organizations lacked adequate financial resources, paid staff, or even permanent offices. This lack of resources resulted at least partly because the members did not demand the money and staff required to enable them to exert influence in the community. Full support was withheld lest the planning organizations themselves attain the power to control the resources needed by the members themselves.

Furthermore, given the vested interests of these planning members (largely social workers and the heads of social-agency-type programs), they resisted attempts to include other types of professionals (e.g., researchers, physicians, attorneys, or the elderly themselves), lest the inclusion of such members dilute their control over planning outcomes. And as noted earlier, because professional researchers and planners were not members of the planning bodies, research or other technical skills usually involved in planning were not considered requisite to the work of the planning bodies. Significantly, the problems of aging were cast *in terms of the disciplines represented* (primarily social work) rather than on the basis of systematic analyses of those problems, followed by the recruitment of members with expertise in the disciplines suggested on the basis of such an analysis.

In actual practice, the planning members did not define the problems of aging on any basis other than their own individual experiences with their elderly clients in the organizations in which they were employed. This aspect of the planners' belief system appears congruent with the social-work perspective which holds that the client cannot accurately perceive his problem. The social worker is seen as the appropriate person to diagnose the client's problem. Frequently, the client's definition of the situation is viewed either with outright disdain or, more posi-

tively, as symptomatic of some deeper problem of which the client himself, by definition, cannot be aware. From such a viewpoint, we could have predicted that the planners would see little to gain (in terms of perspectives on the problems of aging) by actually involving the elderly in the process of problem determination.

In terms of enabling the initial planning members to maintain their control over planning outcomes, beliefs in the inability of the aged to define their own problems are extremely functional. They support the organization of planning dominated by "professionals who work with the aged" and legitimate their claim to expert status and autonomy.

Other factors contributing to the observed goal displacement were (1) the *environmental context* wherein competition among the three planning bodies resulted in the inability of any one of them to achieve adequate resources to function as a formal organization with authority and legitimacy, and (2) the *institutional character* of the planning organizations, fashioned after the welfare council concept (a model developed for harmonious communication and coordination among agencies rather than for instrumental task accomplishment as such), and (3) the *general culture of the larger society* in which solutions to social problems have been conceptualized in terms of a "services strategy" rather than in approaches that result in the redistribution of prized resources to the "victims" (in this instance, older persons). This basic services approach has been given new emphasis in current legislation for older persons (the 1973 amendments to the Older Americans Act), the implications of which are discussed more fully next.

CONCLUSIONS AND IMPLICATIONS

The data indicate that both the nature of the task of planning (conceptualized in broad and ambiguous terms) and the structure of the planning organizations (essentially federative) combined to prevent (1) the objective identification of gaps and needs in the field of aging as a basis for planning, (2) the inclusion of members representing multiple professions, community organizations or institutions, or the elderly themselves, or (3) social action.

In essence, the activities of the planning bodies

appear to have served the primary purposes of (1) labeling the aged as a social problem of consequence in the local community, (2) advancing work in the field of aging as a legitimate profession (with or without a practicing knowledge base), (3) developing and presenting for public acceptance the planners as a core of experts in the field of aging, and (4) attempting to secure the recognition that would enable these professionals to influence any future planning or other community activity in the field of aging. In actual outcomes, planning activities were more symbolic than instrumental, more oriented toward validation and legitimation of the members' work with older persons than actual accomplishment (a classic "goal displacement"). The members studied, then, sought to attain expert status and a claim to control local decision-making activities (present or future) in the field of aging as a means of dealing with the basic survival needs of relatively weak organizations in an adverse environment.

These findings have major implications for the area-planning strategy embodied in the 1973 amendments to the Older Americans Act of 1965, which is receiving congressional support as a continuing strategy under currently proposed 1975 amendments to this act. Under the 1973 amendments and its fiscal year 1974 and 1975 appropriations, close to $100 million has been disbursed annually by the Administration on Aging (AoA) under Title III for area planning and programs funded by these substate Area Agencies on Aging (AAAs). These Title III appropriations utilize approximately half of AoA funding support.

The area-planning concept underlying this legislation ultimately aims to utilize and coordinate existing social agencies at county and multicounty levels, largely through Area Agencies on Aging (AAAs) operating either at the direction of or with the involvement of advisory groups similar in composition to those described in the study reported here (although consumer involvement is also required). To the extent that Area Agencies are so characterized, national policy in aging supports an approach that is likely to assist organizations and professionals more than older people themselves.

Our study also has implications beyond those re-

lated to similarities or organizational structure between AAAs and the organizations studied; they relate to the underlying principles and problems of planning and coordination as organizational tasks. The *central problem* confronting the agencies studied, AAAs, and other organizations that seek to advocacy plan, coordinate, and induce other agencies to perform certain activities is the near impossibility for such planning–coordinating agencies to alter the priorities of organizations over which they have no real authority. Interorganizational cooperation raises issues of territoriality and creates organizational uncertainty. Unless there are perceived inducements of major exchange value, both factors encourage resistance to potentially threatening changes in organizational activities or services which are necessary to effect truly cooperative ventures required by planning agencies to effect comprehensive service delivery systems.

Other problems facing Area Agencies on Aging (AAAs) which are similar to those confronting the organizations studied are that (1) the multitude of AAA functions require many types of staff skills and leadership *and* different types of organizational structures to maximize achievement (e.g., "flat" structures are better for coordination than for planning or service provision); (2) the lack of definitive, teachable skills required to perform some AAA tasks encourages power struggles over task definition and implementation (also augmenting potential influence of self-proclaimed experts who may or may not be knowledgeable in areas critical to goal attainment); (3) the often overlooked fact that many service agencies in aging (which AAAs must coordinate and on whom they depend for cooperation) suffer tenuous and low levels of funding; that is, they are survival-threatened. This problem augments the likelihood of interagency competition and divisive power politics (displacing service goals); and (4) contrary to general belief, AAAs are not free of survival-threatening events that may impede goal attainment, as exemplified in (a) "redesignation" controversies engendered by other agencies' seeking to alter an AAA designation, and (b) requests for an AAA from jurisdictions located in an area already assigned an AAA. Such situations threaten AAA authority and resources and require great expenditures of AAA energies in self-protective efforts, which limit their focus on major goals of direct benefit to older persons.

Significantly, attempts to resolve the problems of aging follow a course similar to that already tried unsuccessfully in other social problem areas. As Warren (1973) has recently described it, the comprehensive planning and coordination strategy receives increasing support as a mechanism for redressing urban social problems in spite of its known weaknesses. He cites research substantiating the "long history of the failure of the strategy to meet expectations," either in terms of implementing "the necessary actions which the planning sequence calls for" or in "obtaining the outcomes in terms of impact on the problem." Why then does such an approach continue as a major strategy, now institutionalized with new emphasis in the field of aging?

Warren (1973) offers insights on this point; the comprehensive planning and coordination strategy is functional in a number of respects: (1) it strengthens and reinforces social agencies at a time when they are "under attack for their ineffectiveness in addressing social problems"; (2) the strategy serves the "viability and expansion needs" of these agencies by defining the solution to social problems in terms of a "services strategy"; (3) with the services focus, the larger social system deficiencies are ignored, thus contributing to the maintenance of existing class, status, and power distributions in the population; and (4) the strategy of coordination and planning "provide the rationale and support for an important growth industry for social scientists and professional practitioners."

The most basic problems of older persons (income, medical care, housing, and transportation) are not likely to be resolved with the current approach. However, its emphasis is consistent with the "politics of aging" as described by political scientist Binstock (1972). Essentially, it is a politics dominated by "middleman programs," in which aging organizations have "been successful in creating a domain of program funds and authority that is available more or less exclusively to aging organizations." While influence is shared among middlemen without singular domination by any one organization, the result is nonetheless predictably beneficial primarily to the

organizations working in the field and to the established social structure itself—and only secondarily to older persons themselves.

Acknowledgments

Research supported by NIMH Special Fellowship 5-FO3-MH4-5336-BEHA. Portions of this paper are drawn and reprinted from "Community Planning for the Elderly: A Study in Goal Displacement," *Journal of Gerontology,* 1974, *29*(6), 684–691.

REFERENCES

Bendix, R. Bureaucracy: the problem and its setting. *American Sociological Review,* 1947, *12,* 493–507.

Berger, P., and Luckmann, T. *The Social Construction of Reality.* Garden City, N.Y.: Doubleday, 1966.

Binstock, R. H. Interest-group liberalism and the politics of aging. *Gerontologist,* 1972, *12,* 265–280.

Blau, P., and Scott, R. *Formal Organizations.* San Francisco: Chandler Publishing Company, 1962.

Collins, R. A comparative approach to political sociology. In R. Bendix (ed.), *State and Society.* Boston: Little, Brown, 1968.

Crozier, M. *The Bureaucratic Phenomenon.* Chicago: University of Chicago Press, 1964.

Cyert, R. M., and March, J. G. *A Behavioral Theory of the Firm.* Englewood Cliffs, N.J.: Prentice-Hall, 1963.

Dahrendorf, R. Out of utopia: towards a reorientation of sociological analysis. *American Journal of Sociology,* 1958, *64,* 115–127.

Estes, C. L. Community planning for the elderly from an organizational, political, and interactionist perspective. Ph.D. dissertation, University of California, San Diego, 1972.

Gouldner, A. Organizational analysis. In R. K. Merton, L. Broom, and L. S. Cottrell, Jr. (eds.), *Sociology Today.* New York: Basic Books, 1959.

Haire, M. Recurrent themes and general issues in organization theory. In M. Haire (ed.), *Modern*

Organization Theory. New York: Wiley, 1959.

Levine, S., White, P. E., and Paul, B. D. Community interorganizational problems in providing medical care and social services. *American Journal of Public Health,* 1963, *53,* 1183–1193.

Merton, R. K. Bureaucratic structure and personality. *Social Forces,* 1940, *18,* 560–568.

Selznick, P. Foundations of the theory of organization. *American Sociological Review,* 1948, *13,* 25–35.

_____. *Leadership in Administration.* New York: Harper & Row, 1957.

_____. *TVA and the Grass Roots.* New York: Harper & Row, 1966.

Thompson, J. D. *Organizations in Action.* New York: McGraw-Hill, 1966.

_____, and McEwen, W. J. Organizational goals and environment: goal setting as an interaction process. *American Sociological Review,* 1958, *23,* 23–31.

Warren, R. *Truth, Love and Social Change.* Chicago: Rand McNally, 1971.

_____. Comprehensive planning and coordination: some functional aspects. *Social Problems,* 1973, *20,* 355–364.

Weber, M. Class, status, and party. In H. H. Gerth and C. W. Mills (Trans. and eds.), *From Max Weber: Essays in Sociology.* New York: Oxford University Press, 1946.

Wilensky, H. L. *Intellectuals in Labor Unions.* New York: Free Press, 1956.

THOMAS O. BYERTS

Thomas O. Byerts is Director of Architecture and Environment, the Gerontological Society, Washington, D.C.

Reflecting User Requirements in Designing City Parks

Population density, congested neighborhoods, economic pressure, expanding technological developments, transportation difficulties, early retirement, and increasing leisure time combine to place a premium on our urban amenities. One of these, city park space, is discussed here. This study describes a research and design process that can also be modified and conducted in a variety of settings for various user populations.

Background

Man-made structures are rapidly replacing the natural forms provided by open space in our sprawling cities. The resultant scarcity of open space and restricted public recreation budgets makes it crucial that urban park design and recreation programs clearly reflect the requirements of the population served. A comprehensive understanding of the needs and capabilities of the actual and anticipated users combined with the systematic application of this knowledge to urban park design and programs will assist in efficiently and effectively developing recommendations for the relevant redesign of existing parks and the satisfactory planning of future facilities.

A growing number of urban park research projects plus the advent of consumer involvement in decision making have pointed to the need for a reevaluation of the process surrounding traditional park planning, design, and programming. These in-depth studies dramatize the need for a comprehensive research and evaluation component to be built into the normal planning and administrative system of park departments and commissions. Summaries from three studies conducted in California illustrate the following issues:

1. The need for designers and administrators to understand better the complex park and neighborhood social structure through in-depth interview and observation procedures (Gray, 1966).

2. The unsatisfactory consequences of an expediently oriented city policy developed by certain pressure groups to "design-out" various undesired user groups (Sommer, 1969).

3. The documentation of opposite perceptions and value systems operating between park planners and park users; planners concentrated on landscape features while users emphasized people and activities (Steinberg, 1968).

The following study of MacArthur Park in Los

317

FIGURE 1
Bench-lined paths near the entrance to MacArthur Park on a
weekend. (Photo by Thomas Byerts.)

Angeles (Byerts, 1970) describes the important factors that should be used in analyzing park performance to generate an informed strategy for a subsequent action phase. The process should be viewed within the following three overlapping urban planning and design goals:

1. The park site—to expand both the active and passive recreation potential of the existing park facility.

2. The adjacent neighborhood—to reach out to the special needs of the community surrounding the park and to maximize the supportive relationship that could exist.

3. The city park system—to respond to the broad-

er needs of other citizens in the city as a viable option within the overall park and recreation master plan.

RESEARCH

Archival Perspective

The first key to understanding the dynamics of a study area is to place it in historical, physical, and demographic perspective.

Historical. General Douglas MacArthur Park (originally named Westlake Park) is located in the Westlake district, an older, once very fashionable neighborhood in west central downtown Los Angeles. It

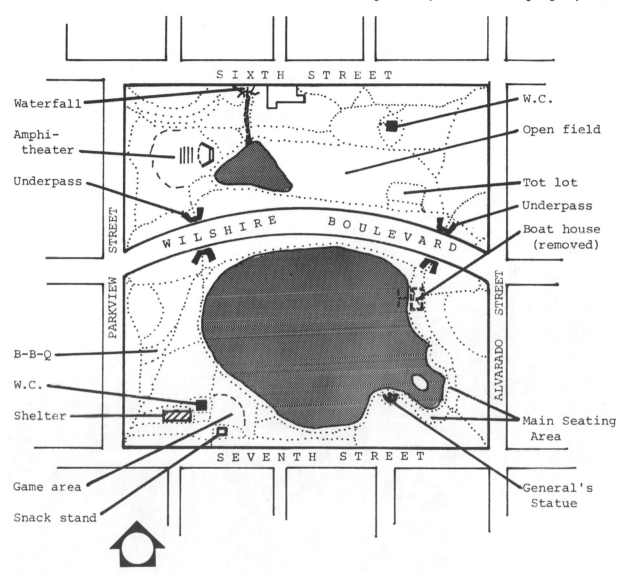

FIGURE 2
MacArthur Park site plan.

was built in 1890 and reflects the Olmstead brothers' outstanding influence on urban park design. The 32-acre park is located in a former low-lying swamp now bounded by two major commercial boulevards and two dense residential streets. Wilshire Boulevard was extended westerly through the park in the 1920s. This elevated six-lane street divides the park space in an appropriate 60 to 40 ratio (see Figure 2). Two pedestrian underpasses connect the northern and southern parts of the park. A 4-acre oval lake dominates the larger park section south of Wilshire Boulevard and is supplied from a smaller spring-fed lake situated in the northern part.

Physical. The intensive commercial uses bordering the park are characterized by a full range of cut-rate shopping facilities, small manufacturing concerns, second-run movie theaters, bars and cafeterias, private medical offices and clinics, several modern office buildings, a small arts college, and a public art gallery. A city-operated club for senior citizens was formed in a large fraternal headquarters, which itself was converted to retirement housing. Several nursing homes, a large number of retirement hotels, apartments,

boarding houses, and older (often run-down) private homes are located in the vicinity.

A city planning effort to revitalize the neighborhood is in the offing. It is a credit to the original designers that the park has remained a vital and stabilizing asset to the community during periods of great social and physical change.

Demographic. Comparing the demographic characteristics of the 3-square-mile Westlake statistical area to the citywide totals, the residential–commercial area surrounding the park is approximately three times more dense in population than the city. The residents are predominantly white and, on an average, are 12 years older, receive two thirds of the city population's average income, and are composed of

FIGURE 3
Main entrance "gates," showing adjacent stores and shoppers. Some park "users" may never set foot on park property.

Urban design and landscaping could help the function and appearance. (Photo by Thomas Byerts.)

FIGURE 4
Benches line the path around the lake, with toilet, snack bar, and game area in background. (Photo by Thomas Byerts.)

one third more single people. Crime statistics show that the four police recording districts surrounding MacArthur Park rank among the five worst districts in Los Angeles in most categories, including all street crimes. This increase in the crime rate is due in part to redevelopment efforts in other central city areas closer to downtown, which forced many indigents to move to the Westlake area.

Inventory of Physical Features

It is important to have an accurate accounting and rating of the quantity and condition of existing furniture and equipment. The 1970 "hardware" inventory in MacArthur Park includes a band shell with 100 fixed-bench seats and a surrounding natural sloping lawn amphitheater seating several hundred more. The southwest corner contains a snack stand, shuffleboard, horseshoes, table game, and card area as well

as a card shelter, which are all used essentially by adult and older people. While primarily male dominated, the table game area provides much of the intergenerational and interracial interchange that occurs in the park.

Many scenic bench-lined paths, a park maintenance area, and two small (shabby) toilet facilities complete the description of facilities.[1]

Many of the benches were the typical dark-green, straight-backed, wooden slat type that are not known for comfortable seating. Most were anchored in concrete or chained together to line pathways. Rows of standard picnic tables are used in the game areas, although they inhibit many activities such as kibitzing and four-handed card games.

Active physical recreation for younger age groups is confined generally to a large open field in the northern section of the park. Many Latin Americans use this area for weekend soccer games. Adjacent to

FIGURE 5
The very active game area. People sit in a sunny area during cold weather but move to the shade as the temperature climbs. This represents the need for options and flexibility in park design. (Photo by Thomas Byerts.)

the field is a traditionally equipped tot lot, which serves as a focal point for children's activity. This playground is surrounded by a row of benches that are restricted for use by adults accompanying children. An intermittently flowing waterfall, large and small lake, several monuments, and a statue of General MacArthur are found amid a wide variety of handsome trees and low-cut landscaping. Some of this landscaping has been removed to improve surveillance by city police and park rangers.

More active recreational facilities, such as basketball courts and baseball diamonds, and a busy senior-center building are located 1 mile to the west in Lafayette Park.

Field Study

A mix of interview and field observation methodology was employed in MacArthur Park to gain an in-depth understanding of consumer attitude and behavior in the setting.

Park interview. A field interview technique was used to gather more specific information on the actu-

FIGURE 6
This functional card shelter is a male-dominated setting. (Photo by Thomas Byerts.)

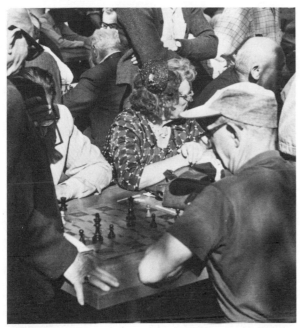

FIGURE 7
Standard picnic tables are not the best solution for games. Three game boards are mounted on each long table. The end boards are used for games, while the middle one gets sat upon. (Photo by Thomas Byerts.)

al users of MacArthur Park. A sample of 35 regular adult park users, defined as adults who make two or more visits to the park per week, was interviewed. Although this sample is too small to afford a representative view of park regulars, a strict random selection method was used. Contacts were made at all times of the day and all days of the week across a transitional spring period to try to achieve cross-sectional representativeness. Of the 103 adults initially approached by McLennan (1969), 68 were not interviewed because they were either not regular park users or they refused to be interviewed.

The final working sample consisted of 28 men and 7 women with an age range of 23 to 85 years (mean of 56.5 and mode of 63+). Eight respondents were foreign born, 30 were white, and 3 had Spanish surnames. Only one Indian and one black were included in the sample. Thirty-three of the 35 individuals were of working-class background or transients. Of these, 11 were currently employed and 24 had retired. Those living alone numbered 25, with the average length of area residence being 12 years, including 5 years at the present address, indicating the relative residential stability of the sample. The large majority of interviewees lived within four blocks of the park.

Self-reported park usage by the 35 respondents indicated that 22 were daily park users; 13 spent their time alone, while 22 spent it with close friends or casual acquaintances. Seventeen passed most of their weekday time in specific areas (amphitheater, large lake area, game tables, etc.); 18 stated they circulated around the park, not relating to particular areas.

Reasons for park use listed in order of frequency were to "get away" from the room, exercise, relate to nature, see and meet friends, and "nothing else to do." Frequently mentioned physical park assets were open landscape with trees and plants, company of interesting people, park wildlife, the lake, and outdoor air.

FIGURE 8
Movable benches in this active conversation area provide flexible relief to the fixed linear pattern. (Photo by Thomas Byerts.)

FIGURE 9
Interviewer making contact with subject in study sample near one of the attractive park entrances. (Photo by Thomas Byerts.)

An important dimension requiring further investigation is why people (especially those who reside near parks) do not use parks. An analysis of park users versus nonusers residing in a boarding hotel adjacent to MacArthur Park can be found in McDonald and Newcomer (1973).

Most of the nonalcoholics cited the "winos" and related panhandling as the greatest park problem. Secondary problems were the general crime situation, inadequate park services, dirty lake water, poor toilet facilities, need for restoration of outdoor gas cooking facilities, overt gambling activity, and desire for more flowers and shrubbery. Most interviewees were unaware of the existing prostitution and homosexual activity in the park. However, almost all respondents stated that they were willing to endure known problems rather than favoring major changes that might disrupt the activities they now enjoy. A large number referred to attempts by the city to "design people out" of certain downtown parks and stated that they did not want such changes to take place in "their" MacArthur Park.

Park observation. To compare the respondents' self-reported patterns with actual behavior, most of the interview sample was unobtrusively observed over a 2-month period. Spot descriptive notations of these observations were compiled; location, number of associates, body posture, and actual activity were noted along with the time, day of the week, and date. The recorded descriptions of the respondents' behavior patterns were then plotted on map overlays, thus graphically representing both individual and collective patterns of spatial use. Individual respondents appeared to follow generally the patterns of activity, social relations, and movement within the park that they reported in the interview. The range of patterns of usage, duration, and repetition of park visits had a much greater variety than had been expected.

Examples of this wide variety include an older woman who often accompanied her husband to his work at the snack stand and then spent two or three hours in the park feeding birds and watching children; a frail elderly man who walked around the park for an hour a day "rain or shine" on an exercise program prescribed by his physician; a middle-aged man who, on the way to work, spent an occasional 10 or 15 minutes sitting on a bench watching the "girls go by"; or the Sunday preachers and panhandlers plying their respective trades in this very cosmopolitan park.

Multiple observations indicated that those who reported circulating around the park and not relating to any specific area did, however, tend to frequent certain areas. Some did seek individual solitude, but the sample population generally was found to gravitate toward locations of large concentrations of people in high-activity areas. However, many subjects were not actually found to socialize in those locations. Observations indicated that many who reported visits with casual acquaintances spent most of their time with the same persons, indicating that there may have been definitional difficulty with the questionnaire in this area. Most of the sample were seen entering and leaving the park alone.

FIGURE 10
The park offers places for solitude as well as places for
socializing. (Photo by Thomas Byerts.)

Research Conclusions

Although MacArthur Park is used by a broad segment of ethnic, economic, and age categories, the
majority of park inhabitants are working-class male
white elderly. Declining health, low socioeconomic
status, fixed incomes, few family ties, and reduced
mobility are all major factors that appear to contribute to the general reduction of options for this central-city user population. Those inclined to use the
park are thus limited to it as a source of inexpensive
recreation and neighborhood associations. For many
the park offers the only expressed enjoyment or relief
from drab and lonely pensioner routines. Others consider park visits less as a matter of positive selection
and more as the best of poor alternatives. Still others
who are encountered as park regulars are there for

strictly expedient (a shortcut), illegal (prostitution), or
non-park participation (waiting for bus) reasons.

The dynamic balance between park and neighborhood is a crucial factor to the success of both enter-
prises. The influence of the park goes far beyond its
arbitrary property line. Both the park and the adjacent shopping and residential area would benefit from
a comprehensive urban design and landscaping effort
that would tie the two together more effectively.

The surrounding population density and composition as well as urban transportation and local parking
all contribute to the generation of the "critical mass"
of a successful leisure space. The needs of casual
visitors, passersby, and passers through should also be
explored.

This park has evolved into a satisfactory and well-
used, basically passive-oriented, recreation space. A

FIGURE 11
The open setting provides a catalyst for intergenerational contact. (Photo by Thomas Byerts.)

range of options are provided within differing landscape arrangements including areas for solitary, small-group, and large-group activities, as well as settings for individual introspection and relaxation. Within this "successful" park, however, there is need for experimentation, gradual improvement, and studied change.

A new range of alternatives reflecting real user needs should be explored. Parks should be viewed as dynamic and changing arenas for social behavior. The real and perceived needs seem to be for a feeling of more security, increased options, revitalization of facilities, and comfort (especially for those who spend long periods of time in the park). Many of these conditions could be corrected in total or in part through a relatively low cost program of physical design modification. Such modification should be accompanied by a built-in evaluation and feedback component to monitor the impact of change and to attempt to anticipate the changing needs of future consumers.

RESEARCH APPLICATION

The following recommendations are based upon the investigation of MacArthur Park; they also serve as an example of general design directives suitable for future action in other such places. The goal of this intervention is the development and design of an attractive, positive reinforcing, "socially connected," and more effective park environment.

General Design Directives

1. The overall park environment should
   a. Contain a variety of settings with focal points for social interaction and "connectedness," which is important to the well-being of high concentrations of older people, who are clearly the primary users in this case.
   b. Present a clear definition of security and safety from criminal action, damage, or physical hazard and be barrier-free by design.
   c. Incorporate a wide variety of functions, ranging from active recreational activities to passive areas of quiet solitude.
   d. Relate to the natural amenities and open space of the site, permitting a range of private to public settings designed for use within broad weather and time options.
   e. Be organized so that the various settings are located at reasonable walking distances and sited with appropriate visual connection, circulation, rest, and observation areas.
   f. Connect with the surrounding community and its urban design.
2. The *park furniture* should
   a. Be attractive, durable, easy to get in and out of, and comfortable, especially for long periods of time spent sitting.
   b. Be portable in some cases to allow for informal placement, depending on the desires of the users as they respond to a range of group sizes, arrangements, and weather patterns.
   c. Lend itself to various options for individual and small-group use as well as help to define space.
3. The *park furniture organization* should
   a. Relate to various group sizes, encouraging a

wide range of peer-group social interaction and activity, as well as between the generations.

b. Promote informal recreation and gaming groups, with special attention given to the role of observer and new visitor.

c. Be oriented to the movement patterns, structures, activities, and natural amenities of the park.

d. Be interspersed within and among activity areas and facilities allowing for appropriate rest and observation locations, with strategic visual overlap that encourages circulation and orientation to the overall park organization.

4. The *park shelter(s)* should

a. Present a focal point for informal social groupings, promote options for interaction between and among generations, and permit a choice of both structured and spontaneous activity.

b. Be sited and designed relative to natural park assets, circulation patterns, and activity areas so as to identify its anticipated function.

c. Regard the historical and cultural backgrounds of the park users and traditions of the park in establishing the theme and spatial configuration.

d. Provide protection from extremes of weather, temperature, and living conditions.

FIGURE 12
The role of spectator is as important as the role of competitor. (Photo by Thomas Byerts.)

    e. Contain, or have nearby, toilets, snack facilities, storage, and other such commonly needed facilities.

    f. Be safe and durable, built on a single level, capable of surveillance, and relatively easy to maintain.

    g. Provide flexible or portable space enclosure (seasonably adjustable) where possible. and be equipped to take care of a range of activity size and type.

Specific Setting Analysis

The design directives and interview—observation results were applied directly to the park context for each of the 30 unique park settings identified during the field research process; a park setting was defined as a homogeneous territory of activity capable of being separated from adjacent settings by natural and man-made perimeters (e.g., the lake, the path and benches surrounding the lake perimeter, and shuffleboard courts). The method employed measured the weekday, weekend, and seasonally adjusted use—kinds of activities, number and characteristics of participants, man-made and natural elements in use, and the like—and compared this with a rating of the estimated amount of use necessary to effectively "consume" each setting. General recommendations for additions, deletions, or no action within each setting were then itemized. Suggestions for combining adjacent settings and subdividing others were also developed.

This process forms a working outline from which to proceed with a park redesign scheme and to set priorities for action. It is also useful in testing the effects of changes in the environment or park programs by providing solid baseline data for future comparison. Periodic reevaluation of the settings can also help predict changing patterns that require future action. A study to develop more objective park-setting use criteria and measurements is called for here.

Since the elderly constitute the major users of this park, an incremental program for environmental modification, phased-in over time, coupled with a public information campaign is highly recommended. This should reduce the stress of change as the environment is modified and "finely tuned." A committee of park users could be formed to serve as a sounding board and communication link to the community.

CONCLUSIONS

Most departments of recreation and parks (or other such agencies) seem to have little or no budget or staff skill for continual or periodic design evaluation research. Decisions and priorities are usually set by political pressure, tradition, esthetics, and/or expediency. The real needs (which are subject to change) of the user population (and nonusers as well) are seldom systematically and periodically investigated. The great challenge that remains is to ask the right questions, to relate the answers to appropriate design and program solutions, and follow-through with the committment necessary to implement the new program.

Most people in the park, and the public in general, have little experience in critically analyzing their physical environment to make constructive recommendations. Few are able to project themselves into future changes. Through the development of a modest research program, based upon interviews of regular park users, observation of behavior, reports by staff, and attention to demography, history, and local trends, a park system can provide better service, resulting in long-term economy.

Resources are needed to conduct pilot studies, refine methodology, and organize a national data bank and clearing house to expedite the development of a comprehensive design and redesign programs. Pieces of such a structure exist in this and other areas of research and design, such as senior centers, nursing homes, barrier-free environments, and children's playgrounds. Perhaps gerontology is the appropriate arena to integrate this vitally needed activity which will benefit all segments of society.

Acknowledgment

A condensed version of this chapter appeared in *Parks and Recreation*, 1975, *10,* 34–36, 62–66, co-authored by Joseph D. Teaff, who was responsible for editing the larger study.

NOTE

1. A $200,000 redesign of MacArthur Park was conducted in 1971 which incorporated some of the recommendations contained in this report and disregarded others. An in-depth follow-up study is warranted.

REFERENCES

Byerts, T. O. Design of the Urgan Park Environment as an Influence on the Behavior and Social Interaction of the Elderly. Unpublished masters thesis, University of Southern California, Los Angeles, August 1970.

Gray, D. Uses of a Downtown Park. Unpublished working paper, California State University, Long Beach, Calif., December 1966 (mimeographed).

McDonald, A., and Newcomer, R. Differences in perception of a city park as a supportive or threatening environment. In D. Gray and D. Pelegrino (eds.), *Reflections on the Recreation and Park Movement.* Dubuque, Iowa: William C. Brown, 1973.

McLennan, L. MacArthur Park. Unpublished masters thesis, University of Southern California, Los Angeles, June 1969.

Sommer, R., and Becker, F. The old men in plaza park. *Landscape Architecture,* 1969, *59,* 111–114.

Steinberg, H. Visual Perception Analysis and Its Design Implications on Urban Parks. Unpublished masters thesis, University of Southern California, Los Angeles, 1968.

M. POWELL LAWTON,
ROBERT J. NEWCOMER,
AND THOMAS O. BYERTS

Conclusion

A look backward through the papers comprising this first attempt to join the forces of physical and social planners in the service of the aging population is likely to show clearly some of the gaps in its coverage. The gerontological literature is surprisingly thin in its treatment of the special problems of aging in nonmetropolitan areas of the country, despite the fact that in general this subpopulation is poorer, less well housed, has fewer transportation options, and is in poorer health than the aging in urban areas. A fresh look at small towns and rural areas is badly needed by a person with an ecological perspective.

Residential migration also deserves more extended treatment, since good neighborhood and service planning depend so much on an assessment of the areas of stability and change in different groups or geographic regions. Excellent work is already at hand in this area (Golant, 1972; Atchley, 1973), and the possibilities for further work with 1970 Census data are most promising.

Environmental barriers to mobility have been referred to repeatedly by many authors, but a focused discussion of barrier-free environments, emphasizing the specifics of building design and site location, remains to be done. The Gerontological Society is currently conducting a project dealing with this problem; its outcome should supplement the more general discussions in this volume.

The main stream of social planning was, of course, deliberately not treated here. We have emphasized the areas where physical and social planning overlap, those where the ecological perspective is most clearly relevant. The strong emphasis on housing is the result of its patent salience to both the physical and social aspects of planning.

Beyond such obviously relevant areas, however, our conviction is that planning should utilize relevant information from both physical and social spheres. A major axiom of the system view of man—environment relations is the equipotentiality of physical and social means to lead to the fulfillment of human goals. The frequent interchangeability of the two means is particularly relevant to the behavior of older people, who are more constrained by environmental barriers because of their biological, social, and economic limitations than younger age groups. Thus the planning of large-scale social programs like Social Security, national medical insurance, and community-based services cannot be performed adequately without due consideration being given to location, access, and the

330

diffusion of knowledge regarding availability. Conversely, community planning cannot be reduced to a strict economic or engineering level and be valid for meeting human social needs.

To conclude this presentation, it seems worthwhile to allude to some planning needs for the future.

Further development of socially oriented market analysis methods. The gathering of primary data from community household surveys regarding needs and preferences has two major limitations. First, it is expensive, and we have little confidence that its cost can be brought down to a level where every group can conduct an in-depth and valid preplanning survey in routine fashion. Second, such data are sometimes of uncertain meaning. Respondents cannot always answer hypothetical questions in a way that will forecast their actual behavior when a completed project or service is offered.

On the other hand, the use of the usual economic indicators to project probable utilization of facilities is likely to be even less reliable for older people. Economic constraints greatly limit the extent to which their behavior resembles that of the younger adult population, and their specific needs are incommensurate with these indicators.

Thus we require methods of estimating need that take into account such environmental factors as homeownership, living arrangement, proximity to family, or location of necessary services and amenities, and such personal factors as age, health, or housing satisfaction. A beginning has been made in this direction by Glassman, Tell, Larrivee, and Helland in their utilization of the best possible estimates of some of these factors to calculate need in local areas. This effort should be extended to include more of the relevant factors mentioned and to include the most useful of the economic indicators and factors on the supply side.

Development of better indicators for assessing both need and supply. In addition to the further development of a planning model, great improvement in the ability to measure the variables utilized in the model is required. The search for social indicators has not to date been particularly encouraging, but we have no other choice than to keep looking. For the present, there appears to be better potential payoff from the development of behavioral indicators such

as requests for specific services, number of physician visits, or number of trips outside the dwelling unit than from attitudinal indicators such as self-reported happiness or housing satisfaction. Even for the behavioral indicators, few national data are now available, and the situation is almost hopeless when one seeks subclassification by ethnic status, level of health, or geographic residence. Such data as exist are also likely to be time-bound, denying the real-world dynamics of change, particularly at the local level.

A methodology that holds promise for alleviating some of these shortcomings is being tested by the San Diego County Area Agency on Aging. This methodology is queuing theory, widely used in management science. Through such a procedure it is possible to predict the expected level of service need during any given time period, the length of service use, the number of persons served, and the optimum number of service units required.

Adequate support of research relevant to planning environments for the elderly. The pessimism expressed over the current state of affairs in measuring need and supply and in deriving usable indicators can be countered only by the investment of energy in problem-solving research. Some federal departments have greatly increased their investment in gerontological research over the past decade, but the most obvious potential sponsor of ecological research, the U.S. Department of Housing and Urban Development, has steadfastly displayed its indifference to the social implications of its programs in its research and development funding priorities. The current surge of interest in man–environment research may lose its impetus significantly if the persistent problems of neighborhood planning, service location, housing design, community alternatives to institutionalization, and market analysis receive only perfunctory acknowledgment by research funding agencies.

Communication of information and utilization of research findings. Although physical planners are now at least talking to social planners, architects to researchers, administrators to legislators, and so on, there are few formalized and dependable sources of information for those who hunger for multidisciplinary knowledge. Some publications are available from HUD, the Administration on Aging, the Gerontological Society, the American Institute of Architects, the American Association of Homes for the Aged, and the National Council on the Aging. But these are useful if by good luck the seeker's problem is one that is covered in this handful of relevant publications. If not, there is no properly indexed archive, data bank, or consultant directory from which to seek direction or retrieve answers to specific questions. Each discipline has its own publications and professional meetings, but these often tend to be parochial and are likely to keep the "foreigner's" interdisciplinary defensiveness mobilized.

Clearly, what is needed is an organized effort to interpret new information from each of the fields related to planning in such a way as to be useful to a multidisciplinary audience. The material itself could be in the form of newsletters, journal articles, computerized abstracts, pamphlets, or audiovisual presentations. A corps of expert consultants for direct interpretation is also called for here. The critical dimension, however, would consist of a staff of planning generalists whose specialty is clear, jargonless writing. A first step in this direction is now being taken by the Administration on Aging through its effort to develop a national clearinghouse of literature and research in aging. The California State Office on Aging has also developed a library system for its Area Agencies. Monthly abstracts of articles, books, reports, and legislation on aging and an indexed library are provided.

Sources of funding for service systems spanning several traditional modes of service. Many problems end up being ignored due to lack of funding. A major step toward implementation would be accomplished if the previous four objectives could be attained. The planning fields are in desperate need of data with which to bolster appeals for the creation of innovative human service networks and facilities. The essence of the ecological orientation is at present extremely difficult to portray in the concrete terms that is possible in the case of traditional single services, such as number of housing units or number of casework sessions. Until planners can use quantitative methods effectively to bolster appeals for funding from political and voluntary sources, their broadly conceived service systems will be poor competition for the traditional single-service organization. This need has suddenly become critical with the diversion of federal funds into the revenue-sharing channel. Aging in many places has been grossly ignored.

The problem-conceptualization process and program-monitoring functions implicit under Area Agency guidelines offer substantial potential for turning around this past situation. An immediate illustration concerns the development of, first, uniform service categories, and, second, uniform project-evaluation criteria. The primary incentive for both these developments is revenue sharing. The Administration on Aging, which has been in the forefront in the development of information and referral systems, and Area Agencies, which have been highly visible social planning bodies, have earned the right to participate in communitywide decision making, such as is required in the establishment of both service categories and evaluation criteria.

Another bright spot concerns the trends in Integrated Grants Administration (IGA). Under this policy, designated agencies assume brokerage responsibility for various funding sources. The IGA can pool disparate monies into a comprehensive service package, relieving service providers of the frustrating process of piecing together several categorical programs. It is likely that many Area Agencies will receive this designation for aging programs.

Appreciation of the political processes in program implementation. Quite apart from the issues of problem definition, needs assessment, and program funding is the matter of politics. Local agencies, such as direct-service providers and organizations like the United Way, have considerable influence on local decision making. Furthermore, they represent a sizable vested interest in the status quo. The ability of these groups to subvert comprehensive planning goals and even program innovation was clearly evidenced during the early years of the war on poverty and the Model Cities program. The rising influence of Area Agencies and heightened priorities for aging programs are both perceived as threats to the status quo. As a consequence, they may meet opposition from agencies normally assumed to be serving the public interest. A chronicle of these processes, as well as an identification of successful Area Agency community organization efforts, is much needed to sensitize the public and policy makers to the petty behavior that can exist within the human care service system.

The editors hope that these objectives for the future will be more easily accomplished as a result of the thinking stimulated by the various contributions in this book. Far more certain is the obvious conclusion that we are not yet out of the Neolithic era in our search for appropriate guidelines and refinement of our methods. The planning process must be both objectified and sensitized for the direct benefit of those elderly who cannot wait for assistance. In so doing, we shall all help to shape our own futures.

REFERENCES

Atchley, R. C. Using census data on residential mobility by age. Paper presented at the annual meeting of the Gerontological Society, Miami Beach, October 1973.

Golant, S. M. *The Residential Location and Spatial Behavior of the Elderly.* Research paper no. 143. Chicago: Department of Geography, University of Chicago, 1972.

Index